Radicals and Realists

IN THE JAPANESE
NONVERBAL ARTS

July 2006

for Ted and Victoria,

all the best,

Tom

Radicals
IN THE JAPANESE

and Realists

NONVERBAL ARTS

The Avant-Garde Rejection of Modernism

Thomas R. H. Havens

UNIVERSITY OF HAWAI‘I PRESS | HONOLULU

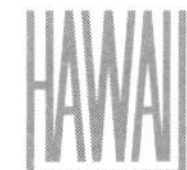

11 10 09 08 07 06   6 5 4 3 2 1

Library of Congress Cataloging-in-Publication Data
Havens, Thomas R. H.
Radicals and realists in the Japanese nonverbal arts :
the avant-garde rejection of modernism /
Thomas R. H. Havens.
   p. cm.
Includes bibliographical references and index.
ISBN-13: 978-0-8248-3011-3 (hardcover : alk. paper)
ISBN-10: 0-8248-3011-3 (hardcover : alk. paper)
1. Arts, Japanese — 20th century.   2. Arts and
society — Japan — History — 20th century.
3. Avant-garde (Aesthetics) — Japan — History —
20th century.   I. Title.
NX584.A1H38   2006
700.952.'09045 — dc22   2006000833

The publisher gratefully acknowledges the support of the
following organizations in the publication of this book:

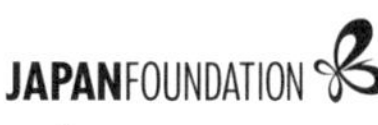

and
THE SAISON FOUNDATION

Designed by April Leidig-Higgins

Printed by Thomson-Shore, Inc.

contents

illustrations

Figures

Color Plates

(gathered after page 150)

preface

Few cultural forms evolve more rapidly than the nonverbal arts of dance, music composition, painting, and sculpture. Today's radicalism is tomorrow's chic; the avant-garde soon becomes the Old Guard. Nowhere was this more true than in the Japan of the 1950s and 1960s, arguably the most transformative decades of the twentieth century for all the countries of East Asia. This book seeks to recapture the fast-paced developments in Japan's nonverbal arts after World War Two before they vanish from memory and their significance for contemporary artistic expression is forgotten. Its larger aim is to shed light on synchronic trends in artistic innovation around the globe as well as on diachronic changes in Japanese culture from prewar imperialism to postwar democracy.

In preparing this account, I've benefited from the help of many persons and organizations. Without exception the individuals listed among the sources at the end of the book answered my questions with courtesy and candor. I'm especially grateful to Hiwatari Nobuhiro and Gregory W. Noble for generous hospitality during 2001–2002, when I was a visiting researcher at the Institute of Social Science, University of Tokyo. As with past projects, Hashimoto Seiko and Hashimoto Minoru provided gracious assistance with my studies, as did the directors and staffs of numerous Japanese libraries, museums, galleries, and research institutes. I'm also grateful to many colleagues in conversation and correspondence, especially Theodore C. Bestor, Beverly J. Bossler, Daniel Botsman, Edward I. Brodkin, Kirsten Cather, Sheldon Garon, Carol Gluck, David G. Goodman, Andrew Gordon, Valerie Hansen, Helen Hardacre, J. Victor Koschmann, Michael S. Molasky, Sayuri Oyama, Jerome Packard, Henry DeW. Smith II, Kent C. Smith, Margaret C. L. W. Smith, Alan Tansman, R. Kenji Tierney, Ronald W. Toby, John W. Treat, Valdo H. Viglielmo, Richard von Glahn, Dennis C. Washburn, Ikuko Watanabe, and Merry I. White. The directors and staffs of libraries at Connecticut College, Harvard University, and Northeastern University assisted with research materials. I'm indebted to Patricia Crosby, Cheri Dunn, Lucille Aono, Susan Stone, Patricia Metz, and the staff of University of Hawai'i Press for expert editorial and production care.

Funds from a Fulbright-Hays Fellowship through the U.S. Department of Education and from Northeastern University speeded my studies, and I'm grateful to these sources for indispensable assistance.

Above all I'm thankful for the advice and support of Karen L. Thornber at every stage of this project. Her deep knowledge of East Asian cultural history and her skills as a scholar of comparative literature helped guide me around many snares, and her personal encouragement is beyond measure or description.

Except for citations of Western-language publications, names of Japanese nationals are given in the customary Japanese manner, with the family name first. Romanizations of Japanese-language terms follow the modified Hepburn system used in the Masuda edition of *Kenkyusha's New Japanese-English Dictionary* (Tokyo: Kenkyūsha, 1974). Macrons are omitted from the most widely known proper nouns. Princeton University Press has consented to my reusing very brief portions of my *Artist and Patron in Postwar Japan* (Princeton, 1982).

introduction

*Postwar Vectors in the Japanese
Nonverbal Arts*

Japanese artists in every genre after 1945 saw themselves as belonging to the contemporary *(gendai)* era of world culture, no longer to the near past connoted by the term commonly used since the late nineteenth century, *kindai* (recent times, hence "modern").[1] Almost uniformly, they regarded the surrender at the end of World War Two as a clean break with Japan's disgraced militarism and as an unbridled opportunity to create a new culture for their country and the world. Yet many avant-garde Japanese artists in the 1950s and 1960s found themselves once again taking up the prewar riddle — "how to grapple with modernism in a partially modernized society,"[2] as the billionaire novelist and arts patron Tsutsumi Seiji (1927–) puts it. For more than two decades after 1945, Japanese thinkers, writers, and arts professionals wrestled with ideas of artistic modernity, eventually joining in the worldwide attack that broke out in the 1960s against high modernism as a mode of thought and culture.

"We are finally at the stage where we can see such things as modernism objectively," the Japanese composer of art music Ichiyanagi Toshi (1933–) pointed out in 2002. "The pace of change was so rapid in the 1950s and 1960s because we were trying so hard to catch up with Western culture. In those days our approach to modernism was superficial and brief. We moved to the next stage, beyond modernism, without deeply experiencing modernism as in Europe or America. In 1970 our understanding of modernism was still shallow; today enough time has elapsed that we can finally discuss modernism, antimodernism, and postmodernism."[3] Although Ichiyanagi probably stints his fellow artists' appreciation of modernism as of 1970, the passage of time has likewise given much greater clarity to other intellectual and artistic currents from abroad, from surrealism and existentialism in the late 1940s to (highly premature) theories of the death of God — or at least the author — two decades later.

Japan was considerably cut off from global artistic developments from the onset of war with China in July 1937 until regaining self-rule in April 1952 — a time of enormous intellectual and artistic upheaval in the rest of the world. Today we know that many wartime artists of the pen, keyboard, brush, and stage brimmed with pride at Japan's military conquests in Asia and the Pacific; others were driven inward in compliance with authority or unspoken resistance to it. The scholar Tatehata Akira says flatly: "The history of the postwar arts cannot overlook wartime painting. Much of it was seized by the Americans right after the surrender, taken to Washington, and only slowly returned to Japan. A reconsideration of this strange wartime era is slowly taking place among art historians on three levels: (1) the rather romantic portrayals of war, together with relations between artists and military leaders; (2) social conditions within Japan itself; and (3) the moral dimension of silence or cooperation, together with subsequent accusations of complicity after 1945."[4] In the same vein, an understanding of the arts of the 1950s and 1960s must be anchored in knowledge of the occupation era.

Once shorn of empire and freed of direct American administration apart from Okinawa, nonverbal artists and other intellectuals began to rethink nationality and cultural distinctiveness while the country as a whole finished recovering from defeat and launched an era of high-speed economic growth in the 1950s. The most forward-looking among them sought to create a new culture that was neither imperially Japanese, as in the 1930s and early 1940s, nor postimperially American, as during 1945–1952. Certain artists constructed idioms reaching beyond the binarisms of national/universal, traditional/modern, Japanese/Western, or ours/others' to become, more simply, commentaries on the human condition, based in the local but extending globally. A number of them ended up producing non-Western or even post-Western contemporary art, although some of it was neutrally nonnational or even transnational in direction. Other avant-garde figures were more mimetic. Many of the most innovative works exceeded syntheses of domestic and Western idioms to develop radically new stances on the relationship between the spatial (Japan) and the temporal (the contemporary). In doing so, some of these works repositioned themselves as transcultural: now deterritorialized as place-specific to Japan and instead engaged in a dynamic, interactive process of cultural creolization that began early in the century and accelerated among artists around the world after World War Two.

The 1950s in Western Europe and North America were years of great artistic creativity beneath an overlay of dour political conservatism and social conformity. The same is true of Japan, where the veneer of conventionality was periodically ripped by labor conflicts, ideological struggles, and political turmoil. Much of the disquiet emanated from Japan's return to world affairs, especially the Japanese government's unswerving support of the United States in the cold war: (1) as staging area for American armed forces during the Korean War of 1950–1953, (2) as steadfast anticommunist ally at the United Nations, and (3) as junior partner in the Japan–United States Mutual Security Treaty of 1952 (known as Anpo, it was revised in 1960 and is still in effect). Thus Japan, while independent, was and is still in-dependence. The 1950s were also a decade of renewed Japanese interest, although little actual participation, in international artistic movements. The Kamakura museum director Sakai Tadayasu points out that "artistic trends from abroad mainly affected Japanese painters and sculptors indirectly. Many Japanese artists created works without much contact with outside ideas. Nor were experiments in Japan during the 1950s well known overseas. There was a good deal of creativity here that wasn't much recognized in Europe or America. For example, the print maker Munakata Shikō was well known abroad, but the equally great print maker Onchi Kōshirō was not."[5]

A decade later Japanese artists grew more knowledgeable about world movements, mainly through travel abroad and visits by foreign professionals during boom years of national economic prosperity. Beginning with vast demonstrations with postcolonial overtones to protest renewal of the Japan–United States Mutual Security Treaty in May and June 1960, the decade simmered with political and cultural ferment, as in other industrialized societies, then boiled over in massive protests against the Vietnam War, university governance, and the security treaty during 1968–1970. Yet this was also a time of creeping artistic decampment, particularly among the younger avant-garde, moving beyond internationalism and especially modernism in all genres. Leading-edge artists searched for local elements to give greater distinctiveness to their cultural projects. This quest was less nationalist than it was a foray into the everyday — the artifacts, materials, and experiences of ordinary life, which are perforce near to hand. By steadily rejecting canonical high modernism and formalism from abroad, Japanese artists partly overcame their anxieties about whether their oeuvre was symmetrically equivalent to that of Vienna, Paris, or New York and instead began to express their ideas in the art of the everyday. This shift meant that progressive artists no longer fantasized about the Western Other,[6] but neither did they indulge in nostalgia, or simple yearning, for an essentialized Japan. Incomplete as the process was by the end of the decade, 1970 marks a surprisingly clear boundary between the artistic experimentation of the postoccupation era and the establishmentarian arts culture of mature capitalism that took firm hold in Japan's bureaucratically administered society thereafter.

The 1950s and 1960s are a germinal but ill-studied era of cultural redefinition in Japan. However conflicted they may have been by war and peace, by Japanese military rule and American military occupation, or by global approaches and local sensibilities in the creative sphere, most avant-garde artists (which in Japan means anyone who is artistically progressive) saw the years after their country regained autonomy in 1952 as ones of challenge, sometimes conflict, often ferment, and nearly always innovation. The painter Enomoto Kazuko (1934–) recalls that for her "the 1950s and 1960s meant that the craving for recovery from the ashes of war produced an energy different from today. Politics, society, and culture were filled with unprecedented vitality. On the one hand, the prewar musical, artistic, and literary establishment was revived; on the other, young artists with a clear understanding of contemporary issues attempted to express themselves outside this framework in progressive ways. I think it was a truly stimulating period."[7] Sakai Tadayasu, a specialist on postwar sculpture, concurs: "The 1950s and 1960s were the most energetic years of modern art in Japan. There was an explosion of creative vigor after war and defeat."[8] A main task facing the historian of culture is to explain how and why this artistic efflorescence took place in a country so devastated by wartime destruction and postwar malnutrition that it began the 1950s with an economy scarcely larger than that of Indonesia or Peru.

This is a book about Japan's avant-garde artists, the work they produced, and the historical environment in which they produced it. Most of them were radicals in two senses: they rebelled against existing canons in their respective genres and against established authority in some form or other, whether diplomatic, governmental, corporate, or artistic. Many were also realists, particularly in the 1960s, in choosing concrete materials, sounds, and themes from everyday life for their art and in gradually adopting tactics of protest or resistance through accommodation rather than confrontation. Yet whatever the means of expression, the production of art was never devoid of historical context or political implication. Like other forms of social knowledge, art is inherently linked with political nuance and the assertion of power, even when the artist repudiates formal party politics (of the left or right) and refuses to engage in public protest. To reject politics entirely, as some claimed to do, was still to make an unmistakable political choice: it was no more possible to be a truly apolitical artist in Japan during the 1950s and 1960s than under the surveillance and censorship that prevailed before 1945.

The focus here is on the nonverbal arts of dance choreography, art-music composition, painting, and sculpture from the end of military occupation in 1952 through the brilliant arts festivals of the Osaka world exposition in 1970 — years rapidly receding from memory as the avant-garde of that era faces inevitable decline and death. Each of these media might well receive separate monographic attention for the period under consideration, yet four reasons particularly justify this choice of art forms for collective examination: (1) they are relatively understudied, both in Japan and elsewhere; (2) they were central to debates across artistic genres in the late 1940s and 1950s; (3) they lend themselves especially well to understanding interactions with the global avant-garde during these decades; and (4) they best illustrate the twin themes of generational and political difference that undergird my analysis. Other equally fascinating realms of artistic expression such as architecture, drama, fiction, film, and poetry are omitted because they are much better known.[9] So too are the sizable domains of popular music, radio, television, and cartoon and commercial art where great innovations — few of them considered avant-garde — took place during the postwar years.

It is true that to dichotomize too rigidly along an elite/popular or a verbal/nonverbal axis is to create false distinctions among art forms that share much in common, in Japan as elsewhere. As the literary critic Howard Hibbett quips, "The main difference between high culture and low culture is that high culture costs more and earns less."[10] The art critic Chiba Shigeo notes that "the art world from Meiji [1868–1912] down to the Pacific War was not clearly divided by genre, and it was so small that many artists in various media knew one another. Even in the 1950s and 1960s, the idea of the arts included everything: literature, film, theater, dance, and music as well as the visual arts."[11] Rather than literally "nonverbal," perhaps "paraverbal" comes closer to characterizing dance choreography, art-music composition, painting, and sculpture, since no medium of artistic expression can exist in the total absence of words. Compared with other genres, are dance, music, and the visual realm less encumbered by the verbal and thus by a need to be translated in order to be cross-culturally significant? Or is their language no less place-specific than creative products that rely on words? Questions such as these rivet the attention of East Asian specialists in all disciplines no less than they engage humanists around the world. The world of the arts in Japan during the quarter-century after World War Two provides rich soil for seeking answers.

While respecting the individuality and diversity of art production in early postwar Japan, this book emphasizes the domestic and transnational interactions of avant-garde genres, each of which must be seen in dynamic collaboration with one another rather than in isolation during the years in question.

Like Deborah Poole, I believe that the "image world" of vision and representation is social: "the specific ways in which we see (and represent) the world determine how we act upon that world and, in so doing, create what that world is."[12] Media of all kinds, including choreographic, musical, and visual texts, reveal both transcultural themes and local practices through the study of art in its social context.[13] I argue that, like many other social groups in postwar Japan, artists were divided as much by generational distinctions as by aesthetic or ideological disputes. This was especially true for those born between 1926 and 1934 — the so-called single-digit generation (*hitoketa*) of the Shōwa (1926–1989) era, who self-consciously stood apart from all others and "virtually captured the memory market in the postwar decades."[14] Internally colonized, in a sense, as youths by Japan's wartime military government, they were profoundly suspicious of authority of any sort, yet after 1945 most of them felt grateful to the semicolonial American occupation of their country for its relative freedom and for the chance to catch up with artistic modernism from the West. This age cohort generally rejected party politics, especially the newly legalized Japan Communist Party, and took little part in protests against Japanese or American foreign policies.

By contrast, younger subsets of postwar artists adopted different, if less unified, stances on both political and artistic questions compared with the Shōwa single-digit group. Generational and political divergences among artists became most apparent in the 1960s, when the internal divisiveness of society, labor, and government of the previous decade was replaced by economic prosperity, bureaucratic management, and the languor of social sameness in the form of middle-class, pret-a-porter consumerism. Younger avant-garde artists, suspicious of the hegemonic aspects of high modernism, often turned to antimodernism to protest this new capitalist conformity, whereas many of their older counterparts took nominally apolitical positions that, in effect, endorsed the new status quo. In moving beyond modernism after the late 1950s, the avant-garde increasingly produced art that was post-Western in method and local in materials, focused on everyday experience. The lavish Osaka exposition of 1970 exemplified the new ascendancy of corporate culture in a country typified until recently by farms and small businesses. In that same year, the collapse of protest movements against the Vietnam War, against Japan's treaty ties to the United States, and against university-governance policies paralleled the "attenuation" of countercultures in all the arts, leading to a "tremendous sense of loss of innocence and idealism," as Ann Sherif has written of the novelist Murakami Haruki (1949–).[15] As a cultural threshold, 1970 stands shoulder to shoulder with Japan's continental turn in 1931 and the debacle of military defeat in 1945.

THE CHAPTERS THAT FOLLOW concentrate on the most progressive individuals in the relatively narrow nonprofit sector of the nonverbal arts where the greatest risks of novelty and experimentation were taken in the name of art. The aim is to discover how some of the most imaginative figures in dance, music, and the visual arts set about devising new cultural modes during two of the most turbulent and fast-changing decades in Japan's modern history. Their activity took place in a balmy climate of considerable postoccupation (and somewhat postcolonial) artistic freedom, in contrast to strict wartime controls on expression by the Japanese state and postwar censorship under American occupation. The genres selected for scrutiny here are particularly useful prisms for refracting the contemporary experience of the arts in both Japanese and comparative culture as a whole. The guiding theme is that generational and political differences largely account for the divergent stances artists took vis-à-vis modernism, the international arts community, Japan's ties to the United States, and the alliance of corporate and bureaucratic interests that solidified in Japan during the 1960s.

Chapter 1 discusses the arts and cultural change in Japan immediately after World War Two. The narrative then divides into two chronological sections dealing with the 1950s and the 1960s, bisected by the rise of an artistic underground in Shinjuku and the security-treaty crisis of May–June 1960. Part 1, "Experimental Voyages: The 1950s," treats Japanese artists who studied abroad as well as the vast palette of experiments in each of the nonverbal avant-garde arts that took place within Japan during that decade, after long years of artistic insularity and near-stasis throughout war and occupation. Chief among the intellectuals who stimulated experimentation were the art critic Takiguchi Shūzō (1903–1979), the painter Okamoto Tarō (1911–1996), and the businessperson-painter Yoshihara Jirō (1905–1972). Each was born in the late Meiji era, each had a following among the early-Shōwa generation, and each held his own distinctive views on art as well as politics. Takiguchi inspired the mixed-media workshop Jikken Kōbō, where composers, painters, and others shared fresh ideas about art between 1951 and 1957. Okamoto encouraged radical innovations in painting and sculpture during the 1950s as well as popularizing art through the media in the 1960s and beyond. Yoshihara founded the Kansai-area Gutai group, a congeries of visual and performance artists active between 1954 and Yoshihara's death in 1972. Other experiments took place in Japanese natural-pigment (Nihonga) painting, calligraphy, and ceramics as well as photography and ballet. By the end of the decade, the key nonacademic locale for innovations in the most cerebral forms of art-music composition, oil painting, and film making became the fashionable Sōgetsu Art Center, founded by the film director Teshigahara

Hiroshi (1927–2001) in the brand-new Sōgetsu Kaikan in 1958. This was a main site of contestation where competing strands of abstraction and the concrete, of l'art informel and the representational, and of serial music, musique concrète, and chance operations vied for favor in Japan's avant-garde arts community.

Part 2, "Alternative Modernities in the 1960s: Locating the Everyday," addresses a multifront assault on formalism (confusingly known as anti-art) led by visual artists nationwide who mainly showed their products at an annual nonjuried exhibition in Tokyo sponsored by the Yomiuri newspapers. Likewise composers of both Western-style and contemporary Japanese-style art music increasingly chose everyday themes from folk music and the premodern musical repertoire for their new presentations. Avant-garde print makers and choreographers similarly moved beyond the modern, and modernism, in their new works. Emblematic of the nonformalist embrace of the everyday was a loose assemblage of sculptors working with natural materials who emerged in 1968, eventually known as the Monoha. It was here, above all, that radical artistic discourse shifted to a post-Western phase where the relationships among unmediated objects — everyday things as they are, with minimal intervention — and the links between locale (Japan, where the cultural products exist) and time (the current moment, especially for temporary installations or performances) superseded the hoary preoccupation with geographical identities — Japan and the West — from Meiji to the early 1960s. Although artists born in the Shōwa single-digit years were not immune to antiformalism during the 1960s, their younger counterparts were the chief antimodernists, offering greater resistance than their elders to established authority in both domestic and foreign-policy matters. A chapter on "Art, Money, and Politics" examines the artistic apex of the postwar period: Osaka's 1970 world exposition, where more avant-garde art music, painting, sculpture, and dance was on display than at any other point in Japan's history, before or since.

RECONNOITERING THE HISTORY of Japan's most progressive art genres during these fascinating decades is complicated by spotty documentation, a dearth of scholarly attention, and the low esteem in which the country's business and political elites held most artists and their works. Segi Shin'ichi (1928–), an art critic and bibliographer of the era, points out that few records exist for any of the avant-garde arts before the 1960s. Exhibit catalogs were seldom produced; little remains from many shows except invitations on postcards and single-sheet lists of works on display. Gradually photographic records began to be retained, in order to document collections and build archives.[16] Although musical scores survive, sound recordings and other materials on music and dance performances from the 1950s are surprisingly scarce. Nor are there many reliable scholarly studies to guide the researcher.

Nevertheless superb exhibition catalogs from retrospectives on postwar culture have appeared during the past decade, and biographical materials abound for composers and choreographers. Writings by major arts figures in high-quality journals published during the 1950s and 1960s constitute excellent primary-source material. Reviews in newspapers and magazines compensate for their occasional lack of sophistication with a flair for conveying the contemporary flavor of an exhibit or performance. Vinyl recordings of musical performances from the 1960s together with compact discs containing the aural record of retrospective concerts held in the 1990s and early 2000s help to offset the diaphanous documentation of the first postwar decade. Numerous interviews with choreographers, composers, and visual artists active in the 1950s and 1960s supplement the archival record, providing considerable insight, little faulty recollection, and a good deal of evidence from the artists' personal files.

This narrative of some of Japan's most innovative artistic forms during the mid-twentieth century invites readers of history to consider the place of art in cultural change as well as cultural continuity. To be sure, artistic ferment at any level of taste, from the most refined to the most earthy, does not necessarily portend upheaval in the distribution of power and privilege. Pierre Bourdieu (1930–2002) is undoubtedly correct that social regimes often use culture and education to preserve themselves: "art and cultural consumption are predisposed, consciously and deliberately or not, to fulfill a social function of legitimating social differences" and thus contribute to social reproduction.[17] But art is far more than a handmaiden of established authority — much more than a safety valve for confirming it by letting off the excess steam of dissent. At certain moments art can also reject conventional criteria of stratification and defy accepted social knowledge by exercising its obligation as critic, as is true for all intellectual, scholarly, and artistic activity whether verbal or nonverbal. The historian must not merely transmit but also examine art,[18] for its own textual integrity and also for its social and cultural significance, first at the site of its production and then in relation to the wider world of learning.

The focus here is on art produced in Japan during two crucial postwar decades by persons native to that country or working there during the 1950s and 1960s. I assume, with Bourdieu, that "it is possible to enter into the singularity of an object" — here, Japanese society — "without renouncing the ambition of drawing out universal propositions." Comparisons with other cultures permit one to "avoid unjustifiably universalizing the particular case."[19] In the chapters that follow, comparative comments are offered where appropriate about transnational artistic phenomena such as the surreal, the modernist, and the many schools of music composition and visual art that swept the globe following World War Two. It should not be expected that these phenomena meant precisely the same things from one culture to another. To examine the field of cultural production is to engage in "a radical contextualization,"[20] Bourdieu's editor notes, far beyond particular social classes toward the total context of culture in a given era as proposed by Mikhail M. Bakhtin (1895–1975).[21] The first level of inquiry beyond the national, namely, the one-on-one comparative method — as scholars from previous generations such as Marc Bloch, Henri Pirenne, and C. Vann Woodward remind us — consists as much in identifying differences as similarities in historical phenomena.[22] Although a compass wider than the comparative is beyond my reach here, future scholars may wish to extend the scope to a second level, regional analysis, by incorporating evidence of artistic counterparts in China, Korea, and adjacent areas.[23] Even more broadly, art forms are attractive grist for research on a third level, the transregional scale long favored by economic analysts of world-systems[24] and, ultimately, for the kind of meta-history being attempted by newly emerging world historians since the start of the twenty-first century.[25]

Yet it is worth remembering the parameters as well as the possibilities of transnational research on the arts. As Julie Rivkin and Michael Ryan point out, "art provides access to a different kind of truth than is available to science, a truth that is immune to scientific investigation because it is accessible only through connotative language (allusion, metaphor, symbolism, etc.) and cannot be rendered in the direct, denotative, fact-naming languages of the sciences" or the quantitative social sciences.[26]

My working assumption is that any text — choreographical, musical, visual, as well as verbal — is susceptible to study in two modalities: (1) that of the moment when it was produced by a specific artist and (2) that of each successive point of retrospect, when a subsequent generation rereads it in different terms, and altered circumstances, for current purposes. Cumulatively the reception and impact of the text can change markedly across time. The challenge of cultural criticism is not merely to engage texts and their artists as timeless artifacts but also to situate them in timeful context: both theirs when produced and all subsequent times when recaptured. No single methodological approach or theoretical position can adequately interpret the multiplicity of artistic expressions found in Japan during the 1950s and 1960s. Instead the reader can be reassured, as Victor Brombert writes, that "eschewing a dogmatic approach and stressing diversity and variation do not preclude a search for underlying patterns and common tendencies."[27] It is to these patterns and tendencies that I now turn.

chapter one

The Occupation and Modernity

Abe Kōbō was part of a most peculiar generation. They had no money or freedom right after the war, only imagination. It's very sad that Abe and his group had to borrow so extensively from the West, just like intellectuals in the early Meiji period. In Abe's case, he borrowed from Kafka. — Arakawa Shūsaku, conceptual artist and urban designer[1]

China for many centuries served as the positional referent for Japanese who thought about their own culture in the round. Not infrequently, Edo-period treatises on international affairs began with platitudes such as "ours is a small and humble country compared with China." Once rapt attention turned to Europe and North America after the mid-nineteenth century, imperial China still remained something of a cultural benchmark for Japan, even when Meiji-era thinkers such as Fukuzawa Yukichi (1835–1901) toyed with "shedding Asia and joining Europe."[2] After the early Meiji fascination with the Atlantic world abated, the art historian Okakura Kakuzō (Tenshin, 1862–1913) famously positioned Japan as a bridge between Western culture and the arts of the Asian continent.[3] Eager as Japan undoubtedly was for ideas from Europe and the Americas during the 1910s and 1920s, it is also true that hundreds of Japanese artists and thousands of Chinese and Korean students crossed the East China Sea during those decades to visit one another's countries in search of knowledge and inspiration. Even at the height of Japan's preoccupation with the European avant-garde after World War One, this cultural turn toward the West took place amid sizable artistic interactions with East Asia that continued deep into the Pacific War.

Defeat, occupation, and autonomy brought about a renewed fascination with the West as cultural cynosure and creative exemplar during a brief but intense interlude lasting through the 1950s. By this time the engagement with Euro-America had grown so deep, the historian Naoki Sakai announced in 1989, that "even in its particularism, Japan was already implicated in the ubiquitous West, so that neither historically nor geopolitically could Japan be seen as *outside* of the West."[4] An example of the artistic enchantment with Europe was the early postwar novelist Abe Kōbō (1924–1993), who as Arakawa Shūsaku (1936–) suggests, emulated Franz Kafka (1883–1924) in letters, and perhaps in life, more than he honored any fellow Japanese writer. Virtually every genre of the Japanese avant-garde repositioned itself after 1945 vis-à-vis the Transatlantic region: Germany and France for composition, Italy, France, and the United States for visual media, New York for choreography. Yet within a decade or so, Yoshino Kōsaku points out, certain artists and writers began seeking a new national identity in "the anti-image of foreigners," to be "affirmed by formulating images of the Other; namely the West."[5] Either way, seeking or shirking, Japan's newly rebuilt cultural bridges all headed in one direction — West.

The American military occupation of Japan from 1945 to 1952, known as SCAP (Supreme Commander for the Allied Powers), abolished wartime controls on expression, only to impose somewhat milder restrictions of its own. At first print censorship was meant to protect the occupiers from harm, but soon it was used to promote democracy and, after 1949, to curb the recently legalized Japan Communist Party and its daily newspaper, *Akahata*. Restraints on traditional theater ended in mid-1947, but film remained suspect throughout. Today most nonverbal artists who were active at the time recall only cultural stimulation, not repression, by the American forces, perhaps forgetting that the public-radio network NHK and private broadcasters suffered a red purge in 1949 in which composers such as Yoshida Takako (1910–1956) and Suzuki Tomoko were driven off the air.[6]

During the occupation many aspiring artists used a library operated by the Civil Information and Education section of SCAP as a porthole for viewing contemporary American artistic currents. Yuasa Jōji (1929–), now the senior composer of art music in Japan, points out that "before 1952 we had no direct access to contemporary music, so we attended C I & E's concerts of recorded works by Aaron Copland, Charles Ives, Roy Harris, Leonard Bernstein, and others. C I & E also operated a library on American culture near the Hibiya Kōkaidō."[7] Like Yuasa, the composer Moroi Makoto (1930–) believes that "there was no occupation censorship of music"; he thinks this was "probably because the Americans did not think Japan was a musical country, in contrast with Germany. Nor did I feel resentment toward the occupation's arts policy, then or later."[8] Ōoka Makoto (1931–), the *Yomiuri* journalist who became a leading poet, acknowledges that "of course there were occasional frictions and odd aspects to the Japanese-American relationship," but he emphasizes that "very few artists felt pressures from American cultural hegemony."[9] Tsutsumi Seiji, who headed a student group affiliated with the Japan Communist Party at Tokyo University during the occupation, flatly states that "my generation of artists felt very little censorship from the Americans. The occupation legalized the Communist Party, and many writers and artists expressed interest in Marxism. But most of them were not Marxists by conviction, just curious about its ideas. Above all, they were interested in artistic freedom."[10]

But a minority of critics believe the occupation enforced a cultural policy that was blatantly antidemocratic. Suda Kunitarō (1891–1961), writing in the art journal *Mizue* in November 1947, decried the "endless importation of new styles" from the West under American rule, with their thick overlay of cultural imperialism.[11] The literary critic Etō Jun (1933–1999) argued that the Potsdam Declaration of July 1945 had promised Japan freedom of expression — hence the occupation censorship was illegal.[12] Etō asserted in 1965 that the conquering Americans had imposed their culture on Japan in much the same manner as the North had forced its way of life on the embittered South after the American Civil War.[13] A decade later the outspoken Yamashita Fumio (1924–) decried popular culture from the United States as "American imperialist cultural aggression," causing the "deterioration of Japanese culture."[14] The anticolonial chorus echoes to this day, and not just in Japan. Whatever the merits of such criticisms, there is little doubt that the occupation's "neocolonial revolution from above,"[15] as the historian John W. Dower puts it, socialized the country for its post-1952 dependence on authority under conservative Japanese governments, a highly unequal security treaty prescribed by the United States, and the presumed superiority of Western cultural models.

Clearly there is no consensus, even today, on cultural life under SCAP. "The Americans put too much emphasis on the ideal democratic world," according to Tanaka Takaki, a gallery specialist on contemporary sculpture. "Many artists were skeptical of this ideal, which they thought too theoretical and oversimplified. Artists also believed that material culture was growing too Americanized."[16] Such criticisms from the creative arena were as predictable as they were acute. Yet after 1945 it was no more feasible completely to exclude the West, artistically or otherwise, than it had been during the Meiji era — indeed, it was much less possible now. Instead the task was to confront modernism, surrealism, existentialism, and the possibilities of cultural accommodation and cultural subjectivity for the postwar era.

Postwar Modernity

The key to understanding Japan's nonverbal arts after 1945, as with their prewar forebears, lies not in determining how Western or Japanese their modernity may be; instead the task, as the literary critic Dennis Washburn has said of writers a half century earlier, is to "examine how Japan's interaction with the West resulted in new expressions of self-identity" through art.[17] Postwar modernity, like its Meiji and Taishō counterparts, was conceptualized by many Japanese as a synthesis: it embraced standards that were neither wholly Western ("modern") nor fully Japanese ("traditional"). To be sure, early in the occupation the cultural critic Kuwabara Takeo (1904–1988) and the architectural historian Hamaguchi Ryūichi (1916–1995) initially dismissed the premodern arts of Japan and, like the novelist Abe Kōbō, glorified the Western artist.[18] But by the 1950s both the arts historian Katō Shūichi (1919–) and the political theorist Maruyama Masao (1914–1996) had popularized the idea that modern Japanese culture, for better or for worse, was tightly interwoven with Western thought into what Katō called hybridity (*zasshusei*).[19] Among the many examples of this early postwar eclecticism were the architecture of Maekawa Kunio (1905–1986) and new hybrids in both calligraphy and pottery, the latter sometimes almost sculptural in appearance.[20]

In seeking new standards for art and thought, some Japanese philosophers sought to submit ethical values to searching criticism by asserting greater selfhood or subjectivity (*shutaisei*). "After defeat in the war," according to the art critic Haryū Ichiro (1925–), "the main theme of Japanese journals of opinion was 'how can we recover our humanity, our subjectivity?' I didn't believe this was possible because I knew the extreme situation of wartime would continue after 1945" through big-power rivalry. "Thus we couldn't reestablish our subjectivity by importing Western humanism" because the cold war imposed limits on artistic autonomy.[21] (Others held that there was no subjectivity to reestablish because it was absent before 1945, accounting for the lack of resistance to war.) Most intellectuals agreed that Japan should shun any fulsome embrace of Western ethics but still believed it possible to achieve democracy and independence by asserting the subject as an autonomous agent.

The sinologist Takeuchi Yoshimi (1910–1977), exponent of a Theory of National Literature (Kokumin Bungakuron), contended as early as 1948 that Japanese could reclaim their subjectivity only by resisting both cultural enslavement by the West and imprisonment by Marxist determinism; instead they should look to the Chinese Communist Party as an expression of selfhood.[22] Three years later Takeuchi began advocating a folk literature, grounded in freedom for the Japanese race *(minzoku)* however imagined, that would revolutionize society by "actualizing the whole human being."[23] At this same time the Marxist Ishimoda Shō (1912–) regarded *minzoku* as a symbol of collective opposition to authority in premodern times, but Takeuchi — like Fukuzawa Yukichi and Maruyama Masao — favored individualism as a route to national independence.[24] In sum, during wartime the notion of race had been monopolized by militarist ideologues trumpeting Japan's superiority over other peoples at a time when Tokyo ruled a multiethnic empire. Now that the nation was reduced to a supposedly monoethnic society, a newly constructed idea of race was coopted by the left in the 1950s and yoked to assertions of a post-Western subjectivity that resisted conservative politics at home and big-power hegemony abroad. This neo-localism found its expression during the next two decades in art as well as in thought.

By no means did the recovery of subjectivity by postwar artists necessarily lead to a specifically anti-Western essentialism; more often it pointed toward a post-Western expression of selfhood in art. In grappling with self-identity in the 1950s and 1960s, nearly all avant-garde artists in Japan were obliged to confront the regnant high modernism of postwar Europe. Modernism was not a movement but a set of attitudes and formal artistic practices that emerged at the turn of the twentieth century in rebuttal to two phenomena: (1) the persistence of the classical Mediterranean heritage of arts and letters and (2) the rise of mechanical culture in the factories and cities of industrializing Europe. Diverse modernists self-consciously separated themselves from the accepted values of the past (in so doing, they partially refigured "tradition" as their foil) and experimented with new forms of expression in current time. Modernists felt fragmented, not whole; they distanced themselves from a shared history and criticized it from the uniquely individual perspective of the self, with "a heightened sense of one's present moment."[25] In virtually every genre, individual self-consciousness regarding the act of narration "is the defining characteristic of the modern"[26] — and usually the modernist as well. The cultural geographer David Harvey spotlights the modernist preoccupation with originality: the artist now "had to assume an aura of creativity, of dedication to art for art's sake, in order to produce a cultural object that would be original, unique, and hence eminently marketable at a monopoly price"[27] — in contrast with popular culture for a mass market. Modernists generally advocated objectivism; some of them also believed that art "embodies or concretely enacts universal truths, what the New Critics called 'concrete universals.'"[28] In this sense a new fixity gradually came to replace the abjected artistic certainties of past centuries.

The avant-garde, which arose as early as 1909 with *Manifesto of Futurism* by F. T. Marinetti (1876–1944), helped to advance modernist attitudes but abhorred the aloof aestheticism of many modernist practitioners. Instead, the avant-garde tried to link art to politics and society, sometimes plunging into ideological controversies that modernists disdained because they preferred to focus their experimentation on form more than on content. An early example of the avant-garde outlook was the famous *Dada Manifesto*, which appeared in 1918 from the pen of Tristan Tzara (1896–1963), a French poet, artist, and terrorist revolutionary. Both the Russian design artist Aleksei Gan (1889–1942), who published *Constructivism Manifesto* in 1922, and the Hungarian artist László Moholy-Nagy (1895–1946), who joined the Bauhaus of Walter Gropius (1883–1969) in 1925 and led a New Bauhaus in Chicago after 1937, opposed purist approaches to the visual and believed that technology should link art to life.[29] During the interwar period philosophers belonging to the Frankfurt School, without renouncing their own fundamental modernism, critiqued the modernist detachment from politics and society. Ironically, not all of them overcame their own aloofness. Writing of one such Frankfurt figure as of 1925, Martin Jay points out that "never during the remainder of his life would Adorno [Theodor W., 1903–1969] abandon his cultural elitism."[30] After the 1920s the avant-garde grew more and more distinct from modernists, sometimes sparring with them over political questions of little interest to those who pursued art for its own sake.[31] An entirely different attack on modernism emanated from derriere-garde Nazi ideologues in the 1930s who regarded it as "the spiritual sellout of national values by decadent artists."[32]

East Asia was washed by these same tides of modernism and the avant-garde almost as soon as they first surged in Europe. In Japan, from the earliest years of the twentieth century, innovative visual and prose-fiction texts privileged the personal self while broadly repudiating all previous conventions of writing, painting, and sculpting. No less than in Europe and North America, film and photography turned the visual into a significant Japanese discourse after World War One. At the same time some of Japan's most daring artists pursued the global values of modernism without yielding their positionality between Europe and Asia. To most of them, modernism was tightly linked to modernization and became what the cultural critic Rey Chow calls a "displaced phenomenon" from abroad — difficult to elude without rejecting the larger modernity of which it was a part.[33] And to criticize modernity might well be to criticize the West *tout court*.[34]

Thus, whereas modernity itself was often transient and splintered into competing modernities, modernism by the end of World War Two grew increasingly attached to holistic certitudes about progress, authority, and global standards for artistic experimentation. Viewed from outside Europe and North America, these standards were tinged with the presumption of Western cultural primacy. Unlike the first modernists in the early twentieth century, postwar high modernism in the West generally accepted "machine rationality" and became closely associated with the dominant power centers in society: corporations, foundations, museums, orchestras, and the state.[35] The focus on experiments in form persisted. During the 1950s these same aesthetic and formalist concerns preoccupied many Japanese artists, some of whom attempted to harmonize the cultural dissonances of this contentious decade: Japan/West, national/international, tradition/modernity, realism/abstraction. A small group of avant-garde artists plunged headlong into the most celebrated political and ideological struggles: the plight of miners, ban-the-bomb campaigns, opposition to American military bases, resistance to extending the Japan–United States Mutual Security Treaty in 1960.[36] Most, however, opted for independence and individual freedom of expression. The artistic and political avant-gardes often clashed with each other during the 1950s, further dividing the disunified forces of the cultural left who felt checkmated by the cold-war confrontation between the United States and the Soviet Union. The literary critic Kurahara Korehito (1902–1999) and others in the Japan Communist Party denounced apolitical modernists for privileging personal subjectivity over class struggle; they declared that surrealism and existentialism were the latest in a series of otiose aesthetic movements spawned by modernism that overemphasized individualism and political disengagement.[37]

Reviving the Avant-Garde

Japan in the late 1940s and 1950s still depended on teletype, short-wave radio, and seamail shipments of art journals and vinyl sound recordings for most of its arts information from abroad. Only in the 1960s did digital technology and new media begin to turn Japanese life into the information society of today. Nonetheless young painters, sculptors, choreographers, and composers, including those born just before or after the Shōwa single-digit subset, showed great eagerness to learn about world artistic currents. At the same time they unanimously avow in retrospect that postsurrender poverty severely constrained their artistic ambitions. The sculptor Iida Yoshikuni (1923–) recalls that "when I was in college at Keiō right after the war, the country was impoverished, there was little to eat, and the country was starting over, as in the *Kojiki*" (Japan's oldest extant book, 712 C.E.).[38] The composer Takahashi Yūji (1938–), who was born just after the single-digit group, points out that "the immediate postwar generation of young composers experienced malnutrition, economic difficulties, and sometimes diseases such as tuberculosis. They had to take whatever jobs they could get to support their composing — for example, Takemitsu Tōru playing piano at an American base during the occupation."[39] To these factors the conductor Iwaki Hiroyuki (1932–) adds determination and perseverance: "The composers born within a few years of 1930 were poor and hungry after the war. Not all of them went to music school. They had dreams to fulfill and felt a real challenge to master new music. Plus they were willing to work very hard, practice incessantly, and fine-tune a work to get it just right."[40] Such sentimental recollections of youthful privation and struggle are widely shared by successful Japanese who were born just before World War Two, yet it is easy to imagine that many young artists in particular faced underemployment and scanty incomes during the first postwar decade.

Under these circumstances, what triggered such exceptional productivity by the early Shōwa group? Many who were then young agree with the composer Mamiya Michio (1929–) that their generation "proved to be so creative in the 1950s and 1960s as a response to the pressure from the military during wartime. All our stored-up creative impulses spilled forth once we were free to compose as we wished."[41] Matsudaira Yoriaki (1931–), a noted cancer researcher as well as a writer of contemporary music, remembers that "in my teens I decided I wanted to be a composer because everything was wiped out by defeat in 1945. The super-spiritualism of wartime was anathema to me. I knew I wanted to find out how far art could express emotion from within."[42] This age group was unique among Japanese artists in experiencing prewar, wartime, and postwar conditions, and it was the first post-1945 cohort not to have taken part in the fighting. Yuasa Jōji, perhaps Japan's most celebrated composer today, points out that "when the war ended, we suffered a loss of credo. As young students, we recognized that older Japanese were confused about their values. We couldn't trust the old ideological canon, morality, or aesthetics. Instead we had to go our own way."[43] What Yuasa omitted was that their own way often led directly to discovering modernism under the aegis of the occupying American overlord.

In short, a combination of resoluteness in the face of material want, rejection of wartime beliefs, and cognitive rupture with artistic practices of the past goes far toward explaining why these young artists of the late 1940s and 1950s were so remarkably productive. So too does the dissonance between the cultural cocoon of wartime and the flood of foreign ideas after 1945, "forcing us young people to think about the human condition," as the businessperson-novelist Tsutsumi Seiji puts it. He adds that many of these artists, such as Takemitsu and Abe Kōbō, "had experience abroad as children, in Korea,

Manchuria, or China, so they were open to other cultures."[44] Perhaps most significant of all, they were ready to chart new intellectual vectors through art — no simple task, given the sizable cultural inheritance from Japan's earlier encounters with modernity dating to the late nineteenth century.

However hard young Japanese artists labored to distance themselves from the past, it was impossible to shed the full weight of prewar cultural innovations or the impact of senior artists who were still active after 1945. Working with the inherited conventions and scarce materials of their era, Japanese artists right after the war richly illustrate Stacy Combs Lynch's point that "it is the ability to use limitations creatively that separates 'art' from 'formula.'"[45] Starting in the late 1920s, a tiny band of composers interested in the modern arts coalesced around the journal *Ongaku shinchō* (New musical tide), forming the nucleus of the New Composers Association (Shin Sakkyokuka Kyōkai); they were complemented in 1930 by the New Composers Federation (Shinkō Sakkyokuka Renmei).[46] After 1945 several important composers from the prewar period championed Western-style art music in Japan. Yamada Kōsaku (1886–1965), trained in Tokyo and Berlin, was the best known, but a handful of artists who in the 1930s wrote syncretic contemporary music incorporating Japanese and European themes had a greater allure to the early postwar generation. Kiyose Yasuji (1900–1981) displayed pride in Japanese culture through his vocal music drawing partly on rural songs.[47] The mainly self-taught composer Hayasaka Fumio (1914–1955) became a music director for the Tōhō film studios in 1939; between the end of the war and his death from tuberculosis in 1955, Hayasaka wrote fifty-four movie scores.[48] The musicologist Judith Herd regards Kiyose and Hayasaka as people's nationalists, seeking identity in aspects of Japanese culture without necessarily embracing government policy in the 1930s and early 1940s.[49]

Other carryover figures made their impact on the young composers after 1945 through teaching and policy making. Moroi Saburō (1903–1977, the father of Moroi Makoto), who studied composition in Berlin during 1932–1934, served as an Education Ministry official responsible for musical education between 1946 and 1964. Ifukube Akira (1914–), considered Pan-Asianist,[50] taught after World War Two at Tokyo Academy of Music (merged into Tokyo University of Fine Arts and Music in 1949), where his best-known pupils included Akutagawa Yasushi (1925–1989, a son of the short-story writer Akutagawa Ryūnosuke) and Mayuzumi Toshirō (1929–1997).

Perhaps the most signal transitional composer was Matsudaira Yoritsune (1907–2001), who linked prewar composers like Hayasaka and Kiyose to members of the early postwar avant-garde, most importantly Takemitsu Tōru (1930–1996). Matsudaira, whose compositions were performed in France and San Francisco as early as 1937, began immediately after World War Two to incorporate elements from ancient Japanese court music (gagaku) into his experiments in twelve-tone technique. Judith Herd points out that, almost a decade before the chance operations of John Cage (1912–1992) became known in Japan, Matsudaira was using an open-notation system based on the free-form structure of gagaku court music.[51] Whatever his attachment to premodern themes, Matsudaira was exceptional in promoting contemporary music, yet his works, like those of other more "neonationalist" composers, were seldom performed (Herd estimates that only 20 percent of Matsudaira's compositions have ever been played in Japan).[52] Within months of the surrender in August 1945, these and other music leaders took advantage of the new freedoms under American occupation to revive prewar composers' associations and establish new ones. By the end of the occupation, performances of new art music sponsored by these groups occurred more frequently than ever, spurred on in part by music criticism from the pens of Yoshida Hidekazu (1913–) and Tōyama Kazuyuki (1922–).[53]

Like the other arts derived from Europe, Western-style dance entered Japan during the Meiji period — but just barely. With its arrival in 1912, Japanese audiences turned ballet into an instant orthodoxy. Together with its offspring, modern dance, ballet in Japan was even more self-consciously iconoclastic than Western-style music, painting, or sculpture because to win acceptance it had to overcome the weighty tradition of classical Japanese dance from the Edo period (1600–1868). Ballet in Japan soon took a sharply Russian turn, particularly after the Anna Pavlova Ballet Company performed in Japan during the 1920s. Tachibana Akiko (1907–1971) developed choreography in this vein that eventually led to the distinctive works offered by her daughter Maki Asami's dance company, founded in 1963.[54] The pioneering choreographer Ishii Baku (1892–1962) staged the first public performance of Western-style dance entirely by Japanese artists in June 1916. Other carryover artists who trained the first postwar generation of modern dancers included Eguchi Takaya (1900–1977) and his wife Miya Misako (1909–), both of whom studied abroad after World War One and eventually brought home expressionist styles from Mary Wigman's institute in Germany and the DeniShawn studios in Los Angeles.[55] The last genro of this dance generation is Ōno Kazuo (1906–), the master teacher of more postwar choreographers in Japan than any other artist, who still appeared onstage at dance concerts, seated in a chair, as recently as 2002.

So eager were Japanese dancers to return to the stage after the surrender that postwar dance reappeared in the sweltering month of August 1946 with a joint performance of scenes from *Swan Lake* at the venerable Imperial

Theater in Hibiya, Tokyo, which had somehow escaped bombardment in American air raids near the end of the war. Members of three prewar companies formed an ad hoc group for the occasion called the Tokyo Ballet Company (unrelated to the Tchaikovsky Memorial Tokyo Ballet Company, which started in 1964). Dancers gamely went through their steps to recorded music because no orchestra was available. The sets and stage art for this production were designed by the oil painter Fujita Tsuguharu (Léonard Foujita, 1886–1968), who had lived in Paris for many years before World War Two.[56] Modern dancers trained abroad during the 1920s and 1930s also reappeared onstage soon after Japan surrendered, quickly putting aside solos and duets in favor of performances by ensembles and full companies. But contemporary dance was fully revitalized only in the mid-fifties, partly because of a brief tour in November 1955 by the Martha Graham Dance Company. By this time classical Japanese dance (Nihon Buyō) was slowly converting from a private salon art to one also seen in the public concert hall, but little of its choreography felt the pull of the avant-garde before the 1960s.[57]

Whereas public schools taught Western classical music while ignoring traditional Hōgaku music and dance for most of the prewar era, both the Japanese-style natural-pigment painting (Nihonga) that emerged in the late nineteenth century and Western-style oil painting (Yōga) were jointly emplaced after 1900 at the state fine-arts academy and in official exhibitions. Both schools of painting were soon buffeted by modernism from abroad and innovations at home. Modernism in Japan meant not a revolt against entrenched artistic conventions but the creation of a contemporary academicism where little formalism existed. Yokoyama Taikan (1868–1958) was the prewar doyen of modern Nihonga, a new style — largely contrived for reasons of cultural nationalism — that commonly used watercolors, ink, the color black, and materials such as silk and gold or silver leaf. Especially in oil painting and sculpture, Japanese embraced the techniques and movements of the contemporary West not as rebellious radicals but as part of the new accredited orthodoxy from Europe that flooded Japan during 1875–1925. Two Western-style oil painters whose prestige ballooned immediately after World War Two were Yasui Sōtarō (1888–1955) and Umehara Ryūzaburō (1888–1986), each of whom had studied at the Académie Julian in Paris early in the twentieth century and did his most skilled work, all of it figurative, during 1925–1940. These carryover artists served as painterly ballast amid the staccato arrivals of abstract expressionism, informel, and other radical movements from abroad during the first years after the American occupation.[58]

Another painter who might have provided guidance to the Shōwa single-digit group of young artists was Fujita Tsuguharu, who reached Paris in 1913 and, except for the 1940s, lived there the rest of his life. The son of a Japanese army surgeon, Fujita learned French in junior high school, graduated from the Tokyo School of Fine Arts, and in France came to know Picasso, Modigliani, Soutine, and members of the School of Paris. Back in Japan during World War Two, he became a renowned painter of army battle scenes but also produced much other art. After the war Fujita was accused of complicity with Japanese militarism by the Japan Art Association (Nihon Bijutsukai, newly formed in 1947) and hounded out of the country in 1949. The critic Haryū Ichirō considers Fujita a scapegoat, the more so because many other Japanese artists turned out military paintings before 1945 but failed to ask themselves about their own war responsibility after the surrender.[59]

The prewar Japanese preference for figurative art exemplified by Yokoyama, Yasui, Umehara, and Fujita continued after 1945 and remains much in vogue today. A frank appraisal by the art historian Chiba Shigeo finds that stylistically "war and defeat probably had no impact on the majority of artists."[60] Yet it is also true that abstract painting flourished in Japan during the 1930s: Murai Masanari (1905–1999), who is best known internationally for his prints, was a pioneering oil painter and mentor to young abstractionists after the war.[61] As with composers, choreographers, playwrights, and poets, Japan's visual artists after 1945 soon set about reinstating the most robust among the prewar artists' associations as well as establishing new ones. Collectively these groups were strikingly open to innovation in all métiers, including painters in both Japanese and Western styles.

The Japan Avant-Garde Artists Club, founded in 1947 as successor to a similar prewar association, held exhibitions in 1948 and 1949 that were veritable coming-out parties for the postwar leaders of the avant-garde arts in that country. Among its top figures were the painter Okamoto Tarō, the critic Takiguchi Shūzō, and the painter Yoshihara Jirō — three of the prime movers behind the arts experiments of the 1950s — as well as the prominent painter Fukuzawa Ichirō (1898–1992). Some of its eighty-four members simultaneously belonged to other artists' associations, and by 1953 most of them had left the Avant-Garde Club for one of two new groups founded that year: Okamoto's International Art Club (Kokusai Āto Kurabu) or Yoshihara's Japan Abstract Art Club (Nihon Abusutorakuto Āto Kurabu). These and many similar short-lived organizations existed mainly to sponsor showings of their members' works at a time when museums were few and gallery exhibits even fewer; most had disbanded by the mid-1960s if not before.[62]

Art historians in Japan often single out certain representational works from the late 1940s or 1950s as "the art of despair," including a focus on the body, whole or in parts. The despair is attributed variously to the distrust and hopelessness of the war years and to Japan's subordination to American culture immediately thereafter, when bodily needs for food and health were pressing.[63] A 1949 oil painting, *Quo Vadis* by Kitawaki Noboru (1901–1951), shows the back of a man in a rumpled brown suit and battered hat, carrying a russet knapsack like that of Ninomiya Sontoku (1787–1856), the peasant sage whose statue stood in every prewar schoolyard (see Plate 1). Unlike the dauntless Ninomiya, who carried a book in his other hand, the bewildered man is staring aimlessly at a distant line of demobilized soldiers trudging through sand waving a red flag, perhaps of revolution.[64]

A further example is the *Bathroom* series (*Yokushitsu*, 1953–1955, oil) by Kawara On (1932–), including an objectified pregnant woman and mutilated body parts in a distorted Japanese bath — "truly our situation after the war, I thought," according to the critic Haryū Ichirō.[65] Intercultural relations during the occupation are sometimes portrayed in gendered terms: the conquering Americans emasculating powerless Japanese males. But Kawara's bathrooms are littered with dismembered corpses regardless of gender, flattened to two dimensions like cut-out figures from a child's book of paper dolls. The Kyushu painter Kikuhata Mokuma, however, had little patience for such images, labeling this preoccupation with the flesh "a form of self-flagellation" by artists "overcome by self-abhorrence."[66] A late instance of the art of despair shows no humans at all: the *Martial Law* series (*Kaigen jōtai*, 1955–1958, oil) by Ishii Shigeo (1933–1962), revealing the artist's belief that wartime imperialism had been replaced by security-treaty imperialism amid the cold war (see Plate 2). The best known is Number V, dating to 1957, showing steel explosives raining down on an urban plaza devoid of people, as though a neutron bomb had already wiped out civilization.[67] Ishii's painting is perhaps the most striking political commentary by a Shōwa single-digit visual artist, abandoning all hope for humanity in the thermonuclear age.

The body also figures prominently in postwar sculpture, as has long been true of the genre. An example more hopeful in spirit than the Ishii painting is *Wadatsumi* (*Poseidon*, 1950, bronze) by Hongō Shin (1905–1980), depicting a nude male from the sea standing with hands simultaneously gesturing power and conciliation (Figure 1). But this work met an unexpected fate, perhaps signaling the confusion of the times. It was commissioned by the peace group Wadatsumikai and first offered to Tokyo University, which turned it down because it was deemed too political. Ritsumeikan University then acquired a casting of *Wadatsumi* (likely the same one refused by Tokyo University) and installed it on its Kyoto campus, where radical students destroyed it during a 1969 demonstration. The Setagaya Art Museum, nestled in spacious Kinuta

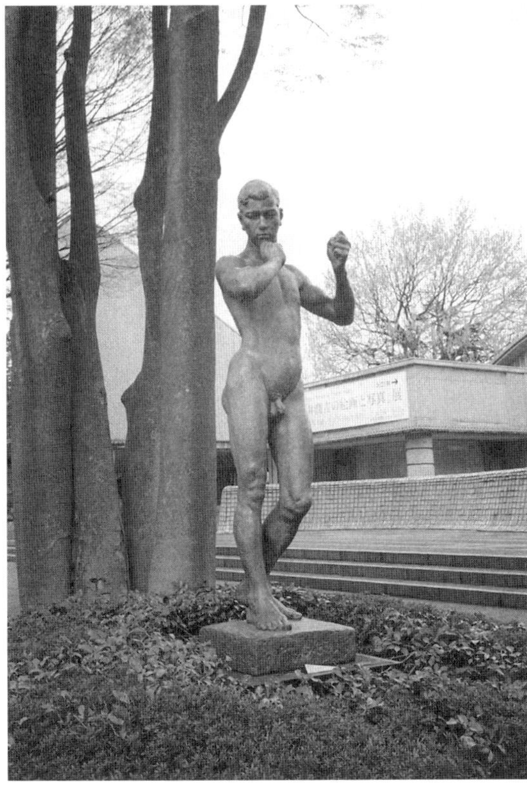

Figure 1. Hongō Shin. *Wadatsumi no koe (Poseidon)*. 1950. Bronze. Setagaya Museum of Art, Tokyo. Photo by the author.

Family Park in western Tokyo, purchased a casting made in 1986 that stands today beneath towering trees before the museum entrance.[68]

By 1954 the internecine squabbles in the various genre-based arts associations had settled down, a second postwar generation of innovative artists was emerging, and the urgency of belonging to a formal organization was starting to abate in each of the nonverbal arenas as new independent art shows, concert halls, recital spaces, and other outlets gradually opened up. By then, too, the avant-garde had been redefined and reinvigorated by two parallel clusters of politically progressive activity taking place amid the occupation-era cultural revivals in music, dance, and the visual media sketched above: The Century Association (Seiki no Kai), founded in January 1947 by aspiring writers at Tokyo University centering on the novelist Abe Kōbō, and the Evening Society (Yoru no Kai), established by Okamoto Tarō and the editor-critic Hanada Kiyoteru (1909–1974) in January 1948. More so than other organizations at the time, these groups encouraged thinking that spanned the boundaries of conventional artistic genres.

Integrating the Arts

At its most engaged, the first postwar generation of avant-garde artists in Japan was more deeply entangled in political questions than many of them later wished to disclose. Like Japan writ large, the avant-garde began its postwar activity without a clear vision of the future but with an inescapable consciousness of a conflicted present. Because society under the American occupation was so highly politicized, young artists regardless of genre could hardly avoid taking up controversial topics even though they may have found politics distasteful. The distinctions between political and artistic progressives were a constant source of debate, yet in many respects the lines became blurred by the overtly ideological character of early postwar discourse. Even more strikingly than during the 1920s and 1930s, one pole was clutched by abstract and surrealist expression, the other by many varieties of social consciousness, including socialist realism. The debates between the abstractionists and the realists turned less on artistic matters than on political outlooks, although within the progressive camp that opposed capitalism or American hegemony lurked important differences of artistic approach. As the critic Taki Kōji points out, most artists of the era lacked critical perspective on world events and were ill informed of the outlooks on international affairs held by their counterparts in other countries.[69] Amid the chaos of the early occupation, the most energetic young Japanese artists formed small groups and carried out transgenre activities of many sorts, searching for ways to make sense of the political contention and economic dislocation confronting Japanese society.

The tangled web of art and politics during the occupation was woven from strands reflecting the rapid rise and fall of small coteries that illustrate how inescapably politics encroached on art during the late 1940s and 1950s. "A big goal of our work right after the war was the integration of the arts (*geijutsu sōgō*)," according to Segi Shin'ichi, one of the small circle of writers and artists then in their twenties who attended gatherings of the Century Association initiated by Sekine Hiroshi (1920–) to discuss principles and possibilities across the creative spectrum — talking across but not dissolving the boundaries of existing genres. Segi agrees that Japanese artists were at the forefront globally in trying to unify goals across genres after World War Two, but he acknowledges that the inspiration "came from Russian constructivism and French surrealism."[70] The same was true of the Evening Society when it began as a salon of more than two dozen avant-garde figures mainly in their thirties. Sekine Hiroshi, a poet who was interested in proletarian theater, and the writer Abe Kōbō, who had just finished his medical studies at Tokyo University after returning from Manchuria in the million-person repatriation of 1946,[71] belonged to both the Century and Evening groups and served as liaisons between the two.

Antecedent to both these clubs was the New Japan Literary Association (Shin Nihon Bungakukai), established immediately after the war to carry forward the spirit of the former Japan Proletarian Writers Federation (Nihon Puroretaria Sakka Dōmei), which had disbanded under threat of governmental pressure in 1934. Takeuchi Yoshimi, the sinologist who expounded the Theory of National Literature after the war, pointed out that the New Japan Literary Association, after debating whether proletarian literature could be turned into democratic literature, ended up as a very different organization from its prewar forebear.[72] Referring to one of its leading lights, the composer Hayashi Hikaru (1931–) noted that "Abe Kōbō had his own individual way of participating in the peace movement. Abe was a part of the New Japan Literary Association, which was closely tied to the Japan Communist Party [JCP], until the party divided in 1950 and many members of the literary group scattered. It may seem strange to say this, but the New Japan Literary Association was purely artistic"[73] — and little concerned with politics.

When the Century Association was launched in 1947, followed by the Evening Society in early 1948, surrealism and existentialism from interwar Europe dominated many discussions at both. The surrealist artists and writers who gathered in Paris between 1924 and 1940 traced their antecedents to Jean Arp (1877–1966) and other antiwar, artistically nihilist poets and painters in Zurich who began using the nonsense term Dada in 1916. Surrealism, with its emphasis on fantastic images through odd juxtapositions, rejected other more structured doctrines of modern art to focus squarely on subject matter, exploring dreams and fantasies with a view toward eventual social change. Man Ray (1890–1976), Joan Miró (1893–1983), Giorgio De Chirico (1888–1978), and Salvador Dalí (1904–1989) piloted surrealist visual culture. Although some of these artists sympathized with communism, surrealism was anathema to official Marxists because of its denial of socialist realism.[74] Japanese interest in the European avant-garde predated World War One, but surrealism drew special attention after 1925 through lectures by the Keiō University poet Nishiwaki Junzaburō (1894–1982), whose advocacy helped to insure that surrealist ideas had as much currency in the literary world as in the plastic arts. Five years later the views of surrealism's prime mover, André Breton (1896–1966), became well known through a Japanese translation by Takiguchi Shūzō of Breton's slender *Le surréalisme et la peinture*, originally published in Paris in 1928.[75]

Twentieth-century existentialism portrayed the dilemma of the individual cut loose from clear standards of right conduct and forced to exercise free choice in daily life without any certainty of outcomes. Morris Dickstein, the contemporary literary critic, pointed out in a 2002 interview that existentialists presented the individual "as perched over an abyss; we had to act in the face of absurdity, knowing the futility of our actions." Such writers "moved away from absolute moral values and toward the sense of contingency, a feeling that life was unpredictable and we had to live fully."[76] Existential views, particularly those from Germany, appealed to Japanese philosophers caught in a "pessimistic mood"[77] after defeat in war, whereas the French existentialism of Jean-Paul Sartre (1905–1980) and Simone de Beauvoir (1908–1986) emphasized individual responsibility and prompted many postwar artists in Japan to seek "that creative freedom which finds ultimate expression in being a law unto one's self."[78] Although existentialism and especially surrealism are sometimes seen as part of Japanese modernism, their respective demurrers from notions of formalist universals added importantly to the nascent anti-modernist tenor of the avant-garde shortly after the war.

The Century Association began as a literary coterie but soon embraced all the arts. Among the visiting speakers in 1949 were Okamoto Tarō, Hanada Kiyoteru, and the philosopher Tsurumi Shunsuke (1922–), followed the next year by Takiguchi Shūzō, the leftist writer Noma Hiroshi (1915–1991), and the playwright Fukuda Tsuneari (1912–1994), a youthful radical who later became an outspoken neoconservative. "Okamoto Tarō was an artist no one could resist," the art critic Kanazawa Takeshi points out. "He was the only source Japan had for information about European art once Fujita Tsuguharu left the country."[79] Starting in late 1950 the art-film director Teshigahara Hiroshi hosted the group's offices at his Shimizuchō home in the Ogikubo area of Tokyo, a house formerly owned by his wife Aiko's father, the New Sensationalist (Shinkankakuha) writer Kataoka Teppei (1894–1944). Here members of the group helped Teshigahara bind copies of its publications, printed by mimeograph on rough paper without permission from American censors.[80]

Okamoto and Hanada's Evening Society began shortly after the Century Association and at first operated quite independently of it. But soon their shared interests in the philosophy and practice of the avant-garde drew the two organizations together: like the Century group, "in terms of aesthetic principles the Evening Society played an important multimedia role during the late 1940s," says the composer Takahashi Yūji.[81] Abe, Sekine, Noma, and a number of prominent painters who joined this contentious group after September 1948 found themselves agreeing more often about artistic principles — especially the place of realism — than about politics.[82] A reorganization implemented by Okamoto and Hanada in the spring of 1949 resulted in closer coordination with the Century Association. Yet despite its efforts at integrating the arts, by mid-1949 the Evening Society separated in two when its visual artists formed their own division to prepare for upcoming exhibitions sponsored by others. Segi Shin'ichi, a leading chronicler of the early postwar avant-garde, points out that the Evening group was "never far from the ideological disputes taking place within the Japan Communist Party,"[83] which suffered severe criticism by the Cominform in January 1950 and split into a mainstream calling for violent revolution and a gradualist antimainstream. Riven with dissent and antipathy, the Evening Society disbanded that same year.

The Century Association was likewise not immune to fissure, particularly when Abe became its undisputed archon in April 1950. By that point he had shown a sudden disposition toward the Communist Party, thanks in good measure to his political (but not artistic) affinity with Noma Hiroshi, to whom he drew closer after Abe had a public falling out with Hanada, his erstwhile literary patron.[84] A number of painters from the Century group had defiantly taken part in Takiguchi's Second Modern Art Exhibition, sponsored by the Avant-Garde Artists Club in September 1949 at the Mitsukoshi Department Store in Nihonbashi, Tokyo. Most of them seceded from the Century Association as soon as Abe was chosen to head it; many joined Kitadai Shōzō (1921–) in forming a new artists' organization, Pouvoir no Kai (1950), which itself soon divided into a politically engaged wing and a supposedly pure-art wing. As one member of the Century group recalled, 1950 was the beginning of "a deep political shadow" over the avant-garde,[85] driving a number of its nonverbal artists into antiformalist experimentation that they believed was unconnected with political ideology.

During these stormy times all three doyens of the postwar avant-garde, Takiguchi, Okamoto, and Yoshihara Jirō, managed to step aside from both party politics and political activism: Takiguchi to write poetry and art criticism, Okamoto to take on the fine-arts establishment single-handedly, Yoshihara to paint and patronize other painters in Kansai. In so doing, they tacitly accepted the 1952 compromise whereby a new conservative government led by Prime Minister Yoshida Shigeru (1878–1967) deferred to the United States in an unequal mutual-security treaty in return for the right to virtually unrestricted trade with all other countries.

Abe, Teshigahara, and the remainder of the moribund Century Association now reached out to artists from the Vanguard Art Association (Zen'ei Bijutsukai), founded in 1947 to carry forward the radical spirit of proletarian art from the 1930s. Among the best-known Vanguard members were the sculptor and future video artist Yamaguchi Katsuhiro (1928–) and the Hiroshima painter Maruki Iri (1910–1995), who together with his wife Akamatsu Toshiko (Maruki Toshi, 1912–2000) produced the well-known *Genbaku no zu, daiichibu (Atomic Bomb Portrait, Part One)* in 1950.[86] The majority of the Vanguard group belonged to the Communist Party but felt bewildered by its rapid changes of dogma and welcomed the chance to discuss surrealism, Franz Kafka (whom Abe considered fresher than Sartre), and what Abe called "social existentialism" or "subrealism," a clear repudiation of the sterile socialist realism espoused by the party.[87] A cognate movement centering on architecture gained momentum when Tange Kenzō (1913–2005), Maekawa Kunio (1905–1986), and others founded the New Works Association (Shinseisakuha Kyōkai) in 1949 to stretch architects' imaginations; two years later reformist Japanese-style painters from a group called Creative Arts (Sōzō Bijutsu, founded January 1948) joined the New Works Association in pursuit of transmedia inspiration.[88]

Nonetheless, by 1951, when the Century Association officially dissolved, most of Japan's early postwar impulses toward integrating the avant-garde arts had redirected themselves in a confusing surfeit of directions, appropriate to that year's turmoil over the occupation's red purge, the Korean War, continuing economic dislocations, and debates over security relations once the country regained autonomy, scheduled for the following spring. Although many progressive artists turned their backs on political activity in favor of developing their art, a number of them resorted to social involvement in various forms, most notably the school of reportage art that flourished briefly in the early 1950s.

Nonparty Activists

The ties between the Japan Communist Party and avant-garde artists speedily attenuated after 1951 and reached the snapping point by mid-1955. At Noma's behest, Abe, Teshigahara (briefly), and the visual artist Katsuragawa Hiroshi (1924–) from the Century-Vanguard circle had joined the party in March 1951. Two months later, with the demise of the Century Association, Abe and the mainstream JCP established a short-lived People's Arts Federation (Jinmin Geijutsu Shūdan), "where his true nature as a surrealist became evident," according to Hayashi Hikaru.[89] Ironically, Abe won acceptance in the conservative literary establishment that same summer by being awarded the Akutagawa prize for a story in his 1951 collection *Kabe* (The wall), the first avant-garde writer to be so recognized. He learned this astonishing news while organizing factory workers in Ōtaku, Tokyo, at the same time the People's Arts Federation was collapsing around him because so many of its artists did not wish their work to become politicized.[90] Abe turned next to writing social documentaries, forming the Contemporary Association (Genzai no Kai) in January 1952 together with the prolific writers Shimao Toshio (1917–1986) and Manabe Kureo (1920–). This step allowed activists beyond the grasp of the JCP to develop reportage on socioeconomic problems and stimulated major demonstrations by literary and visual artists against American military bases the following year.

During the brief lifetime of the People's Arts Federation a parallel group of seven visual artists spearheaded by Ikeda Tatsuo (1928–), Kawara On, and Nakamura Hiroshi (1932–) broke off in June 1951 from Kitadai Shōzō's Pouvoir club, founded the previous year, to set up an activist society with the contrarian name Non. This unit undertook direct resistance by supporting local struggles against environmental disruptions caused by dam construction, military installations, and power plants. It also held monthly discussions and presented a group project on contemporary conditions at the Yomiuri Independent art exhibition in early 1952. Meanwhile, dismayed at the irretrievable fissure in Pouvoir, three members of its painterly wing — Kitadai, Yamaguchi Katsuhiro, and Fukushima Hideko (1927–1997) — bolted in August 1951 to the newly formed Experimental Workshop (Jikken Kōbō), a fresh effort at integrating the nonverbal arts under the guidance of Takiguchi Shūzō.[91]

Despite its tiny size, the Non group thrived under its new name Energy (Enāji) and in the fall of 1952 effectively declared its solidarity with the activists in Abe's Contemporary Association: "We are a group of young artists who seek to establish a new people's art *(minzoku geijutsu)* based on amity and fusion with the revolutionary proletariat and laboring masses who champion the independence and peace of the people *(minzoku)*."[92] These words show a strong affinity with socialist politics, if not with the Japan Communist Party itself, and they reflect the same preoccupation with the Japanese people as a racial group, distinct from conservative elites, that marked so much progressive discourse in the 1950s. Members of Energy, still few in number, prized creative work based on "recognition and implementation,"[93] both in their realist documentary paintings and in their street activism. The main site of Energy's practical action was Sunagawa, where a lengthy struggle was carried out throughout the 1950s by local residents opposed to expanding the United States military air base at Tachikawa in western Tokyo, building on momentum generated by nationwide protests in 1952–1953 against constructing a firing range in Uchinada village, Ishikawa prefecture, for use by American troops training for the Korean War.

Energy was central to Abe Kōbō's last stab at connecting the Japan Communist Party to activism in the arts: the Youth Artists Alliance (Seinen Bijutsuka Rengō), unfurled in March 1953 as an umbrella group to include many unaffiliated painters of social conscience as well as Teshigahara Hiroshi, Katsuragawa Hiroshi, and Yamashita Kikuji (1919–1986) from the Bread and Roses Association (Pan to Bara no Kai), an offshoot of the Vanguard Art Association with ties to the JCP. Members of the former Century Association who had refused any involvement with the Communist Party also took part. Certain members of the Youth Artists Alliance joined in antibase and antinuclear demonstrations under the slogan "peace and liberty" inspired by the Korean War,[94] and some of them produced paintings on these subjects. Many others, nonactivist by instinct but progressive in outlook, remained in their studios and documented social issues through realistic works. The first showing of alliance paintings took place in June 1953 at the inaugural Nippon Exhibition of mainly representational art cosponsored by the Vanguard Association.[95] Included were sixteen items from Kawara On's shocking *Bathroom* series.

The Nippon Exhibition, which continues today as the Scene (Shaku) show, began in 1947 as an exhibit by members of the Vanguard Association who rejected the socialist realism of the Japan Art Association (Nihon Bijutsukai), founded in April 1946 under JCP sponsorship. Earlier in 1947 the Japan Art Association had begun sponsoring the country's first free-submission, nonjuried show, known as the Japan Independent Exhibition (Nihon Andepandanten), to "wave the banner of socialist realism."[96] The Vanguard event was organized in response, but it staked out turf that differed far more artistically than politically from that of the Japan Independent, which likewise still exists. Once transformed into the Nippon Exhibition in 1953, this annual show stole much of the thunder from works produced under the direct impress of official Marxism. In this way, as the critic Sawaragi Noi points out, the Japan Art Association clung to the barren heritage of socialist realism and "lost its critical ground vis-à-vis modernism."[97] Haryū Ichirō adds that the Communist Party's insistence on socialist realism became "a strongly conservative force," dismissing all art since impressionism as "modernist" and driving away many artists as a result.[98]

Another approach to activism emanated from mountain-village operations units set up by the Japan Communist Party during 1951–1955 to agitate against landlords who had ducked the occupation land reforms and to organize liberated zones where oppressed farmers could resist dam construction, oppose planned industrial sites, or carry out postcolonial protests at the nearest American military installations.[99] A number of avant-garde artists took part, including Teshigahara Hiroshi, Kawara On, and Yamashita Kikuji from the Bread and Roses group. Teshigahara told his biographer "there was certainly an anti-imperialist atmosphere among us then"; postwar "Japanese-American relationships had started in a totally colonialistic way, and we couldn't help being critical at that time."[100] The mountain units were a predictable political failure but an unexpected artistic success, for they were the seedbed of a nonparty movement known as reportage painting that focused on social, but not socialist, realism. Socialist realism as promoted by communist parties worldwide addressed political reality through art that was revolutionary only in subject matter, not in style or technique. Marxists regarded art not as the expression of universal ideals but as a social phenomenon born of the particular historical context in which it was produced.[101] By contrast, social realism or critical realism, as the literary critic Leo Ou-fan Lee points out, represents "a social stance of discontent" and "an overriding obsession with the ills of contemporary society" that is political in implication but "remains anchored in the subjective perception of the individual,"[102] not in ideological positions.

Social-realist reportage art in Japan repudiated the antimodernist critical stance of the Communist Party as too theoretical, too politicized, and insufficiently based in observable reality. Reportage painters are especially interesting because of their marriage of the seemingly irreconcilable — realism and surrealism — a union made possible by leaving aside the irrational elements of the latter. Reportage works often reflected both the external conscious reality of society and the internal unconscious reality of the artist's psyche, as informed by surrealism. The masterpiece in this métier is Yamashita's *Akebonomura monogatari* (*Tale of Akebono Village*, 1953), painted in oils on dungaree, a powerful statement about the harsh life of a farm household that evokes surrealism yet echoes Japanese wood-block prints of folk subjects (see Plate 3).[103] On the one hand, its simplicity conveys the rough-hewn poverty and narrowness of rural living; on the other hand, its compositional imbalance and clutter suggest the confusion of domestic existence in the countryside. The critic Dore Ashton observes that Teshigahara's films of the 1950s likewise took an "almost documentary approach,"[104] one the cinema historian Donald Richie calls "existential."[105]

Realist photographers such as Domon Ken (1909–1990) joined in the documentary effort in the early 1950s without being closely connected with reportage painters. Domon photographed antibase demonstrations, Hiroshima survivors, and poor miners in Chikuho throughout the decade, in line with his activist belief that "realist photography is an expression" of the "spirit of resistance that honestly sees reality and tries to steer reality to a more correct direction."[106] An early affinity with Walter Benjamin's ideas about art and mechanical reproduction became evident at this time.[107] Although photographers used black and white images to record people's daily lives, a number of them such as Ishimoto Yasuhiro (1921–) seemed less interested in specific themes of poverty or political protest than in documenting rural life before it receded in the face of urban development. Still others, as the world wanderer Abe Nobuya (1913–1971) put it, "came to understand how the international can be achieved by looking at the national in a convincing way"[108] through photographs. Only with the rise of conceptual art in the late 1960s and 1970s, when painters began using camera images in their works, was photography fully recognized as a contemporary art in Japan.

Reportage paintings displayed at the annual Nippon Exhibition starting in 1953 provided "an unsparing caricature of the distortions and contradictions"[109] of fatherless households, grim industrial scenes, prostitutes, the homeless, poor, and sick, and sites of political opposition to American military bases and Japanese police brutality. At its core, the critic Kondō Yukio believes, "reportage art was a reaction to the tragedy of World War Two. Artists asked, What does it mean to be human?"[110] Although as for most avant-garde art there was little market for such works, the mixed-media artist Nakanishi Natsuyuki (1935–) unequivocally states that "reportage art in the early 1950s actually showed the most political consciousness" of anything involving the visual arts in the postwar era.[111] Such may be the case, but the novelist Tsutsumi Seiji correctly adds that reportage painting showed "more idealism than Marxism."[112] Although individual artists such as Nakamura Hiroshi continued to turn out documentary works, the number of reportage paintings on display had dwindled significantly by the fourth Nippon Exhibition in 1956.[113]

The era of nonparty activists gained special attention from intellectuals when a dispute broke out over art and politics during the winter of 1955–1956 among the literary critic Takei Teruo (1927–) and the art critics Hanada Kiyoteru and Haryū Ichirō. Haryū argued that socialist realism was "a bit removed from our reality" and held that "first you have to produce new art as it should be . . . based on the reality of where you are"[114] — that is, from within the self. Takei defended a more romantic position, praising the artists' front as part of Japan's social transformation in the mid-1950s. The art critic Nakahara Yūsuke (1927–) seized this opportunity to attack abstract painting as a "contemporary myth" and agreed with Takei that "art should change society."[115] This controversy immediately preceded the first invasion of informel art from France in late 1956, Haryū later recalled: "I wrote that informel was of real interest. The reportage painters accused me of switching my position, although Yamashita Kikuji did not join in the denunciation."[116] By now it was clear that "revolution in politics and revolution in art were incompatible," concluded a more recent critic, because the would-be revolutionaries in the Communist Party had created their own official art that was impervious to further innovation, in effect a "reactionary modernism."[117]

The Youth Artists Alliance and the Nippon Exhibition were magnets of the politically engaged visual arts of the mid-1950s and ended up drawing the avant-garde ever further from the Japan Communist Party. Alliance members increasingly worked independently and grew sharply critical of the autocratic rule of the JCP chieftain Miyamoto Kenji (1908–) after 1955. In part they took their cue from the leftist painters Maruki Iri and Akamatsu Toshiko, who by now had taken an anti-Stalinist, anti-Chinese position of independence and let their party ties lapse. Artists such as Kawara On, Ikeda Tatsuo, Iida Yoshikuni, and Ishii Shigeo wandered off in 1955 to establish a Producers Council (Seisakusha Kondankai) to explore mixed-media possibilities.[118] Although many members continued to agitate on social and political questions, as an organization the Youth Artists Alliance had lost its vigor, its antiestablishment tilt, and most of its radical wing by the time it disbanded in 1957.[119]

TAKEN AS A WHOLE, the avant-garde of the Shōwa single-digit group experienced its apex of political activity from the late 1940s through the mid-1950s. Most of its members retreated from activism in 1960 if not before, in the aftermath of failed protests against the Japan–United States Mutual Security Treaty that year. By consciously avoiding much engagement thereafter, they acceded to the political status quo and left most resistance and protest by the avant-garde to the next generation of artists. A number of the early-Shōwa group are now well-known painters, including some who belong to elite circles, and a few are senior university professors and gallery operators with firm ties to Japan's contemporary art world.

part one

Experimental Voyages
The 1950s

overview

On Monday, April 28, 1952, the day Japan regained self-rule, *Asahi* ran a front-page editorial titled "A New Start for Japan." The occupation had been "almost like colonialism," making the public "irresponsible, obsequious, and listless." The editorial admonished the "Japanese people to seize this opportunity to turn over a new leaf."[1] In seeking to rouse the public from complacency, *Asahi*'s remarks contained broad hints of a postcolonial perspective, even before the term came into wide use. Because each generation of Japanese artists and other intellectuals since 1952 has had to live with the legacy of American hegemony, it is worth considering whether the artistic vanguard adopted critical viewpoints now recognized as postcolonial.

Like modernism, postcolonialism is not a unified analytical theory based on commonly accepted criteria of evaluation. Instead it is a cluster of rapidly changing perspectives, varying by time and place, on privilege, power, participation, social equality, and economic justice for those who were until recently colonized by a foreign overlord. Gendered, ethnic, and racial dimensions are usually found in postcolonial discourses as well,[2] thus minimizing the nation as an exclusive category. Most writers agree that, in the historical period, the Japanese islands were never colonized by outside powers before 1945, although exceptions are sometimes granted for Hokkaido and the Ryukyus. Instead Japan's most prolonged experience of modern colonialism was as colonizer, administering Taiwan, Southern Sakhalin, Korea, and Pacific islands under various international agreements in the earlier twentieth century. Postcolonial viewpoints, which critique the continuing cultural imperialism of the former colonial power after political independence has been achieved, are often found in studies of Japan's colonies, for example, the sexual slavery of Korean "comfort women" *(ianfu)*. Postcolonialism also regularly criticizes the politics of assimilation, such as the mobilization of women for state service in the twentieth century or the absorption of Okinawa by Japan both before and after formal reversion in 1972.[3]

Postcolonial perspectives may also sharpen our vision of Japan's experience with the Western Other after 1945. While recognizing laudable intentions on the part of American-led occupiers after World War Two, today a number of scholars acknowledge the "neocolonial" aspects of Allied military administration of Japan during 1945–1952.[4] It is of course true that the United States fought two world wars denouncing colonialism and always intended its rule of postwar Japan to be temporary. It is equally true that most Japanese, then and now, regard the occupation as more benign than malevolent. Yet almost none of them regretted its end in 1952, and nearly all agreed with *Asahi* that it was time to "turn over a new leaf."

To the extent that Japan was subjected to elements of colonial rule during the occupation, postcolonial standpoints may offer insights into Japanese cultural life during the first two decades after 1952. The country's relationship with the West, especially the United States, remained out of balance throughout the 1950s and 1960s in several respects. First and most apparent was the continuing presence of American military power, legalized by the Japan–United States Mutual Security Treaty of 1952 and embodied in 50,000 soldiers, sailors, marines, and air-force personnel assigned to bases on Japanese soil. The bulk were concentrated in Okinawa, which the United States directly administered as a military colony until May 1972. Their legal relationship with the host country was defined by Status of Forces agreements widely regarded as unequal, even by those Japanese who welcomed the alliance for reasons of security during the cold war.

A second item out of balance was Japan's economic dependence on American markets and technology for many years after the occupation. Businesses welcomed the opportunities for selling their goods around the globe under the Yoshida system, with its shallow slogan of "separating politics from economics" (*seikei bunri*), yet the United States remained Japan's chief trade partner in many product lines. Even though Japan exported no more than 15 percent of gross domestic product during the postwar era, this margin of economic activity was crucial to its overall growth of 11 percent annually in real terms between 1955 and 1973.

A third factor of particular significance for artists was Japan's unequal cultural relationship with Europe and the United States. The inequality, partly self-inflicted, traced at least to the mid-nineteenth century but carried unusually great weight after 1945 via Hollywood films, popular music, and yearnings for consumer lifestyles — as well as through the vast prestige of modernism, surrealism, existentialism, and other hallmarks of postwar intellectual life in the West. There is no gainsaying that avant-garde Japanese artists often subordinated themselves to ideas current in the West and willingly accepted the patron-client relationship that drew a few of them abroad for study in the early 1950s. But Western cultural dominance among the Japanese vanguard began to ebb by the early 1960s, whereas the trade dependence and particularly the unequal diplomatic-military relationship between the two countries persist to this day.

These and other legacies of the occupation may justify a postcolonial outlook on certain forms of artistic production during the 1950s and 1960s, but in many ways the fit is awkward at best. As Chapter 1 explains, artistic resistance to American military hegemony by the early Shōwa group, who were always conflicted by ambivalence toward the Japan Communist Party, had largely spent its steam by 1957 and nearly collapsed after the security-treaty crisis three years later. The four sites of artistic output discussed in the next chapters showed a much greater reluctance to engage political questions directly than was true of Abe Kōbō and the other creative figures who threw themselves into activism immediately after the occupation. Then in the mid-1960s some members of a younger subset of artists took up renewed protest against the security treaty and, to a lesser extent, consumer capitalism. By far the most salient evidence of withdrawal from Western cultural norms occurred in the avant-garde's rejection of formalism and modernism in art starting in the late 1950s. Yet it is difficult to call this shift to anti-art or post-Western art truly "postcolonial," since the denial of modernism was a worldwide phenomenon originating mainly among elites, not subalterns, and eventually assumed a firm authority of its own.

Although they seldom engaged in overtly racialized discourse, innovative choreographers, composers, and visual artists became more and more outspoken about difference once the cultural catch-up with the West in the early 1950s was finished and the attack on modernism grew vigorous. This difference of outlook most often chose the local and the everyday as its terms of reference, no longer the globe or even the nation as a unit. Many postcolonial viewpoints elsewhere embraced not only differences of perspective but also a populist quest for social and economic equality. Such populism was uncommon in Japan: the postwar avant-garde took little interest in issues of justice or fairness, partly because such questions were preempted by their government in the 1960s. Nor did Japan experience outright postcolonial movements, unless the environmental protests of the late 1960s and early 1970s qualify. Postwar Japanese leaders aspired at all times for their country to rank high among the world's trading powers; far from portraying themselves as subaltern, these officials willingly accepted diplomatic and military inferiority in order to achieve economic might. The most interesting positions taken by the artistic vanguard that might seem postcolonial occurred in the 1960s:

criticism of the Western-derived modernist canon and of the bureaucratically administered society of consumer capitalism that took firm root in Japan during that decade.

Artists Head West

Writers and other artists from East Asia who traveled to Europe in the early twentieth century often found themselves pursuing a romanticized Other, a projection of the West created by their own curiosity and imagination. Such was seldom the case for the tiny band of young Japanese dancers, musicians, painters, and sculptors who managed to make their way to Europe or North America as students in the early 1950s. Now the purpose was practical, instrumental, and urgent: to catch up with the contemporary international arts after years of semi-isolation during wartime and military occupation. Ichiyanagi Toshi recalls that "in 1952 we were close to fifty years behind the West in composing contemporary music, but artists faced a poor situation then. Only one musician per year was permitted to study in Europe. There were also stiff restrictions on taking money out of Japan."[5] The visitors in this first postwar stage of direct contact with the Euro-American avant-garde took Western artistic predominance for granted and understood that their task was to transport the latest creative ideas back to their culturally démodé homeland.

When they arrived abroad, Japanese artists eager to absorb the latest styles encountered orientalist attitudes among the Europeans, involving images of Zen thought, Nō drama, calligraphy, ikebana, and other traditional arts. Some of the best talent of the Shōwa single-digit cohort had to grapple with expressing their own individuality in the face of such condescending European expectations.[6] A few of them won the favor of their hosts, including the painters Dōmoto Hisao and Imai Toshimitsu (1928–2002), as did the film director Kurosawa Akira (1910–1998) for his *Rashōmon* (1950), which was awarded the grand prix at the Venice festival in 1951. Compared with those who went to Europe, Japanese artists who chose the United States in the 1950s felt less exoticized, at least in the biggest cities where aspiring artists of every nationality competed for advantage, but they usually found living conditions no less harsh. Regardless of overseas locale, the postwar group returned home bearing far more fresh ideas about art and far less nostalgia for Japan than their forebears in the early twentieth century.

Young Japanese composers of art music who traveled to Europe in the 1950s developed ideas and techniques that were cerebral but quite nonacademic when contrasted with the modernism that still prevailed in the Western-style curricula of Japan's major conservatories. The world of contemporary music, so vigorous today, was minuscule when they encountered it in France and Germany soon after World War Two. Some of the visitors were especially drawn to Schönberg's experiments in twelve-tone serialism and to those of Karlheinz Stockhausen (1928–). Others immersed themselves in the theories of postwar French composers such as Olivier Messiaen (1908–1992), who exposed his students to traditional African and Asian music, and Pierre Schaeffer (1910–1995), whose innovations in sound transformation beginning in 1948, known as musique concrète, made electronic music possible. In 1951 Moroi Makoto in Darmstadt and Mayuzumi Toshirō in Paris became the first Japanese to study composition in Europe after the war.[7] As Moroi recounted in 2002, "I learned atonal music from my first music professor, who was much drawn to Paul Hindemith. But I preferred Schönberg, perhaps because I had lived in Berlin as a small boy while my father was studying composition there in 1932–1934."[8] His *Composition for Orchestra* was the first non-European work to be awarded a prize in a concours held in Belgium in 1952; *Partita* for unaccompanied flute (1952–1953), a work he composed in his own twelve-tone system without any previous knowledge of the method, was honored at Oslo in 1953 by the International Society for Contemporary Music.

Today most Japanese remember Mayuzumi Toshirō for his outspoken endorsement of neonationalist causes late in life, perhaps forgetting that he was a dazzling innovator of the musical avant-garde in the 1950s. As soon as he graduated from Geidai in 1951, Mayuzumi headed to the Paris Conservatoire on a French government scholarship. Originally assigned to study with Tony Aubin (1907–1981), Mayuzumi quickly soaked up the music of Olivier Messiaen, Edgard Varèse (1883–1965), and Pierre Boulez (1925–) and also visited Pierre Schaeffer's studio, where he learned about musique concrète. Schaeffer notably toyed with the sounds of trains, improvising by isolating a single sound, reversing or repitching it, and superimposing sounds on one another, all without notation or replicable performance. Soon Karlheinz Stockhausen and others turned Schaeffer's innovations into a synthesis of pure electronic sound.[9] When he returned home in 1952, Mayuzumi claimed not to have learned much in Paris, but his fellow composers disbelieved him when, in a tornado of creativity, he wrote works honoring Varèse, composed Japan's first musique concrète (X, Y, Z, 1953), using everyday noises, voices, and instruments, and produced the first example of synthetic electronic music in his country (*Study I*, 1955).[10]

By the time Yuasa Jōji, a devotee of contemporary German music, took up electronic composition in the early 1960s, interest in musique concrète among the avant-garde had given way to the sudden popularity of its American equivalent, indeterminate music. As discussed in Chapter 5, Ichiyanagi Toshi returned from New York in 1961 and introduced the chance operations of John Cage (1912–1992), in which any sound material was considered musical, without regard for aesthetic properties. From this point forward the number of writers of contemporary music in Japan expanded rapidly, and a great variety of compositional approaches blossomed. As is true everywhere, contemporary music was highly controversial even within the Japanese vanguard; Cage proved to be the last major source of compositional techniques to be introduced from abroad during the 1960s, and his later work was almost never heard in Japan or anywhere else.

The handful of young composers who studied abroad after World War Two spurred their colleagues at home to experiment with nearly every major form of contemporary music from Europe and the United States in the 1950s, the high-water mark of interaction between Japan and the West in terms of musical ideas. In subsequent decades Japanese composers, much less in thrall to the Europeans than the first postwar travelers abroad, were increasingly welcomed into the international company of contemporary-music professionals even as they pursued distinctive intellectual directions that had no Western counterparts.

Young Japanese painters in the Western style took a great interest in abstract art in the 1930s, but the outbreak of the Pacific War drove most of them to paint more realistically so as to avoid official disfavor. Abstract compositions reappeared almost immediately after the surrender, but their allure to the early postwar avant-garde dimmed a bit amid the enthusiasm of nonparty activists for the social realism of reportage art. Nonetheless many young oil painters in the early 1950s were drawn to the forms and colors of abstract works from Europe. Still it is true that most of the oils and watercolors produced in Japan — and nearly all that commanded handsome prices — were representational, both at the height of abstractionism in the 1950s and after. Sculpture, too, remained figurative for the most part.

Like composers from Japan during the 1950s, the handful of Japanese visual artists who lived and worked in Paris starting in the early 1950s freely acknowledged the predominance of contemporary French art. They soon found themselves submerged under waves of abstractionism, especially l'art informel. By then the center of avant-garde gravity had already begun shifting from Europe to New York, but "French and Italian art still had a great following among Japanese in the Fifties,"[11] the critic Nanjō Fumio points out. French art has long exerted a special draw, partly because the Barbizon school, impressionism, postimpressionism, and the school of Paris were dominant when Japan first encountered modern European art in the Meiji era. Between the world wars, more than five hundred persons identified as Japanese artists lived in Paris at any given time,[12] dwarfing the numbers who gathered there in the early 1950s.

Among the earliest to arrive after World War Two was Tatehata Kakuzō (1919–), originally a figurative sculptor of the full human body who learned to emulate informel and pop sculptures while studying in France during 1953–1955.[13] Young avant-garde painters who lived there in the mid-1950s included Imai Toshimitsu, Dōmoto Hisao, Sugai Kumi (1919–1996), and Tabuchi Yasukazu (1921–), each of whom did notably different work from the others, yet all of whom were taken with the vogue of informel no less than their musical compatriots were captivated by serialism and musique concrète at the time. Soon after reaching Paris in 1952 Imai immersed himself in informel, which he translated as "unformed" or "not yet formed,"[14] and soon became known for being "as hard-working as any artist there," according to the comparative-literature scholar Haga Tōru (1931–).[15] Another comparatist, Hirakawa Sukehiro (1931–), recalls getting to know Imai in Paris and writing a poem in 1959 about "Imai Samurai," as he was affectionately known.[16] For a time Imai applied thick red and green paint to his canvases with a knife, then dripped black paint over them. In this way he aided the development of informel as a Japanese style.[17]

Dōmoto Hisao has painted in many styles throughout the past half century, almost always producing abstract compositions since first taking up oils when he moved to Paris in 1955. Trained in Kyoto as a Japanese-style artist by his uncle Dōmoto Inshō (1891–1975), Hisao quickly learned that "academicism in the Japanese art establishment was hardly touched at all by defeat and military occupation. When I got to Paris I found the atmosphere much freer than in Japan. What especially struck me was that artists from countries that had been enemies ten years before — America, Japan, China, Germany, France — were now free to get together in Paris and share ideas."[18] The encounter with informel led Dōmoto to create works displaying a welter of galactic swirls in contrasting light and dark colors, notably the series called *Shūchūsuru chikara (Tension d'esprit)* (1957–1958, oil).[19] These paintings seem chaotic but purposeful and allusive all at once, energetic, intense, and yet somehow playful (see Plate 4). In Paris he befriended the novelist and art historian André Malraux (1901–1976) and won a certain degree of acceptance among the French artistic elite. By the time of his first solo exhibit in Tokyo, at the Minami Gallery in the politically roiled month of May 1960 amid demonstrations over the Japan–United States Mutual Security Treaty, Dōmoto stood at the center of a new establishment of Japanese sympathetic to abstractionism and the avant-garde (see Figure 2).

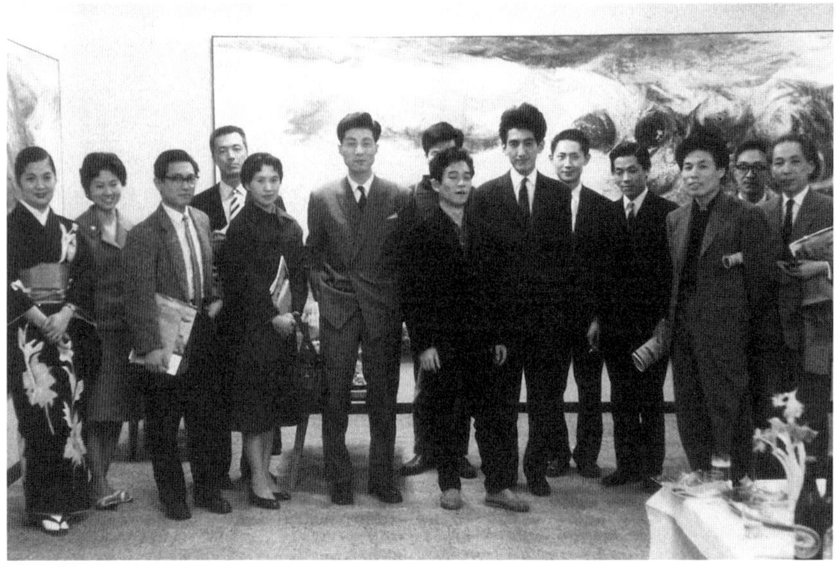

Figure 2. Artists and critics at Dōmoto Hisao solo exhibition, Minami Gallery, Tokyo. May 1960. From left, Dōmoto Mami, unidentified, Ōoka Makoto, Teshigahara Hiroshi, Ms. Haga, Haga Tōru, Tōno Yoshiaki (in front of unidentified), Dōmoto Hisao, Hirakawa Sukehiro, Takashina Shūji, Nakahara Yūsuke, Ōta Sankichi, Takiguchi Shūzō. Courtesy Dōmoto Hisao.

As much as any other artist, Iida Yoshikuni carried home new approaches from Europe that spurred the growth of abstract sculptures in Japan. Iida studied oils at Geidai with the representational painters Hayashi Takeshi (1896–1975) and Umehara Ryūzaburō and never lost "a strong emphasis on the visual element" in his later sculptural works.[20] "It was difficult to study in Europe in the 1950s," Iida recalled a half century later. "You needed an invitation from an institute, and the Japanese government imposed restrictions on taking currency out of the country."[21] In Rome Pericle Fazzini (1913–1987) taught him both classical and renaissance modeling, leading Iida to turn out a *Hito* series (1961–1965, bronze, wood) emphasizing the human body. After viewing sculptures in Munich by Henry Moore (1898–1986) in 1960, Iida focused increasingly on producing abstract works in wood, with rounded forms, while living in Vienna and West Berlin during the 1960s.[22] He returned permanently to Japan in 1970 and began using stainless steel for its mirror effect, while also continuing to produce oil paintings. In effect Iida was a faithful sherpa of European sculpting techniques and materials to Japan, where he was soon embraced by big business as a corporate artist.

Nearly all of the young Japanese artists who studied in the West during the

1950s did so in Europe, but a small group headed by Okada Kenzō (1902–1982) went instead to the United States, where abstract expressionism was in full flower. Another noted émigré was the painter Hasegawa Saburō (1904–1957), who went to America in 1953 to introduce abstract elements of Japanese culture but died suddenly in San Francisco four years later.[23] Another San Franciscan, albeit briefly, was the conceptual painter Yoko Ono (Ono Yōko, 1933–), who spent part of her early childhood there, studied piano after the war at Jiyū Gakuen in Tokyo, and began writing music while an undergraduate at Sarah Lawrence College in Yonkers, New York. After marrying the composer Ichiyanagi Toshi, then a Juilliard student, in 1956, Ono turned to performance art and became known in New York as "the high priestess of the happening."[24] She went back to Japan in 1962 to help nurture both performance and conceptual art at a time when each was in its infancy. The same was true of modern dance: Akiko Kanda (Kanda Akiko, 1935–), whose teacher Itō Michio arranged for her to study with Martha Graham (1893–1991) in New York starting in 1956, pioneered Graham's technique in Japan after arriving back home in the summer of 1961.[25] By contrast, Ichiyanagi, who spent 1952–1961 in the United States, discovered when he returned to Tokyo that "Japanese composers were very ambitious and very spiritually healthy. Information about contemporary European and American music had spread widely," recouping in one decade the fifty-year lag he noted in 1952.[26]

For these and many other nonverbal artists in the 1950s and 1960s, going abroad for de facto certification by the dominant artistic culture was often the quickest route to success at home. The composer Miyake Haruna (1942–) explains:

> I chose to go to New York not just for the quality of musical training at Juilliard but also because, to me, New York was the most interesting place to live — art and music were both exciting there.   It's difficult for artists to develop a reputation here in Japan. Some get started here and then move abroad, hoping to win a good reputation and earn recognition when they come back. But if you return to Japan right after finishing music school abroad, you lack the credentials to win acceptance. What matters is authority — in this case, Western approval — not true assessment of the quality of your art. Japanese music critics provide little real evaluation; they just reiterate the authority of Western acceptance.[27]

Miyake, who studied at Juilliard from 1962 to 1965, pinpoints a phenomenon no less common in Rio or Cairo than in East Asia even today: the tyranny of approval by the Euro-American artistic Other. Ichiyanagi Toshi concurs: "My experience in the United States is what established me when I returned home in 1961."[28] Even film audiences become loge-chair travelers to the exotic: so great is the prestige of arts from abroad that the cinema critic Donald Richie (1924–) estimates that "90 percent of Japanese moviegoers never see a Japanese movie."[29] It is no wonder that even today aspiring young musicians flock to Vienna or Boston and visual artists to Berlin, London, or New York for exposure to, and possibly even the approval of, the international Other.

Producing Art in the 1950s

> Japanese artists now express themselves almost unconsciously, but in the 1950s most of them copied Western art, largely because Western-style painting is taught in the education system. But Japanese Western-style painting is very strange and is not respected in France. The Japanese avant-garde art groups arising in the 1950s are an exception: rather than copying Western art, they placed themselves somewhere between Western art and their own cultural heritage. But these groups were in the minority through the 1960s, and they were not internationally recognized. — Hara Toshio, Director, Hara Museum of Contemporary Art[30]

Japanese society in the 1950s was ripped by ideological dispute, political conflict, and labor unrest, yet for most citizens a growing cultural conformity and social homogeneity became normalized as they had not, during peacetime, for more than half a century. This paradox stems in part from the politicization of public life that began near the end of the American occupation and in part from the creeping standardization of civic behavior through urbanization, the media, the reimposition of uniform schooling, and universal aspirations to middle-class status symbolized by electric refrigerators, television sets, and washing machines, all of which became widely available during this decade. The Japan Housing Corporation (Nihon Jūtaku Kōdan) was created in 1955 to provide inexpensive apartments for urban workers; its first units were immediately subscribed ten times over. The economic white paper (*Keizai hakusho*) for 1956, reflecting the new era of high-speed growth, boasted that "economic recovery has been completed" and "the postwar period is over."[31] Six years later the population of Tokyo exceeded 10 million for the first time.

Amid such unsettling expansion, artists during the 1950s had to be alert to the twin snares of political turmoil and cultural blandness, the latter reflected in a growing uniformity of taste and leisure. More and more arts specialists congregated in the largest cities for incomes, audiences, and ideas. Particularly great homage was paid to Tokyo's preferences and policies, at some cost to regional variety. Both the traditional arts (some of them dating only to the late nineteenth century) and contemporary genres turned into routine, almost routinized, forms of endeavor not only for professionals but also for millions of amateurs among the public at large.

With the visual and performing arts more widely accessible after World War Two to a relatively inexperienced citizenry, many people looked to established organizations to certify acceptable styles. Japan's most innovative artists faced the special challenge of overcoming institutionalized arts culture, such as the official art exhibition known as Nitten and the state-supported Tokyo University of Fine Arts and Music (Geidai). Although Hara Toshio is undoubtedly correct that the education system enforced production standards for Western-style painting, it is curious that Geidai, "which in those days was a bit inflexible, should have produced so many graduates who became top avant-garde artists in the 1950s and 1960s," according to the critic Minemura Toshiaki.[32] Mamiya Michio concurs: "I studied at Geidai from 1948 to 1952 and found the professors rather orthodox, but we students were very free to compose whatever we wished."[33] Would-be professional artists continued to face grim job prospects in the early 1950s, Hayashi Hikaru recalls: "There were very few conservatory posts, orchestra jobs, or even gigs through private music studios. I had a lot of time on my hands, it seemed."[34] Painters and sculptors had to make do with a dearth of art supplies, including high-quality canvases. Yet, as the art conservationist Koyano Masako notes, "sometimes the development of new materials affects changing styles of art. In 1948 the Nakazawa Company began producing cheap new pigments that brought about important changes to Nihonga,"[35] the Japanese style of painting that developed an avant-garde of its own in the 1950s.

Even if they were undaunted by established standards, financial insecurity, or a shortage of materials, painters and sculptors faced the dilemma of choosing between compromising their integrity if they submitted to the discipline of an art association, with its annual exhibit, or isolating themselves and forsaking a guaranteed venue for displaying their output. Most of them elected to join narrow groups, cut off from their counterparts in similar organizations and ill-positioned to draw on a very broad range of fresh stimuli. Whether artists worked individually or collectively, whether they were still politically active or not, three developments in the 1950s offered painters and sculptors fresh ideas and audiences: exhibits sponsored by the major newspapers, newly opened museums of contemporary art, and a fledgling gallery system to showcase both familiar faces and unknowns, including the avant-garde.

In June 1947 the Mainichi newspapers held the first privately sponsored exhibition of the postwar era outside the aegis of the art associations, with 743 works by Japanese artists and an audience of at least 60,000 in Tokyo alone, including the emperor and empress.[36] Yomiuri began organizing exhibits in 1949 and Asahi a year later (Asahi was also a stalwart music patron). The motive in each case was commercial: the newspapers hoped to build circulation by creating a cultured image for their publications. Mainichi and Yomiuri competed fiercely to sponsor shows of Western art, most of which had rarely, if ever, been seen in Japan.[37] Interestingly, none of the large-scale exhibits mounted by the newspaper companies in the 1950s relied much on Japan's fine-arts establishment for advice, scholarship, or liaison with overseas institutions.

By far the most significant exhibition for avant-garde artists was the nonjuried, free-submission show known as the Yomiuri Independent, held annually between 1949 and 1963 at the Tokyo Metropolitan Art Museum. Anyone, regardless of affiliation, was free to display one or two original works not previously seen, a protocol tracing to the first Salon des Indépendants exhibit held in Paris in 1884. Within a few years the Yomiuri Anpan, as it was called, annually presented as many as 1,500 new items of mixed interest but great earnestness.[38] Although unconnected with the JCP, the Yomiuri show was unmistakably antiestablishment in its attack on the government-sponsored exhibitions, the fine-arts establishment *(gadan)*, and the hierarchical system of selection by jury used by most other shows. As Chapter 6 explains, the Yomiuri Independent increasingly renounced modernism and sometimes even capitalism, while trumpeting democracy and equal access for all artists — positions consonant with a postcolonial perspective vis-à-vis prevailing global art standards.

Far better than exhibiting in a temporary locale is to have your work acquired by a museum for its permanent collection — provided the curators place it on display. When the Museum of Modern Art, Kamakura (Kanagawa Kenritsu Kindai Bijutsukan) opened in November 1951, it became Japan's first public facility devoted to the art of the past century, both Japanese and foreign. The private Bridgestone Museum at Kyōbashi, with its large European holdings, made its debut the next January, followed by the Tokyo National Museum of Modern Art at Takebashi in December 1952.[39] With in-house curatorial and planning staffs, the two new public museums conferred an unprecedented status on contemporary art in general and Japan's current visual culture in particular. Yet "modern art" in its Sino-Japanese form *(kindai bijutsu)* denoted everything produced in Japan since the late nineteenth century — much of which wasn't especially modern, let alone avant-garde, by international standards. Understandably, most avant-garde artists harbored mixed feelings toward the new museums as they acquired numerous works from the Meiji era simply because of their date of origin, not because of their style or content.

Significant as newspaper-sponsored exhibitions and the new museums were for making contemporary art available, perhaps most salient were the handful of dealers willing to take a risk on the avant-garde at their commercial galleries. Fewer than a dozen of Tokyo's hundreds of galleries in the early 1950s were devoted to contemporary art. Of these, two stand out: Takemiya at Kanda Surugadai and Minami in Nihonbashi. Two more, the Tokyo and Nantenshi galleries, played similar roles in the 1960s. Starting in 1951 Takemiya, which had been an art-supply store before World War Two, commissioned the poet-critic Takiguchi Shūzō to select new talent unknown to Japan's art establishment for rent-free solo exhibitions lasting ten days each. During the next six years this gallery sponsored shows by more than two hundred individuals.[40] Minami was founded in 1952 by Shimizu Kusuo (1926–1979), "a leading figure in promoting contemporary art"[41] whose business later turned sour in the poor climate of the 1970s. "His suicide was a huge blow to the avant-garde," recalls the journalist-poet Ōoka Makoto, who worked with Shimizu in the 1950s. "He was truly a victim of the second oil shock"[42] that rocked the Japanese economy in 1979.

The newspaper-backed shows, the new museums, and the budding gallery system invoked much greater attention to contemporary cultural products than ever before, especially through publicity in art journals that had previously focused on older styles. *Atelier* and *Mizue* (Watercolors), both of which resumed operations in 1946, were soon joined by new publications such as *Bijutsu techō* (Art notebook, 1948), *Geijutsu shinchō* (New art waves, 1950), and the short-lived *Bijutsu hihyō* (Art review, 1952–1957). Apart from tigers like Takiguchi Shūzō, most critics at the start of the 1950s were practicing artists, not researchers, journalists, or professors (many of the latter favored premodern art and were poor judges of the current output).[43] But gradually the triad *(gosanke)* of Haryū Ichirō, Nakahara Yūsuke, and Tōno Yoshiaki (1930–2005) emerged in the pages of these journals to set the tone for Japan's first generation of knowledgeable critics of contemporary art.

Opportunities to compose and perform art music in Japan, and to a lesser degree ballet and modern dance, likewise multiplied in the 1950s. Several newly established orchestras brought the number of professional symphonies in Tokyo to eight, but patronage of contemporary music and dance could not compare to the combined impact of newspaper companies, museums, and galleries for the visual arts. Most composers made a living from radio, television, or teaching the myriad parents who began studying music and other arts, both traditional and contemporary, in quest of cultivation, ethical training, and middle-class standing for themselves and their children. Yet somehow, the composer Mamiya pointed out in 2002, "it's probably true that Japan now has more composers than anywhere else, although on a per-capita basis Iceland leads the world."[44]

Today the unruly decade of the 1950s offers up little agreement about the achievements of the early Shōwa generation of avant-garde artists, even among those who knew them best, such as the poet Tanikawa Shuntarō (1931–): "How many of the artists I was close to in the 1950s and 1960s have died. . . . I wonder if most people won't have diverse opinions on matters" involving cultural life during those years.[45] Perhaps most enigmatic is the great imbalance of reputations between the musical and visual-art titans of a half century ago. The gallery owner Kawatsuma Sachiko summarizes the contrast: "The avant-garde composers of the 1950s are still thriving these days, but the avant-garde painters of the 1950s have all lost their influence except possibly for those who moved to New York. Every young music student today knows the important composers of the 1950s, but only one art student in a hundred recognizes the avant-garde artists of the 1950s such as Ishii Shigeo."[46]

The following chapters take up the attractions and disappointments of high modernism to the first generation of avant-garde artists in Japan after 1952. They examine four distinct sites of artistic production, two of which avidly promoted cross-pollination among genres and all of which professed detachment from political activism. Perhaps unwittingly, each of the four helped subsequent generations of avant-garde radicals to find their own footing, from which they ended up rejecting the Western-derived universals of modernism and engaging in renewed political critiques during the 1960s.

chapter two

The Experimental Workshop

The 1950s in Japan were unprecedented, even when measured against the famously innovative 1680s and 1910s, for their outburst of artistic study groups, mixed-media events, and collaborative endeavors of all sorts by painters, sculptors, poets, novelists, film directors, composers, playwrights, photographers, graphics specialists, choreographers, architects, lighting designers, and others in expressive fields. Any residual corks on creativity remaining from wartime controls and occupation censorship now popped from the irrepressible artistic ferment that bubbled over during this decade. One participant, the banker and gallery owner Satani Kazuhiko (1928–), boasts that "it was a pioneering intermedia effort; nowhere else in the world was such mixed-media activity happening before the 1960s."[1]

The amateur ideal *(bunjin)* of the government official or city merchant who cultivated the arts has a long history throughout East Asia, but the professional artist as a social type emerged much more recently with the rise of a market economy and the growing differentiation of artistic genres. The early postwar impulse toward integrating the arts *(geijutsu sōgō)*, especially through the Century Association in 1947 and the Evening Society a year later, represented not a throwback to an earlier era of gentlemanly *bunjin* refinement but a spirited effort to fashion common conceptual and aesthetic ground for art forms that by now had each evolved its own distinct character. This impetus toward cross-genre stimulation in Japan had been anticipated by the Mavo arts group in the 1910s and 1920s.[2] The momentum for testing the possibilities of interaction among genres reached its crescendo in the Experimental Workshop (Jikken Kōbō) of 1951–1957.

The Experimental Workshop was not a physical site, with an atelier or a sound studio, but a study society formed by fourteen young artists, mostly from the Shōwa single-digit generation, who staged mixed-media events several times a year in the Tokyo region. Unlike most such groups, its presentations included works by artists belonging to other associations as well as items from abroad. Asked where its headquarters was, the composer Yuasa Jōji replied, "We met here and there, at different locations each time,"[3] in Tokyo restaurants and homes, to discuss books, ideas, and technologies relating to the contemporary "high-brow avant-garde," as the art critic Tatehata Akira terms it.[4] Although they were unable to travel abroad, these young painters and composers were fully as obedient to the formalist and aesthetic teachings of postwar high modernism as were their fellow Japanese artists who visited Paris, Rome, and New York in the 1950s.

The Experimental Workshop included "new artists who cultivated virgin land," Yuasa recalled in 2002: "At a time when most older composers were conservative, Jikken Kōbō had a strong desire to learn about the West — Jikken Kōbō members were exceptional." The workshop opened a virtual window on contemporary Western culture via books, journals, films, and sound recordings imported from overseas. "We were always thinking, 'What's the essential difference between East and West?'" Yuasa remembers. "We read and discussed Jean-Paul Sartre, Herbert Read, and D. T. Suzuki. We did not wish to be nationalists, but rather cosmopolitans instead. Yet we wanted to know about Japan, and through Suzuki we learned about Zen Buddhism, Nō drama, Zeami, and Bashō."[5] Surely it a sign of their infatuation with the West that the young avant-garde artists of the Experimental Workshop, deprived by war of an education in Japanese culture, learned about Japan's premodern aesthetics from a romantic Zen apologist who lived for eleven years in Illinois and later taught philosophy at Columbia. To a considerable extent the Japan they absorbed from Suzuki was one his Western audiences wished him to confirm for them.

Two interrelated characteristics sharply distinguished the Experimental Workshop from parallel activities taking place at the same time on the artistic left. First, unlike the many groups led by the novelist Abe Kōbō or by the Japan Communist Party, the workshop was militantly nonpolitical — which was itself a clear political position subject to "criticism as bourgeois avant-gardeism."[6] Instead the focus was unflinchingly cerebral, driven by ideas without reference to activism. Most members agreed with the veteran painter Okamoto Tarō, writing in 1951 just before the workshop was founded, that "the concerns of art are becoming internationally similar. . . . Of course different social environments create different artistic concerns. However, if we are too preoccupied with these social concerns we will lose the real essence of art."[7] In the hothouse climate of the late occupation years, there was no mistaking

Okamoto's stance against socialist realism or his willingness to cooperate with the alternative path chosen by the Experimental Workshop. Artistically gifted as the workshop members undoubtedly were, they shared elite social origins and an establishmentarian preference not to resist political authority, instead remaining "oblivious to the spiritual conflict and division in postwar Japan," as the critic Minemura Toshiaki points out.[8]

Second, the group was self-consciously "ultramodernist," preoccupied with experiments in form and in representations of beauty — in this sense "united under Bauhaus ideals."[9] Most of its members shared Walter Gropius's fascination with new technologies and applauded his Bauhaus method, first articulated in 1919, of bringing specialists from diverse media together in a workshop where "the artist is an exalted craftsman" — the more so because crafts and fine arts have been tightly interwoven for many centuries in Japan. But the Bauhaus analogy is only partial: no architects belonged to the Experimental Workshop, no heed was paid to the Bauhaus goals of functionality, mechanization, or mass production, nor did workshop members agree with Gropius that "the ultimate aim of all creative activity is the building!"[10] (See Figures 3 and 4.)

Most who joined this small study society already knew one another when it was formally launched in August 1951 through an "accelerating centrifugal energy" propelling the workshop "out of the rigidly defined orbit called art" as it had been taught in Japan before the war, according to one of its founding members.[11] A main catalyst was the photographer-sculptor Kitadai Shōzō, an eclectic thinker who was steeped in Russian constructivism, a 1920s sculptural approach that used manufactured materials to form planes and express volumes. Kitadai also held far-flung interests in musique concrète, cosmology, and quantum theory. Two other prime movers were Fukushima Hideko, a painter scarcely remembered today, and Yamaguchi Katsuhiro, who eventually became Japan's most lauded media artist.[12] Also from the visual arts came the painter and print maker Komai Tetsurō (1920–1976) and the photographer Ōtsuji Kiyoshi (1923–2001). Imai Naoji (1928–) was a lighting specialist who later made his career in theater; Yamazaki Hideo (1920–1979) was a mechanical engineer. The rest had musical backgrounds: the composers Takemitsu Tōru, Yuasa Jōji, Fukushima Kazuo (1930–), Satō Keijirō (1927–), and Suzuki Hiroyoshi (1931–), the pianist Sonoda Takahiro (1928–), and the critic Akiyama Kuniharu (1929–1996). "These people represented the next artistic generation following Okamoto Tarō, Abe Kōbō, Hanada Kiyoteru, and Teshigahara Hiroshi," according to the slightly younger composer Takahashi Yūji.[13] Yuasa Jōji recalled in 1997 that the workshop members were very independent and very busy with their own projects, yet it was never difficult

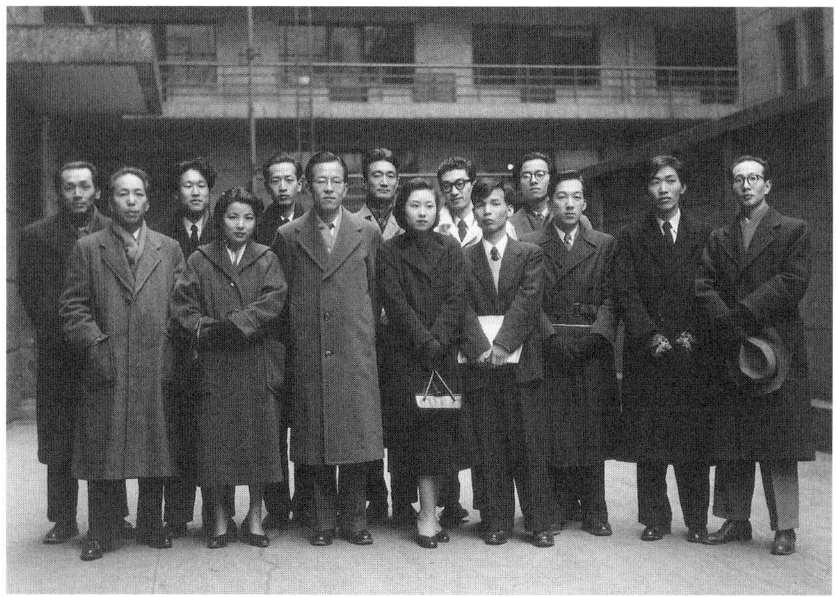

Figure 3. Jikken Kōbō group, courtyard of Nōrin Chūō Kinko, Hibiya, Tokyo. 1954. From left, Kitadai Shōzō (painter), Takiguchi Shūzō (art critic), Akiyama Kuniharu (music critic), Ms. Sonoda, Yamaguchi Katsuhiro (media artist), Sonoda Takahiro (pianist), Komai Tetsurō (print maker), Fukushima Hideko (painter), Fukushima Kazuo (composer), Takemitsu Tōru (composer), Imai Naoji (lighting artist), Yuasa Jōji (composer), Suzuki Hiroyoshi (composer), Satō Keijirō (composer). Photo by Ōtsuji Kiyoji. Courtesy Satani Gallery.

to get them together for an event. He also pointed out that the group never formally disbanded, just ceased its joint activites.[14]

Takiguchi Shūzō: "The Spirit of Experimentation"

Japan's most celebrated composer, Takemitsu Tōru, paid homage to the poet-painter-critic Takiguchi Shūzō at a 1991 retrospective of Takiguchi's works: "My music would not have been possible without the 'Jikken Kōbō' experience. He [Takiguchi] was truly my spiritual patron."[15] Yuasa Jōji agrees: "I started my career as a composer in 1952 when I joined Jikken Kōbō. Before then, I had written some works by myself. Takiguchi Shūzō did not formally belong to Jikken Kōbō, but he was its Godfather — our mentor and spiritual leader."[16] Members of the Experimental Workshop, like the French surrealists Takiguchi helped introduce to Japan in the 1930s, rejected dadaism as too destructive, but they soon moved beyond surrealism to experiment creatively with the newest art forms and aesthetic forays. Takiguchi acquainted

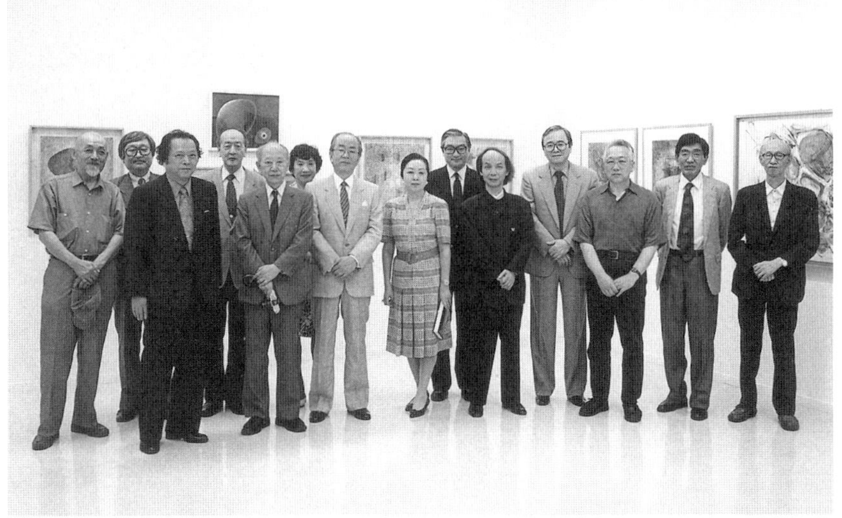

Figure 4. Jikken Kōbō group reunion, Satani Gallery, Tokyo. 1991. From left, Kitadai, Akiyama, Satani Kazuhiko (gallery owner), Yamaguchi, Ōtsuji Kiyoji (photographer), Ms. Komai, Sonoda, Fukushima Hideko, Fukushima Kazuo, Takemitsu, Imai, Yuasa, Suzuki, Satō. Photo by Saitō Sadamu. Courtesy Satani Gallery.

the group with various contemporary Western theories of art, including the striking book *Icon and Idea* (1955) by the British iconoclast Herbert Read.[17] Takiguchi urged the workshop members to pursue the postnational through art by seeking the spirit of modernity throughout the world — a stiff but enticing task for young artists who thus far had no opportunity to travel abroad. Yet Takiguchi's world was centered in Europe, and he never succeeded in creating a denationalized arts discourse of his own that transcended Western theories. (See Figure 5.)

Takiguchi and the small band of fellow Japanese surrealists before World War Two highly esteemed the puckish work of Marcel Duchamp (1887–1968), not the more bizarre aspects of surrealist painting derived from fantastic, sometimes grotesque, images from the unconscious. Nonetheless Takiguchi was detained by the Special Higher Police (Tokkō) in 1941 because the authorities suspected connections between surrealists and members of the illegal Japan Communist Party. He turned out to be a liberal and internationalist, not a subversive, and was released after eight months in jail.[18] For the duration of the war, Takiguchi lived quietly in the Seijō district of Setagaya, Tokyo, a favorite home for artists ever since the Kantō earthquake and fire of 1923. During the American occupation he worked for a news agency, helping to produce *Nichibei Weekly,* and soon met young unknowns such as Yama-

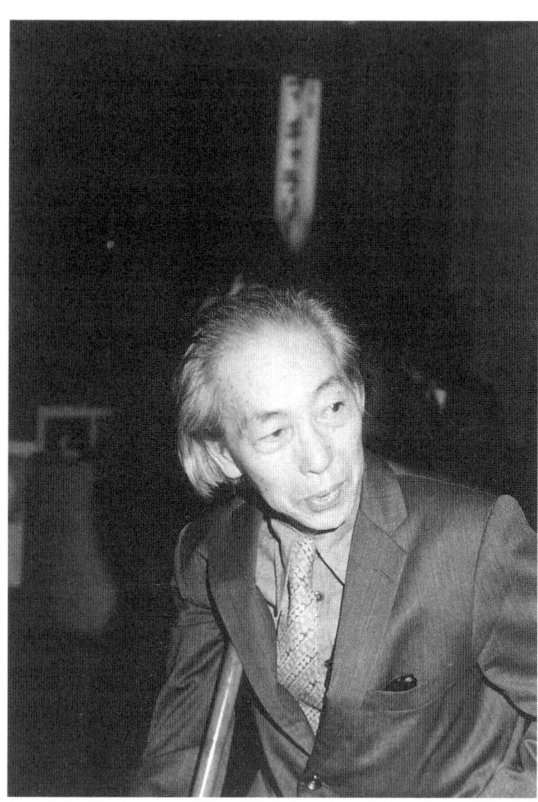

Figure 5. Takiguchi Shūzō, artist and doyen of the Jikken Kōbō group. 1977. Photo by Hanaga Mitsutoshi. Courtesy Satani Gallery.

guchi Katsuhiro, Kitadai Shōzō, and Fukushima Hideko through reviewing their works on display at the Yomiuri Independent, first held in 1949. He began giving young avant-garde painters and sculptors a platform at the Takemiya Gallery in Tokyo's Kanda Surugadai, where Takiguchi was charged with organizing its exhibition schedule starting in 1951, a year after he agreed to write arts criticism for *Yomiuri*, covering painting, sculpture, photography, and music. Through his role as critic, Takiguchi helped to bring together most of the young artists who created the Experimental Workshop in August 1951. The art historian Chiba Shigeo points out that "Takiguchi Shūzō was the last of the true Shōwa *bunjin*"[19] — persons with a renaissance command of talents, or at least a multimedia knowledge of art.

Takiguchi provided encouragement to the avant-garde artists in the Experimental Workshop in early 1952, when he wrote: "In order to strike the same tone as world art, above all a firm outlook is needed. It is essential to nurture a spirit of experimentation. The established modern art of Europe underwent an experimental phase before it attained fulfillment. Artists must endeavor to carry through with their experiments, and society must understand that it has to be generous with supporting them." As intellectual and standoffish as workshop members might have seemed, Takiguchi reminded them that "experimentation is not only a phenomenon of the laboratory. Work is work, so artists too must do their work by interacting with society and reality."[20] This injunction, however, never extended to overtly political questions.

Writing in the art journal *Bijutsu hihyō* later that spring, Takiguchi emphasized that experiments were preferable to relying on the artistic conventions of the past, particularly those imparted in Japanese academies. Artists, he said, could experiment by seeking "a new image of the world and new expressions."[21] Not all experiments could be expected to work, but artists should keep trying — not merely to overcome the conformity of the annual shows put on by the Japanese art establishment but also for two fresh reasons: (1) the rise of film, television, and photography as new media with deep implications for art; and (2) the growing power of big capital with the means to reach mass audiences. Both new factors enhanced uniformity, he pointed out, "leaving artists little time to experiment," but avant-garde artists "need to avoid this sameness" and not give in to the pressures toward standardization.[22] Experimenting, learning from abroad, and engaging with society were Takiguchi's chief lessons for the Jikken Kōbō, not a legacy of surrealism, even though for the rest of his life dreams inspired his own art.

Although few workshop members embraced surrealism, most accepted its premise that the lines between painting and writing, as well as those separating other artistic genres, were indistinct. In an interview published in 2001, Yuasa Jōji said that "in today's terms, Takiguchi encouraged borderless intermedia works."[23] Both Okamoto Tarō's encouragements of the avant-garde and Takiguchi's call for experimentation attacked the established, often dogmatic, distinctions among genres and sought innovations that drew freely from various art forms. Thus it was no surprise that Okamoto, Takiguchi, and the workshop painters all kept a certain distance from informel when it descended on Japan, with certitudes of its own, in 1956.[24]

Takiguchi continued his youthful experiments (1927–1931) with poetry after World War Two but primarily engaged the visual realm: he immersed himself in painting, film, photography, design, calligraphy, écriture, drawing, décalcomanie, and collage. He also took an interest in music and, through his acquaintance with the avant-garde choreographer Hijikata Tatsumi (1928–1986), in the postmodern dance form Butō. He parted ways with the Takemiya Gallery in 1957, disappointed that he had not been able to do more to advance the careers of avant-garde artists, and gave up writing criticism four years later to begin producing his own art rather than promoting the work of others.[25] The process of production — the challenge of creation through experimentation — was what mattered most to Takiguchi, prompting artists in the Experimental Workshop and elsewhere to try new words, images, materials, sound techniques, and forms of human movement.

The Workshop at Work

Ikiru yorokobi (Joie de vivre) was the Experimental Workshop's public premiere, a ballet staged at Hibiya Public Hall (Kōkaidō) on November 16, 1951, in connection with Japan's first exhibition of the art of Pablo Picasso (1881–1973), sponsored by the Yomiuri newspapers. Takemitsu Tōru and Suzuki Hiroyoshi wrote the music and Kitadai Shōzō did the stage design and lighting for this specially commissioned work, named after Picasso's 1946 painting by the same title. As with many of its productions, the workshop reached outside its membership for performers: the ballerina Tani Momoko danced a role choreographed by Masuda Takashi.[26] In 1955 the group cooperated with the Matsuo Akemi Ballet Company to stage performances of *Illumination, Kojiki ōji (The Pauper Prince)*, and *Mirai no Ivu (L'Ève future)*. Workshop members designed sets and costumes; Takemitsu and nonmembers Mayuzumi Toshirō and Akutagawa Yasushi wrote the score. It was entirely predictable that the workshop selected ballet, the dance form most indebted to European originals, for its productions. Japanese dance troupes of every style in the 1950s were quite isolated, few in number, and small in membership compared with the following decades;[27] the Experimental Workshop was almost alone in providing moral and aesthetic support to Western-style dancers by connecting them with artists in other genres through jointly sponsored productions. Far more typical was the outlook of Iwaki Hiroyuki, the conductor who has done more than any other artist to promote contemporary music in Japan since the 1950s: "I don't conduct ballet because I don't like it."[28]

Avant-garde painting played a big part in most of the workshop's sixteen other events between 1952 and 1957, all but three of which also included concerts of contemporary music. The group preferred the term *happyōkai*, or presentation, for its exhibitions and performances, focusing on the unadorned works themselves rather than on their creators or performers. Yamaguchi Katsuhiro, the future media artist, later recalled that "we were dealing with only one issue, the discovery of human vision and music through the use of machines: the automatic slide projector and the tape recorder" as well as film. In terms that evoked Walter Benjamin, Yamaguchi declared that "this experiment of expressing humanity with machines is a task artists must undertake as they advance into the latter half of the twentieth century."[29]

Satani Kazuhiko, who organized a retrospective on Takiguchi Shūzō and the Experimental Workshop at his Ginza art gallery in 1991, believes Yamaguchi may have overstated the group's absorption with mechanical culture: "technology was just one of their many interests."[30] But all parties agreed with Yamaguchi's observation in 1982 that little had been written about the Experimental Workshop during the quarter century since its dissolution.[31] He pointed out that "the group was ahead of its time in relation to Europe as well as Japan. The Experimental Workshop would have been more suited to the 1960s."[32] It likewise sailed a different course from most of the contemporary Western-style music being written in Japan at the time. Few if any artists had closer interactions with contemporary composers in the 1950s than Iwaki Hiroyuki, who first conducted the NHK Orchestra in September 1956, yet he claims that "I had no connection with members of the Experimental Workshop — they were very avant-garde. I was closer to Mayuzumi Toshirō and Moroi Makoto, and later with Takemitsu Tōru"[33] after the workshop ceased activity in 1957. Both Yamaguchi and Iwaki probably exaggerate the radical character of the group's art: as with many organizations in Japan, the differences may have been based more on interpersonal squabbles or factional separatism than on genuinely artistic divergences.

Through their experiments in the 1950s with practically every form of nonverbal art, members of the workshop cleared the track for spectacular mixed-media events in the 1960s and beyond, yet avant-garde music is where the group left its firmest footprint — mainly through the works of its five composers. It is a commonplace that these five were more self-taught than subsequent generations of Japanese composers, but such was probably the case for artists of all sorts in the Shōwa single-digit cohort. Even though the musically inclined participants in the workshop took pains to listen to whatever recordings and read whatever scores from abroad they could find, Akiyama Kuniharu admitted that at first they "were completely unaware of Pierre Schaeffer's work" with musique concrète in Paris.[34] Their early postwar mentors, sometimes quite informally, included carryover composers from the prewar era such as Ifukube Akira, Kiyose Yasuji, Matsudaira Yoritsune, and Moroi Saburō. Hayasaka Fumio, who wrote music for the movies, had a particular charm for composers in the Experimental Workshop, doubtless because of his successes outside the established conservatories but also because of how he linked his striking innovations in sound to familiar aspects of Japanese visual culture.[35] But the impact of each of these was more personal than intellectual. The musical fireworks inspiring the young composers' experiments came from Europe.

The early performances produced by the Experimental Workshop were artistically innovative but far from popular, even by the modest standards of audiences for contemporary music in other countries at the time. Yuasa Jōji remarked that "by 1953 'Jikken Kōbō' had been around for two years, but it wasn't at all recognized yet. Young composers from the music universities who didn't attend our events were acting selfishly, we believed."[36] Three of its programs presented works by Olivier Messiaen; other composers who were introduced included Béla Bartók (1881–1945), Norman Dello Joio (1913–), Erik Satie (1866–1925), Darius Milhaud (1892–1974), Arnold Schönberg (1874–1951), Aaron Copland (1900–1990), Leonard Bernstein (1918–1990), and Samuel Barber (1910–1981)[37] — an all-star lineup of composers seldom, if ever, heard previously in Japan.

The group's two most notable concerts, held in February and August 1956, were devoted to musique concrète and electronic music, signaling a permanent shift in Japan, as elsewhere, away from the compositional techniques of Schönberg's modernist generation. Even today, many composers remember February 4, 1956, as a threshold: under the banner of "Musique Concrète and Electronic Music Audition," the Experimental Workshop drew an overflow crowd to Yamaha Hall in Ginza for a recital of works by members and other avant-garde composers of the day. Some of the enduring compositions on the program included Akutagawa Yasushi's *Maikurohuon no tame no ongaku* (*Music for Microphone*, 1952), a tape-recorded performance of Mayuzumi Toshirō's *X, Y, Z* (1953), and Takemitsu Tōru's first electronic-music experiment, *Ruriefu sutateiku* (*Relief statique*, 1955). Moroi Makoto, Suzuki Hiroyoshi, and others contributed innovative pieces as well. This gala, which was cosponsored by Okamoto Tarō's Contemporary Arts Institute (Gendai Geijutsu Kenkyūjo), helped to dissipate Yuasa's angst about a lack of attention to contemporary music, the more so because critics began to pay it more heed in the press thereafter. As the workshop member and music critic Akiyama Kuniharu noted, Jikken Kōbō turned out to be "less antiacademic than simply filled with the creative spirit of experimentation" with current techniques and ideas from Europe.[38]

Takemitsu and Yuasa in the 1950s

Takemitsu Tōru and Yuasa Jōji were not merely the most productive composers in the Experimental Workshop but also the most widely emulated writers of contemporary art music in postwar Japan. Takemitsu was born in Tokyo in 1930 but grew up in Dalian, in the former Manchuria, returning to Japan when his father died in 1938. He quit middle school, played piano in a music hall on an American military base during the occupation, and eventually graduated from Tokyo Keika High School in 1949.[39] Gradually he became known abroad as well as at home for his scores for ensembles, orchestras, ballets, movies, radio, and television. "Takemitsu may have gained worldwide recognition precisely because he was mostly self-taught, not the product of academic musical training in Japan," the business tycoon and novelist Tsutsumi Seiji thinks. "In this sense, he's like the renowned print maker Munakata Shikō, who never went to art school but taught himself after being inspired by the Nebuta festival in Aomori."[40]

Takemitsu acknowledged in a 1984 discussion with the conductor Ozawa Seiji (1935–) that he had had no real teachers,[41] but elsewhere he wrote of his attraction as a teenager to works by Japanese composers who chose local, not international, idioms: "As I look back over the path I've traveled as a composer, I can't overlook that I've been strongly affected by two composers, Kiyose Yasuji and Hayasaka Fumio." In 1948 when he first met Kiyose, Takemitsu waited more than six hours at Kiyose's Soshigaya Ōkura house in Setagaya for the senior composer to return — as it happened, from visiting Hayasaka in Kamakura. Kiyose started him off with Hayasaka's works for piano, which "had a very high degree of Japanese feeling." Takemitsu found Kiyose's music, too, to be "very Japanese and very humorous, very light." Kiyose tried to extract ideas from his contemporary surroundings; Hayasaka sought them in archaic Japan. Takemitsu concluded: "When I try to think of 'Japan' as a composer, it's always in relation to these two outstanding composers. I learned from these two teachers not to take 'Japan' from the static viewpoint of the state but from the dynamic conditions of the people."[42] Later Takemitsu was similarly impressed by Abe Kōbō's scientific approach to daily life: "He gave new meaning to the word 'everyday.' . . . It was something amazing."[43]

Takemitsu also quickly developed an ear for the musical possibilities found in the cacophony of urban bustle: "One day in 1948, while riding a crowded subway train, I came up with the idea of changing noise to tuned musical tones. To put it more formally, composing means giving meaning to the stream of sounds in the world all around us."[44] Here Takemitsu dates his earliest interest in environmental noises to exactly the same year that Pierre Schaeffer produced his first example of musique concrète. The curiosity with everyday noises was entirely coincidental with Schaeffer's use of the sounds made by passing trains: musique concrète was introduced to Japan five years later with Mayuzumi's X, Y, Z. Once tape recorders became available, Takemitsu preferred to archive sounds in "tape design," not on the usual five-line score, because many images he had in mind couldn't be expressed within the confines of linear notation.[45]

Like the other members of the Experimental Workshop, Takemitsu devoted great energies in the 1950s to learning about recent Western music. He admired Arnold Schönberg, Alban Berg (1885–1935), and Anton von Webern (1883–1945) but was especially fond of the works of Claude Debussy and Olivier Messiaen. Takemitsu's *Saegirarenai kyūsoku (Uninterrupted Rest)*, an instrumental composition in three parts first performed at a workshop concert on August 9, 1952, owed some of its tonal inspiration to Messiaen.[46] Takemitsu's approach was often to integrate melodic phrases with their enveloping silences, especially with closing sounds that faded gently into noiselessness.[47] He wrote that "*Saegirarenai kyūsoku* is a sketch based on Mr. Takiguchi's poem of the same name. However, it does not portray the poem; it touches on the beautiful transparency of this poem."[48]

Takemitsu had evidently read *Yōsei no kyori* (1937), the Takiguchi volume containing this poem, shortly before he met the poet in 1950. The following year Takemitsu wrote an etude for violin and piano titled *Yōsei no kyori (Distance de fée)* that provided an impression, not an analog, of Takiguchi's text.[49] The curators of a 1999 exhibition at the Setagaya Literary Museum on the lives of these two artists suggest that Takiguchi was a virtual "father" to Takemitsu, who had lost his natural father at age eight. The composer visited Takiguchi's house several times a week during the Experimental Workshop years, when Takiguchi was Japan's most prominent art critic. Takiguchi, who had no children, offered to adopt Takemitsu, but the latter reportedly declined on the ground that he respected Takiguchi too much. The two remained close until Takiguchi's death in 1979.[50]

Commenting on his experiments with musique concrète, Takemitsu wrote that "conventional music expressed concrete images by means of abstract musical sounds. Conversely, musique concrète tried to express an abstract image by means of everyday sounds."[51] *Ruriefu sutateiku* (1955), Takemitsu's initial experiment in electronic music as introduced by Karlheinz Stockhausen in 1951, was the first of many examples of his effort to create a "stream of sounds." *Vōkarizumu A.I. (Vocalism A.I.*, 1956–1960), a pun on the word for "love" *(ai)*, was planned as a 72-hour marathon work but eventually was compressed to 4:09 minutes of alternating male and female voices, interpreting a love poem by Tanikawa Shuntarō. *Mizu no kyoku (Water Music*, 1960) used the sounds of water dripping rather ingloriously in a Tokyo toilet tank — electronically compressed, elongated, spliced, transformed — to create yet another example of musique concrète.[52]

Among Takemitsu's many other compositions dating to the 1950s, *Gengaku no tame no rekuiemu (Requiem for Strings*, 1957) won him an especially wide audience. His program notes for the premiere spoke of the "stream of sounds flowing through people and their world" and said parts of this stream were "produced by chance."[53]

The core motif of this highly structured work is modified (rather than developed, as in orthodox German compositional technique) in what Takemitsu called "double variations" to advance the sound stream. *Requiem,* which Igor Stravinsky (1882–1971) highly praised during a 1959 visit to Japan, was commissioned by the Tokyo Symphony Orchestra and seemed to be a memorial to Hayasaka Fumio, the film-score composer who had taken in the young Takemitsu as an assistant. The music writer Peter Burt suggests the composition was equally a requiem for Takemitsu himself, who wrote it during a lengthy and serious illness, producing a work played with a "dark, monochromatic *film noir* sonority."[54]

By the end of the decade, Takemitsu had launched his dazzling career, which lasted until 1996, by writing at least twenty-four works for instruments, chamber ensembles, orchestra, tape, broadcast, or stage — and another thirteen scores for movies, including Teshigahara Hiroshi's 1959 documentary *José Torres.*[55] He later commented that "for a long time Japanese music has been entirely imitative,"[56] and indeed during the 1950s Takemitsu absorbed himself in experiments with contemporary music from France, and to a lesser extent Germany and the United States. In those days Darmstadt was the focal point of serial music, but Takemitsu found its approach too rigid. In 1960 he criticized the "dangerous aspects" of twelve-tone technique: it was "too mathematical, too geometrical, too intellectual."[57] Already he had established his bent toward more intuitive compositions drawing on the rich quality of sounds heard in everyday life,[58] a direction discussed more fully in Chapter 8.

Yuasa Jōji, who was a year senior to Takemitsu, followed a more conventional path as a youth. The son of a doctor who headed a large hospital in Kōriyama, he abandoned his medical studies at Keiō University in 1951 to become a composer and wrote his first work of note, *Futatsu no pasutorāru (Two Pastorals)* for piano, the following year. Yuasa studied contemporary French poetry and felt particular sympathy with the ideas of Jean-Paul Sartre and the postwar French existentialists.[59] These literary interests provided an easy link to Takiguchi Shūzō and the Experimental Workshop, many of whose members were reading French surrealist poetry at the time. Yuasa says he was attracted by the group's eagerness "to reject established ideas" about art and open up a new world through new media.[60]

"At the start of my career I was much taken with Copland, Bartók, Messiaen, and other French composers,"[61] Yuasa remembers. For the next decade he steeped himself in Western composing methods, usually taking an approach more intellectual than Takemitsu's, but one no less sensitive to sound qualities. Yuasa's works from the start were consistently objective; he called many of them "projections," to emphasize his conviction that "creativity is to plan for the future."[62] Yuasa was one of the first in Japan to experiment with musique concrète, sometimes combining his compositions with slides of photographs and drawings. He made regular use of NHK's electronic-music studio, turning out his most famous electronic composition, *Icon*, in 1966–1967 as "five-channel electronic music for white noise."[63] He later remarked that the musique concrète and electronic music of the 1950s eventually merged in the domain of computer music.[64]

Yuasa points out that, at first, members of the Experimental Workshop were so fascinated by contemporary European music that they felt little concern to coordinate Western art forms with Japanese sensibilities. "But by 1954 we were having many discussions about problems in the arts, always focusing on differences between East and West and how to integrate them." For the next two years he experimented with bitonal, polytonal, and atonal music, then turned to twelve-tone composition. "I wrote a lot of pieces in twelve-tone technique, but then I realized it was based on European foundations in Bach, Beethoven, and Mozart — motif and variation. For three years I tried to express Japanese temporality through twelve-tone technique, then I abandoned it." To resolve these problems between the West and Japan, "I turned to Nō music, which sounded unnatural vis-à-vis Western music. From this, I found that the essential differences between Japanese and Western music were their senses of time and space." In Yuasa's view, the term *ma*, which can mean both time and space, is best understood as the "timing and spacing" of sounds in a composition.[65]

Yuasa moved beyond his earlier fixation on contemporary German idioms toward a somewhat postcolonial stance in the late 1950s, freely using elements from early Japanese theater and poetry. Even so, his work showed little evidence of musical nationalism or Pan-Asianism. "I've always wanted my music to appeal to all peoples, so my musical ideas should come from the genesis of human culture, in prehistory. The religious feelings of people are deeply connected with musical expression in this early genesis of mankind, before any differences between East and West." This conviction eventually led him to seek universal musical meaning. Although he was fascinated with D. T. Suzuki's idea of cosmic unconsciousness, Yuasa's search for the cosmic (*uchū*) through music stemmed also from science: "I've always been interested in physics and cosmology, including the works of Stephen W. Hawking. I think of music as musical energy moving, reflecting mankind's cosmology. My music shows my individual cosmology, based on my own experience and my own language. My ideas come from thinking about differences between East and West and about the polarity between the commonality of mankind on the one hand and my own individuality on the other."[66] He has also been indebted throughout his career to Herbert Read's concept of touch-based perception, most recently in *Cosmos Haptic V* (2002), for which he received NHK's Otaka Prize in 2003, the fourth time he won this award.[67]

What of Yuasa's works themselves? Many are quite playful with sounds, such as his *Toi* (Question, 1971) for mixed voices, especially its brief number "N to n," in which male and female singers alternate asking "hmm?" and answering "hmm."[68] Although he produced far fewer works during the 1950s than Takemitsu — just six instrumental pieces and two movie scores — Yuasa's repertoire thereafter became astonishingly diverse: instrumental, chamber, orchestral, electronic, computer, and choral and solo vocal compositions as well as songs for children, music for radio and television, and eleven film scores. Like Takemitsu, he was also a prolific writer of books, one of which, *Ongaku no kosumorojī e* (Toward a cosmology of music), expressed his views on the ultimate meaning of music.[69] From 1981 to 1996 Yuasa served as a professor of music at the University of California, San Diego, by chance returning to Japan permanently the same year Takemitsu died. Yuasa's works were the subject of a weeklong retrospective held in late May 2002 at Opera City in Tokyo, displaying anew his skill at employing avant-garde sounds favored by Western composers while showing a sensitivity to Japanese aesthetics through spacing and timing, sometimes using a nonlogical structure of time, as in *nō*, to allow his music to unfold with the boundless feeling of an unrolling *emaki* painting in medieval times.[70]

Counterpoint: Mayuzumi, Akutagawa, Dan

Of Japan's many innovative composers of art music in the 1950s, the Experimental Workshop's chief rivals for attention among the avant-garde were three sons of the Tokyo artistic elite — Mayuzumi Toshirō, Akutagawa Yasushi, and Dan Ikuma (1924–2001) — who constituted the Three-Person Society (Sannin no Kai) between 1953 and 1962. This group was even more successful than the Experimental Workshop in mobilizing audiences for contemporary music, even though (or perhaps because) its programs were less musically daring and more stylistically indebted to prewar precedents. Four decades later, Dan recalled that the Three-Person Society belonged to an era of "centripetal vectors" in Japanese music when Japanese composers sought wide audiences. The ideal of music as a common experience was abandoned in the late 1960s, and the period thereafter was one of fragmentation, dispersal, and niche markets — symbolized by the introduction of the Walkman in 1979.[71]

Akutagawa maintained that the Three-Person Society was formed "by chance" in the summer of 1953 "when all three of us happened to be in Kyoto" on "movie business."[72] They agreed to share the considerable costs of hiring the Tokyo Symphony Orchestra to present their new works, at a time when the typical program of contemporary music featured chamber music, which was much cheaper to stage. Altogether this group put on five full-scale concerts before disbanding in 1962, the first of which took place in January 1954 at Hibiya Public Hall offering a fresh composition by each of the three, who took turns conducting the ensemble. Although some criticized their extravagance for employing a full orchestra, others pointed out that these well-heeled composers helped make it possible for musicians to subsist.[73] The pinnacle for this group came on April 2, 1958, when Akutagawa premiered his *Erōra* symphony, Dan a suite called *Arabia kikō (Arabian Travelogue)*, and Mayuzumi his signature *Nehan (Nirvana)* symphony — three of the best-known works in the postwar Japanese repertoire.

Mayuzumi, who together with Takemitsu was as eclectic as any avant-garde composer of his era in Japan, in 1957 became the first in his country to write for prepared piano;[74] he then began using the NHK electronic-music studio to analyze the sound structure of seven temple bells, including those at Byōdōin in Uji and Tōdaiji in Nara. He measured their average pitch and used it in twelve-tone system for his basic chords in the *Nehan* symphony, augmented by a large choir of male voices chanting texts used by the Tendai and Zen schools of Buddhism. These elements, chosen from living religious practice, were Asian in provenance but culturally contemporary to the composer's age, not revivals from the past.[75] While he was composing *Nehan*, Mayuzumi was also writing on Webern, Boulez, Cage, and Stravinsky, particularly praising their antirational characteristics.[76] His attraction to Western compositional techniques slackened in the 1960s, yet Mayuzumi remained one of Japan's foremost experimentalists well after other avant-garde composers, including Takemitsu, began churning more familiar ground.

Akutagawa Yasushi, who like Mayuzumi and Dan graduated from the Tokyo Academy of Music, soon became known for the lyrical melodies in his movie scores, written while serving as an assistant to Hayasaka Fumio. His string compositions were notable, doubtless because he admired the works of Igor Stravinsky, Sergey Prokofiev (1891–1953), and Dmitry Shostakovich (1906–1975). In 1954, when it was still illegal to do so, he traveled throughout Hungary, the Soviet Union, and China, meeting musicians and developing ties with fellow composers. Two years later he visited cave temples in India and was surprised to discover erotic stone sculptures, which inspired his 1958 symphony *Erōra*, played by separate men's and women's orchestra sections.

Without abandoning his musical progressivism, Akutagawa entered a more spare, astringent phase with his 1960 opera *Hiroshima no orufue (Orpheus in Hiroshima*, originally titled *Kurai kane* or *Somber Bell*), written in collaboration with the novelist Ōe Kenzaburō (1935–). Rather than adding sounds, as in most Western contemporary music, Akutagawa preferred to play all the notes at the beginning of a work and then remove certain ones thereafter, after the fashion of much indigenous East Asian music.[77] Although closely identified with the Three-Person Society, Akutagawa reasserted his trenchant individualism in a 1966 article: "People must fight to improve their circumstances by challenging their natural, social, and political environments. There are many ways for each individual to do this, one by one; there is no single way. It's absolutely essential for composers and performers to assert themselves according to their own lights"[78] — watchwords for the avant-garde in Japan ever since.

Dan Ikuma, the son of an art historian and grandson of the Mitsui mogul Dan Takuma (1858–1932), who was assassinated in a right-wing plot in 1932, was best known for his opera *Yūzuru (Twilight Crane*, 1952), with a libretto by the playwright Kinoshita Junji (1914–) based on a Japanese folk tale. This work, using five-tone melodies, had been performed more than six hundred times by the time Dan died in Shanghai in 2001.[79] No postwar Japanese musician was more fascinated by China and Asia than Dan, as his orchestral suite *Arabia kikō* for the Three-Person Society concert in 1958 shows. Dan considered himself an heir of the mainstream prewar composer Yamada Kōsaku and soft-pedaled his inventiveness in a 1980 interview: "my music doesn't touch on electronic processes, chance operations, or other avant-garde techniques, so I may be criticized for being a little unprogressive."[80] Yet of the three Sannin no Kai composers, Dan was probably thematically the most wide-ranging, combining elements from Yamada, Russian, and Chinese music.

Dan, who was one of very few composers invited to join the establishmentarian Japan Art Academy, was also a prolific and expansive essayist. He pointed out that until the late nineteenth century "the history of Japanese music is a history of poetry rather than of music,"[81] because up to that time composition was called "adding a tune" *(fushizuke)* to a literary work.[82] Dan was thoroughly trained in contemporary Western-style composition, calling it "thinking in sound" wherein "sound is subservient to thought." Unlike Asian music "Western musical forms are based on Western ideals of logic and symmetry."[83] Although Dan found himself increasingly drawn toward the Asian continent after the finale of the Three-Person Society in 1962, he was careful to distinguish difference, rather than a hierarchy of value, in Western and East Asian music: "It is not enough to write Japanese-sounding compositions using Western forms and harmonies," he said in 1961. "Those who have tried to do so have had no real or lasting success. The purpose of the composer, first of all, must be to write good music, and this we are not likely to have through mere rearrangement of traditional music for Western instruments. Something new, but at the same time fundamentally Japanese, must be created."[84] Here Dan defines one of the critical artistic questions of the 1960s in Japan: how to produce art that is postnational ("good" in the global arena) while also being thoroughly local (true to the Japanese context). Like the other composers in the Three-Person Society, he was far more sensitive to the arts of Asia than was the Experimental Workshop, yet the musicologist Judith Herd is surely right that the Sannin no Kai fostered an outlook that was "neither openly patriotic nor narrowly nationalistic."[85]

COMPARED WITH ABSTRACTION in other arts, contemporary music in Japan progressed calmly during the 1950s, probably because, ever since the onset of modernism, no alternative to the abstract could be found in Western-style composition until at least the discovery of musique concrète. Although everyday noises found their way into a number of Japanese works starting in the 1950s, the critic Tone Yasunao correctly pointed out in 1961 that to most avant-garde composers musical tone continued to be less a matter of sound than of the concept of sound[86] — more so with Yuasa than Takemitsu, but largely true of their entire generation, despite Dan's reservations about "thinking in sound." Gradually the composers in the Experimental Workshop, who were distinctly nonacademic, made common cause with the Three-Person Society and other leaders of academic contemporary music through the Twentieth-Century Music Institute (Nijūsseiki Ongaku Kenkyūjo), founded in 1957 to promote all styles of contemporary art music with particular focus on serialism.[87]

Two years earlier the Tokyo Symphony Orchestra began including a Japanese work in every regular subscription program. The composer Takahashi Yūji, who remembers seeing Takemitsu riding the train from Kamakura as both traveled to Tokyo for concerts in the mid-1950s, recalls the Symphony Orchestra's performances especially for presenting much contemporary music by Japanese as well as foreigners.[88] In 1957 the Japan Philharmonic Orchestra started up and immediately began commissioning works by Japanese composers, the same year the Twentieth-Century Music Institute launched its annual contemporary music festival in Karuizawa (relocated to Osaka before the series concluded in 1965). Moroi Makoto, a cofounder of the institute, notes that "Mayuzumi had just returned from Darmstadt and I had just returned from another summer festival in Europe. We believed the level of contemporary music in Japan was very low, so we organized summer festivals in Karuizawa" for music professionals and their students.[89]

By then the visual artists who belonged to the workshop likewise felt the appeal of the Producers' Conference (Seisakusha Kondankai), established in 1955 by Ikeda Tatsuo, Iida Yoshikuni, Ishii Shigeo, Kawara On, and others to experiment with a new realism in painting, sculpting, and print making. This group came to supplant the Experimental Workshop in displaying some of the greatest critical acumen of the era.[90] The Alpha Art Circle (Arufuā Gei-jutsujin), also founded in 1955 by the poet and visual artist Matsuzawa Yutaka (1922–) and others, brought together composers, poets, painters, economists, and scientists for transdisciplinary explorations. Even though the Experimental Workshop yielded its leading position to newer experimental groups after 1957, more recently its mixed-media efforts have been recognized in retrospective exhibitions and performances, starting with a Jikken Kōbō show at the Satani Gallery in 1991 and a concert of works by the workshop's composers at Hama Rikyū Asahi Hall in 1996. Still, the Experimental Workshop is little remembered today, a victim perhaps of its own ultramodernism and devotion to Europe in an ultra-postmodern and artistically postnational age.

chapter three

Avant-Garde Visual Culture
Local and Historical

While Mayuzumi Toshirō, Yuasa Jōji, and other composers of contemporary art music were starting to modify their European-inspired experiments by using indigenous elements from living religious or secular practice in their new works during the 1950s, Japan's most recognizable advocate of avant-garde painting and sculpture — Okamoto Tarō — began to exemplify a shift away from modernist visual culture toward the historical and local. Writing serially in the weekly magazine *Shūkan asahi*, Okamoto said that by energetically studying Japan's actual history, not the distorted narrative spun out by the modern Japanese state since the 1880s, "gradually we'll become aware that the past has value for the present. Thus the present will be enriched."[1] At the same time, he pointed out in 1954, artists are citizens of the world but also Japanese who "are absolutely part of an everyday environment."[2] Far from representing an attachment to the bygone, the study of history has meaning today because it refines our skill at seeing our current milieu: "artistic technique is always revolutionary and develops as perpetual creativity. This is the essence of art."[3] In this way Okamoto became the first major avant-garde figure in Japan to champion art that set aside the concrete universals of high modernism and sought standards that were at once contemporary and Japanese, rooted in lived experience.

Okamoto was a bridge across artistic eras in several respects. Like Takiguchi Shūzō, he was born in the late Meiji era, acquainted himself thoroughly with European artistic ideas about art during the interwar period, and tirelessly promoted unconventional approaches to contemporary art in Japan after World War Two. He was born to creative parents: the novelist, poet, and Buddhist scholar Okamoto Kanoko (1889–1939) and the cartoon artist

Okamoto Ippei (1886–1948). Unlike Takiguchi, he helped smooth the path for aspiring artists of the Shōwa single-digit cohort who wished to innovate without necessarily emulating Western practices. His own paintings and photographs provided transitions from the immediate postwar art of despair to a modified form of abstraction and finally to works that confirmed the historical and the everyday in the present. Okamoto also helped the avant-garde shed the confines of party-based political activism without abandoning a critical consciousness about contemporary society.

In moving beyond the modern, Okamoto made it plain that he was no neonationalist: "the fine term 'love of country' is a narrow outlook," and "in feelings of dislike for others, I don't think true love is to be found."[4] Okamoto founded no school, nor was his painterly style much imitated, yet his outlook on the place of history and art in Japanese society was shared by some of the most imaginative avant-garde artists of the 1950s in media ranging from oil painting and sculpture to calligraphy, pottery, and the natural-pigment painting of Nihonga. Their experiments drew less on a purely imagined tradition than on Japan's partially documented past, such as the archaeology of the Jōmon era (10,000–2,300 B.P.), and helped to update, revivify, and stir new interest in their respective genres — internationally as well as at home.

Okamoto the Mentor

Takiguchi Shūzō and Okamoto Tarō were close personally, even though their approaches to the arts differed. To us, Takiguchi was our uncle, Hanada Kiyoteru our eldest brother, and Okamoto our second-eldest brother. Takiguchi was most important for the personal encouragement he offered. In terms of ideas, Hanada had the most powerful effect, especially his knowledge of avant-garde art in the prewar period. — Segi Shin'ichi, early postwar art critic[5]

Hanada Kiyoteru often went drinking with artists and exerted an important, if old-fashioned, effect on them, but like Abe Kōbō, his intellectual magnetism faded after the 1950s. Okamoto Tarō, like Hanada, seemed very "cultural" to us young hippies, not so radical intellectually and not at all part of the artistic underground in Shinjuku. He was significant for calling attention to the Jōmon period. — Yoshimasu Gōzō, poet and photographer since the 1960s[6]

Although separated in age by just eleven years, Segi and Yoshimasu disclose in these remarks, made in 2002, both how revered Okamoto and Hanada were and how transient their impact on successive generations seems from today's vantage. Segi (1928–), the intimate of artists who established the Century Association in 1947 and the Evening Society a year later, reflects the esteem felt by many avant-garde painters in the 1950s for Hanada as editor and organizer and for Okamoto as sponsor of new art that was as daring as it was distinctive. Yoshimasu (1939–), a poet much given to verbal experiments, expresses the eagerness of many underground playwrights, choreographers, painters, and sculptors in the 1960s to find new artistic spaces free from the authority of the Shōwa single-digit generation and those, like Okamoto, Hanada, and Takiguchi, who were its mentors.

Unlike Hanada, Okamoto had direct experience with the prewar European avant-garde from living in Paris during 1929–1940. He studied philosophy, psychology, and ethnology at the Sorbonne, graduating with a degree in anthropology. In Paris he painted under the tutelage of Kurt Seligmann (1900–1962) and absorbed surrealism from André Breton and Max Ernst (1891–1976), while also learning about abstract art through contact with the poet-painter Jean Arp (Hans, 1887–1966), the sculptor Constantin Brancusi (1876–1957), and the painter Wassily Kandinsky (1866–1944). He became fascinated by primitivism through his studies of Picasso and African art. Okamoto thrived on what he took to be the opposition of extremes in pure abstractionism versus surrealism.[7] By the time he returned to Japan in 1940, the year France fell under Nazi occupation, he had already embraced three of his main precepts for postwar Japanese art: the importance of trying new techniques, the creativity arising from polar opposites, and the lessons provided by ancient history.

Okamoto's early postwar oil paintings verified his commitment to destroying old artistic values and seeking new ones in the avant-garde. *Jūkōgyō* (*Heavy Industry*, 1949) and *Mori no okite* (*Rules of the Forest*, 1950) used the familiar European device of visual symbolism to address contemporary problems of human society, as did the apocalyptic *Moeru hito* (*Burning People*, 1955), inspired by Hiroshima and Nagasaki as well as by the exposure of a Japanese fishing vessel, the *No. 5 Fukuryū maru* (*Lucky Dragon*), to hydrogen-bomb tests in 1954 by the United States in the South Pacific. *Mori no okite*, which might also be rendered "law of the jungle," could be read as autobiographical, expressing the artist's wartime experience as a thought-police (Tokkō) suspect for harboring "dangerous thoughts" and as a draftee into the Imperial Army, who did a portion of his service in China, from which he returned in June 1946.[8] Okamoto wrote that the painting presents "a torn-apart state between being real and unreal. One can certainly see an allegory of today's political events; but one can also find the symbolism of a fundamental humanity. The fundamental exists as a polar opposite to the historical and social."[9] This

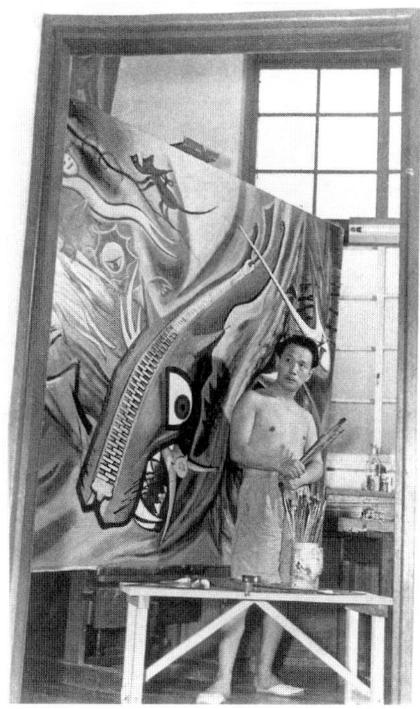

Figure 6. Okamoto Tarō
with *Mori no okite (Rules of
the Forest)*. 1950. Courtesy
Okamoto Toshiko and Oka-
moto Tarō Museum of Art,
Kawasaki.

disturbing scene of violence and confusion, executed in vivid primary colors, centers on a crocodile-like animal with a zipper as well as teeth, as though the mechanical culture of warfare were now more menacing than the natural order. (See Figure 6.)

Moeru hito mixes civilization and nature in the chaos of a nuclear explosion: a quasi-geometric design of two ships tossed asea, a mushroom cloud, human eyes and limbs, the earth in flames, the planet given over to plants and snakes.[10] These and other abstract works completed in the first postwar decade verified Okamoto's 1948 dictum that "art today must not be nice, it must not be pretty, it must not make you feel good," whereas Umehara Ryūzaburō's soothing postimpressionist oils did precisely that.[11] He also dismissed fellow Japanese artists, as the art historian Bert Winther-Tamaki points out, who "he thought produced a traditional sort of Japanese aesthetics that easily and predictably charmed foreigners."[12] Because of his decade-long encounter with the European avant-garde before World War Two, Okamoto's paintings were chosen to represent Japan at the Venice and São Paulo biennales in the early 1950s, but by far his greater impact was felt at home through encouraging new styles, techniques, and ways of seeing the past in the present.

Okamoto relished the antithesis of extremes *(taikyokushugi)* evident in the art versus life conundrum, what he once called "the contradictory opposition and bipolarism of abstract and hyperreal elements" in the avant-garde.[13] Like many in his generation, his thought reveled in the dialectics of binary opposition: rational/irrational, real/surreal, figurative/abstract, West/Asia — but without proposing any synthesis, because *taikyokushugi* shirked continuity and stasis in favor of creative energy to transform how ideas were expressed through the visual.[14] The architect Isozaki Arata (1931–) sees in this unresolved confrontation of opposed elements some tendency "to advocate a Japanese uniqueness against modern Western painting."[15] Such may be true of certain canvases by Okamoto, yet he warned artists not to situate themselves in a unitary polar position but instead to draw vitality from the dynamic tension between opposites. The collision of ideas and the creative spirit, he believed, would produce resplendent art. Okamoto's *taikyokushugi* was a vivid component of the early postwar debate over realism and abstractionism, in which he and Hanada Kiyoteru were the clearest voices for an abstract art that was nonpolitical but not detached from civic life.[16] The idea of polar opposites faded after the mid-1950s, and most avant-garde artists, no matter how controversial or iconoclastic, staked out their positions thereafter with little reference to the binarisms that fascinated Okamoto.

Okamoto Tarō's most conspicuous contribution to postwar visual culture was his rediscovery of the pottery from Japan's prehistoric Jōmon era. His widow, Okamoto Toshiko, reveals that "Okamoto had known Marcel Mauss [1872–1950] and studied cultural anthropology in Paris during the 1930s." When he paid a return visit to Paris after the war, "he was shocked that André Malraux could identify Jōmon artifacts that Okamoto himself did not recognize. So he began learning about Jōmon, discovering it was a wide-open field."[17] Okamoto helped touch off the 1950s debate about the place of the past in Japanese culture with an article on the then-rare topic of Jōmon earthen vessels in the February 1952 number of *Mizue*, a premier art journal. He found the pottery of the subsequent Yayoi era (300 B.C.E.–300 C.E.) too balanced and formal, perhaps reflecting the highly stratified nature of Yayoi society, whereas he maintained that Jōmon materials displayed a "primitive strength, purity, that is, the fundamental passion of humanity"[18] — an exemplar of energy and boldness for the postwar avant-garde, especially to those young artists willing to help excavate newly discovered archaeological sites.

Like many antiestablishment intellectuals after World War Two, Okamoto reviled the canonical reading of Japan's history proffered by the Meiji state, with its saccharine paeans to Buddhist temples as the sources of the Japanese arts: "sentimentalism dragged in from the past is foolish."[19] *Nihon no dentō* (Traditions of Japan), published in 1956, launched a series of books in which

Okamoto attacked the dry, often twisted traditions promulgated by the authorities in their effort to place the premodern arts safely under glass and key in the gallery of the past.[20] Instead, he wrote in 1963, "each of us must create our own tradition" by discovering the values of Japan's actual history. "We should not live in ignorance of the past. Because tradition persists so robustly, it's our responsibility to live properly mindful of both the past and the future. This is the reason I've begun to write about Japanese tradition."[21]

Okamoto turned to Jōmon culture partly because he believed all subsequent Japanese eras were too socially hierarchical or, as with Muromachi (1336–1573) aesthetics such as *wabi* (poverty of means) and *sabi* (imperfection), too associated with Japanese nationalism during World War Two. Primitivism, which in the 1950s was still linked with modern art, reinforced the view of Japanese archaeologists at the time that Jōmon society was classless and egalitarian.[22] Okamoto believed "primitive art had a certain power not found in modern art — a power of life, an energy, the real source of Japanese art," says the art historian Kondō Yukio.[23] Like Okamoto, the American sculptor Isamu Noguchi (1904–1988), the painter Hasegawa Saburō, and the sculptor Teshigahara Sōfū (1900–1979) all spent time in the 1950s seeking the roots of Jōmon culture, which the art historian Chiba Shigeo believes became something of "a historical creation, a constructed vision of a precontinental past in response to the post-1945 uncertainty many Japanese felt about their culture."[24] Thus, even though Okamoto attacked the traditions invented by the Meiji state, he too helped to erect an alternative past for present purposes.

The camera was essential to Okamoto's way of viewing vestiges of primitive culture in remote parts of Japan during the 1950s, a decade when he wrote more than he painted. The poet Ōoka Makoto thinks that "Okamoto Tarō's biggest impact on all the arts was his discovery of early culture, especially the photographs he took of Okinawa,"[25] published in 1961 as *Wasurerareta Nihon — Okinawa bunkaron* (Forgotten Japan — Okinawan culture).[26] Kondō points out that Okamoto's photographs of Jōmon sites had a "big influence on sculptors in the 1950s and 1960s. He turned them back to early forms and unpolished materials such as clay, iron, and ceramics."[27] Some of his avatars were Teshigahara Sōfū, who produced rough cast-iron sculptures; Tsuji Shindō (1910–1981), whose *Kanzan* (1961) was done in clay; Inoue Bukichi (1930–1997), a sculptor whose work celebrated the history of Nara, his home region; and Ueki Shigeru (1913–1984), whose abstract wooden sculptures addressed ancient motifs.[28]

Okamoto Toshiko recalls that archaeologists at Tokyo University cooperated willingly with Okamoto's photographic expeditions but that the United States government did not. He had been denied a visa in 1952 to attend an exhibit of his own work in New York because the Department of State deemed him "a progressive artist" (the show was moved to Paris). Moreover "it was even difficult to get a visa in 1959 for his ten-day research trip to Okinawa," then under American military administration. Okamoto's explorations of Jōmon sites, the Ise Shrine, and remote Okinawan islands led him "to think 'this is Japan,' not Nara or Kyoto," his widow believes.[29] Yet his preoccupation with the past was more than simply essentialist. He criticized the notion of a Japanese patterned form *(kata)* in the premodern arts because it rarely measured up to world standards. Two years after his book on Okinawa appeared, Okamoto wrote that "the most urgent task of contemporary art is to synthesize the global *(sekai-sei)* and the particular *(koyū-sei)*; to understand the particular in a global perspective; and to achieve a global perspective that is based on the particular"[30] — an apt summary of the postnational aspirations of avant-garde artists everywhere in the late 1950s and 1960s.

Bringing Artists and Critics Together

While the Experimental Workshop was at its peak of activity in the mid-1950s, Okamoto and Hanada Kiyoteru took the helm of a comparable assemblage of critics and artists who tried to rekindle the mixed-media spirit of the occupation-era Evening Society. The new group, which held its first public event in December 1955, called itself the Contemporary Arts Society (Gendai Geijutsu no Kai), the umbrella organization for a subunit known as the Contemporary Arts Institute (Gendai Geijutsu Kenkyūjo) established earlier the same year. This society became the chief platform for Okamoto's ideas about the avant-garde, creative oppositions, and Japanese primitivism. The Contemporary Arts Society, together with the Experimental Workshop, served as a bridge from the early postwar study societies that sought to integrate the arts to the transmedia experiments sponsored by the new Sōgetsu Art Center, led by Teshigahara Hiroshi, in the late 1950s and early 1960s.

Hanada Kiyoteru was a novelist, playwright, editor, and critic of the creative arts who tirelessly labored to bring artists and their genres together, despite the centrifugal effects of specialization, depoliticization, and market forces as Japan's economy heated up after the Korean War. The art critic Haryū Ichirō recalls:

In the late 1940s I attended meetings of the integrated-arts group Yoru no Kai [Evening Society], held at a restaurant in Higashi Nakano, near Shinjuku. I met Hanada Kiyoteru there; because of his influence, I learned to sympathize with avant-garde art and literature. Hanada initially thought well of Okamoto

Tarō. Hanada thought Takiguchi Shūzō was too favorable in his appraisals of art, whereas Hanada tended to be quite critical. However, Takiguchi did criticize the Congress for Cultural Freedom [a CIA-sponsored organization of anticommunist intellectuals founded in 1950].[31]

Haryū's words evoke the interweaving of the avant-garde during the American occupation and the cold-war vortex confronting even the most detached artists. Hanada worked closely with Okamoto in the Evening Society but joined the Japan Communist Party in 1949 when the occupation authorities imposed their red purge. Okamoto stoutly resisted involving the Evening Society in politics and felt abandoned by Hanada's turn to the JCP, according to another society participant, Segi Shin'ichi.[32] Segi recounts that Okamoto told him many years later of the regret he harbored: "Exceptional circumstances must have made Kiyoteru feel obliged to engage in such activity at that time."[33]

Hanada avoided taking sides in the ideological rumpus between the party's mainstream and antimainstream factions during 1950–1951, then agreed in March 1952 to edit *Shin Nihon bungaku* (New Japan literature), the journal of the New Japan Literary Association (Shin Nihon Bungakukai), which had begun to distance itself from the JCP when the factionalism set in. Soon he ran afoul of the writer Nakano Shigeharu (1902–1979) and others from the prewar proletarian group, who resented his growing influence over the association and eventually finagled his dismissal as editor in July 1954.[34]

Disillusioned by the infighting, Hanada now resumed his friendship with Okamoto and his earlier search "for ways to synthesize different genres of the arts"[35] by setting up the Documentary Arts Society (Kiroku Geijutsu no Kai), a salon that resembled the former Evening Society. Also in 1954, another small circle of politically wary architects, writers, visual artists, and critics known as Contemporary Critics (Gendai Hihyō) began to gather monthly at Okamoto's newly built studio in the Aoyama section of Tokyo "to rectify [i.e., depoliticize] the relationship between politics and the arts."[36] Okamoto, the intellectual historian Hashikawa Bunzō (1922–1983), and especially Takei Teruo, a literary critic, focused the group's discussions on questions such as artists' war responsibility, as well as Okamoto's ideas about infusing contemporary art with the energy of antiquity, from a skeptical but non-Marxist stance.[37]

Considerable criticism, countercriticism, and contention prevailed among members of each organization; in particular, Contemporary Critics experienced a good deal of internal confusion. By early 1955 certain members of these groups had established the Contemporary Arts Institute, which in turn became the core of the Contemporary Arts Society that started up in December 1955 to bring critics and both verbal and nonverbal artists together from the entire creative spectrum.[38] One of the biggest challenges facing the transgenre Contemporary Arts Society was to liaise with the International Art Club (Kokusai Āto Kurabu), founded by Okamoto in July 1953 as the Japanese chapter of the Rome-based organization of the same name.

Okamoto had returned to Paris in November 1952 for a solo exhibition of his works, hastily rescheduled from New York after the United States denied him a visa, and went back to Tokyo the next May determined to set up a branch of the International Art Club as analogue to the Japan P.E.N. Club — although the latter was far more establishmentarian than the avant-garde visual artists who joined Okamoto's new group. "This club has absolutely no connection with politics,"[39] its manifesto declared, signaling its openness to conservatives as well as progressives of all ages — although few who were politically committed responded. Soon it took in members of the rival Japan Abstract Art Club such as Onchi Kōshirō, Murai Masanari, and Takiguchi Shūzō. Onchi became managing director of the International Art Club, administering its affairs from his Ogikubo home until his death in 1955. The club, which was never an art movement, sponsored exhibitions at galleries in Ginza and Shinjuku by avant-garde and other abstract artists chosen by Okamoto, both independents and members of other art associations. Renamed the Japan Art Club (Nihon Āto Kurabu) in 1961, the organization reached its peak membership of nearly two hundred in the mid-1960s and then slowly contracted, as artists went their individual ways.[40]

Okamoto was the principal link between the International Art Club and the Contemporary Arts Society, especially because each group met regularly at his Aoyama atelier. The Contemporary Arts Society was smaller in membership but broader in purpose: to promote "interchange among genres." The aim was to tie the arts to daily life, because "until now the arts have been managed by specialists, but in order to liberate the arts as something for all persons, we must link specialists and the general public closely together."[41] To pursue this objective, during 1955–1956 the Contemporary Arts Institute published four volumes of lectures for educated audiences to serve as a catch-up on the arts after two decades of semi-isolation from international currents. Among the contributions were essays by Okamoto on contemporary visual art, Tange Kenzō on architecture, Mayuzumi Toshirō on art music, and Noma Hiroshi on the novel. Hanada wrote on "The Typology of the Contemporary" and Takiguchi on "Directions in Contemporary Arts."[42] But despite its popularizing intentions, the Contemporary Arts Society mainly functioned as an elitist lecture and study group, with one program in 1956 featuring the novelist Abe Kōbō and another presenting electronic music in collaboration with the Experimental Workshop. Print makers, novelists, and photographers addressed the society from time to time, and in March 1957 the philosopher Tsurumi Shunsuke spoke on "Mass-Market Film Theory."[43] In this fashion Okamoto, Hanada, and their followers among the avant-garde managed to relight the fires of mixed-genre collaboration that had first flared in the late 1940s. Their activities marked a pathway down Aoyama Dōri, a broad Tokyo thoroughfare now known as route 246, to the new Sōgetsu Art Center where even bolder and more controversial transgenre events took place beginning in late 1958.

In the politicized artistic climate of the late 1940s and early 1950s, Okamoto ducked the most polemical exchanges while urging painters and sculptors to see that art is tied, but not hostage, to the real world. His faintly elitist outlook comported with Theodor W. Adorno's observation that "whereas the line separating art from real life should not be fudged, least of all by glorifying the artist, it must be kept in mind that works of art are alive, have a life *sui generis* . . . they have life because they speak in ways nature and man cannot."[44] Okamoto's fence-sitting about politics and foreign policy satisfied neither activists nor those who remained aloof. He grew famous in the 1960s as a popularizer of contemporary art on television, which diminished his impact on the young avant-garde artists who completed the rejection of modernism that Okamoto helped launch.

Downstream Ripples

Okamoto's chief enduring effect is that he sought the global in the local without privileging the cultural products made in Japan as "Japanese." What mattered was their spirit of primal energy, not their specific geocultural provenance, much as Yuasa Jōji's compositions in the late 1950s and 1960s began to draw on the cosmic energies and religious sentiments of prehistoric peoples everywhere. But beyond the circles of avant-garde painting and sculpture, other visual arts in the first postoccupation decade were washed by ripples, and sometimes waves, from the effort to fashion from everyday surroundings an art that addressed ideas of worldwide significance. What place, for example, did Japanese-style Nihonga painters define for their genre — originally created by the mid-Meiji state to express a new tradition of Japanese art — in the de-essentialized, nationally decentered orbit of cultural production in the 1950s?

By the postwar period it was not possible completely to renounce world trends in the arts, above all those from the West, any more than to incorporate them fully. Pure Japanese painting was a fantasy: "There was no possibility of a short-circuit return to premodern values," the art historian Tatehata Akira argues; the egg cannot be unscrambled. "Nor would there be much 'pure' Japanese culture left having subtracted from modern Japan all that had been assimilated from the West." Indeed, "the very idea of 'Japanese-ness' or 'East Asian-ness' presupposes a sense of opposition, a resistance to a more powerful occupying force"[45] — that is, a whiplash against cultural colonization. As the art historian Dore Ashton notes, there is "no nation that has developed a purely national art."[46] Instead of thinking of Nihonga as essentially Japanese painting, it is more useful to see it as owing debts to European neoclassicism and, to a degree, the postimpressionists. Like all the arts in post-1945 Japan, Nihonga was a product of the synchronic hybridity identified by the cultural historian Katō Shūichi in which an international artistic style is modified from one culture to another by a "particularity of sensibility" specific to each ethnos. Likewise Katō recasts Okamoto's diachronic approach to history in the contemporary: "artistic traditions in Japan are alive in the sense that the past unmistakably conditions the present, and the present constantly redefines the past."[47] In the case of Nihonga, the Meiji authorities created a past for present nationalist purposes that hardly mattered any more in the postnational arts milieu of the late 1950s and 1960s.

Scholars of the subject rarely maintain that Nihonga was unaffected by oil painting from Europe throughout the twentieth century, but most of them detect a much greater realism in the Nihonga produced after World War Two. In place of line drawing came a greater attention to composition across the entire surface. Many Nihonga were now painted from a plank suspended over a horizontally spread surface. New natural pigments and adhesives made it possible to mix colors to achieve a thickly painted effect similar to oils, giving play to a freer expression of ideas and emotions than was possible in more stylized and decorative Nihonga executed according to earlier rules. Some critics detect hints of action painting and informel in how conventional themes such as landscapes were addressed.[48]

Few dispute that the distinctions between Western-style and Nihonga paintings were largely ones of generations and artistic factions after World War Two, because in theme and technique the two were often indistinguishable. Hara Toshio, director of Japan's first private museum of contemporary art, nonetheless points out that "Nihonga after World War Two remained very oriented toward the headmaster system; even today, two artists dominate major lineages. Contemporary art, by contrast, has no hierarchy or headmasters."[49] Nihonga and Western-style painting have divided the art market almost equally since 1960 in a country that produces more paintings than any other.

Avant-garde ideas touched two prominent groups of postwar Nihonga painters, Creative Arts (Sōzō Bijutsu, founded January 1948) and the Kyoto-based Pan-Real Art Association (Pan-Riaru Bijutsukai, dating to May 1948), both of which engaged in a decade or more of experiments before settling back into more comfortable, less innovative approaches in the 1970s. Creative Arts declared at the outset, "We seek creativity in Japanese painting based on world standards," and the group focused on expressing realism through strength of form, not line.[50] Dissociating themselves from the art establishment and the government-sponsored art shows, the painters in Creative Arts held their own exhibitions, starting in September 1948, committing themselves to learning from Cézanne, Gaughin, Matisse, Picasso, and other modern masters. Haryū Ichirō summarizes the critical consensus that Creative Arts was not especially pathbreaking: "its shows were conventional juried exhibits, and its 'progressivism' merely amounted to Westernizing Nihonga."[51] In 1951 this group became the Nihonga section of the New Works Association (Shinseisakuha Kyōkai), the stronghold of postwar visual modernism, with particular emphasis on formal experimentation.

Pan-Real was formed by a handful of Kyoto artists who challenged the established conventions of Nihonga by ignoring the customary natural-pigment materials and instead using sand, concrete, boards, and canvas as well as Japanese paper *(shikishi)*. Some members did collages. The group held its own events rather than exhibiting at the open-submission, juried shows sponsored by the art establishment, in accord with its declared purpose of defying "the guild system of the Nihonga" schools and "the conservative anachronisms in Nihonga."[52] Through its bold innovations Pan-Real far outstripped Creative Arts in shedding natural-pigment painting techniques, and it eventually became a leading site for experiments in abstract expressionism, pop art, and op art. Still it is true, as the curator Matsumoto Tōru points out, that Nihonga and Western-style painting differed far less than their respective adherents usually claimed: oil paints, water colors, and mineral paints all come from natural sources such as ores, plants, or seashells,[53] so it is little surprise that avant-garde Nihonga artists took up materials and themes similar to their counterparts in Western-style painting.

An excellent example of how Nihonga artists responded indirectly to abstract expressionism is the large painting *Tō* (*Pagoda*, 1957, mineral pigments on cotton) by Yokoyama Misao (1920–1973). Executed in super-broad strokes of black ink, this work is a semiabstract rendering of a five-story tower at Tennōji temple in Yanaka that had burned to the ground. The composition is angular, rough, unkempt, almost tactile. The pagoda's eaves, some of which protrude toward the viewer, are cut off at all four margins, as though in a detail of a larger work. The tower is free-floating and decontextualized; the viewer can see nothing of its surroundings. Yokoyama was associated with the Seiryūsha (Green Dragon Society), a group of Nihonga painters that, like Creative Arts, "served as a reformist movement to help tide over the crisis in Nihonga"[54] after World War Two, until many Nihonga artists settled into the more familiar role of producing decorative paintings starting in the late 1960s. A few persevered with surrealist fantasies, almost indistinguishable from oils, into the 1970s.

Japanese calligraphy and crafts during the 1950s were likewise carried by the tides of seeking the past in the present and the global in the local. Bert Winther-Tamaki aptly notes that "calligraphy and pottery are serviceable to the definition of national identity on a dimension" far surpassing Nihonga: "the everyday life of the vast majority"[55] of Japanese. When vanguard calligraphy was shown abroad, audiences were surprised to find abstract forms, not just time-honored Chinese characters, yet the use of space in calligraphic art appealed widely to abstract expressionists in and out of Japan.[56] In this sense a historic art form evolved provincially, within Japan, into a contemporary visual expression that excited transcultural interest.

The Hattori Wakō Gallery at the Ginza 4-chōme intersection in Tokyo, its occupation-era duty as a commissary for the American military now at an end, became a main venue for exhibits of contemporary crafts after 1952. The Kyoto-based ceramics group Sōdeisha (Mud-Racing Society), formed in 1948, used Wakō as its window on the world at the most international — and during 1945–1952 the most neocolonial — of Tokyo crossroads. Sōdeisha artists took sharp exception to academic ceramics, including the pottery associated with tea ceremony, and instead produced avant-garde vessels and, increasingly, highly abstract objects.[57] Between 1947 and 1956, the curator Moroyama Masanori has calculated, fourteen new groups were organized with the conviction that "crafts are rooted in everyday life."[58] Modern crafts, as "art for actual use," together with innovative industrial design, thrived in successive eras of economic catch-up and high-speed growth, particularly as popular export items in the 1950s.[59] In this way both abstract and applied ceramic artists used materials from daily life to revamp time-honored pottery techniques in imaginative ways that contributed to, much more than mimicked, world trends in craft production. Like the painters and sculptors sympathetic with Okamoto's ideas, as well as creative artists in calligraphy and Nihonga, this generation of ceramists shirked romanticism (which uses the past to overcome the present) in favor of modifying an everyday culture of ancient origins, in effect crafting the past to meet contemporary needs and fitting the artists' own context to the creative world beyond Japan.

chapter four

Concrete Abstractions,
Abstract Expressions

Looking back in April 1968 at two decades of radical innovations in the arts, the critic Haryū Ichirō commented that he'd traveled widely in the United States and Europe, but "no other country has such an 'out-of-town' complex" as Japan.[1] So powerful was Tokyo's lure as a magnet of media, audiences, markets, and ideas that artists outside the capital, even those in large cities, regularly asked him to come to their rescue. And with good reason, for Tokyo's galleries and exhibitions, its concert halls and performance spaces offered exposure to a public larger than any other in Japan — in East Asia's most cosmopolitan intellectual and artistic hub at the time.

Yet two of the most original art groups of the late 1950s and early 1960s sprang up far from Tokyo and initially had little to do with that city until curators and exhibit organizers from the capital went afield to invite their members to display their work in the metropole. The Gutai Bijutsu Kyōkai (Concrete Art Association), founded in 1954 by the Osaka businessperson-painter Yoshihara Jirō, and the Kyushuha (Kyushu School), a group of painters centering on Kikuhata Mokuma (1935–) who first gathered in 1957, spearheaded Japan's anti-art movement at the turn of the 1960s. Each of these organizations adopted premises antithetical to both premodern and modernist art, yet the two knew virtually nothing about each other, let alone about the Neo-Dada coterie in Tokyo, which in 1960 became the third tine of Japan's anti-art trident.

When they started up, neither Gutai nor the Kyushuha had much specific knowledge of abstract expressionism or its French counterpart, informel, nor did either group understand a great deal about contemporary Western art in general, because in those days information was sporadic at best.[2] This degree of isolation meant that neither Gutai nor Monoha was specifically anti-Western or overtly postcolonial in rhetoric or action. Yet both felt waves from the splash of informel art, introduced to Japan in late 1956, and Gutai painters became particular favorites of informel's chief sponsor, the French critic Michel Tapié (1909–1987). The artists in each group, many of them from the early Shōwa generation, lacked the social standing of Takiguchi Shūzō's and Okamoto Tarō's followers in the capital. The Gutai association was as chary of political activism as the Tokyo groups, whereas the Kyushuha yoked its pursuit of the everyday in art to a leftist concern for local economic justice.

Roughly fifty progressive art groups proliferated outside Tokyo during 1955–1965, including a few that developed an indigenous performance art despite almost no awareness of its variants in New York or elsewhere. Especially notable were Vava in Gifu, Group Kurai (Group Situation) in the dry bed of the Nagara river, and Zero Jigen (Zero Dimension) in Nagoya. These troupes shared with the Gutai artists in Osaka a preference for non-Marxist praxis, not poesis.[3] Although all these avant-garde associations felt a degree of anger at the establishment exhibitions in Tokyo, Haryū believes that only the Kyushuha showed truly independent activity, although surely the Gutai group did too. Members of all the others "rushed to Tokyo" whenever they could, "vitiating their local focus."[4] Only Gutai and the Kyushuha enjoyed able leadership. Both kept their attention on innovations in the visual media, whereas members of the others often diverted their energies seeking social reforms at cost to their art — particularly during the tumult of demonstrations against the Japan–United States Mutual Security Treaty in 1960. For all these groups, the focus was on new relationships between art and daily life.

Gutai: Embodying the Material

> I had no conception of the new art. Then and now, I looked for interesting materials not used by any other artists and turned them into art works. I used water, smoke, rocks, etc., as materials for my works. My style drew inspiration from nature. — Motonaga Sadamasa, Gutai painter[5]

> The Gutai group wanted to make finished works. Their art was a bit too fixed, too unified. We in the Neo-Dada movement wanted instead to destroy, not to unify, and we made art out of daily-use items. — Akasegawa Genpei, Neo-Dada painter[6]

As George Orwell (1903–1950) knew, hints of the particular could be found amid the enervating sameness of twentieth-century industrial urbanism around the globe: the Englishwoman of a certain age, riding her bicycle in tennis shoes to vespers in the evening mist, or the familiar circle of hardy regulars crowding the neighborhood pub. Social critics of capitalist modernity, writing in the tradition of Karl Marx (1818–1883) and Max Weber (1864–1920), often identified such manifestations of the local as "everydayness" — rich sources of provincial variation and difference in the face of monotonous industrialism and the commodification of consumer culture.[7] As the postwar Japanese economy entered a stage of high-speed growth and oppressive consumer conformity after 1955, progressive artists who were unmoved by, or even untutored in, high modernism from Europe often turned to the everyday as a site of connection and difference for their ideas, even if they sometimes criticized the everyday as an outcome of capitalist production. No matter how abstract their modes of expression, members of the Gutai group chose materials from their daily surroundings that embodied what they called the material *(gutai)*. Although their approach varied greatly from that of the Kyushuha or the subsequent Neo-Dada Organizers, all three helped to transform the relationship of contemporary art to everyday life in Japan.

The Gutai society, which traced its origins to painting classes first offered by Yoshihara Jirō in 1947, differed considerably from Okamoto Tarō's approach in that it was the first group in Japan to escort the avant-garde away from its theoretical underpinnings and apply it to the everyday local environment. The curator Alexandra Munroe calls its works "concrete enactments of individual character, emotion, and thought in opposition to cerebral and abstract aesthetics."[8] Yoshihara was the son of a wealthy petroleum dealer in Osaka who taught himself to paint abstract works and transmitted to his pupils the dictum of his mentor in prewar Paris, Fujita Tsuguharu: "do things others haven't done."[9] Yoshihara was politically conservative but impatient with the conventional in art. His goal with his followers, he said, "was not to give them a set of directions or ideas, but to encourage them to work in their own way," to give their ideas "concrete form" *(gutai)*.[10] Surprisingly, he offered no comment on the artist's technique and judged only the finished work, usually just "good" or "not good."[11] Even though the Gutai group paid little heed to preserving its products — burning all of them after its first outdoor show in 1955 — Yoshihara's preference for evaluating the completed work, not the process of dismantling canonical norms of Western-derived painting and sculpture, irritated many other avant-garde figures, including Akasegawa. (See Figure 7.)

The Gutai Bijutsu Kyōkai was inaugurated in late 1954 by Yoshihara and sixteen young artists, many from the Shōwa single-digit cohort, "to show concrete evidence of spiritual freedom," including complete dissociation from

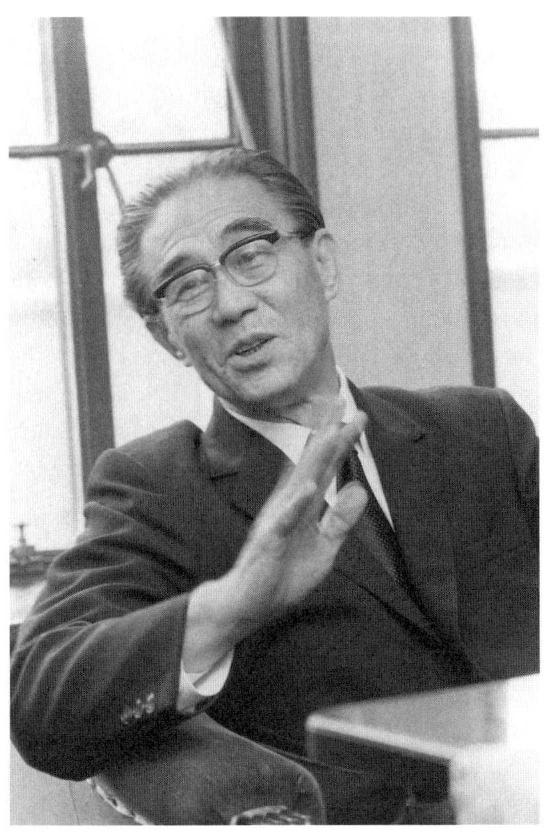

Figure 7. Yoshihara Jirō, painter and leader of the Gutai group. 1971. Courtesy Kyōdō Tsūshinsha.

politics — but not from authority: within a year half of the original members had quit to protest Yoshihara's heavy hand.[12] In January 1955 it published the first issue of a yearly journal, *Gutai*, with English summaries in the first few numbers, and later that winter twelve members exhibited at the Yomiuri Independent in Tokyo. Each of their submissions was titled *Gutai*; oddly, Yoshihara did not participate. Although their works were strikingly concrete, many Gutai painters admired the abstract expressionism of Jackson Pollock — evidently for the material properties of the enamel more than the decorativeness or use of space.[13] Indifferent though he was to most contemporary art from Europe, Yoshihara is considered the first important artist in Japan to appreciate American action painting and abstract expressionism, partly because he thought they were value-free. But the curator Matsumoto Tōru rightly observes that Gutai deliberately opposed mind to matter, unlike Pollock, and indulged in "a hot expressionism, the direct application to canvas of the artist's immediate desires," rather than the cool expressionism of precise geometric forms found in many previous abstract works.[14]

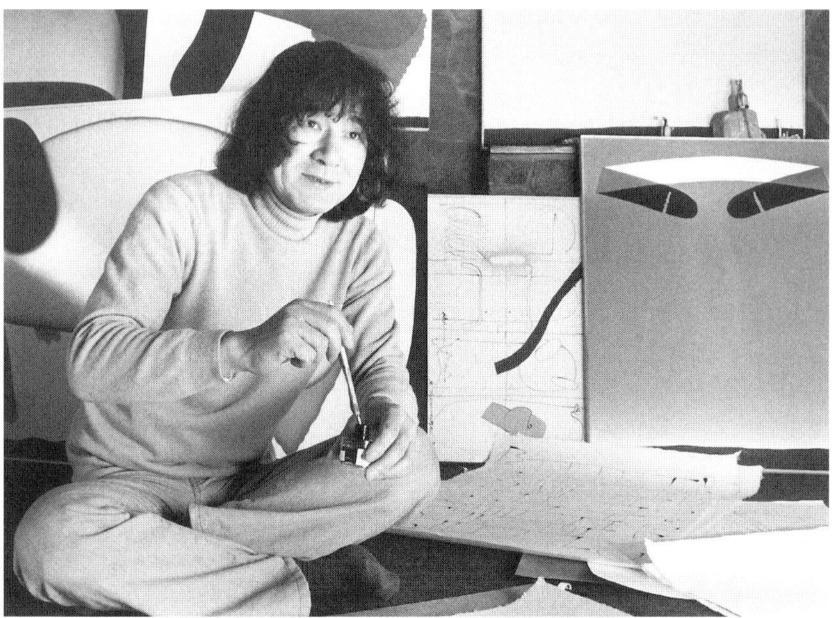

Figure 8. Motonaga Sadamasa, painter. 1980. Courtesy Kyōdō Tsūshinsha.

Almost alone among Japanese art styles in the 1950s and 1960s, Gutai drew a measure of international attention because of its supposed spontaneity and physicality. But modernists decried its lack of formal maturity, and many others in Japan and abroad impugned its lack of theory. "In the 1960s," Motonaga Sadamasa says, "critics in the Kantō region said there were no ideas in Gutai works, so they weren't true works of art. They liked my works, but Gutai was dismissed as no good."[15] Even the Gutai manifesto, belatedly issued by Yoshihara in October 1956, drew the scorn of the sociologist Daniel Bell as "an empty echo of Marinetti's Futurist Manifesto of 1910."[16] (See Figure 8.)

The first part of Yoshihara's hyperbolic manifesto focuses on respect for materiality (matter or physical properties, *busshitsu*), a concept familiar to Japanese since the 1920s through the writings of Karl Marx and Henri-Louis Bergson (1859–1941) as well as the paintings of Jean Dubuffet (1901–1985). In Yoshihara's formulation, "The arts we have known up to now appear to us in general to be fakes fitted out with a tremendous affectation. . . . Their materials such as paint, pieces of cloth, metals, clay, or marble are loaded with false significance by human" intervention. By contrast, "Gutai art does not change the material but brings it to life. Gutai art does not falsify the material" in any way. "If one leaves the material as it is, presenting it just as material, then it starts to tell us something and speaks with a mighty voice."[17] Clearly Yoshihara's bombast exaggerates for effect: the Gutai artist might "present" the material, not craft it, yet most works by members of this group ended up as completed projects, purposeful and self-contained, although not set apart from daily life like most paintings and sculptures in the West.

A second theme among the Gutai artists was shedding conventional abstractionism, no easy task for a group whose leader had just taken up abstract art in 1953 and never stopped producing it. Yoshihara said, "It is obvious to us that purely formalistic abstract art has lost its charm," so the Gutai society "would go beyond the borders of abstract art" to the tangible, by concretizing abstract space. "We want to be centripetal, not centrifugal" vis-à-vis daily life by privileging the materiality of objects in the environment and in art, not emphasizing the abstract form, however materially it might be presented.[18]

A final point, shared with Okamoto Tarō and the rest of the avant-garde, involved experimentation: "Gutai art puts the greatest importance on all daring steps which lead to an undiscovered world," Yoshihara declared, yet he made sure to add that "we think differently, in contrast to dadaism; our work is the result of investigating the possibilities of calling the material to life" by embodying it tangibly.[19] The act of expression established its own purpose, aided not by art supplies but by material objects, to be accomplished without explicitly repudiating the principles of Western art theory, merely ignoring them. As the French art editor and autobiographer Catherine Millet has pointed out, Gutai stemmed partly from abstract art and rejected surrealist characteristics. Rather than glorifying nature or materials, its followers simply used them as tools.[20] In short, materiality, reifying the abstract through everyday objects (both natural and human), and experiments in expression were Yoshihara's three chief teachings for the fifty-nine artists associated with the group between 1954 and his death in 1972.[21]

Gutai's first exhibition took place outdoors in a grove of Suma pines along the Ashiya river in Hyōgo prefecture in July 1955, including a few seemingly spontaneous experiments with bags of colored water suspended from tree limbs and cedar logs chopped with a hatchet. Touting "progress beyond abstraction," its debut in Tokyo took place three months later to complete critical silence. Twenty-three members displayed works at the Tokyo exhibition, including a few who performed activities such as jumping through a frame of kraft paper, slithering in mud, and inflating a balloon to fill an entire room — what remained after the artists finished were said to be action installations. Later Gutai events included attacks on the conventions of painting through experiments by Shiraga Kazuo (1924–), who not only hacked timbers but also painted with his feet; by Shimamoto Shōzō (1928–), an artist fond of shooting paint from a gun or breaking bottles of paint on rocks placed on a flat canvas; and by Murakami Saburō (1925–1996), who hurled rubber balls soaked in india ink onto the canvas.[22] The group's records mention twenty exhibits in its eighteen years of existence, in which more than forty members presented about two hundred visual works, mainly large paintings, installations, environments, and constructions, some accompanied by music, light, smoke, or physical actions by the artists. Eventually recognized in Tokyo as well as the Kansai region, Gutai chose Takashimaya department stores in Nihonbashi, Yokohama, and Osaka as locales for many of its undertakings.[23]

Performance art was barely recognized internationally when Gutai began its first experiments with site-specific action events in 1955, most of them resembling folk theater, none of them surviving except in photographs. "Gutai music," a form of musique concrète, was played at the group's second outdoor art show in 1956 and at a few indoor exhibits. Yoshihara and a dozen followers presented "Gutai theater" on July 17, 1957, at Sankei Hall in Osaka, billed as the world's first onstage art exhibit. Although Shimamoto says "our performances" were not drama and "were limited purely to the presentation of art,"[24] several of the works were studies in time and space, crossovers from visual to kinetic and performance art: the artists leaped through sheets of paper, used smoke, vinyl, and other materials, and "wore jackets with electronic devices to produce sounds," the composer Takahashi Yūji recalls.[25] The only other stage show by the Gutai group occurred the following year, although some of its members appeared in a joint performance with the Morita Masahiro Modern Dance Company in 1962.[26]

Also in 1962 Yoshihara opened a museum in the Nakanoshima area of Osaka, called the Gutai Pinacotheca, where he displayed avant-garde art from abroad as well as works by his students. The opening of the Gutai Pinacotheca was a sign that painting, however unconventionally executed, remained primary to Gutai artists. By now most of them were producing two-dimensional canvases, in good part because of strong overseas demand for their products starting in 1958 through the efforts of Michel Tapié, who helped to organize exhibitions of Gutai works at the Galerie Stadler in Paris, the Martha Jackson Gallery in New York, and an exhibit space in Oakland.[27] Putting Gutai art in a museum made it more widely accessible but also tamed it. As a curator at another institution, Yamamoto Atsuo, puts it: "Early Gutai had a sort of primitive charm which was rough but generated vitality and spirit through the chance discovery and meeting of unique materials and techniques. This trend reached a peak around 1960 as the use of both materials and techniques was strengthened and became mature, yet this mode of working was turning into a style somewhat stiff and controlled"[28] — in effect, a partial reversion to formalism.

Materiality remained the key motif in Gutai paintings in the 1960s, particularly the use of bright enamels in decorative designs and, later in the decade, high-tech elements such as strobe lights, bubbles, and kinetic components. Yoshihara himself never gave up painting; by the early 1960s he was turning out circular forms such as *Sakuhin* (Work, 1962, oil on canvas), a semi-abstract, lopsided circle of off-white paint dashed on a black background dappled with deep browns. This work seemed to embody what Gutai said it opposed: forms and abstractions. It showed Yoshihara's limitations as a painter and reemphasized that his real significance was as patron, not artist. Although some critics detected a narrative or lyrical tendency in later Gutai art, Motonaga Sadamasa said in 1966: "I try very hard to avoid being literary in my work. If one's work is generous in 'stories,' his role as a painter is weakened. Among other things, I never give titles."[29] The Nara artist Tanaka Atsuko (1932–2005), a pupil of Yoshihara who joined the Gutai association in 1955, began painting mandala-like groups of circles, in bright colors, "like dancers in motion,"[30] that soon won her opportunities to exhibit in Italy, Tokyo, and, in 1964, at the Guggenheim in New York. Shiraga Kazuo, who trained as a Nihonga painter and Buddhist priest, took up oils to pursue realism in portraying war and defeat, then turned to abstractions painted with his toes and feet in brief bursts of emotion. His *Tenkeisei Henmi Sanrō* (1964, oil on canvas) is a riot of reds and blacks honoring an ancient Chinese literary hero (see Plate 5).[31] The graphic artist Tanaka Ikkō (1930–2002) got his start as an assistant to Yoshihara designing sets for a fashion show, working with the materiality of textiles, and became a member of the Gutai organization before branching out to book design, typography, and poster art after 1961.[32]

In spite of its temporary works and onstage activities, Gutai contributed above all to artistic innovations that linked ready-at-hand materials to everyday life. As Motonaga points out, the Gutai group was criticized for lacking theory, although the same might be said of contemporaneous Western movements such as minimalism and conceptual art.[33] The painter Hikosaka Naoyoshi (1946–) chided Gutai members for not squarely addressing the "two-sided coin of stabilizing Japanese democracy in the wake of defeat in war and American cultural and military aggression in Asia"[34] — a context entirely absent from the group's manifesto or from Yoshihara's hopes for his followers. Even Okamoto Tarō joined in the catcalls, once Gutai became associated with informel art from France. The group became well known abroad thanks to Tapié's embrace of Gutai as a Japanese variant of l'art informel (Tapié preferred the term *un autre art* to informel), although Yoshihara and his followers had little patience with the French critic's theories. Okamoto had worked with Tapié in Paris but grew scornful of his aesthetics when Tapié visited Japan in 1957 and 1958. Okamoto now criticized Gutai artists for not confronting the social context of their art and ended up dismissing the group as representing "exactly the same ideas as Tapié's."[35] Moribund since the mid-1960s, the Gutai association disbanded after Yoshihara's death in February 1972 but received a good deal of retrospective attention in the 1980s for its stance against more conventional art, thanks mostly to drum beating by Hikosaka.[36] Gutai became the subject of major reappraisals at the 1993 Venice Biennale and at several retrospectives on the postwar avant-garde held in Tokyo since the mid-1990s. Its most vibrant paintings have outlasted many other Japanese visual products of the 1950s and early 1960s in freshness and appeal.

Informel: Discarding Forms

L'art informel was the French counterpart of American action painting, which was a branch of the abstract expressionism that emerged in the United States immediately after World War Two. The critic Harold Rosenberg (1906–1978) began using "action painting" in 1952 to describe the work of abstract expressionists such as Jackson Pollock and particularly Willem de Kooning (1904–1997).[37] The notion of l'art informel originated as early as 1909 in Paris and gained currency after 1951 as a way of characterizing abstract and expressive paintings that were neither geometric abstractions nor expressions of socialist realism or documentary art.[38] As often happens with translingual practices, in Japan the term informel came to mean both l'art informel and action painting, or indeed abstract expressionism overall. This usage began the moment the idea of art that does not rely on form became known in November 1956 through a major show, based on Michel Tapié's collection, called Sekai Konnichi no Bijutsuten (Exposition Internationale de l'Art Actuel), held at Takashimaya in Nihonbashi.

It is sometimes said that abstract artists, of whom Japan counted many by the mid-1950s, produced a preconceived visual effect, whereas action painters and informel artists produced an accidental result, without premeditation.[39] In fact many action paintings and informel works, such as de Kooning's *Woman* series (1950–1953), displayed forms in some degree of configuration.[40] Abstract expressionists and informel artists were also assumed to express intense emotion at the moment of creation, more out of idealism than radicalism, but the art historian Erika Doss observes that Pollock had a "social-critical agenda" that belied his reputation as a devotee of art for art's sake.[41] The critic Clement Greenberg (1909–1994), noting that representational art was often thought to be superior to the abstract, argued instead that both approaches were valid so long as quality was maintained. Greenberg praised the best abstract-expressionist canvases but drew the line at abstract art that went beyond painting, although he made an exception for the canonical sculptures of Henry Moore and Alexander Calder (1898–1976).[42]

Abstract expressionism had gradually become known in Japan even before the informel exhibition of November 1956, partly through a longstanding interest in Asian thought, especially Zen Buddhism, expressed by American artists such as Mark Tobey.[43] Tobey's works, together with those by Pollock and Mark Rothko, had first been displayed in Japan at the 1951 Yomiuri Independent. During the early 1950s Japanese artists living in the United States, including Hasegawa Saburō and Okada Kenzō, relayed news of the latest works and exhibits there to their counterparts back home, who learned that action painters, in particular, had largely abandoned forms in favor of "a vital, intense expression of the material as a physical entity,"[44] choosing paints over compositions in ways scarcely seen in Japan.

The 1956 informel show is remembered even today as an irreversible crossing for the Japanese avant-garde: "Okamoto Tarō was important to us young artists mainly as the organizer of the Sekai Konnichi no Bijutsuten exhibit at Takashimaya. This show had a very great effect on my generation,"[45] says the Neo-Dada painter and arts critic Akasegawa Genpei. During a visit to Paris the previous year, Okamoto had spoken with many persons, including Tapié and the expatriate painter Imai Toshimitsu, about arranging an exhibition of contemporary paintings in Japan. After the mainstream Nikakai art association declined to show informel works belonging to Tapié, Okamoto persuaded the Asahi newspapers and the International Art Club chapter, of which he was the leader, to sponsor an event featuring paintings by both Japanese and international artists on the theme of "world art today."

Altogether 60 Japanese and 46 foreigners were represented among the 136 works displayed, of which the informel paintings by Jean Dubuffet, Jean Fautrier (1898–1964), and Georges Mathieu (1921–) stirred particular interest. Also notable were works by the American abstract expressionists de Kooning, Tobey, and Sam Francis (1923–1994), the latter of whom was later married briefly to Idemitsu Masako (Mako), the third daughter of the oil baron Idemitsu Sazō (1885–1981), who in 1966 founded a gallery in Tokyo that acquired Francis' paintings for a collection otherwise devoted to Asian art.[46] The mixed-media artist Shinohara Ushio (1933–) recalls the impact of the 1956 informel show: "The exhibit of Tapié's collection at Takashimaya gave us all a big shock. Tapié liked the works of young artists whom the Japanese critics, obsessed with surrealism and other schools, had ignored."[47] Doubtless the shock has ballooned in retrospect, but the show was useful in introducing informel to Japan at a time when modernism was starting to grow stale among the avant-garde.

After closing in Tokyo, the informel exhibition toured Nagoya, Osaka, Hiroshima, and Fukuoka, drawing numerous contemporary artists at each stop. The art historian Chiba Shigeo believes that the Gutai group, heretofore isolated in Osaka and Ashiya, felt both stimulated and vindicated by seeing that such cutting-edge work was taking place abroad. The impact of informel was evident at the late-winter 1957 Yomiuri Independent in paintings by Gutai as well as other artists, some of them imitations of the French art they had just viewed. More works in the informel manner by Japanese artists followed at the 1958 and 1959 Yomiuri exhibitions. In Chiba's opinion, certain better-established Japanese oil painters were mainly impressed by informel stylistically, whereas younger, more progressive artists saw in informel "a different character compared with heretofore,"[48] permitting greater spontaneity and expression of sentiment without being bound by the formal properties of modernism. In this instance the impetus to transcend European modernism came to Japan from Europe itself.

Tapié returned to Japan in September 1957, joining Francis and Imai at a gathering of Okamoto's International Art Club that took place during the brief run of a solo exhibition by Mathieu at the Shirokiya (now Tōkyū) department store in Nihonbashi. Tapié also met that fall with the eccentric flower master Teshigahara Sōfū, whose son's biographer says Sōfū's "baroque sculptures, often composed of gnarled wooden stumps or mosaic on wood, seemed remote from any traditional modernist art,"[49] and thus of interest to Tapié (see Figure 9). (Akasegawa, speaking for a younger crowd, acknowledges that "Teshigahara Sōfū had links with Michel Tapié, but his artistic views were rather anachronistic.")[50] More important, Tapié visited Osaka at the suggestion of Dōmoto Hisao to learn about the group of young artists working with Yoshihara Jirō. As Dōmoto recalls: "Actually it was I who introduced the Gutai school to France and America. I had known Yoshihara Jirō when I was a young painter in Kansai, years before he formed the Gutai group in 1954. I was able to speak with the critic and collector Michel Tapié about Yoshihara's group and to play a part in arranging exhibits of Gutai works at the Galerie Stadler in Paris and the long-since closed Martha Jackson Gallery in New York."[51] Dōmoto is far from alone in taking credit for the introductions, but he undoubtedly played a useful role in both cities.

The encounter with Yoshihara and his pupils led to a show, held in April

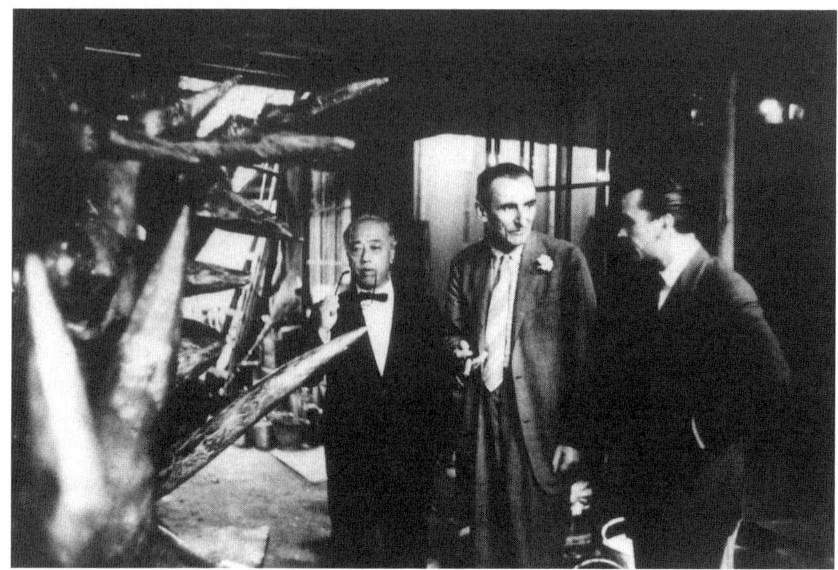

Figure 9. Teshigahara Sōfū, Michel Tapié, and Georges Mathieu at Teshigahara's atelier, Mita, Tokyo. 1957. Courtesy Teshigahara Akane and Sōgetsu Art Museum.

1958 at Takashimaya in Osaka, called World Exhibit of New Painting — Informel and Gutai, which subsequently toured France and the United States. Included were twenty-two Gutai artists, of whom Tapié particularly praised Shiraga Kazuo; he arranged a contract for Shiraga with the Galerie Stadler starting that same year.[52] Shiraga and the other Gutai members met Tapié's expectations for an alternative to the late modernism dominant in France immediately after the war, such as the Salon de Mai painters. Not unlike informel, Gutai emphasized action and materiality; its performances particularly delighted the French critic. Although informel eschewed the concrete, both informel and Gutai paintings (titled simply *Gutai*), largely effaced the artist's individuality, and each favored an outpouring of sentiment (and paint) rather than a preoccupation with aesthetic ideas.[53] More generally, informel stimulated all sorts of anti-art and nonart activity in Japan, while at the same time reassuring at least some Japanese artists that their largely isolated attempts at new approaches to the visual had counterparts abroad.[54] And the attention from foreign visitors such as Tapié, Mathieu, and Francis forced art critics in Tokyo to take Gutai and similar groups more seriously than before. Informel affected sculptors and print makers, too; its formless abstract expressionism was easy to emulate in almost any medium, resulting in much watered-down copying and, soon enough, a loss of vitality and appeal.[55]

The vogue of informel painting in Japan during 1956–1959 provoked a predictably mixed reaction from Japanese art critics, both then and since, and it had the incidental consequence of helping to establish the professional position of critics, as opposed to publicists and patrons, in the world of contemporary Japanese art. The older generation of genuine critics, such as Takiguchi Shūzō and Hijikata Teiichi (1904–1980), were generalists familiar with many media in world art across broad expanses of time but lacking much knowledge of current trends. The serious critics who emerged in the 1950s, mainly born in the Shōwa single-digit years of 1926–1934, were deeply read in modern philosophy, literature, and aesthetics, and many of them, such as Haryū Ichirō, Segi Shin'ichi, and Tōno Yoshiaki, belonged to various artists' associations during the late 1940s and 1950s. The brief informel boom provided critics a fresh voice in art journals and the popular press for deciphering the importance of such strikingly different art. The emergence of knowledgeable critics, together with artists riveted with the everyday, helped to emplace contemporary art side by side with architecture as a cultural practice — an art form that can contribute to public discourse.[56]

Sawaragi Noi, a critic from a later generation, wonders in retrospect whether the fervid embrace of informel by Japanese artists showed the emptiness of their previous efforts at visual expression.[57] Evidently Okamoto agreed with such skepticism at the time because he was angry that very few strong painters were emerging in Japan in the late 1950s, although Haryū Ichirō adds that friction developed between Tapié and Okamoto in 1958, after which Okamoto was "regarded as an enemy by Tapié."[58] Equally outspoken was Segi Shin'ichi, who declared that "informel is not an art movement" but a commercial campaign by a French gadfly with close ties to the galleries of Paris.[59] Segi attacked the elitism of the informel painters in Paris, claiming that few authorities there took them seriously. He concluded, "There was a strong feeling that Tapié was seeking a new market in Japan" for informel paintings, not promoting art itself.[60]

Haryū, by contrast, recognized the importance of the 1956 informel show and wrote in the January 1957 number of *Mizue* that Japanese artists should set aside geometric abstractionism and surrealism and return to Dada, in effect abandoning his earlier advocacy of reportage painting.[61] By 1961 he acknowledgeded that French informel and American abstract expressionism had caused many in Japan — not just the partisans of anti-art in the Gutai, Kyushuha, and Neo-Dada groups — to reconceptualize contemporary art.[62] Two years later he conceded in *Bijutsu techō* that the effect of informel had been great turmoil, but he also predicted that Japanese art would thereafter move toward diversification and individuality[63] — as quickly proved to be true.

In the wake of the informel show and Tapié's 1957 visit, Haryū and Tōno began writing about international art movements more often, especially developments in the United States. Unlike the Hijikata-Takiguchi generation, which worshiped French art, these young critics were stimulated by informel but ended up dazzled by contemporary American painting. Tōno, a critic for the art journal *Bijutsu hihyō* starting in 1954, became an expert on the anti-art groups of the early 1960s, particularly Neo-Dada Organizers and the partisans of pop art. Nakahara Yūsuke, who with Haryū and Tōno formed the triumvirate of postwar art criticism in Japan,[64] plunged vigorously into organizing exhibitions as well as writing criticism and proved to be adept at bringing together divergent groups of artists into a single large show.[65] Nonetheless it was another young critic, Miyakawa Atsushi (1933–1977), who in 1963 established the dominant view of informel to this day: it was not an art movement, just a stimulus for rethinking the place of cultural products in contemporary life.[66] Thirty years later, however, it gained unexpected retrospective attention in rural Japan with the opening in 1993 of the Informel Nakagawa Village Art Museum (Anfuorumeru Nakagawamura Bijutsukan) in the Ina valley, Nagano prefecture,[67] a site comfortably removed from the political and artistic mainstreams — but also from the urban fabric of daily life where informel received its most sustained expression in Japan.

The Kyushuha: The Art of Everyday Living

Perhaps the most critically overlooked, and possibly the most radically innovative, of all art groups in Japan after World War Two was the Kyushuha, formed in 1957 by a dozen or more painters and sculptors in Fukuoka who decried the continuing poverty of Kyushu farmers and miners while the big cities on Honshu prospered. Kikuhata Mokuma, their most vigorous spokesperson, estimates that this small association produced more than one thousand works during its first four years, including "perhaps a foolish number of anti-art items."[68] Of this sizable output, only ninety are believed to remain,[69] consigning the Kyushuha to near oblivion in the narrative of contemporary Japanese art. Yet the most striking aspect of this vigorous group was its focus on the social realities of its immediate local environment. Self-consciously antagonistic toward the Tokyo art establishment, the Kyushuha was a truly provincial society of artists who developed their own antimodernist styles along lines quite different from the Gutai association or the most innovative Kantō painters.

Sakurai Takami (1928–) served as chief organizer when this loose band of artists first came together in 1957 to exhibit at the Yomiuri Independent and at their own outdoor shows. By 1960, in the view of one critic, they were "the stars of the Yomiuri exhibition."[70] Some members were drawn to agrarian fundamentalism, a potent antimodern ideology of hard times long associated with the Kyushu city of Kurume. Many took up the plight of nearby miners, especially in the town of Miike, where 75,000 coal workers were fired in the course of a bitter 282-day strike during the first ten months of 1960 that brought an end to union radicalism and sapped the Japanese mining industry.[71] The anti–security treaty protests that spring drew artists' support but did not deflect their attention from trying to build community solidarity *(kyōdōsei)* with the less fortunate in their own undermodernized region. As Kikuhata wrote, the arts of the 1950s were generally infected with individualism produced by the rise of media and monopoly capitalism: "the arts escaped politics; the arts shed humanism." This "shows the inner frustrations of modern capitalist society."[72] The goal of the Kyushuha was to locate in both the past and present a new ethical vision that would rekindle an awareness of human problems in Fukuoka and the nearby region.

The way to do this, Kikuhata argued, was to link materiality to people's daily lives — seemingly more so even than was true of Yoshihara and the Gutai association. Kikuhata denounced modernist painting in a 1964 essay on "Facing the Commonplace": "Conventionally, to paint has been to sham, to hide, to delude, to camouflage. It is never the true essence. Painting has meant using the extra, the frivolous, to attain a complete falsification of matter itself. Worthless things mock the material *(busshitsu)* and cover it up." But for Kikuhata and his confreres in Kyushu, "today humanity and everyday materiality *(nichijō no busshitsu)* do not stand in clear opposition but instead have started to unite." He added, "I'm seeking a new image of people and the material in the relationship between things and myself, by painting both."[73] Kikuhata held that "the only way to rescue the idea of contemporary art is to be found in 'the commonplace.'" It was precisely in the traces of the particular, the everyday, amid the stifling sameness of contemporary economic and bureaucratic institutions that Kikuhata held out hope for local society: "In my work I never forget to open a small window to the commonplace. My materials are coins, teeth, false eyes, shields, frames, lumber. I think it's important that the starting point for creativity be the commonplace."[74] Such workaday materials and concerns for local economic inequalities clearly distinguished the Kyushuha painters, most of whom held office or retail jobs, from the generally well-born artists in Takiguchi's and Okamoto's circles.

Other Kyushuha members used cardboard, vinyl boards, tires, and asphalt — the latter a low-tech material suggesting both its origins in Kyushu mines and its usefulness to city road builders encroaching on the countryside. The curator Kuroda Raiji points out that despite placing positive value on everyday items, these artists were not producing pop art, which instead used highly processed manufactured goods.[75] If anything, Kikuhata's *Rūretto* (*Roulette*, 1963, enamel on wood) approached conceptual art in its use of everyday letters, numbers, and solar symbols (*kigō*, or signs) painted on an ordinary wooden packing crate (see Plate 6). This work shows the confused symbolic world of consumer capitalism that masks and deflects attention from the difficulties of Kyushu living, as though nothing but chance reigns.

In its most active phase, from 1957 to 1960, the group turned out paintings bearing some resemblance to informel. By the early 1960s it was producing more objets in the form of sculptures, assemblages, and collages of ordinary materials, much like the three-dimensional works by the Gutai artists at the time. Soon the Kyushuha members also created installations and staged a number of street performances and other temporary works of "living art" to connect with everyday experience through audience participation, for which they became almost as well known as for their initial squabbles and infighting a few years earlier.[76] They mainly presented their work in Fukuoka after the final Yomiuri Independent closed its galleries in 1963. Then in the mid-1960s two members moved to San Francisco, and the organization gradually weakened until it ceased activity in 1968 with a final exhibit and the publication of the concluding number of its irregular magazine, *Kyūshūha*, which appeared eight times between 1957 and 1968.[77]

Dissent within the Kyushuha cropped up again when the group turned to public theatricals. Kikuhata, who had joined at the start and was most active in 1958–1959, said "I was the first among the founders to leave,"[78] in 1962, apparently because of differences over access versus excellence (one critic labeled his outlook "elitist").[79] What is more, rapid economic growth in the early 1960s sapped the group's social message by changing the character of people's everyday lives. Yet Kikuhata battled on in the pages of the avant-garde journal *Kikan*, railing against the rise of consumerism and the administered society *(kanri shakai)*, with everyone on a structured lifecourse, in the 1960s and 1970s.[80]

If Kyushuha was "a failure as a movement" and left behind little significant art, as Kuroda Raiji believes,[81] nonetheless it engaged, as had no previous Japanese art group, even the prewar proletarians, with the everyday lives of ordinary people in its own neighborhood. The Kyushuha artists represented a weighty force in the larger anti-art movement at the time, in that they rejected modernism and also the placid designs of geometric abstractionism, but even more important was their positive contribution: they related their art to social actuality in their locale as fully as any Japanese avant-garde group of the era. In this fashion they incorporated the idea of everydayness into Japanese visual culture more completely than others before. Together with their overtly nonpolitical Gutai counterparts in Osaka and the informel whirlwind in Tokyo, the Kyushuha members helped break the thick ice of established modernist art in Japan and freed new channels for the expressive realm in the 1960s.

chapter five

The Sōgetsu Art Center
Avant-Garde Refinement

While the Gutai group, Kyushuha, and other out-of-town progressive artists in the late 1950s were connecting visuality and movement to people's everyday surroundings, three Tokyo-based currents of artistic innovation — the Experimental Workshop, Okamoto Tarō's Contemporary Arts Society, and the sudden vogue of informel painting — began to flow together in a new creative whirlpool, the Sōgetsu Art Center of 1959–1971. The center was based at the new Sōgetsu Kaikan, designed in violet ceramic tile by Tange Kenzō and opened in 1958 on Aoyama Dōri in Tokyo's Akasaka district (see Figure 10). Its director, the politically progressive artist Teshigahara Hiroshi, intended the Sōgetsu Art Center as a site for fresh transmedia thinking: "above all we wanted to establish a place for fellow artists to exchange ideas," where they could "freely gather from various genres to create, express, and criticize."[1] Enormous abstract-expressionist paintings by Sam Francis and Georges Mathieu decorated the concrete side walls of the 370-seat basement auditorium, where artists associated with the center produced their own events with no restrictions on approach. They introduced jazz, contemporary music, art film, photography, animation, dance, performance, and a broad palette of avant-garde visual art — much of it presented by socially elite artists and performers from the Kantō area.

Although Japan remained somewhat cut off from artistic developments overseas, the Sōgetsu Art Center probably brought as many contemporary painters and composers from abroad to Japan as any other institute, conservatory, university, gallery, or impresario of its time. By the late 1950s and early 1960s the most gifted Japanese nonverbal artists of the Shōwa single-digit group had developed their avant-garde ideas and techniques to a point where

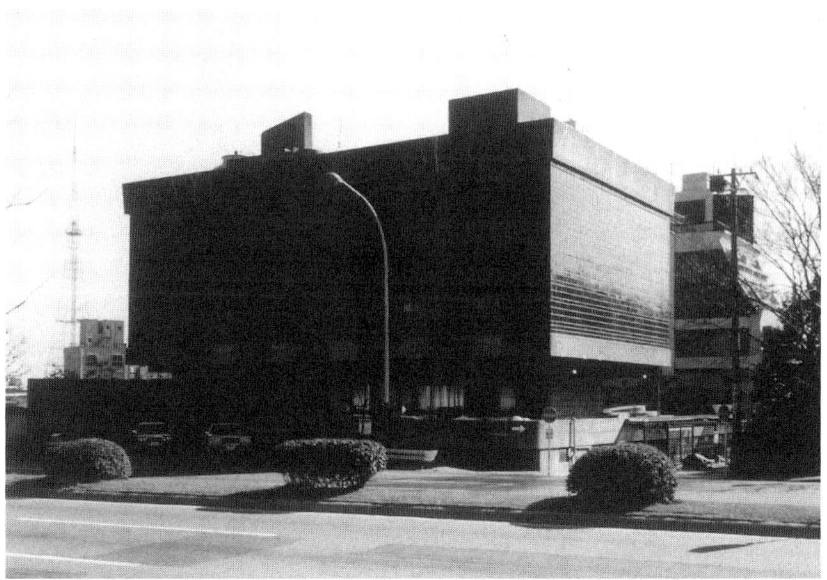

Figure 10. Sōgetsu Kaikan, Akasaka, Tokyo, designed by Tange Kenzō, as it appeared when completed in 1958. Sōgetsu Hall, the main venue of the Sōgetsu Art Center during 1958–1971, occupied the lower level. Courtesy Teshigahara Akane and Sōgetsu Art Museum.

interconnectivity with their overseas guests as peers, not just disciples, was beginning to be possible. International figures such as Mathieu, Francis, Mark Tobey, Olivier Messiaen, John Cage, and Iannis Xenakis (1922–2001) could now visit as colleagues, even equals, to share thoughts and to gain stimulation as well as to inspire. The ambitious programming at Sōgetsu marked a gateway from the era of Euro-American dominance to a transitional moment of artistic collaboration, exchange, mutuality, sometimes even symbiosis (e.g., contemporary dance) in the early 1960s — soon followed by divergence and advance beyond the creolization that flowered, for a time, in the stark Sōgetsu basement in Akasaka.

Teshigahara Father and Son

> Teshigahara Sōfū was very talented, filled with great creative vitality. He was a true modernist. His son Hiroshi was quite intellectual but less vital than his father. It's sad that he was a victim of the headmaster system, caught in a role in which he was uncomfortable because he was an artist. — Tsutsumi Seiji, poet, novelist, businessperson[2]

Teshigahara, father and son, were especially influential because they headed their flower-arrangement school, so their followers took an interest in their avant-garde art. Teshigahara Hiroshi was important as a film director and avant-garde calligrapher. His bamboo installations resemble flower designs. He was an interesting person, but his works aren't included among the more than eight hundred items in my museum. — Hara Toshio, Director, Hara Museum of Contemporary Art[3]

Teshigahara Sōfū was far more than a pure floral artist. He produced uncounted paintings, drawings, sculptures, constructions, and calligraphic works as well as an astonishing variety of ikebana designs. A retrospective of his works held at the Setagaya Art Museum in 2001 contained no items of ikebana at all.[4] His son Hiroshi followed his own lights as a youth and did no flowers, only avant-garde images. Soon after World War Two Hiroshi befriended artists in many genres by joining the Century Association and the Evening Society. Through these contacts he brokered a number of avant-garde ideas with his father and helped steer Sōfū's mature arts career, even though the two enjoyed rather "neutral" interpersonal relations.[5] To be sure, Sōfū's postwar products were a mixed success. The curator and sculpture specialist Sakai Tadayasu dismisses his three-dimensional works as "very large and numerous, but many are undistinguished." Yet he was a major friend of progressive art after the war: "his chief value to the avant-garde was his energy and his array of contacts abroad."[6]

Sōfū remained headmaster of the flower school throughout the twelve-year existence of the Sōgetsu Art Center but left artistic decisions about the center to his son. Yet Sōfū, despite suggestions to the contrary, was no mere indulgent father bankrolling Hiroshi's artistic proclivities. The composer Ichiyanagi Toshi credits Sōfū with a deep and probing interest in avant-garde music: "When I returned to Japan from New York in 1961, I found that the Sōgetsu Art Center was very active and sympathetic to new things. There were artists from many fields. Teshigahara Sōfū showed a great interest in contemporary music. Sōfū was the first real patron of contemporary music in Japan; Tsutsumi Seiji was the second, supporting it into the 1980s. The third great patron of contemporary music was Saji Keizō [1919–1999], the head of Suntory Whiskey."[7] Whatever the constraints on father and son imparted by the headmaster system, as Tsutsumi and Hara Toshio point out, the Teshigaharas' combined vigor and imagination promoted remarkable mixed-media and transcultural exchange in the sleek purple temple on Aoyama Dōri built by revenues from the ikebana faithful.

Teshigahara Sōfū inherited from his father Wafū a fascination with the final Meiji-era literatus painter, Tomioka Tessai (1837–1924), whom he met shortly before Tessai's death. Sōfū thereupon introduced new materials in addition to plants in his floral arrangements, transforming the Sōgetsu style from an alcove ornament into a modern art. The term "objet," first used in Japan in the 1920s, soon acquired many meanings — doubtless explaining Sōfū's preference for *zōkei* (forms) to describe his postwar works. After 1945 "objet" was commonly used for three-dimensional structures that couldn't be called sculptures, including many of Sōfū's. Progressive, or objet, ikebana flourished during the late 1940s and early 1950s as Sōfū created forms using dried wood, stone, glass, vinyl, and scrap metal as well as ceramics, eventually producing "ikebana" without any living plants at all. He stated, "When I say ikebana, this truly means 'to make something live'"[8] — even giving life to the inanimate. Sōfū welcomed the popularization of floral art during the ikebana boom of 1960–1965, but he found it hard to reconcile the broader access afforded by rising family incomes with the avant-garde thrust of his works.

Today Teshigahara Sōfū is an object of hagiography like no other twenti-eth-century visual artist in Japan, doubtless because the profitable flower-arrangement school he founded in 1927 supports the exhibitions and publications honoring his memory. A recent encomium comes from Ōshima Seiji, director of the Setagaya Art Museum: Sōfū "was gifted with the power of discerning artistic elements immanent in every detail of our life. This immediately suggests today's avant-garde activities in contemporary art."[9]

In truth he was formidably productive, particularly in the first decade following Japan's surrender, creating forms and assemblages that resembled sculptures, especially three-dimensional objets fashioned from scrap metal and wrought iron during the American military occupation. Like his contemporary Takiguchi Shūzō, he was deeply absorbed in current European art even before the war, especially Russian constructivism, cubism, and the Bauhaus.[10] Such ideas found their way into his early postwar works, first displayed at a solo exhibit in Tokyo in 1951 and then in group exhibitions he attended in New York, Paris, Spain, Turin, and Venice between 1952 and 1960 (*Time* called him the "Picasso of flowers" in 1956).[11]

At the same time, like Okamoto Tarō and others in the mid-1950s, Sōfū began looking to the *Kojiki* (712 C.E.) and other early sources to discover the nature of ancient Japanese life, although neither his avant-garde ikebana designs nor his sculptures suggesting prehistoric haniwa figurines enjoyed much critical or popular following.[12] In the late 1950s he turned from making small iron objets to huge, often spiky wooden sculptures fashioned from pine roots and trunks. He called these works primordial wooden beasts *(jujū)*, also regarding them as "half gods, half beasts."[13] Sōfū often gave away his creations from this period without titling, dating, or documenting them, like flowers that faded away after a few days. Also, he sometimes deconstructed his sculptures in order to obtain materials to make new ones — an art without legacy or commercial advantage. By 1963 he accorded prehistoric Japan almost empyreal status, giving every work in a solo exhibit a designation drawn from the *Kojiki*. "When I look at a Miró painting, or at a Chagall or a Klee, it is fun to see the *Kojiki* come forth," he wrote in 1966. "The essence of the *Kojiki* is in the depth of its imagination. . . . For me the *Kojiki* wipes out time and space and is a book for today."[14] Sōfū professed to discern an "avant-garde spirit" in the earliest era of Japanese history, an age he considered truly revolutionary from an artistic point of view,[15] although the value of using such anachronisms to characterize ancient times is limited.

In the light of his mixed success with sculpture and other media in the 1950s and 1960s, Sōfū's chief contributions to the contemporary arts were the publications issued by his school and the productions sponsored by the Sōgetsu Art Center. Especially significant to the early postwar avant-garde was the flower school's publication *Sōgetsu,* which first appeared in 1951, changed its name to *Ikebana Sōgetsu* four years later, then reverted to the original title in 1970. As Haryū Ichirō has written, this periodical was the first important journal dedicated entirely to the contemporary arts in Japan, giving young critics such as himself, Segi Shin'ichi, and Tōno Yoshiaki a forum for introducing new styles and ideas.[16] Even Takiguchi, then at the height of his critical powers, used the February 1953 special number of *Sōgetsu* to express admiration for Sōfū's modernism as an addition to contemporary aesthetics.[17]

Teshigahara Hiroshi, in contrast to his father, was an aloof but illustrious figure among the avant-garde, mainly because of the art films he directed and the calligraphic works he executed, but he was also a skilled photographer and produced well-regarded ceramics and bamboo installations later in life. Like a number of other progressive artists in the Shōwa single-digit generation, he entered the Tokyo School of Fine Arts immediately after World War Two and studied conventional oil painting with the modernist Umehara Ryūzaburō, as well as Nihonga with Kobayashi Kokei (Shigeru, 1883–1957). But he was soon stirred by Okamoto Tarō's encouragements to experiment with new endeavors, notwithstanding Okamoto's iconoclastic attacks on Umehara's technique.[18] Film proved to be Hiroshi's most brilliant métier, even though "his movies all failed financially, costing lots of money and angering his father Sōfū," according to the Sōgetsu chronicler Segi Shin'ichi.[19] Hiroshi's first trip abroad, in 1959, led to the unpolished but intense twenty-five-minute documentary *José Torres* (1959), which the journalist-poet Ōoka Makoto calls "Teshigahara Hiroshi's greatest work, although *Suna no onna* (*Woman in the Dunes*, 1964) is very fine as well."[20]

As Dore Ashton has written, Hiroshi's overseas tour of New York and Europe reinforced the importance of border crossings among arts genres that he had first experienced with the Century and Evening associations a decade earlier. He returned to Japan with redoubled determination to convert the new Sōgetsu Kaikan into a transgenre center for new expressive forms where artists could interact across the entire creative spectrum.[21] He collaborated closely with Takemitsu Tōru, as music and sound director, on all his films from *José Torres* forward. He also brought Ichiyanagi Toshi and Takahashi Yūji into subsequent film productions, as well as sponsoring performances of works by all three composers at the Sōgetsu Art Center. *Suna no onna* won Hiroshi an enduring international following and epitomized the mixed-media collaboration trumpeted by the Sōgetsu center. This finely wrought film, based on Abe Kōbō's classic existential novel of the same title (1962), contains Takemitsu's stunning musical score and other sound effects to accompany Hiroshi's visual inventiveness and skilled use of timing. After the center ceased activity in 1971, Hiroshi continued to direct movies while also founding a pottery workshop in Fukui prefecture, taking up garden design in the 1980s and displaying his mixed-media versatility by turning out sculptures, tea vessels, india-ink paintings, and bamboo installations into the 1990s.[22]

Sōgetsu Culture

Like Seibu culture at the Seibu Theater and Seibu Art Museum two decades later, Sōgetsu culture in the late 1950s and early 1960s, backed by the financial wallop of a major flower-arrangement school, instantly became synonymous with hip, leading-edge arts events among the urban elites who were drawn to the latest vogue onstage or in the exhibit hall. But even more significant than chic patronage was the transgenre collaboration fostered by the Sōgetsu Art Center, a cross-pollination of artistic varietals that propelled Japan's renunciation of mature modernism at the level of highbrow culture fully as much as the anti-art movement, in and out of Tokyo, provoked rebellion against solemn modernist certitudes at the intersection of visual expression and the everyday.

Sōgetsu's first Tokyo building, a modest three-story structure in immodest Kōjimachi Sanbanchō, opened in December 1933 but was destroyed in an American air raid at the end of World War Two. Its replacement, an imposing four-story building in a premier location across the street from the crown prince's residence, was completed in June 1958 and soon became home to the Sōgetsu Art Center under Teshigahara Hiroshi's leadership. At length this building proved inadequate for the burgeoning flower-arrangement business, and the present Sōgetsu Kaikan, a many-storied glass affair designed like its predecessor by Tange Kenzō, opened on the same site in December 1977, less than two years before the death of Teshigahara Sōfū. It is said that Sōfū, who met Georges Mathieu through Okamoto Tarō in September 1957, commissioned Mathieu to produce a two-by-eight-meter informel canvas for the Sōgetsu building then under construction — and that Mathieu, who painted directly from the tube, finished it in a single day. Sōfū then asked Sam Francis, who arrived in Japan the day Mathieu departed, to provide an abstract painting of the same size, which required a month to complete.[23] These decorative works, mounted on either side of the auditorium, gazed silently down on virtually every event at the Sōgetsu Art Center for the next twelve years, witness to the charismatic power of abstract expressionism to awe as well as inspire.

With contemporary photographs, paintings, and sculptures on exhibit as mise-en-scène, including many by Teshigahara Sōfū, much of the programming under his son Hiroshi's direction featured the performed arts, often in novel combinations: jazz concerts, experimental animation and film, performance art, postmodern dance, underground theater, and many types of contemporary music. Hiroshi repeatedly said the center's goal was "exchange and experimentation among the various arts,"[24] which took the form of publicity and education as well as presentations by both Japanese and international artists. Much of the criticism once appearing in *Ikebana Sōgetsu* now shifted to the new journal *SAC* (later *SAC jānaru*), which issued thirty-four numbers ending in 1963. The center sponsored lectures, workshops, and panels on the contemporary arts intended for professionals but also for the au courant audiences who thirsted for the latest productions, particularly from abroad. For several years Hiroshi hosted an experimental-film series, Sōgetsu Cinemathèque, including discussions after each showing led by critics, directors, and scholars. Experimental theater had its Sōgetsu debut in 1960, including studio performances of works by the avant-garde playwrights Terayama Shūji (1935–1983) and Kara Jūrō (1940–), two of the most ingenious and defiant minds of postwar Japanese theater. The underground "dance of darkness," ankoku butō, was scarcely known in 1961 when Hijikata Tatsumi put on an earthy demonstration of his choreography at the Sōgetsu center.[25]

Contemporary music claimed pride of place among the center's events, especially during the four-year run of the Sōgetsu Contemporary Series, which put on twenty-four concerts starting in 1960. These performances stirred the critic Tōno Yoshiaki to call the Sōgetsu Art Center "the epicenter of the avant-garde arts of the 1960s" in Japan,[26] even though the series offered mixed fare: both innovative composers from the Experimental Workshop (1951–1957) but also others, particularly at the outset, whose newest work was not quite avant-garde. One of the first concerts took place in April 1960 when Takemitsu presented his taped experiment in musique concrète using various sounds made by water, *Mizu no kyoku* (*Water Music*, 1960). The conductor Iwaki Hiroyuki helped Teshigahara Hiroshi corral other young composers of mainstream contemporary music such as Akutagawa Yasushi, Miyoshi Akira, and the folk-music devotee Mamiya Michio as well as more daring figures such as Hayashi Hikaru, Matsudaira Yoriaki, Mayuzumi Toshirō, and Moroi Makoto. These individuals, together with Takemitsu, were associated with an informal group called the Composers Federation (Sakkyokuka Shūdan). Starting in 1962 the series turned increasingly to avant-garde compositions, often featuring members of another association, New Directions, formed that year by Ichiyanagi Toshi, Akiyama Kuniharu, and Takahashi Yūji.[27]

One other composers' organization of momentary note at Sōgetsu was Group Ongaku (Music Group), formed in 1960 by antimusic performers at Tokyo University of Fine Arts and Music who renounced European academicism and instead used instruments, household utensils, and advanced technology in their recitals. Led by Kosugi Takehisa (1938–), who sought a "dramaturgy for the age of indeterminacy" connecting art music with the everyday well beyond musique concrète,[28] these improvisatori produced noisy, deformed sounds at their lone Sōgetsu appearance in September 1961. Evidently they were quite unaware of John Cage's similar ideas about chance operations, which Ichiyanagi had just begun to introduce via scores he brought back from New York that summer. Two decades later members of Group Ongaku earned acclaim when they appeared worldwide with the Merce Cunningham Dance Company.[29]

An implicit purpose of the Sōgetsu Art Center was to tumble the fences dividing indigenous and overseas arts in an effort to transcend locus of origin and build a dynamic site of mutual artistic exchange, what today might be called dynamic hybridity, even creolization. For this project no one was better suited than Ichiyanagi Toshi, the versatile young composer who had spent nine years in the United States, including 1954–1957 at Juilliard, before returning to Japan in 1961. Ichiyanagi first encountered John Cage in 1957 while the latter was teaching at the New School in New York. He embraced Cage's ideas about indeterminacy almost at once and began performing with Cage's associate, the pianist David Tudor (1926–1996). Arriving home in mid-1961, Ichiyanagi helped to introduce works by Cage and others at the first Osaka Contemporary Music Festival, held in August of that year, and then at a concert at the Sōgetsu center in November (see Figure 11). Even in such a magnet of the avant-garde, according to its authorized history, the November performance was "a true shock to the audience."[30] Veteran aficionados in Tokyo likewise remember vividly the spectacle of a follow-up event at Sōgetsu presented by Ichiyanagi in May 1962: an unrehearsed New York–style happening staged by the dancer Hijikata, Neo-Dada painter Akasegawa Genpei, and music critic Akiyama, with Yoko Ono recumbent atop the piano, striking keys at random with her elbows.[31]

The most arresting chapter of Sōgetsu culture unfolded in October 1962, when Ichiyanagi brought John Cage and David Tudor to Japan for six performances, including two at Sōgetsu Kaikan, of works by Cage, Ichiyanagi, Takemitsu, Karlheinz Stockhausen, Morton Feldman (1926–1987), and others. This visit, followed by a return trip in 1964, taught Japanese composers that music was no longer intended to express philosophical ideals of beauty and that there were no borders between music and everyday life. Cage's theory of chance operations assumed a mix of sound, space, and daily activity: musical production depended on the spontaneity of performers in their everyday environment, not on the composer's intention. Such notions of indeterminacy made it possible for a pianist to present Cage's well-known 4'33" (1952) by sitting at the keyboard, playing nothing for four minutes and thirty-three seconds, closing the lid, and departing.[32]

Cage's lectures and performances liberated Japanese composers from the rigidities of serialism and notation on a five-line staff. Ichiyanagi said Cage's most meaningful teaching was that "the concept is more important than *écriture*"[33] — explaining Cage's preference for diagrams of his works. "The music of indeterminacy immediately excited great interest in Japan,"[34] the critic Chōki Seiji says, and it also led to unusual reciprocity between local composers and their counterparts abroad who used chance operations. The reasons went beyond Cage's close creative affinities with Ichiyanagi to the American's deep immersion in Asian philosophy. "When we heard John Cage was interested in Zen," Yuasa Jōji recalled in 2002, "we were skeptical of his ability to understand it. But once he visited Japan, it was clear that his knowledge was far from superficial."[35] Ichiyanagi adds that "Cage was very sensitive and developed his interest in Zen thought from within. He acted in his daily life in accord with the Asian way of living that he embraced intellectually."[36] This appraisal may seem tantamount to conferring honorary cultural citizenship on Cage; at least it shows the deep personal respect in which he was held by certain avant-garde composers in Japan.

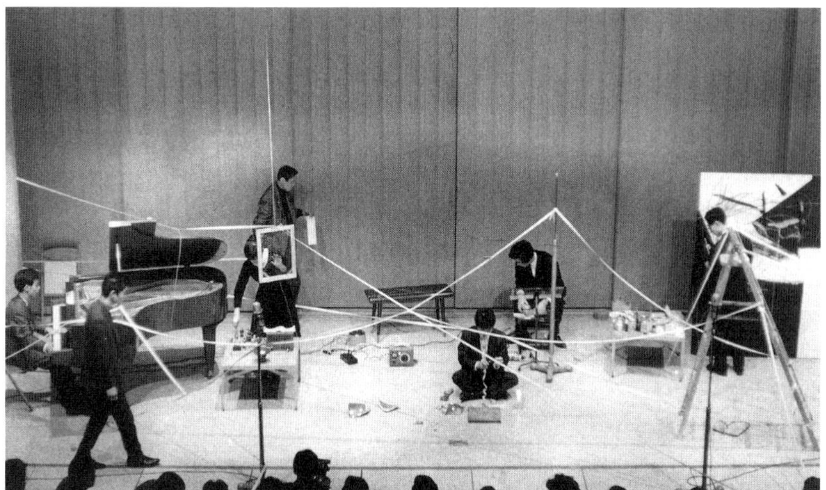

Figure 11. Performance of Ichiyanagi Toshi works, Sōgetsu Hall, Tokyo. November 30, 1961. From left, Takemitsu Tōru, Takahashi Yūji, Shiomi Mieko, Mayuzumi Toshirō, Kosugi Takehisa, Mizuno Shūkō, Ichiyanagi Toshi. Courtesy Ichiyanagi Toshi.

Cage's modesty, indeed humility, made it easy for him — and to some degree those who practiced his teachings — to accept musical ideas from their colleagues in Japan, much as modern choreographers such as Martha Graham, abstract expressionists such as Mark Tobey, or poets such as Gary Snyder (1930–) opened themselves to creative endowments from that country. At the same time, Ichiyanagi is quick to add that Cage's impact, although forceful, was soon spent: "I admired John greatly; he had marvelous ideas, but regrettably his musical expression was not cumulative. Only his music from the 1940s and 1950s is ever played today." Cage's precepts did not comport well with the concert stage, whereas to Ichiyanagi "the basis of music is performance. We composers have to connect with the performers."[37] In this he concurs with Iwaki Hiroyuki, who observes that "nowadays people specialize in performance, composition, or conducting. Yet the best composers are usually also performers,"[38] as is true of Ichiyanagi himself.

What Cage began was soon repeated by other visitors to Sōgetsu. Cage's longtime collaborator Merce Cunningham (1919–) brought his dance company to the arts center in 1964, "causing a shock to the Japanese dance world as great as Cage's was to music."[39] The painter Jasper Johns (1930–) arrived at Sōgetsu for intergenre performances in May 1964, followed by Robert Rauschenberg (1925–) in November. Ichiyanagi presented the drip music of the American composer George Brecht (1927–), and the center also staged a performance of *The Maids* by the French playwright Jean Genet (1910–1986) as well as an off-Broadway musical. Interspersed were a large exhibit on the Bauhaus and a series of jazz performances, mostly blues, called Sōgetsu Music Inn. From 1965 on the center's programming focused increasingly on experimental films, among which Iimura Takahiko's *Love* (1962, music by Yoko Ono) caused a hubbub when it was shown in its fifteen-minute entirety in 1966 because of its explicitly erotic content.[40]

Early 1960s Crosscurrents

John Cage, Olivier Messiaen, Iannis Xenakis, and other marquee figures in contemporary music who visited Japan in 1961–1962 arrived at a moment when Japanese composers were searching for new avenues of expression beyond the experiments, often under French and German impress, of the 1950s. The versatile writer of people's *(minzoku)* folk music Mamiya Michio highlights both the personal and the political elements that now came into play: "I felt exhilarated by John Cage's visits to Japan. I was also excited by contemporary Polish music in the 1960s. The clash of left and right, capitalist and socialist, was very stimulating to musical culture in Japan."[41] Messiaen's music was already familiar to the avant-garde when he toured Japan in 1962, the year he completed *Sept Haikai* for piano and small orchestra.[42] Xenakis ended up working closely with the youthful Takahashi Yūji, mostly in Berlin during 1963–1966. It was Cage, above all, whose ideas affected some of the most imaginative composers in Tokyo, especially Ichiyanagi Toshi and Takemitsu Tōru, in the first half of the decade.

The critics Akiyama Kuniharu and Takiguchi Shūzō began writing shortly after 1945 about Cage's theories of indeterminacy, but not until Ichiyanagi moved back from New York in mid-1961 did Cage receive sustained attention in Japan. Born in Kobe to a musical family and reared in Tokyo since age two, Ichiyanagi was invited by acquaintances of his Oberlin-educated mother to study music in Minnesota as a teenager. He received conventional training in composing, especially serialism, at Juilliard in the mid-1950s before encountering Cage at the New School. He began using graphic notation, and in 1962, with *Sapporo* for small chamber orchestra, followed by *Nagaoka* two years later, he emulated Cage by introducing long silences into his compositions. Ichiyanagi's orchestral work *Za fuīrudo* (*The Field*, 1966), featuring a solo flute (shakuhachi), challenged the performers to calibrate their own sounds and silences based on a sketchy score.[43]

Partly because Ichiyanagi realized that Cage's teachings remained static, and partly because he linked composition with performance more closely than Cage, he moved beyond his teacher's approach in the late 1960s to collage, pop art, and minimalism. During this period, as recorded by Takemitsu in 1971, Ichiyanagi stated that "result is a thing of the past. If you are concerned with results no vital action takes place because you don't know the present. Motivation and process are the important things"[44] — the contemporary arts in cameo. Then, as Ichiyanagi became absorbed in how people relate to technology and the urban environment, the critic Akiyama Kuniharu wryly commented that he "blurs the borders between noise and music and between contemporary music and popular music."[45] In the four decades since returning from New York, Ichiyanagi has been one of the most prolific and versatile contemporary composers anywhere, writing orchestral, chamber, instrumental, vocal, and electronic works, as well as music for classical Japanese instruments, computer, stage, and film.[46]

Although Takemitsu knew some of Cage's ideas about indeterminacy via performances in the late 1950s of works by Stockhausen, he too felt the "Cage shock" from the moment the New Yorker appeared at the Sōgetsu auditorium in 1962. "John Cage had a profound effect on me," Takemitsu wrote nine years later. "Cage is trying to corroborate the importance of the basic act of listening. . . . Listening to his sounds is what John Cage's music is about, like any music."[47] Already Takemitsu had produced his first major work based partly on chance operations, *Ring* (1961) for flute, guitar, and lute in four movements, which evidently could be played in any order. Another experimental composition, *Corona II* (1962) for ensemble, emulated Cage in using graphic rather than staff notation.[48]

During these years, to be sure, Takemitsu was also writing in some debt to Webern's serial technique, as well as carrying out experiments in timbre. However, as the musicologist Chōki Seiji notes, Takemitsu ended up deciding serialism was too structured and chance operations not structured enough.[49] Taken to an extreme, Takemitsu said in 1989, Cage's randomness becomes "just the opposite — it seems terribly logical," although he added that Cage's immersion in Asian thought helped Takemitsu "recognize the value of my own tradition."[50] Takemitsu's music often flirted with radical experimentalism, yet its recurring eddies of emotion, especially a deep sadness that sometimes seemed a slough of misery, ran at crosscurrents with Cage's utter lack of intentionality, with its absence of emotion, just tones for tones' sake. Still, despite their differences and their lack of sustained interpersonal contact, Cage and Takemitsu displayed a degree of momentary creolization in their shared interests in Asian philosophy, their independent discoveries of silences as compositional basics, and their mutual use of the sonorities of single sounds. Such cooperative feedback, as Peter Burt observes, also helped to confirm the growing use of Hōgaku instruments by local composers in the 1960s.[51]

While Ichiyanagi, Takemitsu, and others were interacting with Cage, Takahashi Yūji, a twenty-three-year-old musician who had studied with Dan Ikuma, encountered the stochastic works of Iannis Xenakis when the Greek-born French composer gave a lecture-demonstration at Sōgetsu Kaikan in 1961. Xenakis had worked in Le Corbusier's studio after reaching Paris in 1947 and based his music on architecture and mathematics.[52] His technique drew on the laws of probability, not unlike the indeterminacy favored by Cage. Takahashi recalls that "Xenakis came to Japan in 1961 for the Tokyo World Music Festival organized by the anticommunist Russian composer Nicolas Nabokov [1903–1978], who had been supported by Radio Free Europe. A dispute broke out among Japanese composers over whether to participate. Hayashi and Mamiya were opposed; Takemitsu and Yuasa took part."[53] Undeterred by political disagreements, Takahashi sought out Xenakis as a way to study in Europe. When Xenakis was invited to Berlin in 1963 under a new Ford Foundation program to showcase contemporary arts to East Germany, "he was allowed to bring along one student and chose me." But evidently no real synergy developed between the two.

In Berlin and Stockholm from 1963 to 1966, Takahashi "did no composing for piano while in Europe, only occasionally for computer, so I kept performance and composing quite separate. Only later did I begin to bring the two together."[54] He then spent six years in the United States, including Boston, New York, Buffalo, and Bloomington, Indiana, before returning to Japan in 1972 to launch a prolific career writing mainly instrumental and vocal music, in addition to many appearances as a concert performer. His time in Europe notwithstanding, Takahashi is not considered one of the more progressive composers of his generation, even though he wrote electronic music well into the 1990s. Like Ichiyanagi, he emphasizes that "music is a process, an activity to be shared, not with an end-conscious method, but as a technique of the body."[55] He adds that "music is not pure creation, but also appropriation" from one's milieu.[56] During the past decade Takahashi has promoted works by Asian composers, particularly those from Southeast Asia, through an informal association known as Kerbau (Suigyū, or water buffalo).

Through Ichiyanagi and Yoko Ono, artists associated with the Sōgetsu center and other groups also made contact with the New York community of painters, composers, and mixed-media specialists who belonged to Fluxus, an avant-garde movement originating in Germany in 1961. This loosely organized society, grounded partly in dadaism, fused various artistic disciplines to produce puckish visual and musical works, many of them minimalist. Performances, street-theater events, and happenings verified these artists' engagement with the evanescent qualities of everyday life implicit in the name Fluxus ("change, flow"). Starting in 1965 this group began to use the term "intermedia" for fields of artistic expression that fall between or merge conventional media. The curator Alexandra Munroe calculates that twenty-three Japanese participated in the group during its most active years in the 1960s and 1970s.[57] In addition to Cage and Ono, its most prominent members included the visual artists Joseph Beuys (1921–1986) and George Maciunas (1931–1978), the video artist Nam June Paik (1931–), and La Monte Young (1935–), a composer who learned from Cage that everything could be music.[58] Fluxus enjoyed neither the financial resources nor the social cachet of the Sōgetsu Art Center, but its activities offered Japanese participants avenues of experimentation even wider than Aoyama Dōri, the Tokyo thoroughfare linking Okamoto Tarō's studio to the Sōgetsu Kaikan.

THE OFFICIAL HISTORY of the Sōgetsu School acknowledges that Teshigahara Sōfū patiently supported the arts center, even as his own focus shifted more and more to ancient Japanese history in the early 1960s. Its programs brought left-leaning artists such as Mamiya and Teshigahara Hiroshi together with politically more complaisant individuals who believed they were devoting themselves entirely to art. (Indeed, the ikebana world tilts noticeably toward Japan's establishment and frequently supports conservative politicians with votes and cash.) However much they differed about politics and foreign policy, father and son collaborated amicably on the agenda of the arts center. Hiroshi candidly stated that "the deficit of the Sōgetsu Arts Center at the time was covered by my father Sōfū."[59] Thanks to Sōfū's cash and Hiroshi's unflinching commitment to borderless arts, the interactions among practitioners across genres and the communication with like-minded peers from abroad, concentrated as they were in 1959–1964, opened up new fields of collaboration for Japanese artists who had little previous experience with the outside world. The Sōgetsu center cleared the path for younger artists from diverse backgrounds to challenge the premises of modernism by connecting more completely with the everyday and the local — and sometimes to criticize the technobureaucratic state that was firmly entrenched in Japan by the mid-1960s. The center also helped to establish the contemporary Japanese arts on a more equal footing with those abroad, making it possible to speak with greater confidence of a transcultural, yet grounded, art movement in Japan ever since.

part two

Alternative Modernities
in the 1960s
Locating the Everyday

overview

For the ancients in East Asia, like scholars in medieval Europe, the idea of culture referred to dominant groups and always included music and literature (as rhetoric), and it often extended to architecture, figurative sculpture, and sometimes painting as well. Modern anthropology took as its focus culture in the sense of patterns of social expression transmitted from one generation to the next. Marxism in the nineteenth century argued that culture in every form was political, both as an instrument of capitalist manipulation and as a mechanism of resistance. In the latter vein, as Julie Rivkin and Michael Ryan indicate, culture began to be utilized increasingly in the 1960s as a means of opposition, as analyzed by the Birmingham school of cultural studies in England.[1] The same questions of culture as domination or resistance arose in Japan in the 1950s and 1960s, but the artistic responses, particularly in the nonverbal arena, took on different colorations after 1960 — usually less anticapitalist than a decade earlier, doubtless because of rapid enrichments of national economic life rather than "as a result of any real change in Japanese art" itself.[2]

The 1960s in Japan were bracketed by widespread protests against extending the Japan–United States Mutual Security Treaty in 1960 and nationwide pride at the country's economic and technological progress, showcased at the Osaka international exposition of 1970. Part 2 of this book discusses how avant-garde nonverbal artists responded to each of these temporal bookends and to generational, political, and artistic shifts in between. To paraphrase Andrew Gordon, in diet, dress, housing, and transport the Japan of 1960 seemed more like the Japan of 1930 than that of 1970.[3] Tokyo in 1960 offered train rides for 20 yen (5.6 cents at the time) and taxis for as little as 60. Networks of utility wires were suspended from wooden telephone poles above streets lined with open cinder-block storm sewers. Vacuum trucks visited residential areas to pump out household septic tanks every few months; merchants and restaurants offered home delivery of small items by bicycle, not yet motor scooter. Hand-pulled carts *(riā kā)* piled high with flattened cartons foreshadowed a vogue of recycling at the end of the decade. Air conditioning was virtually unknown, locomotives on long-haul passenger trains burned bituminous coal, and the neighborhood public bathhouse was the usual site for personal grooming. National economic performance was strong and political and social institutions were secure, but the amenities of daily living that were taken for granted a decade later were still scarce in 1960.

Deliberately isolated by the occupying Americans during 1945–1952, Japan became open by degrees to the outside world during the 1960s. Jet aircraft went into service across the Pacific in 1958 and joined the Japan Air Lines fleet two years later. Except for American military personnel and their dependents, few international visitors arrived in Japan as of 1960; those who did discovered that the Japan Travel Bureau maintained mimeographed lists of the handful of Japanese-style inns willing to accommodate them. For outbound Japanese travelers, restrictions on taking currency out of the country were eased in stages and had largely disappeared by the Tokyo Olympics of October 1964. Even so, at the end of the decade the number of Japanese making trips abroad for all purposes was just 663,000, a figure that multiplied twenty times during the subsequent quarter century.[4] A trans-Pacific telephone cable from California to Japan via Guam was completed in February 1964, providing connections favorable in quality if not price. Such improved communications and travel opportunities now made it easier for Japanese artists to keep abreast of international developments. Urbanization and the rise of new international architectural styles, above all metabolism, also helped to stimulate interest in the avant-garde. The mechanical reproduction of visual images became easier with the use of the air brush, silkscreen, and other techniques. The combined sum of this transnational flow of people, capital, cultural artifacts, and artistic ideas was far weightier than during the 1950s, so that in art, as in material life, the Japan of 1970 was greatly transformed from ten years earlier.

At the pivot of this transformation was a deliberate government policy of economic growth and social integration under central bureaucratic oversight. Shortly after nationwide demonstrations failed to block approval of the revised security treaty, a new conservative cabinet controlled by the Liberal Democratic Party unveiled an economistic design to nurture a guided form of consumption as a middle-class habit, if not yet a virtue. Prime Minister Ikeda Hayato opportunistically rode the wave of an income-doubling plan, formalized in late 1960, that promised fulfillment within ten years but ended up requiring only six and one-half, thanks to high-level increases in real gross domestic product already under way since 1955 that continued until 1973.[5] In effect, the postwar era ended not in the mid-1950s, as the economic white paper for 1956 had proclaimed,[6] but in the mid-1960s — benchmarked by the Tokyo Olympiad of 1964, the opening of the Shinkansen bullet train the same year, Japan's first postwar trade surplus with both the United States and multilateral partners in 1965,[7] and the unexpected speed of income doubling. As Japan entered the age of high mass consumption, in Walt W. Rostow's smug phrase,[8] advertising agencies developed clever marketing techniques that harnessed new media, above all the iconic power of television, to generate and channel consumer demand. "Today's consumption patterns," the historian Kano Masanao wrote in 2000, "are based on this era" of the 1960s, when "we can see the advent of abundance, the Americanization of lifestyles, and the attenuation of interpersonal relations."[9]

In exchange for a calm, noncontentious daily life of controlled consumerism, albeit at prices often unfavorable to shoppers, Ikeda and his successors perfected bureaucratic politics that imposed an administered society *(kanri shakai)* on the country — the immediate target of cultural critics on the left. Scholars today recognize that a systems society — that is, the integration of state and society — began to emerge in industrialized countries worldwide in the 1930s through centralized education, electronic media, information management, new regimes of taxation and conscription, standardized factory production, and mobilization for total war. Interrupted in Japan by the American occupation, this process accelerated in the 1960s, resuming the prewar interpenetration of state and civil society wherein individuals surrendered a degree of autonomy to the authorities while demanding social programs and services not previously considered the responsibility of the state.[10]

The administered society that took shape in the 1960s gave Japan something notably absent a decade earlier: a degree of "governmentality" enabling "activity thinkable and practicable both to its practitioners and to those upon whom it was practised."[11] If the political scientist James Scott is correct that modernizing governments take pains to make cities "legible" by rationalizing civic spatial arrangements to facilitate governing,[12] Japan's administered society of the 1960s was a virtual space on which a bureaucratic modernity could be overlaid to guide the interpenetration of state and civil society. The administered society was never completely attained in Japan; multiple narratives and alternative modernities, including some proposed by "habitually marginalized groups"[13] such as the youngest avant-garde artists, continued to defy both the authority of modernism and the authorities in Tokyo's governing ministries. By the 1990s there were clear signs that civil society had succeeded in eroding, but not overturning, the managerial state.[14]

Certain choreographers, composers, and visual artists responded to the Ikeda government's program of induced prosperity and social management with dismay or outright asperity, consistent to some degree with the perspectives of postcolonialism. "With sovereignty achieved," writes the literary critic Robert J. C. Young, "postcolonialism seeks to change the basis of the state itself." It "eschews the high culture of the elite and espouses subaltern cultures and knowledges which have historically been considered to be of little value but which it regards as rich repositories of culture and counter-knowledge."[15] To the extent that Japanese artists in the 1960s critiqued the marriage of corporate and bureaucratic power underlying the administered society, they sought an alternative basis for rule. Insofar as they denounced the modernism espoused by elite Japanese artists of the 1950s, they searched for equivalent knowledge in the everyday artifacts and lives of ordinary people — in farm dances and community festivals in the northeast, in folk music throughout the nation, in discarded construction materials and junked household items from both city and countryside. Like artists in many countries, they rejected the high-modernist faith in science and technology. They mocked social hierarchy and the homogenizing tendencies of consumer culture through their open submissions at the egalitarian Yomiuri Independent, street-theater performances, spontaneous happenings, and an alternative exposition in Osaka to disparage corporate patronage of art at Expo '70.

Countercultures around the world attacked the iron triangle of military, industrial, and state dominance in the 1960s, including the modernist beliefs that helped undergird it — what David Harvey calls global "resistance to the hegemony of high modernist culture."[16] Antimodernist members of the avant-garde, partly echoing a July 1942 conference of Japanese intellectuals devoted to "Overcoming the Modern," began to erect a new artistic edifice that was both contemporary and international, but also post-Western in its autonomy outside the norms of North Atlantic modernism. For certain artists this meant repositioning themselves via new eastbound bridges: "By the late 1960s," observes Tsutsumi Seiji, "it proved difficult for many artists to sustain their interest in Europe and America. A number of them turned to Asia, especially China. For example, Dan Ikuma's music had noticeably Chinese rhythms."[17] An unintended outcome of this post-Western turn was that it deceived many Western critics, and even some Japanese, into discovering in avant-garde works a neotraditionalism that was seldom actually there. The art historian Kondō Yukio tactfully summarizes this misperception:

> While it is desirable to find a common language to discuss contemporary art transcending national boundaries, we often expect art to reflect national characteristics, and many people look for connections with the clichés of a certain tradition. . . . These stereotypical ideas about national traditions are not as self-evidently

true as they may seem, and they have seldom developed naturally. . . . Many things that the Japanese consider to be traditional characteristics of Japanese art were established or created by government officials and others in the process of forming a modern nation state.[18]

The post-Western seen in the most inventive aural, choreographic, and visual arts of the late 1950s and 1960s aligns favorably with Japan's literary artists of a generation earlier, who in Dennis Washburn's view sprang "free from the authority of two traditions — the native tradition, which seemed inadequate to express their sense of the modern, and the Western tradition, which threatened their cultural autonomy"[19] — and instead placed personal experience above the concrete universals of modernism.

The rejection of modernism in Japan after the 1950s took place in Western-style oil painting and musical composition, in Japanese-style watercolors and traditional music, in both contemporary and classical dance, in every genre and every part of Japan. Also gone was the tyranny of uniform standards set by the elite art, dance, and music associations established well before World War Two; these organizations were now fractured less over schools of thought or artistic sensibilities than because of personalities, factionalism, and especially generations. The decline of modernism in Japan shows the merit of Katō Shūichi's observation that artistic alienation can be found worldwide and is not caused by anything peculiarly Japanese.[20]

At the end of the 1960s it was clear that both surrealism and existentialism, so prestigious among modernists and the avant-garde a decade earlier, had been tamed, popularized, and eventually discarded, especially by the local countercultures that produced Japan's versions of the worldwide antiestablishment protests at the end of the decade. As Martin Jay observes, culture disarms its critics: modernist art eventually turns into an accredited object of consumer desire, and "the avant-garde, if indeed the term can still be used, has become an honored ornament of our cultural life, less to be feared than feted."[21] By the time of the Osaka World Exposition in 1970, many avant-garde artists in Japan feared that even their most radical products had been absorbed by the corporate and governmental institutions whose authority their art was meant to critique.

Rather than explicitly postcolonial, the Japanese avant-garde in the 1960s is best understood as searching for modernities alternative to those offered by Western-derived modernism or by the administered society of sponsored consumerism. As more art and artists arrived from the West in the 1960s, fascination with foreign cultural products reached its zenith among the general public. At the same time "pret-a-porter," first used in 1959, epitomized women's styles during the 1960s as shoppers bought off-the-rack copies of fashion lines that were reassuring in their sameness. Many vanguard artists were enervated by this popularity of Western culture and consumer conformity among Japan's new middle classes. Instead they sought other modernities that were increasingly post-Western but not necessarily nationalist or culturally essentialist. Well-established composers such as Mayuzumi Toshirō, Yuasa Jōji, Dan Ikuma, and Takahashi Yūji found stimulation in the various musics of Asia during the 1960s, as did choreographers and painters such as Lee Ufan. Other expressive sources were found in everyday lives and local contexts, in consumer protests, and in environmental movements at the end of the decade.

The pursuit of alternative modernities included a gendered perspective, although mainly one of greater continuity than change.[22] The subordination of women found in other areas of public life during the 1950s and 1960s generally characterized the nonverbal arts as well. The majority of art, dance, and music students were female, as were most neighborhood teachers of each. Yet males disproportionately occupied the leadership positions in these genres. As in other countries, both male and female choreographers were prominent in creative dance after World War Two, and a number of female painters took part in groups like the Experimental Workshop and the Gutai Association. Yet males dominated the anti-art Neo-Dada Organizers in 1960 and the Monoha at the end of the decade, much as male authority prevailed in the antiwar organizations and student movements of the later 1960s. A few notable females such as Yoko Ono, Kusama Yayoi (1929–), the choreographer Akiko Kanda, and the composer Miyake Haruna spent extended periods abroad and won recognition there, but most Japanese émigré artists were male. In Japan itself, apart from dance, avant-garde female artists were obliged to seek success in a largely male world, as with most other professions in a society where role separations between genders were sharply distinguished. Much greater opportunities for female artists opened up in the 1970s and after.

Alienated from communism and aggrieved by the fate of postwar democracy after the treaty crisis of 1960, particularly as the glue binding state to society hardened in the next years, a number of avant-garde artists once again railed against their government's foreign policy after the Vietnam War escalated in March 1965 and the cabinet of Prime Minister Satō Eisaku began cooperating more fully with United States military operations in Southeast Asia. Although many Japanese now say art and politics did not mix in the 1960s, significant productions in underground dance, tent and touring theater, protest music, and the visual arts suggest otherwise.[23] Yet it is also true that Japanese largely accepted Ikeda's program of economic growth and did not mount significant movements to empower the poor, the exploited, and the abused such as were often found in genuinely postcolonial settings. Whatever their antielitist proclivities, many vanguard artists who appeared in the 1960s came from comfortable backgrounds that afforded them the leisure for, or at least no discouragement from, pursuing their expressive interests. And whatever distance they may have felt from their immediate elders in the Shōwa single-digit generation, these emerging artists showed a generational antipathy toward the slightly younger undergraduates who shut down campuses, including art academies and music conservatories, over local governance disputes during 1968–1970.

Few in Japan could deny the compelling presence of innovative art trends from abroad during the 1960s: the music of John Cage and Morton Feldman, the choreography of Anthony Tudor (1908–1987), Merce Cunningham, and José Limón (1908–1972), the dramas of Samuel Beckett (1906–1989) and Arthur Miller (1915–2005). In painting and sculpture, no contemporary artist could remain wholly innocent of abstract expressionism, followed variously by postpainterly abstraction, anti-art, pop art, assemblage, performance, op art, primary structure, conceptual art, minimalism, installation, and kinetic art. By 1970 some of these approaches had fizzled, but others had adapted to the Japanese artistic environment and been parlayed into advantageous local modes of expression.

Still it would be misguided to suppose that the 1960s whisked the Japanese arts to sudden cosmopolitanism. However partial their internationalism in the 1960s, young avant-garde artists of both genders rejoiced that the hitherto closed arts establishment within Japan was losing its authority. By rejecting forms (*zōkei*), the most avant-garde choreographers, composers, painters, and sculptors sank an irremovable harpoon in the flanks of modernism and broadened the borders of their art to touch on nearly every dimension of daily life. Predictably, skeptics showered them with opprobrium. Looking back in 1981, the critic Minemura Toshiaki condemned this avant-garde proclivity toward rejecting external standards and decried the loss of cooperation and the excessive individualism of artists during the 1960s, which he believed was why the era produced no lasting works.[24] Writing in the April 1987 number of *Bijutsu techō*, the French critic Catherine Millet scoffed at radical Japanese art from the 1960s as "nihilistic," surfeited with rough materials, body parts, and violence, occupying "an irredeemable position"[25] from which there was no escape.

The painter Nakanishi Natsuyuki explains that "whatever modernism may mean, it's closely connected with Europe and America. The rejection of modernism in the 1960s took place just when environmental pollution showed us the limits of industrial capitalism and of modernization as a whole. Thus it's difficult to separate modernism in art from overall modernization and Westernization."[26] By the end of the 1960s, many organizations of contemporary painters, sculptors, or composers had disbanded, victims of a "sense of collapse" (*hōrakukan*) of any consensus on what art was. Individuals increasingly went their own ways, some taking refuge in renewed formal experiments but most finding niches of expression firmly grounded in their immediate experience. In short, the works of art emerging from Japan's fitful and incomplete struggle against modernism in the 1960s bear out what the literary critic Victor Brombert has written in another context: It "implies the negative presence of the subverted or absent model. But it is as much a question of mood as of mode. No single theoretical formulation, however ingenious, can possibly accommodate the specific thrust and quality of a given work."[27]

Artists and Foreign Policy

Immured in their country's conservative bunker mentality of the early 2000s, many Japanese artists and critics today believe that the avant-garde of the previous generation mostly remained aloof from the vast public demonstrations against renewing the Japan–United States Mutual Security Treaty (Anpo) in 1960 and against Japan's support of American military intervention in Indochina starting in 1965. An example of the current perception is this essentialist cliché from the art critic Nanjō Fumio: "it is a special characteristic of Japanese culture that artists don't get involved in politics."[28] A second, more pertinent explanation for the supposed standoffishness is a deep aversion to indoctrination. Moroi Makoto, one of the first composers from the Shōwa single-digit group to win acclaim abroad, recalled in 2002: "I have many bad memories of wartime and the malnutrition afterwards. As far as I'm concerned, capitalism and communism share the same roots. I don't trust ideologies"[29] — thus accounting for his detachment from politics. Like Moroi, Yuasa Jōji stayed on the sidelines, he remembers, because he feared dogmatism:

> I went to elementary and junior-high school during the fanatical emperor-based
> ideology of wartime. All of us who were born around 1930 firmly wanted to pre-
> vent such a situation from recurring after the war. We didn't wish to get involved
> in politics of any sort, left or right. Standing against Tōjō or praising him is the
> same thing — propaganda either way. During the Anpo crisis in 1960, I didn't
> support Prime Minister Kishi Nobusuke, but as a composer I couldn't use any

artistic means to stand against right or left. Even during the Vietnam War, Jikken Kōbō members generally didn't commit to Beheiren [Citizens' Federation for Peace in Vietnam], although Mr. Takemitsu was close to Ōe Kenzaburō and may have joined.[30]

Hara Toshio, the museum director, adds that "the political situation in Japan in those days was very severe. Politics, like the avant-garde art groups, were very clear-cut. Either you favored the alliance with the United States or you opposed it, so Anpo became a symbol of the straightforward political climate."[31] If artists were forced to choose between polar positions, they may well have preferred to step aside altogether, but doing so was tantamount to unvoiced support of officialdom, as by closet conservatives who may have been reluctant to admit their views in public.

A third reason often cited for shirking politics is the press of time. The choreographer Tachikawa Ruriko (1936–) says, "I was busy just dancing in the 1950s and 1960s, and I hardly thought about anything else, such as how political movements affected the development of contemporary art in Japan."[32] Matsudaira Yoriaki, the composer and cancer researcher, observes that "by the time of the anti-Anpo movement in 1960, I was too busy as a professor to take part, although I did not support the treaty. Likewise, rather few composers joined Beheiren in opposition to the Vietnam War, although many sympathized with the movement."[33] Whether nonideological, preoccupied, or simply apathetic, artists of the late 1950s and 1960s are said to have preferred individual critiques of society and politics, no longer the collective action of groups like Non, Energy, the Youth Artists Alliance, and the Nippon Exhibition a few years earlier. If so, they abandoned their predecessors' stance of resisting what should be opposed and thus surrendered a portion of their credibility as social critics.[34] By so doing, they also flouted the constrained circumstances of cultural production during World War Two, when individuals who wished to pit themselves against official policy were not free to do so.

Like other Japanese in the years of high-speed growth, composers, musicians, and visual artists were unavoidably swept along by the tides of economic prosperity and a growing middle-class market for their works, swayed by what Minemura calls "the monolithic and unidirectional sense of reality" imposed by consumerism.[35] True, the intellectual critique of capitalism in Japan had already spent much of its force, but in fact many progressive artists were less complaisant about their country's foreign policies than is commonly supposed today. Journalists who covered the anti-Anpo and anti–Vietnam War protests largely agree with the photographer Ishiguro Kenji: "A number of film actors and members of left-wing theater groups such as Haiyūza took part in the Anpo demonstrations by students and young workers in 1960. I remained an observer, behind my camera, and didn't get involved."[36]

Ōoka Makoto, who claims to have known more artists and writers than any other journalist in the 1950s because of his duties with *Yomiuri*, corroborates that "as a reporter, I just watched from the window as the Anpo demonstrations unfolded. I took no part. I was nonpolitical even when Beheiren began in 1965, although it had broad appeal" to artists and other intellectuals.[37] By the end of the decade, Ishiguro recalls, the socioeconomic profile of the demonstrators was more elitist, and class tensions were more apparent: "The police and the student demonstrators in 1960 were the same age, so there was a certain ease of communication. Nor were there very many differences of social status between them, even though the students had received more education. The protests in 1970 were very different, the lines much more sharply drawn, with little communication between police and students" or others, including artists, who joined the marches.[38]

Most young visual artists were less inclined toward activism after the mid-1950s, by then already disenchanted with the Japan Communist Party and with socialist realism. They were particularly dismayed by Soviet Premier Nikita S. Khrushchev's 1956 speech revealing the excesses of former Premier Joseph Stalin and by the Soviet suppression of the Hungarian uprising that same year. But the ongoing protest at Sunagawa in suburban Tokyo was another matter. This effort to prevent the extension of runways at the American air-force base in Tachikawa attracted the painter-sculptor Yoshimura Masunobu (1932–), who was a close artistic ally of Okamoto Tarō, Kawara On, and Ikeda Tatsuo. Yoshimura had abandoned socialist realism in favor of existentialism and then informel, but he had hardly given up political action. He corralled a number of left-leaning artists, known as the New Century Group (Shinseikigun), to join the Sunagawa movement in 1956. The avant-garde painters Yakushiji Yasuyuki and Akasegawa Genpei were particularly effective organizers, laying the basis for demonstrations against the security treaty four years later. Many members of the Neo-Dada Organizers who clustered around Yoshimura in 1960 were drawn from the New Century Group.[39]

The music critic Komiya Tamie, who has documented political agitation by Japanese composers and musicians in the twentieth century, takes pains to say that "compared with theater, the visual arts, and so forth, historically music has been the field with the weakest social consciousness" in Japan.[40] Nonetheless, while politically committed painters were struggling against bases used by the U.S. military in the 1950s, the composer Akutagawa Yasushi completed a choral work in 1956, *Sunagawa*, with words by the labor organizer Sakamoto Banri.[41] When the Goat Society (Yagi no Kai), formed in 1953 by the composers Hayashi Hikaru, Mamiya Michio, and Toyama Yūzō (1931–), held a fifth-anniversary concert on November 30, 1958, inserted in its printed program was a statement opposing a legislative bill revising the Police Administration Law (Keishokuhō) put forward by the Kishi cabinet the previous month. The statement expressed concern that the proposed changes would threaten constitutional freedoms. It was signed by twenty-six members of the newly formed Young Musicians Assembly (Seinen Ongakuka Gikai), including the Goat Society and composers Mayuzumi Toshirō, Matsudaira Yoriaki, Moroi Makoto, and Takemitsu Tōru; the conductor Iwaki Hiroyuki; and the critics Akiyama Kuniharu and Tōyama Kazuyuki. Widely denounced by the Japan Socialist Party, organized labor, and more than four hundred civic groups as a revival of the "hey, come here" tactics of the wartime thought police, the bill was never enacted.[42]

This little-noticed gesture of resistance was followed by a declaration from the Young Musicians Assembly in January 1960 opposing revision of the security treaty. The Japan Society for Contemporary Music (Nihon Gendai Ongaku Kyōkai), Music P.E.N. Club (Ongaku Pen Kurabu), and East Asian Music Society (Tōyō Ongaku Gakkai) all followed suit in March. Musicians' organizations in western Japan similarly protested. Takemitsu, Hayashi, Mamiya, and Akiyama also joined with odd bedfellows who normally conflicted with one another, such as Ōe Kenzaburō, Etō Jun, and Ishihara Shintarō (1932–) from literature, Asari Keita (1933–) from theater, and Hani Susumu (1928–) from film, to form the Young Japan Association (Wakai Nihon no Kai) to resist the revised treaty.[43] As the document was being rammed through the Diet in June, an action group called Association of Musicians to Defend Democracy (Minshushugi o Mamoru Ongakuka no Kai) took shape in the elegantly austere Sōgetsu Art Center. At its first gathering, to which all musicians were invited, 580 members of the new association signed a resolution calling for Kishi's resignation and new Diet elections. It was unprecedented for Japanese musicians to act politically in this manner.[44] Some members of the group lobbied against plans for the Tokyo World Music Festival scheduled for 1961 to mark the opening of the Tokyo Metropolitan Festival Hall (Tokyo Bunka Kaikan), and several refused to participate when the event went forward as scheduled.[45]

As many as 5.8 million persons are thought to have demonstrated against the revised treaty on June 15, 1960, followed by a general strike by 6.2 million workers (according to labor leaders) one week later.[46] Few of the protesters were genuine radicals; most feared being dragged into unwanted wars through the revised and expanded military treaty with the United States. Nearly all sought regularity and predictability in national social life following the fractious 1950s, believing that scaled-back ties with America would restore harmony to civic culture. Japan's premier historian of modern and contemporary dance, Yamano Hakudai, thinks that "dancers' participation in the Anpo demonstrations was reserved: only about thirty dancers protested at the Diet. Most people in the dance world were neither left nor right politically. Their minds were on artistic ideas, not political issues."[47] Still it is the case that some who opposed the 1961 Tokyo World Music Festival ended up founding the Japan Music and Dance Council (Nihon Ongaku Buyō Kaigi) in June 1962, dedicated to political efforts to preserve artistic freedom and, a few years later, to raise money for Vietnamese dislocated by war.[48]

Many avant-garde figures, however, declined to plunge into the antitreaty fracas. Akasegawa, on the one hand, says: "I made my contribution to the antiwar movement by participating in the Sunagawa struggle against American military bases during 1956–1959, so I didn't feel a need to participate in the huge Anpo movement in 1960 or the antiwar Beheiren organization in 1965. Nonetheless I felt very sympathetic to those who resisted the war in Vietnam."[49] On the other hand, the painter and urban planner Arakawa Shūsaku, who threw rocks outside the Diet building with fellow Neo-Dada artist Shinohara Ushio in 1960, recalls that "I took part in the Anpo demonstrations because intellectuals had an obligation to take part — everything was so out of balance."[50] The architect Isozaki Arata agreed. He had been a year above Yoshimura Masunobu at First Ōita Prefectural High School and later designed Yoshimura's White House at Hyakuninchō, in Tokyo's Shinjuku area, which soon became the headquarters of the Neo-Dada Organizers. Isozaki wrote that "for approximately one month, I participated every day in their protests" against the treaty.[51] Nakanishi Natsuyuki, a radical artist not formally connected with the Neo-Dada group, remembers that "I was barely two years out of college when the Anpo demonstrations erupted in 1960. I was independent of both major sectarian groups leading the protests, but I wanted to take part as an individual. It was very dangerous when I went over to the Diet building to see what was happening — there were so many riot police everywhere."[52]

Nakanishi points out that, unlike workers, students, or the Young Musicians Assembly, no organizations of visual artists emerged to oppose the revised treaty in 1960.[53] Instead, the art historian Chiba Shigeo argues, "the Neo-Dada members, on the whole, treated the demonstrations against the Japan – United States Security Treaty as an artistic event, not a political one. Their real message was 'down with informel' (han-anfuo), not 'down with Anpo' (han-anpo)."[54] Whatever the purpose, the Neo-Dada members spent more time in the streets during the treaty crisis than other arts professionals — and then many of them moved to New York in the early 1960s. In fact those who stayed behind, including Akasegawa and Nakanishi, continued to connect politics and culture through their events, performances, and exhibits — at the Yomiuri Independent until its demise in 1964 and then through public events in the streets of Tokyo.

Yet in retrospect a dark cloud of futility overspread many participants' self-assessments of the worth of these activities. Looking back on 1960 many years later, Isozaki, thoroughly disenchanted, poured scorn on the protests he had once embraced: "This passionate intensity was nothing but self-abandonment and self-destruction. The result was the inevitable destruction of an auto-intoxicated radicalism."[55] It is true that most artists who denounced the revised treaty soon resumed their intense fascination with contemporary arts from the United States, but a number of them also joined Beheiren five years later to criticize American mistakes in Vietnam. More measured than Isozaki's dismissive retrospective on the era is this recollection from the abstract sculptor Sekine Nobuo (1942–):

> I was a student during the demonstrations against the Japan–United States Mutual Security Treaty in 1960. We threw paving stones during protests outside Shinjuku station. I was a graduate student during the anti–Vietnam War movement starting in 1965. I was even locked out from my graduate school at Tama Art University for more than a year during the student movement beginning in 1968. Somehow we saw ourselves as politically uncommitted, yet art itself was so revolutionary in those days. We discussed politics a great deal, so it was difficult to separate art and politics.[56]

If art itself was revolutionary, as Sekine believes, surely some among the avant-garde who declined to protest foreign-policy issues imagined that they were capable of even more radical critiques in the studio, concert hall, or onstage than in the streets. Subsequent chapters discuss some of the most clear-cut examples.

Shinjuku and the Artistic Vanguard

Shinjuku today is the hub of Tokyo's city government, transit network, middle-class retailing, and tawdry nightlife. Home to a magnificent imperial garden and a stunning opera and theater complex, the area variously contains a vibrant Koreatown, elegant hotels, the world's busiest train station, and the site of the "west-exit economy" *(nishiguchi keizai)*, named for the ranks of skyscrapers bearing the names of corporate giants like Mitsui and Sumitomo juxtaposed with tiny one-story restaurants, decorated with red paper lanterns, hugging the west side of the JR tracks outside Shinjuku station — a metaphor in architecture for the symbiosis between Japan's postwar business powerhouses and the myriad small-scale suppliers and vendors that depend on them for survival. Presiding over the district is Tange Kenzō's city-hall complex (1991), echoing Notre-Dame de Paris in design, a secular cathedral for the triumph of postwar capitalism.

Shinjuku in 1960 was thronged with sidewalk shoeshine stands, city-operated streetcars on Toden Dōri (now Yasukuni Dōri), camera shops filled with bargain hunters, cinemas surrounding the Kabukichō peace park, commuters switching trains in a tumbledown national railway station — and demonstrators against the revised security treaty in May and June, gathering each evening outside the east station exit directly across from the Nikō grocery store. Where tall buildings and plush hotels now stand was the Yodobashi reservoir, whose eventual demise gave city officials a rare and successful chance at urban planning, much of it financed by corporate behemoths.

To the youthful vanguard in 1960 Shinjuku meant cheap rents, plays and concerts in Kinokuniya Hall, a first-rate bookstore, a handful of galleries sponsoring contemporary art, and tales from an older generation about prewar salon culture in Nakamuraya, a bakery and café long since out of favor with the young. Whereas the postwar epicenter of high-culture experiments was Sōgetsu Hall in sleek Akasaka, some of the first tremors of a true artistic underground in Japan were being felt in workaday Shinjuku. Yoshimasu Gōzō, the photographer and poet, sets the scene:

> In the late 1950s and early 1960s, Shinjuku was the center of artistic ferment in theater, photography, jazz, and dance as well as the visual arts. Takiguchi Shūzō, for example, was very interested in Butō. He used to spend time in Shinjuku with us hippies in a bar called Najda or in other tiny drinking establishments. Those bars, a few jazz coffeehouses, and the Fūgetsudō restaurant on Toden Dōri were the nurses of the underground arts in those days. We young artists, playwrights, poets, and photographers felt the effect of the Beat generation in America, especially in the overheated atmosphere and intellectual energy of Nadja. Yes, Shinjuku was it, wasn't it?[57]

Although the respectable art journal *Bijutsu techō* claimed in 1978 that the term "underground" was first heard in Japan in 1966,[58] experimental film meriting that label goes back at least to *Love* (1962) and *Onan* (1963), brief erotica directed by Iimura Takahiko (1937–).[59] The photographer Ishiguro Kenji affirms that "jazz was very important to the underground in Tokyo starting in the late 1950s. Artists would hang out at Shinjuku jazz clubs like

Nadja, debate artistic ideas at Yoshimura Masunobu's White House in nearby Hyakuninchō, and take part in demonstrations against American bases and the treaty."[60] The historian Joe B. Moore, commenting on the crossovers among jazz, film, and theater at the end of the 1960s, writes that "virtually the only place where new-music advocates were able to experiment and perform in public was Shinjuku, which became the place where the vanguard music movement was able to intersect with the radical political and artistic trends of the times."[61]

Soon the experimental dance of darkness, Butō, attracted a following among the Shinjuku avant-garde, as did the underground plays of Kara Jūrō, who was arrested in 1969 when his Situation Theater (Jōkyō Gekijō) pitched its red tent in a Shinjuku park without a permit.[62] Even the late-1960s sculptors who renounced forms and incorporated materials from daily life imbibed the underground movement, says their founding spirit, Sekine Nobuo: "Monoha members gathered regularly for discussions about art and philosophy at the Toppu coffee shop in Shinjuku"[63] — the least formal, the most formless, the most everyday of Tokyo's major districts, certainly then and probably even now.

THE NEXT CHAPTERS examine generational shifts, political and social consciousness, and the search for alternative modernities by three groups of visual artists, a variety of contemporary-music composers, and several pioneering contemporary-dance troupes. Chapter 10 analyzes the convergence of art, business, and politics in the Osaka exposition of 1970. A concluding chapter reappraises the experiences of radicals and realists among Japan's avant-garde community during 1952–1970.

chapter six

Beyond Form and Formality

Like most other peoples, Japanese since at least the poet Ki no Tsurayuki (ca. 868–945) have pondered the question, What is art? Global flows of culture, first from China and Korea beginning in the third century, then from Europe in the sixteenth, provoked reflection about what, if anything, was indigenous in the arts of Japan. Nativisits in the eighteenth century, such as Kamo Mabuchi (1697–1769) and Motoori Norinaga (1730–1801), concluded that a great deal was distinctive about their country's arts, especially the aesthetic heritage of expressing emotion and sentiment. Mabuchi, Norinaga, and other National Learning scholars rebuffed the rationalist internationalism of the haiku writer and travel diarist Matsuo Bashō (1644–1694), who deliberately distanced himself critically from the poets of old China and Japan and thus might be called one of his country's first modernists. After the Meiji revolution of 1868, artists recalibrated their space/time reference points by veering sharply toward norms used by the European genres of the moment, consigning most previous arts of East Asia to the museum, if not the slagheap, of the past. After slight adjustments to accommodate new traditions such as Japanese-style painting (Nihonga) in the 1890s, Western-derived modernist ideas about the inherent nature and proper function of art continued to set the bar for many painters, sculptors, choreographers, and composers in Japan down to World War Two.

Serious questioning of the widely accepted modernist orthodoxy swept the tiers of Japan's avant-garde only in the 1960s, shaking artists' complacency and plunging them into quandaries about the values of the eye and ear. Their brash skepticism toward inherited artistic verities, presaged a few years earlier by musique concrète, indeterminacy, Gutai, informel, and the Kyushuha, came into full bloom in stages: through the antiestablishment actions of Neo-

Dada and other artists participating in the Yomiuri Independent, through fresh musical idioms drawing on people's everyday experiences, and then through new modes of vision found in sculptures by the Monoha group after 1968. As was sometimes true in the United States and elsewhere, the term "anti-art" began to be used in Japan after 1960 to characterize attitudes and behaviors intended to deconstruct canonical approaches to dance, music, and the visual. The term itself is less important than the spatial and temporal vectors it implies: Japan's most progressive nonverbal artists in the 1960s advanced toward a denationalized, post-Western realm of creative activity while simultaneously shifting beyond the modernist era toward the current condition of artistic expression. In this way the assault on modernism, although never complete, built the foundations for today's citadels of artistic endeavor in Japan.

Anti-Art and the Everyday

An outlook of rejecting conventional elitist aesthetics while seeking aspects of the everyday can be found variously in Dada, futurism, and surrealism originating in Europe early in the twentieth century. As used in the United States and Japan after 1945, terms such as antitheater, antiroman, and especially anti-art "demanded freedom from established concepts of art, and they inevitably opened up a new possibility that everything can be art"[1] — what is sometimes called "pan-art." Anti-art was not necessarily antimodernist in the full sense: the critic Rey Chow cautions that "if the impetus of modernity is a criticism of the past, then much of our cultural criticism is still modernist."[2] Like abstract expressionism in America, informel in Japan during the late 1950s straddled a liminal point between radical innovation and mainstream acceptance as accredited art. Anti-art as a position owed much to informel's iconoclasm, even as it abjured informel's authoritative aura among painters and especially its lingering allegiance to the abstract. By contrast, as the art historian Nakamura Keiji suggests, the tacks taken by anti-art navigators were linked by a quest for precision: not the virtual world of figurative art but the reality of the sensate visual and aural domains.[3] Yet because anti-art was sometimes destructive, usually deliberately formless, and frequently temporary via installations or events, it left behind few works or artifacts for future generations, only a refreshingly critical and questioning viewpoint.

Reviewing the 1960 Yomiuri Independent for *Yomiuri*, the critic Tōno Yoshiaki chose "anti-art" (*hangeijutsu*) to describe works by Kudō Tetsumi (1935–1990) and others who used discarded everyday items as their materials. Two days later Takiguchi Shūzō identified "a certain Dada-like or anti-art tendency" in the scribbled graffiti images displayed by young artists at the exhibit.[4] Both Kudō and Shinohara Ushio from the Neo-Dada group disliked the term "anti-art" yet agreed that art was not an abstract, Western-derived concept but something immanent in the everyday.[5] As Shinohara wrote in 1968, "the critic Tōno Yoshiaki, just returned to Japan from abroad, came up with the terms 'anti-art' and 'anti-sculpture' to describe the Beat works that overflowed the twelfth Yomiuri Independent. We were unhappy. Wasn't it that all we were trying to do was posit avant-garde art as the antithesis of established art? We weren't opposing old authority or old ideas themselves."[6]

Taking anti-art to its most extreme, if nearly any artifact could be used to make art, any sound to produce music, or any movement to create dance, then technique was unimportant, the artist didn't require training, and all that mattered was the certainty of the observed object, sound, or motion itself. Rather incongruously, Kikuhata Mokuma of the Kyushuha claimed that by using junk, rubbish, packaging materials, odd sounds, decaying vegetation, pornography, and dangerous items, anti-art "undoubtedly was art that supported peace."[7] Whether irenic or bellicose, the defiant young artists who decried modernism helped to tie the contemporary arts in Japan more firmly to their insurgent counterparts abroad without minimizing the particularities of their own everyday surroundings.

At heart, anti-art in Japan meant not a true alternative modernity but an antiformalist, iconoclastic mood of cultural production in the late 1950s and early 1960s, yet its appearance roiled the notably placid waters of Japanese arts criticism. Miyakawa Atsushi sprang to prominence in 1963 with a series of articles identifying a sharp break between modern and contemporary art; he noted that anti-art required modernism as its forebear and foil.[8] Tōno Yoshiaki, the first Japanese critic to discuss anti-art, convened a multigenre panel on the topic at the Bridgestone Art Museum in Kyōbashi, Tokyo, on January 30, 1964. This jammed event took place just weeks after the police interrogated the Neo-Dada painter Akasegawa Genpei for possible violations of the currency laws, and it occurred barely a fortnight after Yomiuri canceled the 1964 Independent, permanently closing this important venue for avant-garde works. These unexpected developments, coupled with the government's campaign to project a sunny image for foreign visitors to the Tokyo Olympics later that year, troubled many artists and doubtless swelled the audience for Tōno's roundtable by the Young Seven, including an avant-garde sculptor, two painters, the critics Tōno and Haryū Ichirō, the architect Isozaki Arata, and the composer Ichiyanagi Toshi.[9]

As Miyakawa later wrote, the Bridgestone soiree was "more a scene than a real discussion."[10] He quoted Ichiyanagi: "if you believe it's good to tear down the existing art of others, don't you first have to look inward" and question your own artistic values? In Miyakawa's view, "anti-art *(hangeijutsu)* is not non-art *(higeijutsu)*."[11] Anti-art accepted rather than denied art, but it opposed established schools; indeed, all art was anti-art in the sense of challenging previous approaches. As pioneered by Robert Rauschenberg and Jasper Johns, the anti-art of Neo-Dada and of pop art was the next step beyond abstract expressionism and informel, Miyakawa contended. He reasoned that anti-art used junk and readymade articles, so its "descent into the common everyday negates the final border between art and non-art." Still, he acknowledged, "not everything is art"[12] — to proffer such a claim would be to drop all aesthetic standards. Miyakawa conceded that anti-art raised important questions about the nature of art, even as he lamented the term's vagueness. What may be most notable about his criticism of this highly concrete artistic perspective is that Miyakawa's thesis was purely theoretical — he barely referred to actual works of art at all.[13]

Tōno and Haryū believed that Miyakawa exaggerated the compass of anti-art and made too much of it.[14] Chiba Shigeo later wrote that Miyakawa overstated the similarities between contemporary Western and Japanese modes and undervalued the domestic precedents for anti-art set by Gutai. Thus the reasons for the shift from informel to anti-art "must be sought in Japan's existing context."[15] In 1981 the authoritative art journal *Mizue* concurred that Japanese art of the 1960s was in full flight from the European notion of a work, in favor of local actions, ideas, and materials, but it warned editorially, "Of course this is not to say there was a pure expression of Japonisme."[16] Others acknowledged the amplitude offered by the anti-art attitude of skepticism. Perhaps foreshadowing the poststructuralist criticism of the next generation, the cultural critic Tone Yasunao wrote in 1970 that, in anti-art, the act of painting was enough: "The work is always unfinished, fostering the idea that it is equivalent to the everyday, to real objects and daily activities. Thus it's not at all strange that every concrete object or ordinary action suffices as a painting"[17] — in effect, everything is a text.

Looking back from the vantage of 1982, Kikuhata Mokuma was less generous: he found the anti-art outlook of which he was once a part "idealistic, audacious, self-indulgent, and self-defeating," confecting a spun-sugar orthodoxy against which to rebel even though there wasn't much of an art establishment left in Japan by 1960.[18] At best anti-art was a brief antiauthoritarian phase in the evolution of Japan's contemporary culture — and it sometimes critiqued everydayness after connecting with it, through the street theater of

Terayama Shūji, the Neo-Dada group's happenings, or the shadow paintings of Takamatsu Jirō (1936–1998),[19] all of which questioned the consumption-based social system then solidifying into its current shape.

Neo-Dada in Shinjuku

Shinjuku in 1960 was the focal point of antimodernist and anti-treaty activities by a young subset of avant-garde painters and performers who became the first Tokyo-based group to seek a basis for their art in the everyday. They claimed the anti-art mantle of European radicalism and called themselves the Neo-Dada Organizers. Dadaism traveled a winding route from Zurich in 1916 to Shinjuku in 1960 via Paris in the early 1920s and New York in the mid-1950s. Even before Dada, Marcel Duchamp — a favorite of the interwar Japanese avant-garde — began using "readymade" everyday items in his works, most notably *The Fountain* (1917), a white ceramic urinal signed R. Mutt signaling disillusion with the Great War.[20] Like the dadaist circle, who were most active in 1916–1921, Duchamp sparked questions about the boundaries between art and the ordinary world, much as the anti-art attitude later attempted in Japan. Two transnational Dada slogans from 1919 were "art is dead" and "DADA is the voluntary destruction of the bourgeois world of ideas,"[21] words with resonance for the Japanese avant-garde forty years later. Dadaism also presaged the activities of the Kyushuha and other vanguard groups by showing that performances could be art. Walter Benjamin, among others, noted how Dada used both pictorial and literary means to create effects commonly used in film in the 1930s. Seeing their works as reproductions, not original creations, the Dada members had little interest in the market value of their art.[22]

Like postwar Nouveau Réalisme in Paris, Neo-Dada arose in New York after the mid-1950s, consciously distinct from abstract expressionism, by using ideas, materials, and chance encounters from everyday life. When their approach became known in Japan, the American avatars of Dada in the 1950s affected far more artists than the Shinjuku-based Neo-Dada Organizers alone. The Monoha sculptor Sekine Nobuo affirms this: "I produced my first works in 1961 while I was studying at Tamabi [Tama Art University]. I started by concentrating on painting. The effects of informel were still felt by my teachers and the older students, but by that time the informel surge had peaked. So Tōno Yoshiaki, a very influential critic on the faculty there, began to turn our attention specifically to American art by introducing the ideas of the Neo-Dada painters Jasper Johns and Robert Rauschenberg."[23] The connections with American painters were personal and generational as well as artistic, Dōmoto Hisao adds: "I knew Johns and Rauschenberg in New York in the late 1950s and felt especially close to them because Johns was the same age as I and Rauschenberg just slightly older."[24] By the time the two Americans visited Japan in 1964, their interest in the everyday had led them to pop art and minimalism, and meanwhile several of the Shinjuku Neo-Dada group had settled in New York.[25]

The Neo-Dada Organizers (soon simply Neo-Dada, dropping the leftist "organizers") consisted of about ten young avant-garde figures who gathered regularly during the unruly year 1960, sometimes simply to hang out, at Yoshimura Masunobu's White House residence on the northern outskirts of Shinjuku. Some were interested in surrealist and dadaist aesthetics, others in exhibitions and street happenings to attract notice. The art historian Kondō Yukio points out that these "were unknown young male artists in Shinjuku who used the media as a new-generation strategy. They sought publicity through newspapers, magazines, and TV to call attention to themselves. Anpo was a unifying experience for them, reflected even in play — young children that summer enjoyed *Anpo demo gokko* [pretend demonstrations against the security treaty]."[26]

Several members hailed from Ōita in Kyushu; most were current or recent art students subsisting on part-time jobs, unlike their contemporaries in the Kyushuha in Fukuoka, who were already well established in wage-earning positions. The Neo-Dada artists were mainly associated with elite art schools: a number were teachers or alumni of Musashino Art University (Musashino Bijutsu Daigaku), although Shinohara Ushio had studied at Tokyo University of Fine Arts and Music at the same time as two Neo-Dada sympathizers but nonmembers, Kudō Tetsumi and Nakanishi Natsuyuki. Starting with Shinohara, the most mediagenic of the group because of his "Mohican" (Mohawk) haircut, each of the ten displayed oils, sculptures, or assemblages of everyday materials at the Yomiuri Independent between 1958 and 1963. Even during their White House year, it is difficult to identify a clear group consciousness among them beyond generalized anxieties about the fate of society and the place of art.[27] Far from offering a genuine substitute modernity, their works mostly displayed a cheeky and querulous attitude toward received artistic axioms. Indeed, in 1986 Iwata Shin'ichi, head of the Super Ichiza theater company and a founder of the avant-garde Zero Jigen group, scoffed, "They called themselves Neo-Dada, but their god was Duchamp, or closer at hand Takiguchi Shūzō."[28] But they certainly shared dadaist impulses to struggle against accredited standards, often through what Akasegawa called "action," sometimes via outrageous activities in public places, an art-for-the-moment that has been preserved only in occasional photographs.[29]

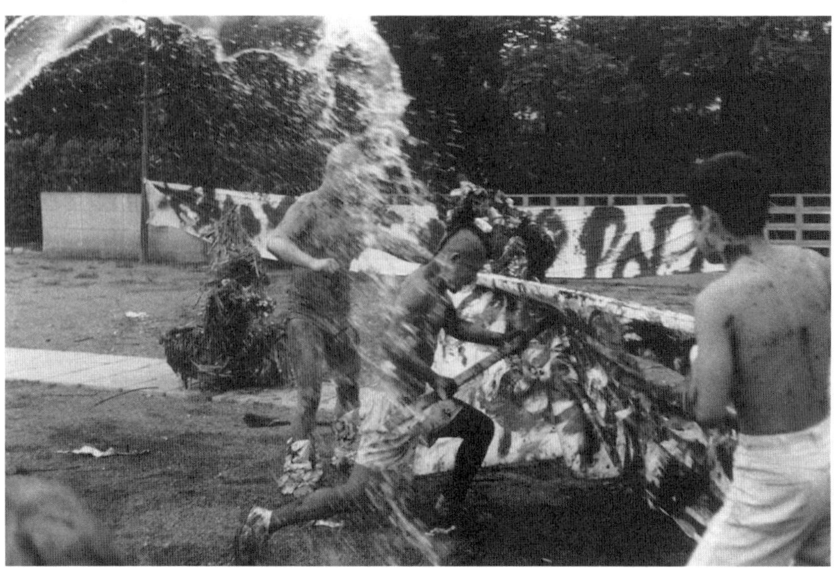

Figure 12. Shinohara Ushio (center), sprayed by a hose, slashes a temporary installation at a Neo-Dada event, Hibiya Park, Tokyo. 1960. Courtesy Ishiguro Kenji.

The Neo-Dada group embarked on the first of its three gallery exhibits with a madcap scene at the Ginza Gallery in April 1960: Yoshimura demolished chair legs with karate chops, Kazakura Shō (1936–) immersed his head in a water bucket, then sputtered imprecations about World War Three, and Akasegawa spoke of becoming butchers in order to avoid being slaughtered.[30] Both in galleries and at casual open houses at the White House, the group's paintings, collages, and other tangible works often seemed completely improvised, from thrown-together rubbish, on a moment's spur, so that the element of time — that is, timing — was paramount. The visual paralleled the theatrical: during the summer of 1960 Shinohara slashed the fabric of a hastily rigged installation in Hibiya Park, Tokyo, foregrounding what the scholar William Marotti calls "the temporality of the act."[31] (See Figure 12.)

Shinohara was the best known of the Neo-Dada organization, not merely because of his antic theatrics, but also because of his showy action paintings at the Yomiuri Independent starting in 1957, as the wave of informel first swelled. The art critic Hyūga Akiko locates Shinohara squarely among Okamoto Tarō's followers, mainly because of Shinohara's often-overlooked canvases executed before he turned to op and pop art in the mid-1960s.[32] "I had nothing to do with politics, nor did other Neo-Dada artists get much involved," Shinohara recalled in 2002, blinking at the rocks he hurled near the Diet building in June 1960. "There was so much pressure on us to succeed and so few outlets for our work. Until the mid-1960s our works didn't sell, so we were very clean and pure,"[33] untainted by revenue streams from rich patrons. The architect Isozaki Arata points out that Shinohara lived at the time near Tokyo's largest dump and used junk he found there. The Neo-Dada artists were transfixed by the discourses of vernacular culture, even as they watched the globalization of contemporary art.[34]

Yoshimura Masunobu proved to be a complex painter who took an interest in virtually every aspect of art in the 1960s, and neither he nor the short-lived Neo-Dada coterie can be easily identified with any critical position on art or politics beyond opposing the modernist canon. Although some of his followers soon grew wary of the Ikeda government's incomes scheme, Yoshimura himself, looking back a decade later, wrote that "Neo-Dada, formed at the time of the 1960 Yomiuri Independent, can be called an exaggerated form of capitalist realism."[35] This apparent acquiescence in industrial materiality led the critic Tōno Yoshiaki to label the group "the post-Hiroshima generation,"[36] too young to feel the political effects of defeat but acutely sensitive to their destitute physical environment of lumber scraps and broken objects immediately after 1945 — the everyday items used in their first works.[37]

As youths, the Neo-Dada artists may have joined demonstrations against the security treaty with the United States, but they did not seriously question the American values of abundance and proliferation of manufactured products that were permeating their country, leading a recent critic to comment that "in attitude they were a part of the postwar generation that affirmed occupation culture."[38] The curator Kuroda Raiji believes that, unlike the politically engaged painters and sculptors of the early 1950s, the Neo-Dada group "did not regard America as imperialist oppressor but instead indiscriminately accepted its mass production and consumption, music, and mores and saw these as sources of new art"[39] — including ever more discarded items. Such a view suggests that, for the future Neo-Dada members who did so, joining the antibase New Century Group in the late 1950s was a bagatelle, and it also implies that their absorption in everyday objects did not translate into deep concern with society's problems or a sustained effort to reach a broader public. Indeed, Shinohara disclosed a cavalier aspect of Yoshimura's White House in 1960: "the Saturday gatherings soon turned into drinking parties."[40]

However apt Yoshimura's gibe about "capitalist realism" may be, it is hard to ignore that some Neo-Dada works, particularly by Akasegawa and Arakawa Shūsaku, explored the dissonant aspects of humans' interactions with material culture. Arakawa's *Mō hitotsu no hakaba yori No. 1* (*From Another Cemetery No. 1*, 1960) is a concrete cocoon laid out on striped red fabric in a wooden coffin,[41] developed from his well-known *Mudai* (*Untitled*, 1958), suggesting the spectacle of a nonordinary calcified body atop workaday cloth inside a box of low-grade wood. (An outraged Tōno dismissed these sculptures as "ferocious materializations of the sickened unconscious mind of contemporary man.")[42] This preoccupation with the body and the passage of time characterized Neo-Dada's street performances, as well as some of the exaggerated aluminum ears cast by nonmember but sympathizer Miki Tomio (1937–1978) starting in the White House period. Arakawa later used washing machines and clothes hangers to mock, not affirm, the materiality of household living.[43]

Mō hitotsu no hakaba yori No. 1 was the talk of the show when Arakawa held a one-person exhibit at the Muramatsu Gallery in September 1960, flouting the group's strictures against solo displays. He was promptly expelled from the White House and soon moved to the United States, the first deep fissure in the loosely organized Neo-Dada circle. Once settled in Manhattan, Arakawa became an important conceptual artist and later, in partnership with his wife Madeline Gins, an urban planner of note. Kudō Tetsumi moved to Paris in 1961 and remained active abroad for many years. Beset with defections, the remaining Neo-Dada members lapsed into desultory exchanges throughout 1961 and finally disbanded when Yoshimura moved out of his Shinjuku residence in January 1962, seven months before relocating to New York.[44] Akasegawa stayed in Japan and that same year joined Nakanishi Natsuyuki and Takamatsu Jirō to form High Red Center, a small art group that staged carefully planned actions in the streets of Tokyo.

"At the time," Akasegawa recalls, "the art critics appreciated about half of what we were doing in Neo-Dada and High Red Center, but they didn't really understand our efforts."[45] One who neither understood nor appreciated them was Haryū Ichirō, who published a testy article in August 1962 called "I'm Tired of Avant-garde Art," slamming Japan's most groundbreaking artists, including some at the Sōgetsu center, for "drifting amid chaos, opening up their own structure of sensibility, trying to give agency to an irrationality that denies every system." Haryū complained that they displayed an "avant-garde neurosis, a disease that's spreading throughout society. This is equally true of artists and of the public."[46] It is also a fact that the Neo-Dada group paid scant heed to female artists, unlike the Gutaiha and Kyushuha, nor did most of its members accord these out-of-town associations much respect. Akasegawa, whose antipathy to Gutai art has been noted in Chapter 6, wrote in 1984 that Gutai "seemed like a rich boys' plaything. So we felt animosity" toward its activities. "We were dissatisfied with 'Gutai' because we could not sense very much dynamism in relation to society"[47] — a charge often leveled at the Neo-Dada members themselves.

With the dissolution of Yoshimura's White House group, the museum director Hara Toshio points out, "many Japanese artists fled to Paris, New York, and other places because the situation in Japan was so confused. One reason was the dominance of the tight avant-garde groups; a second was the uncertain market for their works at a time when Japan was still poor; and a third may have been the political climate of Anpo."[48] It was natural that some of them should move to the major centers of the Western avant-garde — whereas the Gutai artists depended too much on Yoshihara Jirō and the later Monoha artists resisted Euro-American art theory too strongly to relocate.[49] The Neo-Dada renegade Arakawa, who remembers that "Marcel Duchamp was extremely kind and helpful from the moment I arrived in New York in 1961," says "one reason I left Japan was that even intellectuals such as Takiguchi seemed so local, so romantic." In New York he took on the challenges of true criticism: "realistic and metaphysical art are easier to do than critical art," but the latter is the genuine test.[50] Shinohara Ushio, who moved to Brooklyn in 1969, observes that "it's very hard for Japanese artists to penetrate the mainstream art world in New York. They're expected to be very 'Japanese,'" as Imai, Dōmoto, and others found in Paris a decade earlier. In New York Shinohara "set aside all my previous ideas and started over, progressing inch by inch. At least in the U.S. people are willing to pay for art that's good, not just art that's famous, as in Japan."[51] Both Arakawa and Shinohara managed to establish themselves in America, but others grew discouraged and drifted back home, or, in Yoshimura's case, returned mainly because of visa problems.

At heart, the young painters, sculptors, and performers who clustered around Yoshimura in 1960 were artistic rather than political rebels, full of creative energy but with little sense of direction. By the end of the decade, Neo-Dada as an idea had been supplanted by conceptual art, minimalism, pop art, and then environmental and technological art. While the Gutai and Monoha leaders were joining the contemporary-art establishment as jurors for exhibitions and professors at the top academies,[52] most of the young Shinjuku artists remained outsiders, whether living abroad or in Japan. In this they resembled their Dada forebears in Europe a half century earlier.

Yomiuri Ends Its Independent

The Yomiuri Independent was the chief vehicle of postwar democracy for young visual artists in Japan who lacked connections with the clubby fine-arts establishment. "We young artists in the late 1950s had no money but lots of passion," says Shinohara Ushio. "We entered our works in the Yomiuri Independent because that was the only place we could show them. There were hardly any museums or galleries in those days, and no patrons."[53] Akasegawa Genpei remembers it as "a fervent market for young people,"[54] a bazaar of new ideas and materials. From about 1958 on, the show concentrated in a single venue the anti-art impulses breaking out among the avant-garde all over Japan, "shattering the idea of the work of art"[55] by using everyday items to produce objets and installations, discarding the use of frames, and calling into question the nature of artistic expression by denying that form was something to be learned, then passed to the next generation. By 1959 the curator Miki Tamon declared that the Independent gave him "the feeling of a performance space rather than of an exhibition site."[56] Akasegawa called it an "anarchic 'open space'" by 1960.[57] Performances or actions *(kōi)* became even more common at the Independents held in 1961–1963.

Soon the directors of the Tokyo Metropolitan Art Museum, host to the Yomiuri Independent, balked. During setup for the 1962 exhibit, curators summarily removed one artist's vinyl bag of red ink on which spectators were supposed to walk and create art by tracking ink on the museum floor. They also banished certain photographs of the body as obscene, a sword as dangerous, and foodstuffs that might molder. The following December the museum issued a ukase against objectionable items within its walls: works making unpleasant or loud noises, materials that might smell or rot, swords and other dangerous objects, works that might make viewers extremely upset or run afoul of public-health laws, installations using water, sand, gravel, or other materials that might damage floors, and works suspended from ceilings.[58] Takiguchi Shūzō and the League of Art Critics immediately demanded that the museum retract the guidelines; the critics Haryū Ichirō, Tōno Yoshiaki, Nakahara Yūsuke, and Miki Tamon subsequently protested to the museum director, without achieving a compromise.[59] Tōno called the restrictions "very troubling for freedom of expression."[60] Police were called to remove protestors dancing in their underwear outside the Tokyo Metropolitan Art Museum to decry the new rules when the 1963 Independent opened, but in fact the exhibits included works using a bath bucket, a straw mat, knives, glass fragments, a steel drum, a tire, and foodstuffs such as a French roll, udon noodles, bean sprouts, and tofu.[61]

Barely a month before the 1964 Independent was scheduled to open, Yomiuri decided to withdraw its sponsorship and terminate the annual exhibitions. Its statement to artists on January 12, 1964, declared that the fifteen previous shows, 1949–1963, had accomplished the original purpose of nurturing fresh art and free expression: "We believe the time has come for artists to manage their own affairs. Confident that we've attained our objectives, we of Yomiuri

Shinbun have concluded our sponsorship with last year's exhibition."[62] Yomiuri clearly believed it had milked all the public-relations advantage possible from serving as sponsor and saw nothing further to be gained. Many artists were shocked, but by now the antimodernist tendencies cultivated at earlier Yomiuri Independents were well launched, and many works planned for the 1964 show found an alternate locale for display in galleries, small exhibits, and competitions, as well as juried exhibitions sponsored by Mainichi Shinbun. In retrospect, Akasegawa criticized the avant-garde artists who violated the museum's rules: "The unconscious destructive energy of the artworks had destroyed the space itself."[63] Yet many unaffiliated artists among the avant-garde found a toehold after 1964 as Japan's art world diversified and grew increasingly individualistic. The Yomiuri Independent, as Sawaragi Noi points out, was less a unified artistic spirit than an institutional structure for showing unconventional art at a time when it could otherwise not be seen.[64] Now that anti-art and other innovations were widely known, the Independent was less vital to the health of Japan's visual arena, and in a surprisingly short time the annual Yomiuri events were almost forgotten.

SO LONG AS THERE WAS a mammoth independent art show sponsored by a major media company like Yomiuri, the rebels who rejected modernism, abstraction, and elite institutions could not fully attack the art establishment.[65] Once the Yomiuri Independent came to an end in 1964, they were freer to do so, but whatever radicalism they possessed proved to be a temporary unity of opposition, not a rigorous body of theory or an energizing force with long-term consequences. Meanwhile the top museums turned out to be more receptive to avant-garde art in the 1960s, starting with a major show on contemporary painting and sculpture at the Tokyo National Museum of Modern Art in 1961 and another at its Kyoto branch three years later. At the same time, two important private museums of contemporary art began displaying some of the newest work: the Gutai Pinacotheca in Osaka (1962) and the Nagaoka Museum of Contemporary Art (1964). Even the Museum of Modern Art in Manhattan recognized the younger generation with its traveling show called The New Japanese Painting and Sculpture in 1965, featuring twenty-nine Japanese living in Japan and seventeen more abroad.[66]

In short, the need for an Independent or for art-association exhibits was clearly over by the mid-1960s.[67] By then the new Shōwa double-digit generation of those born in 1935 and after were able to criticize modernism, politics, and the managed social system with ever greater freedom, no longer hobbled by the fetters of formal art associations — although now with unpredictable risks to their livelihoods in the emerging consumer marketplace. Increasingly individual artists could follow their own lights in rejecting forms in favor of concrete elements from everyday life, provided they were willing to gamble on making a go of it through the growing number of commercial art galleries that handled avant-garde work. Whether art that succeeded in a capitalist market system could still be called avant-garde remained an open question for the rest of the decade, until it was largely settled by the massive corporate patronage at Banpaku, the international exposition of science and industry held in 1970 in the Tenri hills east of Osaka.

chapter seven

Events, Objects, and Concepts

Among the avant-garde — a term Japanese critics used less frequently in the 1960s as innovative art won acceptance — the collapse of the Yomiuri Independent after 1963 portended the gradual eclipse of painting by sculptural constructions and conceptual art. Yet for visual artists as a whole, painting remained the favorite medium in Japan as elsewhere, often with renewed emphasis on figuration rather than abstraction. An International Figurative-Art Exhibition, held at Nihonbashi Takashimaya in October 1962, declared that the participants, fifteen Japanese and thirteen foreign painters, were committed to "a conception of art based on reality,"[1] what might be called capturing "a sense of life" rather than "the exact depiction of figures."[2] The same was true of more and more natural-pigment painters in the Japanese (Nihonga) style, such as Takayama Tatsuo (1912–), whose *Hokkoku* (*The North*, 1966, mineral pigments on paper) portrays two rural women, one clothed and one nude, against lush fields of yellow with what the curator Matsumoto Tōru believes is "a greater realism than in earlier Nihonga."[3] But the flight from abstraction was most apparent in the concrete works, both visual and performed, of nonconformists who increasingly used everyday objects and materials. This vanguard variously produced street-theater events, sculptures, two-dimensional collages, and three-dimensional assemblages, as well as prints, pop art, electronic and environmental art, and conceptual art by the end of the decade — but very few paintings until the late 1970s. Much of the new work was ephemeral, even trifling, but interspersed was serious social commentary offering alternatives for thinking about art, livelihoods, and politics in an era of rising affluence in Japan.

High Red Center and Early Conceptual Art

A three-person band of visual and performance artists called High Red Center was the immediate successor to the Neo-Dada group as torchbearer of anti-art in Tokyo during 1962–1964. High Red Center was the most mediagenic of the many counterculture art groups of the decade, but it was also intensely cerebral in its calculated challenges to modernism, the Japanese arts establishment, and the cloying predictability of urban life. More trenchantly than any other Japanese arts organization at the time, its activities mocked, and sometimes disturbed, civic order sufficiently to earn occasional surveillance by the authorities. One of its members unwittingly ended up in court questioning the legal authority of the state to restrict artistic expression. In some respects High Red Center adopted positions akin to the postcolonial, and indeed its members felt marginalized in their own society — yet each ended up being embraced by the arts establishment once the group's rebelliousness had spent most of its force.

High Red Center took its name from the English translation of the first characters of the names its founders, Takamatsu Jirō, Akasegawa Genpei, and Nakanishi Natsuyuki. The poet and photographer Yoshimasu Gōzō points to close bonds between High Red Center and the artistic experiments of the 1950s: "Takiguchi Shūzō was a godlike figure even to underground artists like Akasegawa, Nakanishi, and Hijikata Tatsumi — these were the second postwar generation of avant-garde artists affected by Takiguchi, following Takemitsu Tōru and others in the Jikken Kōbō" who were born in the Shōwa single-digit decade.[4] Takamatsu, Akasegawa, and Nakanishi were likewise congenial with the Neo-Dada group, although only Akasegawa was a member. All three perpetuated the Neo-Dada attitude of anti-art iconoclasm yet were eventually absorbed by the elite arts institutions they initially castigated: Akasegawa won the literary establishment's Akutagawa prize for his fiction under the penname Otsuji Katsuhiko, and both Takamatsu and Nakanishi went on to become professors at prestigious art institutes.

More so than the Gutai, Kyushuha, or Neo-Dada artists, the High Red Center members focused on joint efforts to stage carefully planned episodes of social criticism in public spaces, each meant to express a defiant organizing thought, producing one-time-only works that left no legacy except in photograph and recollection. In some respects their projects more closely resembled street satires by itinerant Japanese artists in earlier centuries[5] than performances seeking redress staged by subaltern groups in Asia or elsewhere. High Red Center's presentations emphasized concrete ideas and helped to nurture the growth of conceptual art in the late 1960s, based on Akasegawa's notion of linking thought and action in daily life through his own objects wrapped in kraft paper, Takamatsu's single ropes, and Nakanishi's clothespin sculptures.

Today High Red Center's performances seem unsurprising in retrospect, although sometimes it is still said that "High Red Center shocked ordinary people's common sense with its meaningless, nonsense events."[6] In fact they were the furthest thing from nonsensical: these public productions took art outside conventional exhibit spaces to urban people going about their daily activities, raising unasked questions about the nature of everyday society. The art historian Tatehata Akira, who calls its works "partly conceptual and partly idea-generating," sees the group as "off-museum rather than anti-museum"[7] because it used the city instead of the gallery as its space, partly to test whether art in an ordinary noninstitutional setting could still be considered art. There, Akasegawa later wrote, it was possible "to explore the borders between the everyday and the noneveryday,"[8] using Werner Heisenberg's unproved principle of indeterminacy once "we had all deviated from painting as a fixed form."[9] High Red Center's events tried to shake up the bored but affluent middle class not through the diffuse attention-grabbing street activities of the Neo-Dada group but through well-planned "direct actions"[10] that turned out to be acerbic critiques of the safe, predictable middle-class society then taking shape under bureaucratic management. Insofar as High Red Center offered an alternative, it was a civic culture in which citizens would exercise greater agency by taking an active part in politics rather than resigning themselves to the state's penetration of civil society.

High Red Center's first happening, a grand instance of camp held in the Tokyo suburb of Kunitachi, commemorated the seventeenth anniversary of Japan's defeat in World War Two. Guests invited to a banquet on August 15, 1962, paid a stiff admission charge, then found themselves spoofed: they were allowed only to watch while the artists ate, drank, danced, and brushed their teeth[11] — using vision to taunt, and thwart, unslakable desire and turning impulses to consume inside out. One afternoon two months later Nakanishi led a meticulously planned mobile festival on the Yamate (later renamed Yamanote) passenger line from Shinagawa to Ueno, with stops at Yūrakuchō and Tokyo. He rode the train in whiteface and spilled paint on a station platform, then licked and broke open an egg-shaped object containing ordinary items: hair, an old watch, a mirror, a spoon — a satire on the daily hurly-burly faced by harried commuters. Nakanishi recalls this time-space critique: "In the 1960s I grew interested in street theater from the Edo period [1600–1868] and in the unseen aspects of society in that era"[12] — critical precedent, perhaps even inspiration, from an earlier age of urban materialism and state-administered civic life.

Nakanishi, Takamatsu, and Akasegawa each exhibited at the final Yomiuri Independent, held in March 1963, where the latter displayed an early version of his *1,000en satsu* (*1,000-Yen Note*, 1963), a slightly unfinished simulacrum of the obsolescent national banknote, then worth $2.80, enlarged to the size of a tatami mat.[13] The group held its first formal show in early May 1963 at the Shinjuku Daiichi Gallery, on the third floor of a nondescript building facing the east central exit of the national-railway station. Okamoto Tarō traveled from posh Aoyama to cut the ribbon at the opening.[14] Takamatsu exhibited ordinary hangers, fans, spools, and jackets wrapped in string. Nakanishi displayed assemblages made of clothespins and wore hundreds more pinned to his hair, face, and clothes; his *Clothespins Assert Churning Action* (1963) is representative (Figure 13).[15] Clothespins are meant to restrain, confine, and bind — the opposite of asserting the churning action of frenetic workaday life. Akasegawa showed a chair, coat hanger, and other items wrapped in tan paper — "more in the manner of a scientific idea rather than as an artistic act,"[16] he said — only vaguely aware, through indirect contacts with the Fluxus group in New York, of similar works by Christo (Christo Javacheff, 1935 –).[17] Whether suggesting repression, the negation of restriction, or expansive gestures such as wrapping cars, buildings, or even Tokyo Tower,[18] Akasegawa's bundled works showed his fascination with the cosmos and the possibility of harnessing it by enveloping it, somewhat like the composer Yuasa Jōji's idea of dynamic musical energy drawn from cosmology.[19]

High Red Center ventured deeper into reproducing images in January 1964, when it rented a ¥7,000 suite for a night at the old Imperial Hotel in central Tokyo to shelter artists symbolically from nuclear war. The low neo-Egyptian building in tan and brown stone, designed by Frank Lloyd Wright (1867 – 1959), had opened officially on September 1, 1923, and seemed ideal as an iconic refuge because it withstood the devastating Kantō earthquake and fire at noon the same day. Visitors to this "shelter plan," such as the painter and graphic artist Yokoo Tadanori (1936 –), could pay ¥1,000 to have their bodies measured and photographed, from which life-size plaster replicas were made,[20] as though the individual were now mechanically duplicable — the casts being plan-ahead death masks, as it were, in case the shelter gave way, as it doubtless would in an atomic attack.

The group members thumbed their noses at conventional gallery protocol by holding a reverse-logic "closing" party in June 1964 to mark the first day of a weeklong nonexhibition in Shinbashi at the former Miyata medical clinic, now converted into a gallery called Naiqua, a pun on the term for internal medicine. Prospective guests at this Big Panorama Show received advance announcements declaring: "High Red Center is now holding a gallery clos-

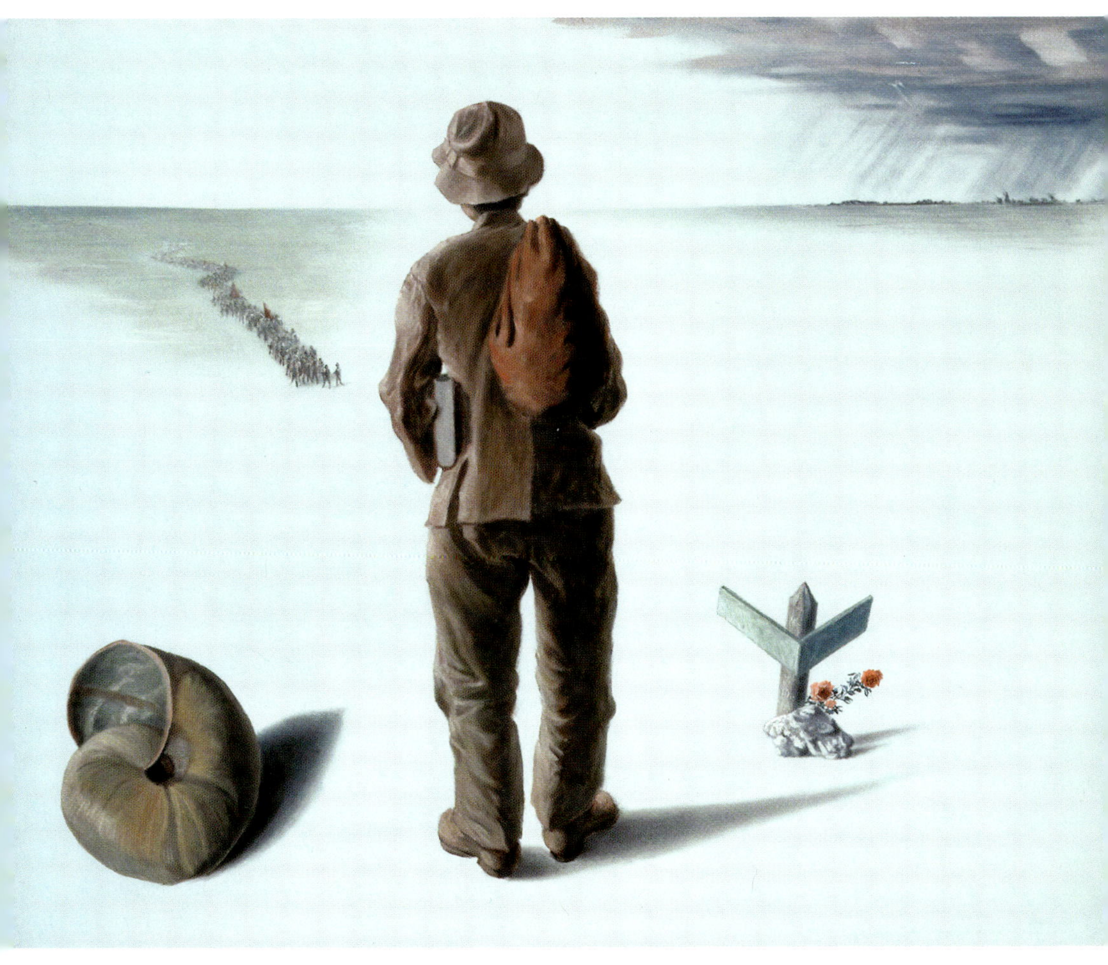

Plate 1. Kitawaki Noboru. *Quo Vadis.* 1949. Oil on canvas. Courtesy National Museum of Modern Art, Tokyo.

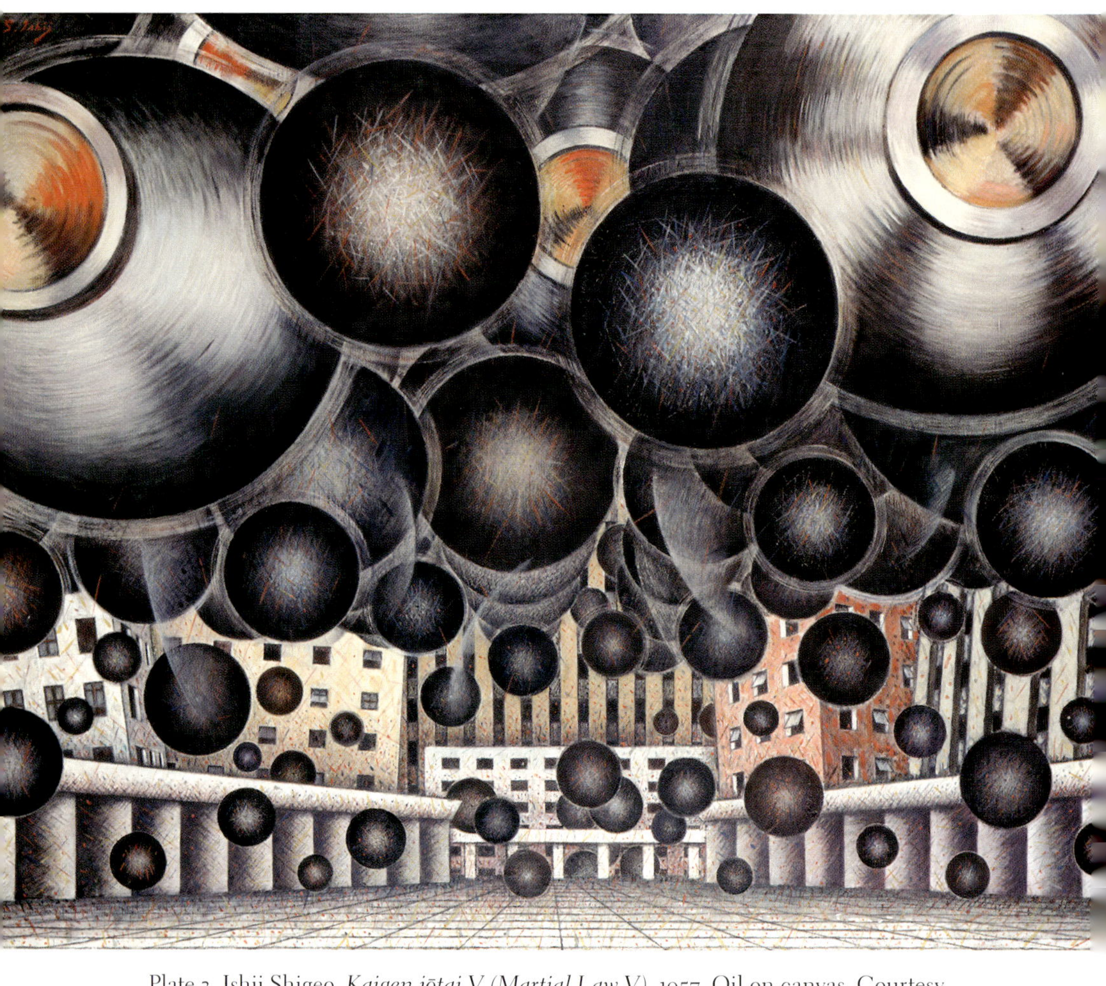

Plate 2. Ishii Shigeo. *Kaigen jōtai V (Martial Law V)*. 1957. Oil on canvas. Courtesy National Museum of Modern Art, Tokyo.

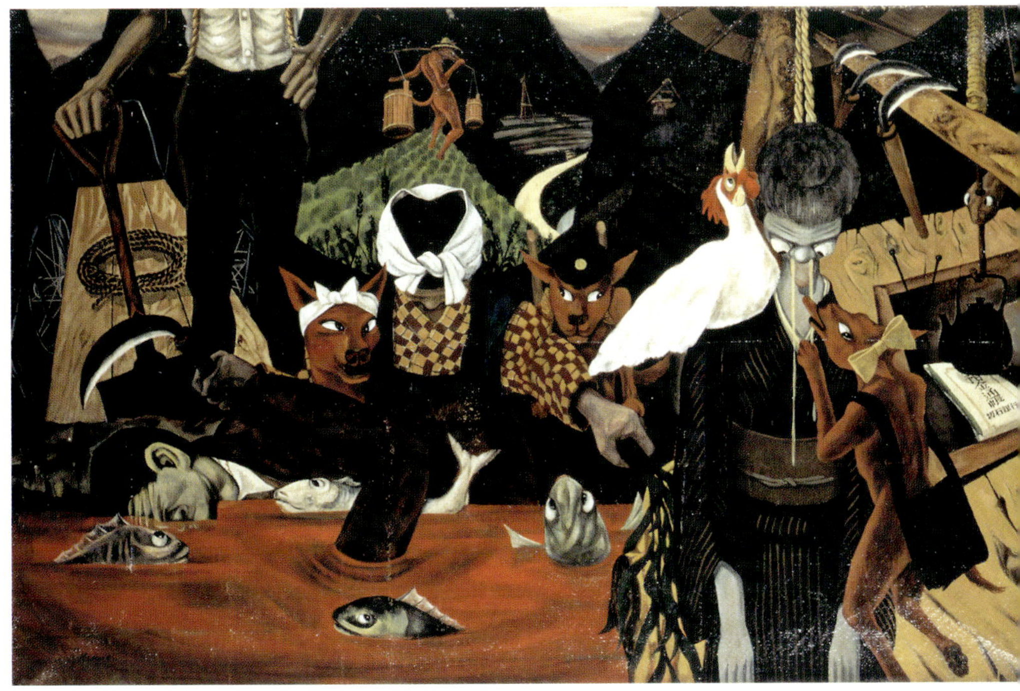

Plate 3. Yamashita Kikuji. *Akebonomura monogatari (Tale of Akebono Village)*. 1953. Oil on dungaree. Courtesy Nippon Gallery.

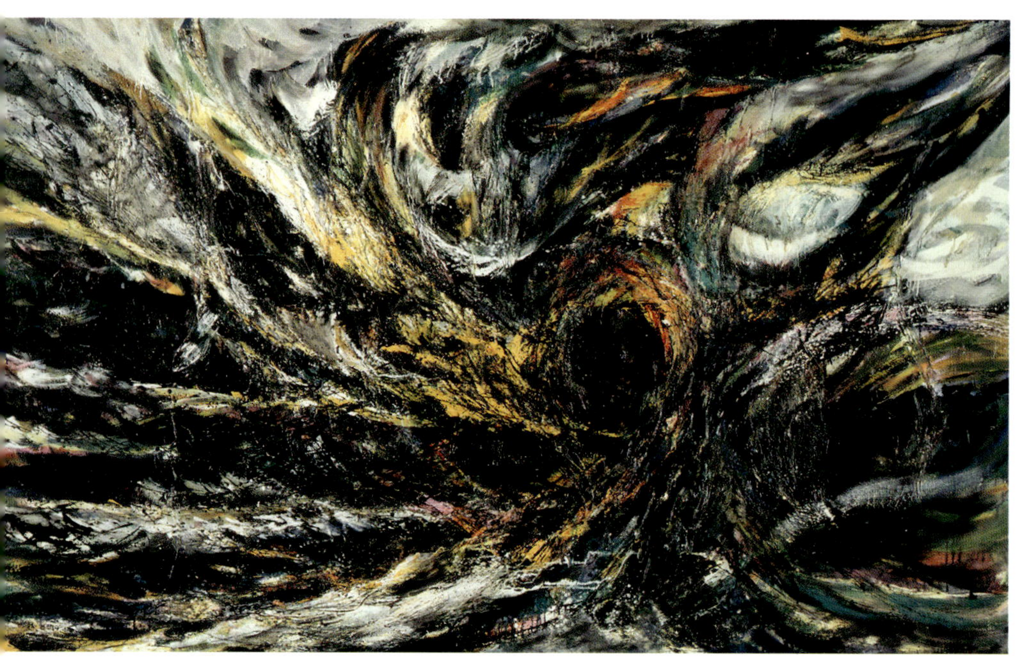

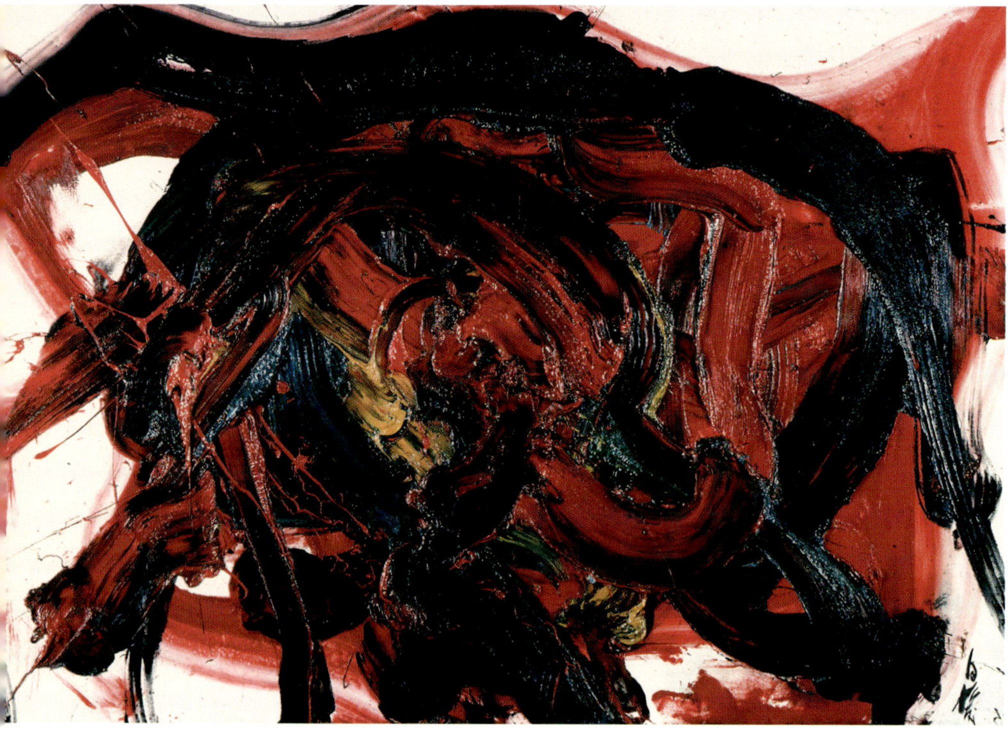

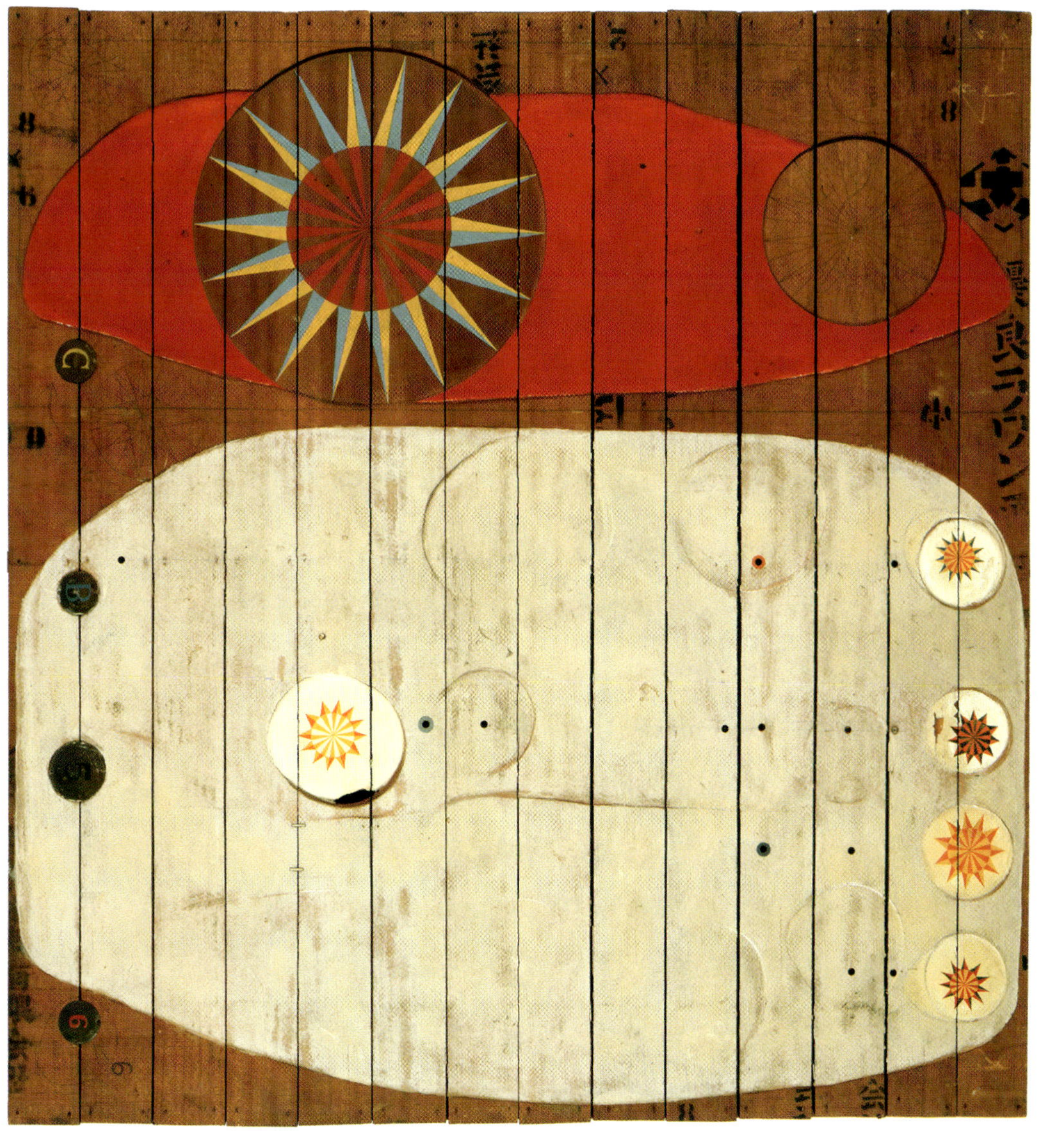

Plate 4. *(Facing page, top)* Dōmoto Hisao. *Shūchūsuru chikara (Tension d'esprit)*. 1957. Oil on canvas. Courtesy Dōmoto Hisao and National Museum of Art, Osaka.

Plate 5. *(Facing page, bottom)* Shiraga Kazuo. *Tenkeisei Henmi Sanrō*. 1964. Oil on canvas. Courtesy National Museum of Modern Art, Tokyo.

Plate 6. *(Above)* Kikuhata Mokuma. *Rūretto (Roulette)*. 1963. Enamel on wood. Courtesy National Museum of Modern Art, Tokyo.

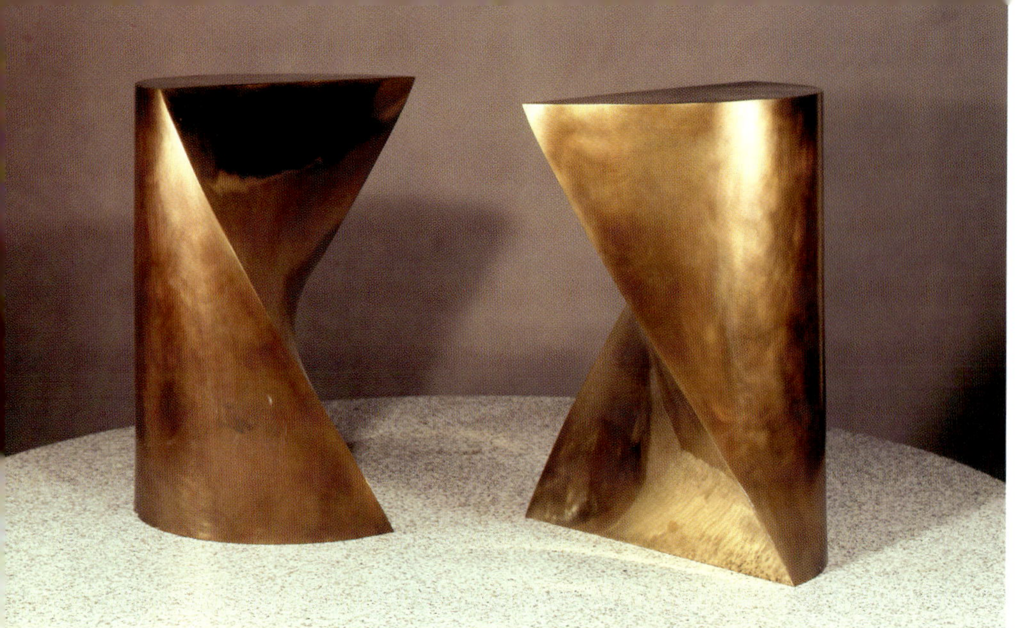

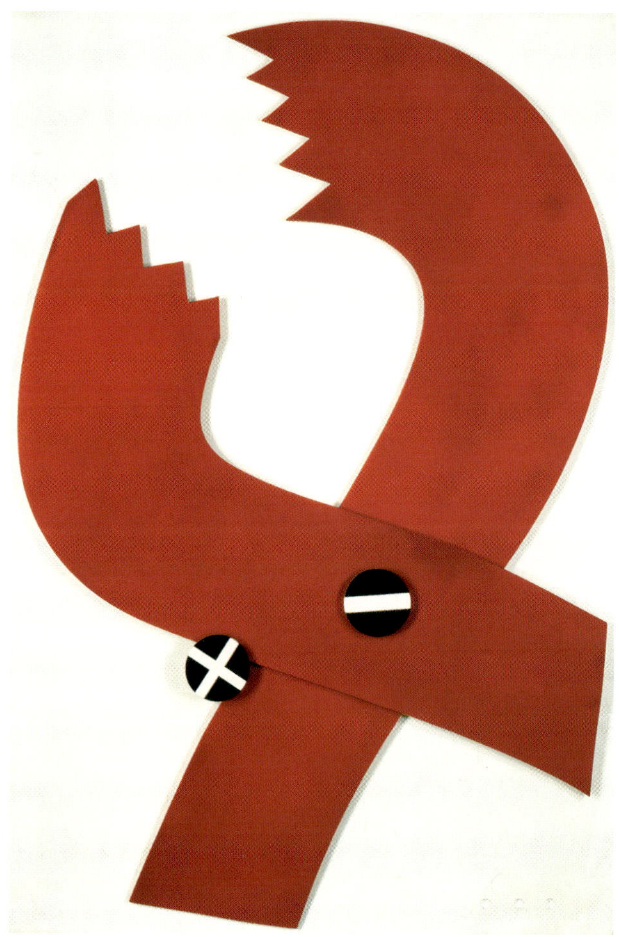

Plate 7. *(Above)* Horiuchi Masakazu. *Entō no nitōbun (Two Half Cylinders).* 1969. Bronze. Courtesy National Museum of Modern Art, Tokyo.

Plate 8. *(Right)* Saitō Yoshishige. *Penchi (Pliers).* 1967. Lacquer on plywood. Courtesy National Museum of Modern Art, Tokyo.

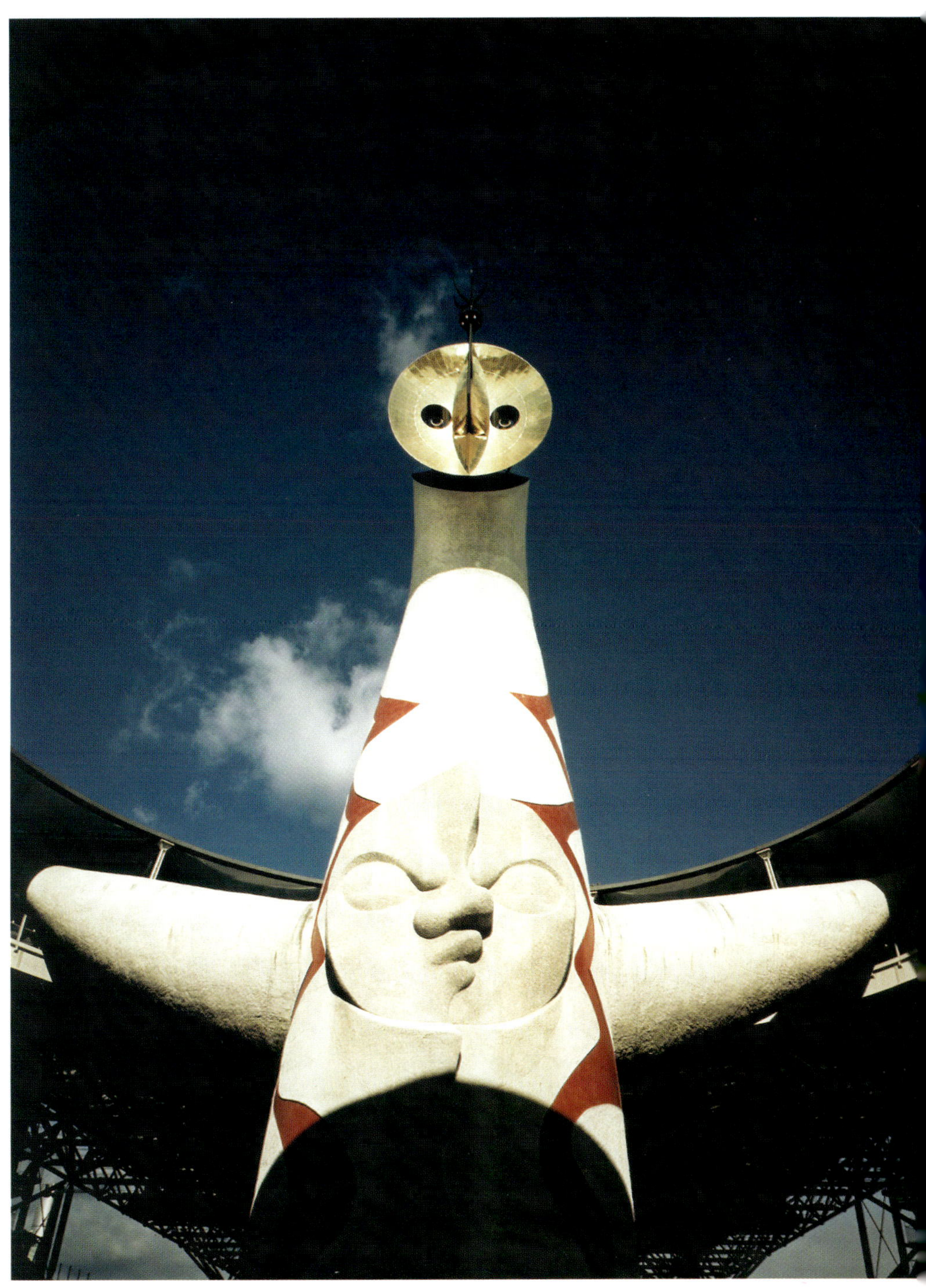

Plate 9. Okamoto Tarō. *Taiyō no tō (Sun Tower)*. 1970. Concrete. Courtesy Okamoto Toshiko and Okamoto Tarō Museum of Art, Kawasaki.

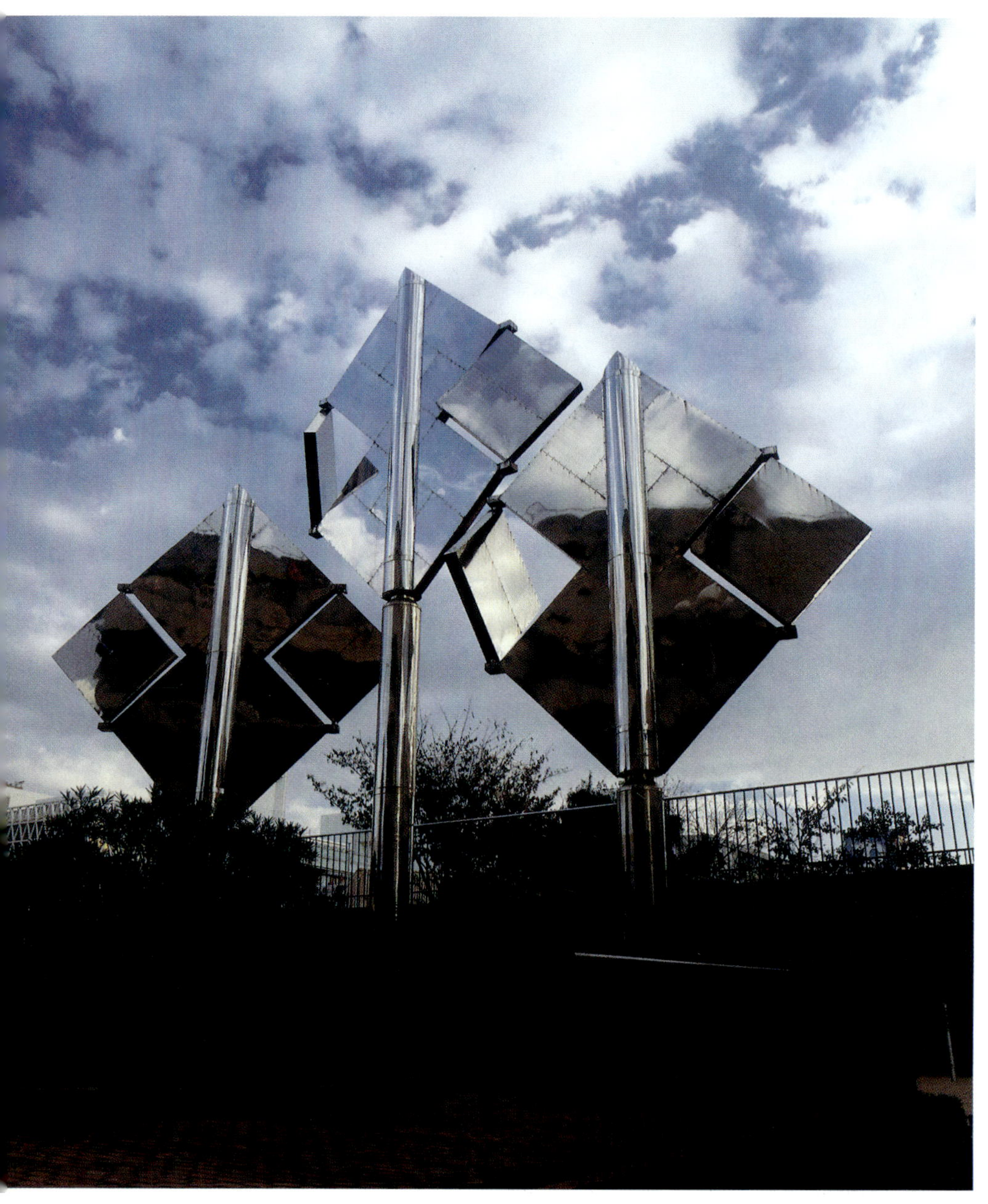

Plate 10. Iida Yoshikuni. *Suteinresu no mori (Forest of Stainless Steel)*. 1970. Courtesy Iida Yoshikuni.

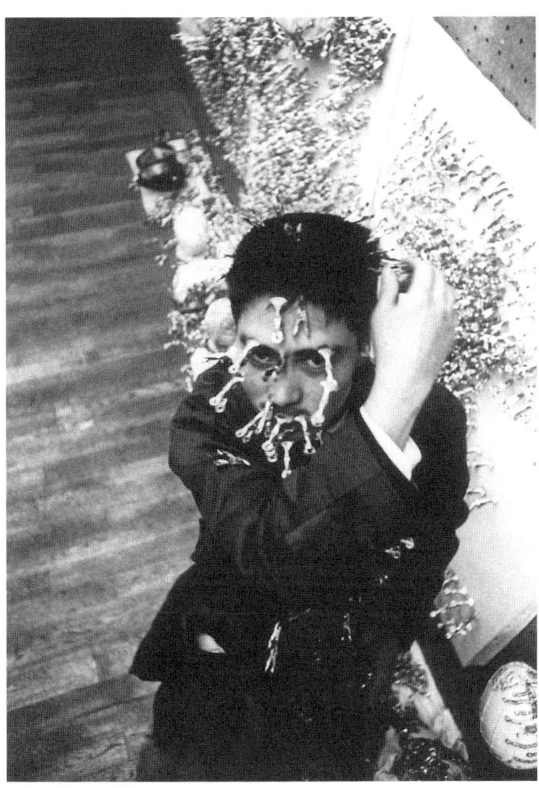

Figure 13. Nakanishi Natsuyuki. *Clothespins Assert Churning Action.* 1963. Temporary sculpture, Tokyo. Courtesy Nakanishi Natsuyuki.

ing. When you have time, please do not attend."[21] Akasegawa and Nakanishi went there on day one, nailed boards across the door, and put up signs saying "closed." Leaving the space that way until the final day, they held an "opening" party attended by Takiguchi Shūzō, Ichiyanagi Toshi, Sam Francis, and Jasper Johns, the latter of whom helped pull nails from the boards barring the entrance. Even the pop art on display was reversed, with labels stuck on the insides of tin cans,[22] a surreal parody of an art form that was itself parodic.

Perhaps lampooning the elite artistic experiments at the upscale Sōgetsu Art Center across town, High Red Center chose a rival flower-arrangement school in quotidian Ochanomizu for its "dropping event" on the first day of the Tokyo Olympics, October 10, 1964. At Sendagaya, six stops west of Ochanomizu on the Chūō line, the emperor of Japan presided over a minutely scripted opening ceremony marked by brassy fanfare, suffocating punctilio, and the release of hundreds of peace doves fluttering skyward. Back at Ochanomizu, Akasegawa and others lugged a haphazard trunkful of ordinary clothes, umbrellas, magazines, and other discarded items to the rooftop of the four-story Ikenobō Kaikan and released them tumbling downward to the sidewalk below to create "art that is not art," producing a pattern that Akasegawa compared to the works of the impressionists or the late Cézanne.[23] He called these everyday articles "paints," replete with palpable materiality just like the pigment-rich canvases of informel or abstract expressionism.

The group's last public performance mocked the cosmetic cleanup campaign proclaimed by Tokyo bureaucrats to make the city sparkle for Olympic visitors. On October 16, 1964, Nakanishi and a half-dozen High Red Center supporters marched to Ginza, Japan's most cosmopolitan window on the world, stopping in front of the Hokkaido Shinbun building at the intersection of Namiki Dōri and the east-west street separating 5-chōme from 6-chōme. They brought buckets, mops, sponges, and soap to give the sidewalks and streets a seven-hour "super cleaning"[24] that would show up the city government's cursory beautification efforts.[25] Wearing lab coats like clinical uniforms and stationing professionally lettered signs to detour traffic, Akasegawa said, gave this private event a certain "authority,"[26] no less than the civic scrub-up ordered by the public authorities. Such hard labor to make a single urban block gleam made it embarrassingly obvious that no amount of official tidying up for foreign guests could mask the sooty mien of industrial Tokyo — or the low percentage of homes connected to sanitary sewers.

Reflecting many years later on the brief High Red Center phase of his long career, Nakanishi commented at a Ginza café thirty meters from the site of the 1964 street-cleaning episode:

> My early work at the beginning of the 1960s was a little different from abstract art. Herbert Read's ideas had been introduced to Japan in the mid-1950s and made a deep impression on me. Throughout the 1950s and 1960s I was very much aware of the social struggles taking place and gave a lot of thought to the meaning of human existence. At the beginning of the 1960s I became aware of how porous and indistinct the boundaries of our vision are. I wasn't especially drawn to action painting's focus on material, nor was I attracted to pure abstraction. I believed art should be for everybody, not just a limited avant-garde.[27]

This outlook comported with Akasegawa's view that art should "attack a depoliticized everyday," as the scholar William Marotti puts it,[28] rather than accepting administrative guidance of consumer society as the norm while taking refuge in elite artistic experiments.

Nakanishi is undoubtedly correct that High Red Center avoided partisan party politics,[29] yet in a broader sense its social criticism was as iconoclastic politically as its visual and public-event commentary was subversive artistically: deeply antiestablishment and antiauthoritarian. More so than has been usually recognized, Akasegawa, Nakanishi, and Takamatsu were heirs both to Takiguchi's fascination with the surreal and the untried and to Okamoto Tarō's sardonic 1955 dictum that "utter nonsense may have more power to change social reality than seriousness. What we call the serious joke may be the foundation of art."[30] Their capers on the trains and sidewalks of Tokyo mattered far less than the concepts underlying these antic performances, which explored the borders of conventional art and bureaucratic authority. Evidently by late 1964 the group thought its parodies had run their course, for Akasegawa declared that after the Ginza Be Clean affair there was nothing more "left to do."[31] But surely part of the reason for abandoning showy events was the police interrogation Akasegawa underwent in early 1964 and the subsequent uncertainty about whether he would be prosecuted for producing images of thousand-yen notes the year before.

After much dither, the government obtained an indictment of Akasegawa and two printers in November 1965 on charges of imitation *(mozō)* in violation of an 1895 law against copying currency or securities.[32] (Pop-art or advertising renderings of currency, no matter how exaggerated, were also illegal in the United States in the 1960s.) That the case went to trial at all, as happened in August 1966, surprised and perturbed artists throughout Japan. Akasegawa later conceded, "It's certainly the case that High Red Center did various things while saying 'this isn't art, it can't be art,' but we never thought we'd get as far as going to court. No, rather than going to court, we were taken to court."[33] The group's activities navigated the buoys between the artistic and the illicit, as well as the limits of governmental toleration, but whether this alone triggered a decision to prosecute is doubtful. Nor should the indictment be attributed merely to the routine rotation of new prosecutors eager to cut their teeth on a tempting case. The most likely cause was the government's determination to crack down in the wake of skilled counterfeits of thousand-yen notes put into circulation in the early 1960s, known as the T-37 episode.[34] After a lengthy and spectacular trial, described by one critic as "the greatest historical event in the record of postwar art,"[35] the court ruled that Akasegawa's *1,000en satsu* was both a work of art and a crime. As was true under the Meiji constitution of 1889 and subsequent legislation, art could thus be art but still violate the law. In April 1970 the Supreme Court upheld the guilty verdict.[36] (See Figure 14.)

Akasegawa argued from the moment he was first interrogated in January 1964 that his thousand-yen note, which he produced in several formats, was "not a forgery" but "a copy" *(mokei,* or model). The "copy is *unusable*: it is the image of a thousand-yen bill stripped of its function as paper money"[37] — a simulacrum, not a simulation as a counterfeit is. Indeed, to imitate — which was the essence of reproductive techniques such as pop art — was the height

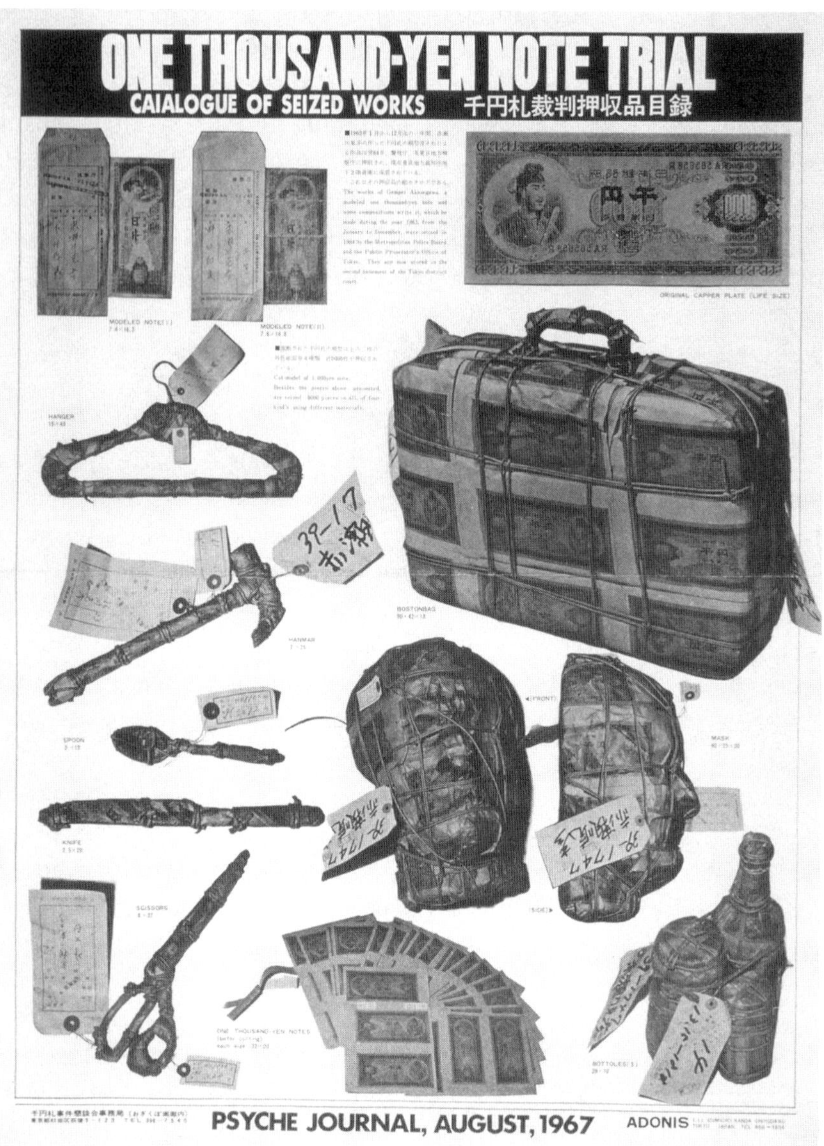

Figure 14. Akasegawa Genpei. Thousand-yen note trial poster. 1967. Courtesy Akasegawa Genpei and SCAI the Bathhouse.

of denying modernism, which instead prized creativity. For example, Akasegawa's erstwhile Neo-Dada colleague Shinohara Ushio, an excellent draftsperson as well as painter, copied with permission Robert Rauschenberg's images of Coca-Cola to produce *Drink More* (1964), in effect a double reproduction by "appropriating another artist's found object as his own,"[38] as the curator Rand Castile has written. Akasegawa and Shinohara were legatees of

Walter Benjamin, a great modernist who nonetheless wrote in 1936 that the growth of photography and film in the early twentieth century had made any work of art reproducible, thus robbing it of much of its originality.[39] Mechanical reproduction, electronic communication, and air travel linked technology with information to help artists everywhere share ideas on a global scale by the 1960s, steeping the avant-garde in popular culture and perhaps leading to the demise of modernist individuality, possibly even of "all conceivable artistic experiments," according to the critic Noguchi Reiichi.[40]

Akasegawa, who mailed three hundred monochrome replicas of thousand-yen notes in registered cash envelopes to invite guests to his solo exhibit in February 1963, also used enlarged copies as wall posters or as wrapping paper for everyday items — an early kind of conceptual art. In the press and at trial, he asked: What is a crime? What is reality? What is art? He said his reproductions of bank notes varied from the originals in size or color and "were not at all a crime," any more so than folding a thousand-yen bill into the shape of a crane.[41] (The court found that his imitations were illegal because they might cause "confusion" with the real thing, regardless of the artist's intent.) Akasegawa said his aim was to question reality and the authority that certified it: he chose paper money as a "point of direct contact between the pictorial world and the real world," in order to "trigger the fusion between the fictitious and the real."[42] He took "more than a little interest in imitation in order to explore the nature of real things," and he claimed that "real things are not absolute things. Real things are the embodiment of a dictatorial system of coercion which maintains that they are real."[43] While the proceedings dragged on, he impishly produced *oen satsu* (*Zero-Yen Notes*, 1968) and sold them for three hundred yen.[44]

The critics Takiguchi Shūzō, Nakahara Yūsuke, and Haryū Ichirō were called to testify and turned the occasion into a seminar on the nature and premises of art.[45] At trial the High Red Center members reversed their earlier denials and now claimed that their works and public events "are all art,"[46] hoping this might absolve Akasegawa. They created a sensation by demonstrating Takamatsu's ropes, Nakanishi's clothespins, and a great variety of other avant-garde work at a judicial showcase portrayed by the media as a struggle over artistic freedom.[47] Of the thousand-yen note, Akasegawa said, "of course it's a joke, but High Red Center always takes its jokes seriously."[48] In the end none of the exhibits or testimony exculpated Akasegawa: his art was ruled illegal. This reassertion of state authority signaled no new wave of repression, but it confirmed to the avant-garde that the law was on the side of those responsible for imposing a highly conformist, bureaucratically administered society in the 1960s and thereafter.

Anti-art in general and High Red Center's drift toward reproduction art and pop art in particular helped to close off the era of formal experiments exemplified by the Experimental Workshop and the Sōgetsu Art Center. High Red Center also acted as a bridge to another major visual movement of the 1960s, Monoha, which began in 1968. Sekine Nobuo, the dean of Monoha artists, points out that "Takamatsu Jirō, Akasegawa Genpei, and Nakanishi Natsuyuki went in different directions after their High Red Center disbanded in 1964. Takamatsu began to explore reality and nonreality through his *Kage [Shadow]* series of paintings, part of an approach he called 'tricks and vision.' His example had a huge impact on me, and until 1967 my paintings closely resembled Takamatsu's, but I learned from him to follow my own ideas, not his or those from abroad."[49] The novelist Tanizaki Jun'ichirō (1886–1965) often used shadows to represent Japanese culture vis-à-vis the West, but Takamatsu's works suggest something more universal. His *No. 273 (kage)* (1969), for example, invites us to question appearances: it deliberately confuses viewer and image by creating the illusion that the blurry double-vision shadow on the lacquered surface is that of the observer standing in the gallery, backlit by Plato-like unseen sources of light.[50] (See Figure 15.)

Nakanishi reverted to painting after 1964 but also threw himself into avant-garde music and dance. "The composers in Group Ongaku were my friends," he recalled in 2002, and "I also worked with Hijikata Tatsumi at the Asbestos Theater" on productions of Butō.[51] Akasegawa, who also collaborated with Hijikata in the 1960s, understandably grew discouraged once High Red Center ceased and prosecutors obtained an indictment against his art: "The movement for reform which had been amassing during the 1950s boiled over momentarily in this way at the start of the 1960s. But it was completely spent before the decade was halfway through."[52] As a result, Akasegawa "soon lost interest in painting," the art critic Minemura Toshiaki contends. "He had little conceptual ability and was more of an improvisational performer, like Shinohara Ushio. Once he won the Akutagawa Prize for his fiction in 1981, he was beyond all criticism and no longer avant-garde."[53] Still, whatever Akasegawa's limitations as a thinker, his visual works were important steps toward the conceptual art that bloomed in the late 1960s.

Sculpting with New Materials

The same was true of three-dimensional art in the 1960s, although contemporary Japanese sculpture evolved more slowly than oil painting after World War Two, leaving much ground to recoup once the grip of modernism relaxed. By the early twentieth century, Western figuration — above all

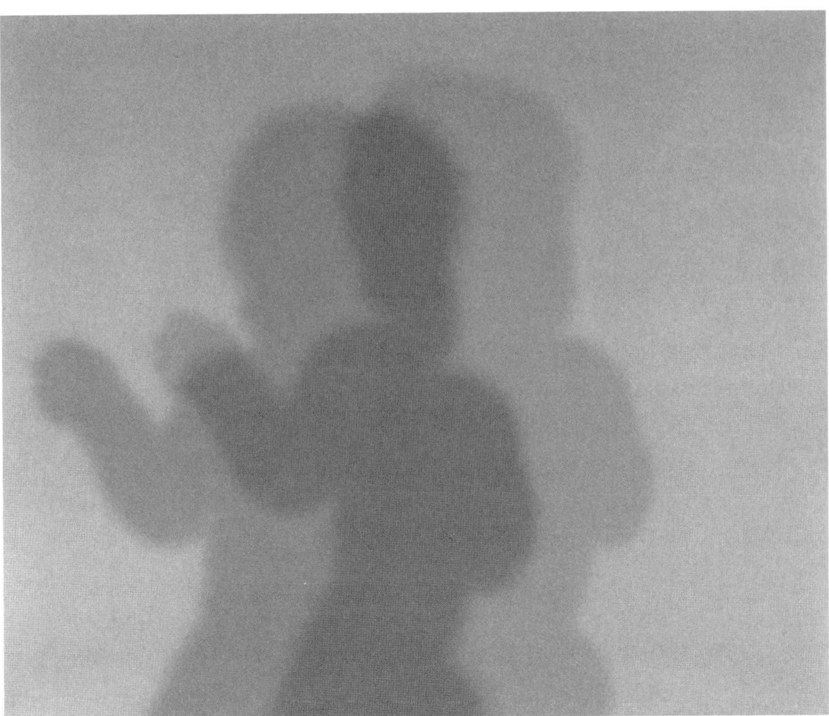

Figure 15. Takamatsu Jirō. *No. 273 (kage)*. 1969. Lacquer on wood. Courtesy National Museum of Modern Art, Tokyo.

the romantic individualism of Auguste Rodin (1840–1917) — overwhelmed the inherited tenets of Buddhist sculpture and Chinese carving among Japan's most innovative artists, of whom the poet-sculptor Takamura Kōtarō (1883–1956) was especially notable. "Japanese sculpture in the 1950s was rather quiet and understated," the museum director Sakai Tadayasu declares, "and it was hard for people to understand. Yet sculpture is the mother of the visual arts, and people are generally sensitive first to sculpture, then to other media."[54] Abstract works of interest were produced during that decade by such artists as Tsuji Shindō, Horiuchi Masakazu (1911–2001), and Nagare Masayuki (1923–). Although Sakai believes "the most important sculptor active in Japan in the 1950s was the American Isamu Noguchi,"[55] the chief international currents flowing into Japan came at first from modern French realism and the even more realistic styles of postwar Italian sculpture.[56] Then in the late 1950s "came a tidal wave from England: first iron sculpture, which was prominent in countries associated with the industrial revolution, then the works of Henry Moore and others."[57]

New materials and new conceptions of space soon gripped the avant-garde, elevating sculpture to echelons of importance that it had not occupied for many decades, in Japan as elsewhere.[58] Industrial and technological development yielded everyday items such as concrete, iron, stainless steel, aluminum, glass, rubber, cloth, and plastics, where wood, marble, and bronze once dominated the artist's choices. As the museum director Takashina Shūji notes, now the texture and color of materials also mattered, not just form and volume.[59] At the same time painting moved closer to sculpture by using rough substances and everyday materials that approached the three-dimensional, and a number of painters ended up experimenting with sculptures. Thanks to the building-construction and art commissions accompanying high-speed economic growth in the 1960s, sculptures were redeployed from cloistered indoor spaces to everyday outdoor locations, especially in city parks and plazas, so that the surroundings became part of the work. The short-lived Contemporary Sculpture Group (Shūdan Gendai Chōkoku, 1960–1962) was founded by Tsutsumi Seiji, Horiuchi Masakazu, Arakawa Shūsaku, Mukai Ryōkichi (1918–), and Tatehata Kakuzō to pursue avant-garde plastic art beyond the bounds of modernism. At its peak it was thirty-eight sculptors strong.[60] Even after it became defunct, individuals from the group exhibited at outdoor symposia and exhibitions that sprang up at Manazuru, Ube City, Kobe, and Hakone beginning in 1963.

Just as small, three-dimensional works that were not formal sculptures came to be called objets after World War Two, larger kinds of three-dimensional modeling were known in the 1960s as open-sided, see-through forms (*rittai zōkei*) that showed "the denial of the sense of weight,"[61] in Miki Tamon's apt phrase. Using such light materials as balsa, aluminum, thin stainless, or plastics, artists constructed abstract sculptures that often seemed temporary and unfinished, without boundaries between interior and exterior space or between materials and daily life. Some seemed merely ornamental and decorative; others evoked the viewer's delight in materiality and shape. The critic Terada Tōru observed that avant-garde Japanese sculptures in the 1960s, including many lightweight, see-through forms, were concerned with human alienation and sardonic social criticism, no longer with glorifying heroes or even the human body.[62] The gallery owner Iino Kiichi added that "the important thing about sculpture since the war is that artists are trying to create dialogue with ordinary people, especially in public, where sculpture is not massive but on the same level and same size as ordinary citizens."[63] Younger sculptors thus turned away from modernist precepts and began using local artifacts to create art, often with a social viewpoint, in everyday places where sculpture had not been seen before.

Okazaki Kazuo (1930–) first showed his iron works at the 1958 Yomiuri

Independent and, at the last Yomiuri show five years later, displayed a construction made of items received in the mail. His iconoclasm toward status boundaries was evident in a solo exhibit at the Tokyo Gallery in 1966 titled *Gyobutsu hoi (Imperial Property)*, which tried to valorize everyday things as worthy of the royals.[64] The European-trained Iida Yoshikuni, who first carved in wood and stone, found himself "drawn to the artificiality and the neutrality of stainless steel. It seemed to me that this material would erase forever the marks of what was personal and individual,"[65] so he worked exclusively in steel after returning to Japan in 1967. Horiuchi Masakazu began experimenting with wire and sheet-metal constructions in 1954 and produced witty sculptures focused on material properties, such as *Entō no nitō bun (Two Half Cylinders*, 1969, bronze), a pair of twisted pieces warily eyeing each other like wrestlers from mutually defensive postures,[66] which can be read as a metaphor for the standoff between state and society amid the tensions of the security treaty and the Vietnam War (see Plate 7). Downplaying both technique and aesthetics, Horiuchi became a key spokesperson for conceptual art in the later 1960s.

Despite the impact of manufactured materials, wood remained a favorite among the vanguard throughout the 1960s. To Iino Kiichi, the local character of such materials was paramount: "Japan is a country of mountains surrounded by water, with a distinctive natural setting of its own, and the best sculpture reflects this distinctiveness rather than mimicking some general international style."[67] One example is Ueki Shigeru, who produced abstract forms in blond woods, usually in multiple linked pieces. Another is Eguchi Shū (1932–), famous since the 1980s for making works from a single tree, who first showed his contemporary wooden sculptures at the Tokyo National Museum of Modern Art in 1963 and, two years later, at the Museum of Modern Art in New York.[68] Recalling the late 1960s, Iida Yoshikuni wrote: "Because I have an instinctive feeling of intimacy with wood, I always felt a vague desire to return to it when I worked with metal. The foundation of my work seems after all to be primary structures, and I would like to try doing them in wood." These words show his devotion to the minimalist principle of primary structure, which creates a space within a space, without boundaries between the work and its surroundings, allowing him "to deal with problems of space in a way which transcends individual consciousness."[69] Soon Iida turned more directly to conceptual art when he met the poet Nishiwaki Junzaburō and created *Chromatopoiema* (1972), which put some of Nishiwaki's English-language verses into shapes and colors[70] — reuniting the verbal and the visual as Abe Kōbō, Okamoto Tarō, and Takiguchi Shūzō had encouraged a quarter century earlier.

An Outburst of Styles

If in the 1960s "all previous assumptions about art were to be put to the test,"[71] the Japanese avant-garde proved to be avid examiners. Nearly every major movement or style of contemporary world art had its counterpart in that country, sometimes among Japanese-style painters as well as artists trained in Western techniques. Although pop art there never became the commodity envisioned by Andy Warhol (1928–1987) or the mirror of mass culture held by Roy Lichtenstein (1923–1997) or Claes Oldenburg (1929–), artists like Yokoo Tadanori, Nakamura Hiroshi, Okamoto Shinjirō (1933–), and Tanikawa Kōichi (1938–) exploited the media-saturated graphics and mass-produced goods of everyday Japanese life in their works without quite mimicking American pop art. Instead, using new technologies of printing and copying, they drew on visual elements from underground dance, theater, film, and popular music in designing works linking ordinary people to their burgeoning consumerist environment.[72] Important as individual artists such as Yoshimura Masunobu and Yokoo Tadanori became, pop art was overshadowed by Neo-Dada and never became "a flourishing movement in Japan," as Haryū Ichirō and many other critics have agreed.[73]

Print making in Japan was likewise transformed by new technologies, including silk screens using photographic plates. One of the most versatile technicians of graphic art was the young print maker and future Geidai professor Noda Tetsuya (1940–), who today is well known to the international art world. Although modern prints by Onchi Kōshirō, Saitō Kiyoshi, and especially Munakata Shikō were favorably regarded abroad, Noda believes that "ever since the Edo period, Japanese critics have looked down on prints. Yet Japanese artists have great skills and produce a wide variety of prints. The 1960s, when I began, were freer for artistic expression than the 1950s."[74] Noda's mixed-media images regularly included his own photographs of everyday scenes, variously using wood-block backgrounds and silk-screen stencils and often incorporating words, phrases, or reproductions of newspapers as conceptual symbols. His prints formed a diary of personal experiences, intimately connected with his daily surroundings.[75]

Minimalism, happenings, and radical theater in the 1960s also cleared paths toward conceptual art and other destinations, some of them blind alleys. Minimalists produced sculptures even less wrought than the lightweight, open-sided constructions of *rittai zōkei*; they minimized the artist's intervention and merely "presented" materials, oftentimes impersonal, industrial objects placed directly on the ground or floor. Their de-emphasis of artistry resembled the chance operations of John Cage and his Japanese colleagues such as Ichiyanagi Toshi. Minimalist sculptures were typically untitled, although seldom anonymous, directing attention to materials drawn from ordinary surroundings, not painted canvases or carved marble from specialized art-supply merchants. Minimalism soon spilled over into painting and print making. An early example was the large lithograph *Mudai (aka)* (*Untitled [Red]*, 1961, silver foil and Japanese paper) by Kuwayama Tadaaki (1932–) executed shortly after he relocated to New York. This work displays an exaggerated H pattern in silver foil against a crimson background, typical of minimalist paintings in its contrast of primary and nonprimary colors.[76] Minimalism gained a toehold in Japan at the beginning of the 1960s but achieved its chief expression, in slightly altered form, through the Monoha group of sculptors starting in 1968, discussed in Chapter 10 below.

The painter Ay-O (Ai Ō, 1931–) provided a pipeline to the Fluxus artists in Manhattan, who were as opposed to the consumer orientation of pop art as they were to the European biases of high modernism. The poet-photographer Yoshimasu Gōzō notes that "the New York-based Fluxus group, led by George Maciunas, had some links to the Neo-Dada group and the playwright Terayama Shūji in Tokyo. But the Japanese avant-garde was more earthy, and stranger. Terayama came from Aomori and shared origins in the northeast region of Japan with Hijikata Tatsumi, who grew up in Akita. Terayama wrote haiku and other forms of poetry, as well as plays. He was as multitalented as Takiguchi Shūzō, but less cerebral and more down to earth."[77] In this fashion minimalism, happenings, Hijikata's underground dance, and the daunting theater staged by Terayama connected with everyday urban culture in ways sharply different from the reproductive techniques of pop art, film, or print makers like Noda. None of these took art theory much beyond the denial of modernism inherent in anti-art at the start of the 1960s, yet collectively their activities, together with the experimental sculpting taking place at the same time, created many small but important breakthroughs in how Japanese regarded art.

"The artists in the 1960s all thought about how we see things, about our ways of looking," says the art critic Minemura Toshiaki. "It was a very thoughtful generation. One of the key gathering spots for their discussions was a Tokyo art-supply store and free exhibition space called the Ogikubo Gallery, especially in 1966–1968."[78] A big topic was conceptualism, which was a slightly contrarian counterpoint to minimalist art both in Japan and abroad. Known in Japan as *gainen geijutsu*, conceptualism drew on the enhanced access to information, images, signs, and other forms of documentation of everyday life that became newly available through electronic and copying technologies in the 1960s. Images and language were seen as interchangeable: the artist thought through an idea and then executed it in art, sometimes almost as an afterthought.[79] Japanese conceptual artists were not a formal group, but most saw themselves as heirs to the Gutai and anti-art movements — as distinct from the Monoha group, which is often labeled "minimalist."[80] But the differences may be minor. The Monoha sculptor Suga Kishio (1944–) believes his own work is consistent with conceptualist principles: "I rejected all previous ideas about art, and yet I was impressed by conceptual art from the United States. But whereas American conceptual art depends on language, Japanese conceptual art means thinking carefully about physical substances and the relations among them. I think a great deal first, then put together my sculptures very fast."[81] Many of Suga's works are geometric relationship studies using simple materials and cannot require much time to assemble. His a priori contemplation is rather different from conceptual art as understood by others.

Kawara On and Arakawa Shūsaku, both resettled in New York by 1961, immersed themselves in conceptualism after 1965, as did the former High Red Center painter Takamatsu Jirō in Japan.[82] Yet the acknowledged pacesetter of Japanese conceptual art was the Waseda-trained architect, Matsuzawa Yutaka, who began writing poetry and also painted a *Mandala* series in the late 1950s and, at the same time, another called *Psi*, the latter often featuring birds in flight.[83] By 1964 he had shifted from using signs to words in his paintings, having found sensate visual expression and tangible materials inadequate for conveying his conception of art, which he henceforth sought in the realm of ideas.[84] The art historian Okabayashi Hiroshi locates much of Matsuzawa's thinking in Suwa, Nagano prefecture, particularly the shrine there, but he also acknowledges Matsuzawa's claim that he chose the mandala as "the handiest shape for thinking about the structure of the universe" and that the *Psi* series was partly inspired by Heisenberg's unproven equations regarding uncertainty.[85] Perhaps it is safest to see Matsuzawa as a searcher for artistic truth in word and thought rather than in concrete works, whereas Suga Kishio and many others produced their art by moving sequentially from concepts to physical objects.

WITH THE SUCCESSIVE FIREWORKS launched by High Red Center, new sculptural designs, pop art, minimalism, and conceptual art, it is no surprise that among progressive artists, "until the late seventies, painting experienced a long cold winter, during which the word 'painting' became virtually unmentionable,"[86] as the art historian Reiko Tomii has written. Abstract and figurative painters, as well as those in natural pigments, continued to create large numbers of works that enjoyed far more commercial than critical success. International subgenres such as color-field painting, postpainterly abstraction, hard edge, and optical art found small followings in Japan, and a good deal of indigenously generated contemporary art appeared as well.[87]

Meanwhile the standoff between idea and praxis persisted. On the one hand were clusters such as the Jikanha (Time School), which took a new look at time as an element in art. As Akasegawa Genpei noted: "The Jikanha was an intellectual group. Whereas the Neo-Dada, Kyushuha, and Zero Dimension groups tended to rely on art theory for ideas about destroying present-day reality, the Jikanha purged parasite elements in art theory from abroad."[88] On the other hand were organizations such as the nine-member Group Kurai (Group Situation), which worked from practice (motorcycles, beds, small daily-use items) to theory in almost direct opposition to Matsuzawa's conceptual art.[89]

Environmental art, led by Yamaguchi Katsuhiro and Isozaki Arata, had its season starting in September 1966 with an exhibit on space and color at the Minami Gallery in Tokyo. As practiced in Japan, environmental art also became known as "multimedia" or "intermedia" art and relied heavily on technology: moving objects, sounds, and lights, ostensibly anticipating the upcoming world exposition of science and industry (Banpaku) scheduled for Osaka in 1970.[90] High tech triumphed when the Sony building at Sukiyabashi, Tokyo, held an international ultratechnological art show without reference to environmentalism in April 1969[91] — a year that was almost the nadir of industrial pollution in Japan. Kinetic sculptures, especially ones fabricated from stainless steel, sprouted in Japan no less frequently than elsewhere. Three-dimensional stainless-steel works with polished mirrored surfaces reflected the natural and built surroundings, extending the principle of relating the sculpture to its whereabouts.[92]

These and other experiments with light, sound, and image, sometimes aided by computers, verified that Takiguchi's exhortations to innovate, Okamoto's encouragements to go against the canon, and Yoshihara's precepts about doing art unimagined by others had been taken to heart during the 1960s, often in unexpected ways, by both the Shōwa single-digit avant-garde and their slightly younger successors. By the end of the decade, in Japan as abroad, the political, social, and environmental context of cultural production had come to define a work of art even more than the formal considerations associated with modernism.[93] The alternative modernity of the local and the everyday was now widely, although not universally, distributed throughout the many varieties of Japanese visual culture, much of it ridiculing the homogeneity of middle-class existence and some of it attaining outright political heterodoxy.

chapter eight

*Contemporary Art Music
and Dance in the 1960s*
Transcultural Idioms

Japanese composers of art music and choreographers of contemporary dance in the 1960s redrew their creative boundaries by forsaking modernist abstractions, reaching out instead to avant-garde collaborators around the world with one hand and to their concrete local environments with the other. Having played catch-up with contemporary Western dance and music in the 1950s, progressive Japanese composers and choreographers during the next decade began to set aside European and North American patterns, producing a range of denationalized works that were at once transcultural and yet locally positioned. Speaking in 2002, Ichiyanagi Toshi explained how this creative process, far from reverting at a stroke to an essentialized Japanese métier, was instead a methodological amalgam spanning many years:

> Nearly all composers of contemporary music in Japan since 1950 started by writing Western-style works, partly because Western music dominated musical education and partly because of the general cultural prestige of Europe. Only in the 1960s did we begin to understand the importance of traditional Japanese and Asian arts. We began to look at the East Asian arts through our Western-trained eyes, using Western logic and analytical approaches to help identify the concepts behind our indigenous arts. Without Western methods, it would be impossible to find the principles inherent in the East Asian arts, because when you study a traditional instrument or visual medium, you merely imitate the teacher, not question the underlying rules. Traditional teaching uses no words; Western training gives us the words with which to understand East Asian concepts. So one has to go through Western culture to understand East Asia. This was not possible fifty years ago.[1]

Ichiyanagi and his fellow vanguard composers in the 1960s freely employed Western musical vocabulary to write alternative music that was thoroughly contemporary — usually antimodernist, sometimes outright post-Western — and also grounded in the specific musical culture of their everyday environment, without dreams of cultural difference, let alone conscious nativist intent. Such bridging propensities began with the Goat Society in the 1950s and matured through interplay between Japanese Hōgaku and Western music a decade later. The same held true for classical Japanese and contemporary dance forms in the 1960s. These homegrown and foreign styles never achieved the same degree of rapprochement, in either compositional or performative technique, that marked postwar Nihonga and oil painting, but the transcultural interactions produced vast registers of intriguing music and dance about which critics still disagree.

The Goat Society: People's Music

While the marquee composers Akutagawa Yasushi, Mayuzumi Toshirō, and Dan Ikuma were establishing their well-financed Three-Person Society in 1953, three other avant-garde musicians with modest backgrounds and leftist outlooks formed a similar musical organization, the Goat Society (Yagi no Kai, active 1953–1958). The founders, Hayashi Hikaru (see Figure 16), Mamiya Michio, and Toyama Yūzō (1931–), were members of the Shōwa single-digit generation without overseas experience. They were eager to produce a nonmodernist people's music *(minzoku ongaku)* combining themes from Japanese folk songs with the style of Russian ethnic music, sometimes yielding "very inferior" results.[2] Paralleling the Communist Party's focus on the Japanese as a racial group, the Goat Society resembled the Energy art association and Abe Kōbō's Contemporary Association, both dating to 1952, in seeking freedom for ordinary people under reconstituted conservative rule amid the cold war (see Chapter 1).

Hayashi, Mamiya, and Toyama first gathered in the fall of 1953 in a two-story wood-frame building at Shin Ōkubo station on the northern fringes of Shinjuku, near the future site of the Neo-Dada group's White House in Hyakuninchō, to discuss poetry, plan concerts, and write music. "Like goats, we consumed lots of paper — the five-line kind for scores," Hayashi noted in an autobiography.[3] Although they worried about American cultural hegemony and talked a good deal about socialist realism, the three were mainly attracted to contemporary Russian composers and the avant-garde music of Central Europe. They also admired Mao Zedong's ideas on literature, science, and history. Most important, Hayashi recalled in 1978, was that "to

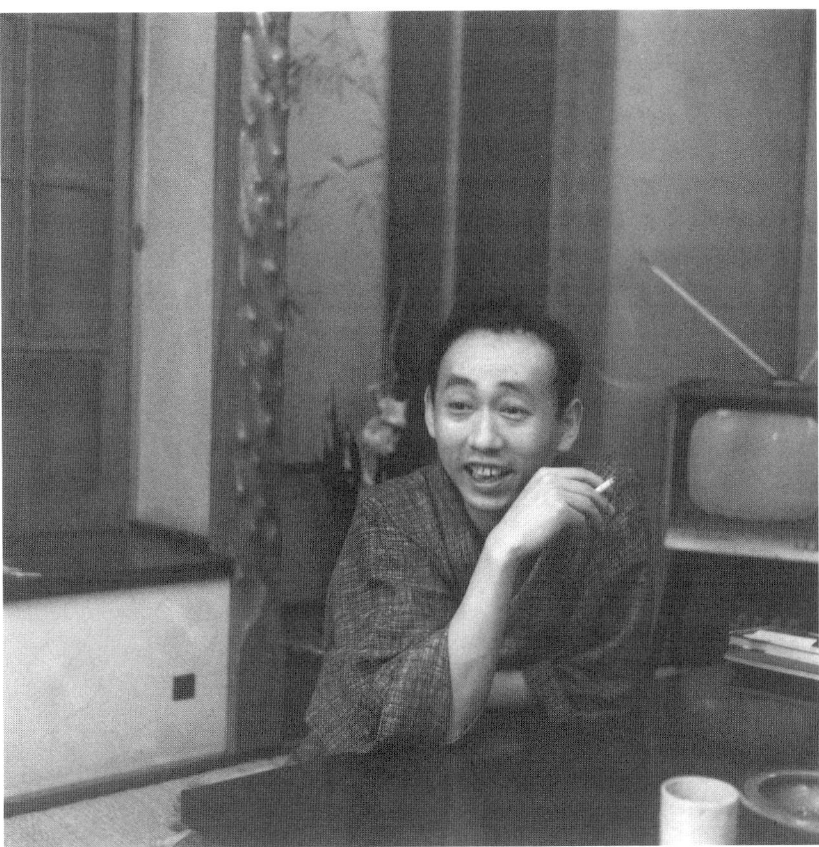

Figure 16. Hayashi Hikaru, composer. 1965. Courtesy Kyōdō Tsūshinsha.

us, people's music was less a matter of style than of attitude." In the vortex of Soviet-American tensions and the recent Korean War, "we sought to hoist our political agenda" to promote people's autonomy as the backbone of postwar democracy.[4] Looking back in 2002, Hayashi said: "The Yagi no Kai was somewhat nationalistic in the sense of *minzokushugi* [racial or people's nationalism], but not statism or patriotism. We were like the Russian composers of ethnic music. Our work was half socially focused on folk music and half experimentally focused on musical composition."[5] Toyama, who is best known today as a conductor, incorporated folk melodies extensively into his works across four decades.[6] Hayashi and especially Mamiya also drew on folk rhythms, literature, folklore, and children's themes in their predominantly vocal compositions.

Hayashi has been the most socially engaged of the postwar composers in Japan, as well as one of the most versatile and prolific.[7] Among his many interests in the 1950s and 1960s were Western and Japanese operatic styles, Japanese theater and poetry, and the folk music of Okinawa. Hayashi studied Western-style composition at Tokyo University of Fine Arts and Music (Geidai) from 1951 to 1953, then dropped out to make a living in music, including writing early works for stage and film. He took part in cultural diplomacy with the People's Republic of China arranged during the Hundred Flowers Movement in 1957: his ballet *Hakumōjo* (White-haired woman, 1955) was performed by the Matsuyama company during a tour of China amid the Great Leap Forward in 1958.[8]

Hayashi has written more than one hundred pieces for orchestras, ensembles, and solo instruments, several hundred vocal works, and scores for at least 130 films, yet the composition for which he is probably best known is *Genbaku shōkei* (*Little Landscapes of Hiroshima*, 1958–2001). He produced the first part, "Mizu o kudasai" ("Give Me Water"), when he was twenty-seven and finished the last, "Towa no midori" ("Eternal Green"), when he was sixty-nine: "I have been writing it, that is, for virtually my entire life as a composer,"[9] perhaps unwilling or unable to let go of it until the apex of his career. "I became interested in writing music about Hiroshima starting in 1950, when I began reading the poetry of Hara Tamiki [1905–1951] in journals such as *Mita bungaku*. I was also quite interested in poems by Tōge Sankichi [1917–1953]. I knew both their names through the peace movement, but I never met either of them before their deaths," Hayashi recounted in 2002.[10]

When the time came for Hayashi to compose his Hiroshima work, Mamiya and Toyama helped him choose appropriate poems by Hara and Tōge. Tanikawa Shuntarō, another poet with whom Hayashi occasionally collaborated, also advised him about the project at a summer resort in Kita Karuizawa.[11] The sections of *Genbaku shōkei* vary tonality (1958) with mixed atonal and tone clusters (1971), then tonality again (2001), but Hayashi says "their spiritual contents have remained constant throughout."[12] In some ways Hayashi could be seen as an early postcolonial composer. The conductor Iwaki Hiroyuki, who led the Tokyo Philharmonic Chorus in a riveting performance of "Mizu o kudasai" at the new Daiichi Hall in Kachidoki on March 20, 2002,[13] says: "Hayashi was very moved by the suicide of Hara Tamiki [March 13, 1951, on the Chūō line west of Nishi Ogikubo] and was inspired to write 'Mizu o kudasai.' When it was finished in 1958, NHK refused to broadcast it, out of concern not to offend the Americans. It was as though Japan was still semi-occupied by the U.S. Army."[14]

The first concert by the Goat Society in 1953, however, presented completely uncontroversial works by Mamiya Michio. Known today as a seasoned scholar of musical folklore as well as a prolific composer, Mamiya was trained in Western music at Geidai during 1949–1952. "In the early 1950s," he recalls, "I focused entirely on European music, above all Bartók's works evoking the folk tunes of Hungarian farmers and the Hungarian ballads and folk songs of Zoltán Kodály [1882–1967]. Then, starting in 1955, the researcher Uchida Ruriko and I began studying folk songs from all over Japan, with the help of NHK's extensive archive of folk music at its old Uchisaiwaichō offices, built up partly at the behest of the folklorist Yanagita Kunio [1875–1962]."[15] The oldest recordings there dated only to the early 1940s, but "because I grew up in Aomori, I knew the tunes from the northeast best. I then researched music all over the country, short of Okinawa, and learned that there were something like four or five thousand folk songs extant in Japan. Some have since been lost, especially from rural areas."[16] Between 1955 and 1965 Mamiya composed the piano accompaniment for five series of songs, using folk themes of his invention based on the rhythms and nostalgic verses he found throughout Japan, including many associated with local rites and festivals. The purest, he found, were work songs and other ditties associated with daily life, especially those with "a great simple roughness."[17]

Mamiya began writing choral works using elements of folk songs in 1958, the year he won a Mainichi music prize for *Gasshō no tame no konpojishon daiichiban* (*Composition No. 1 for Chorus*, 1958), which is still played in arrangements for men's, mixed, and children's voices with various accompaniments. Structural elements of folk songs even appeared in his orchestral, chamber, and instrumental works, as well as in his scores for stage, film, and television.[18] Mamiya said in 1975 that his aim throughout was to develop "a new Japanese language of music based on the musical heritage of ordinary people,"[19] a course he was still pursuing at the end of the century. But long before, "in the 1960s, I branched out to African, Scandinavian, and other world folk musics. I discovered parallels between folk songs from Lapland and those of the Ainu. I also studied the oral traditions, both literary and musical, of American Indians and Eskimos,"[20] incorporating these into his compositions as well. He also showed a high regard for the supposedly authentic, precontinental Jōmon era, in concert with artists such as Okamoto Tarō, Isamu Noguchi, and Teshigahara Sōfū.

Immersed though Mamiya was in the folk music of ordinary Japanese, his approach was more adaptational than preservationist, creatively evoking folk rhythms and melodies rather than simply replicating them. Nor was he a romantic with accompaniment: far from insisting on Japanese Hōgaku instrumentation, he wrote primarily for piano and other Western instruments. The same was true of his orchestral and chamber music during the 1950s and 1960s. When he composed for combined instrumentation, the result was syncretistic. For example, Mamiya's *Hachimen no koto to shitsunai ōkesutora no tame no kyōsōkyoku* (*Concerto for Eight Kotos and Chamber Orchestra*, 1957), scored for eight kotos, two flutes, oboe, bassoon, cello, double bass, four violas, and percussion, was first performed on a Bunka Hōsō radio broadcast in November 1957. Mamiya said idealistically of this work, "The separation of these two genres, Hōgaku and Western, is gradually eradicated, and they must become a single entity." He added, "We can avoid many pitfalls if we can think of both Hōkagu and Western-style music as sharing the common problem of addressing the music of Japan, establishing conditions in which we can speak of them in the same language."[21] Mamiya's vision of conflating Hōgaku and Western instruments to express musical idioms based on local folk songs differed radically from Takemitsu Tōru's method a decade later in his well-known *November Steps* (1967), where a biwa (lute) and shakuhachi (flute) were juxtaposed and alternated, but not combined, with a Western-style orchestra.

Hōgaku and Contemporary Japanese Art Music

Mamiya's bold move to establish equivalence by blending Japanese and Western instruments may have been suitable for his folk-based material, but few other avant-garde composers followed in his wake, even during the so-called Hōgaku boom of the 1960s, when a number of them wrote contemporary music for native instruments alone. Using biwa, koto, and shakuhachi made such works no less contemporary, but Takahashi Yūji points out a basic constraint on the composer: "In Japanese traditional music culture in general, all the instruments were considered as percussion" — even tapping the finger holes on a flute or stroking the koto strings.[22] At heart Hōgaku and Western music are incompatible "sonic treasures,"[23] representing "equally logical but different systems," as the musicologist William P. Malm puts it,[24] ruling out true hybridity.

Historically Japanese music was subordinate to verse, which was sung to instrumental accompaniment. Works for ensembles were linear, percussive, and disjunctive, making ample use of spaces between sounds, with instruments entering at different intervals.[25] The result, according to Takahashi, is that "timing, color, posture and coordination are constantly and intentionally made to float."[26] Since antiquity Hōgaku relied on a headmaster system of instruction permitting variation but little innovation. In modern times Japanese musicians, almost always trained on Western instruments, have found it hard to master native music: it is just as unnatural for them as for the foreign students, mainly from the West, who have been partly responsible for keeping Hōgaku alive in recent decades. Only in 2002 did the Ministry of Education require public junior-high schools to teach at least one Japanese instrument, but it will probably be a decade or more before this mandate can be met.[27]

Yamada Kōsaku pioneered the use of Hōgaku instruments in his Western-style compositions as early as 1917. His landmark *Kōkyō nagautagaku tsuru-kame* (*Congratulatory Music for Song and Orchestra*, 1934) mixed traditional song, samisen, and Western-style ensemble.[28] Efforts began in the 1920s among koto artists to bring Hōgaku closer to European music through a movement known as New Japanese Music (Shin Nihon Ongaku), led by Miyagi Michio (1894–1956). Contemporary Hōgaku (Gendai Hōgaku) dates to experiments by koto players shortly after World War Two. It was institutionalized in 1957 when the Hōgaku Quartet (Hōgaku Yonin no Kai) became the first of several groups to present concerts of both traditional music and new works by contemporary Western-style composers written for koto, shakuhachi, and samisen. Many of the latter sounded "somehow European in style," the critic Sano Kōji and others believe.[29] But the avant-garde composer Moroi Makoto, who wrote forty pieces for the Hōgaku Quartet, observes that "shakuhachi and electronic music both use glissando and have other similarities, so it was easy to compose contemporary Hōgaku for Japanese instruments. Both electronic and Hōgaku music use interesting noises. I liked the relative formlessness of contemporary Hōgaku, although after 1964 I composed both it and contemporary Western-style music"[30] — in the aggregate, an idiom temporally current and spatially local: contemporary Japanese music.

Until the versatile avant-garde composer Mayuzumi Toshirō began to pay attention to Hōgaku in the late 1950s, Chōki Seiki argues, "most composers of contemporary music scorned Hōgaku because of its nationalistic associations with wartime. Because they were trained in Western music, when they turned to Hōgaku in the 1960s, they did so with entirely fresh eyes, causing quite a shock" even among the Hōgaku reformers.[31] Near the end of the decade the government allowed ensembles to use Heian-period instruments from the Shōsōin imperial storehouse in Nara for performances of contemporary Hōgaku, sometimes juxtaposed with huge harps. The National Theater, which opened at Miyakezaka, Tokyo, in 1966, began commissioning contemporary composers to write Hōgaku music to be played on these ancient instruments.[32]

Another stimulus for renewed interest in Hōgaku came from abroad: the composers John Cage, Olivier Messiaen, Karlheinz Stockhausen, and Lou Harrison (1917–2003) showed the same respect for Japanese aesthetics as had Mark Tobey, Sam Francis, and other visual artists a few years earlier. When

Cage, in particular, expressed admiration for Hōgaku, Japanese composers of contemporary music began to notice its current possibilities — as did programmers at NHK, Bunka Hōsō, and government-aided arts events.[33] Cage overcame the differences in rhythm between Western music and Hōgaku by setting aside European notions of timing and introducing moments of quiet. Hirose Ryōhei (1930–) reflected Cage's chance operations in *Konpojishon daiichiban (heki)* (*Composition No. 1 [thunder]*, 1964), scored for three shakuhachi, two violins, viola, and cello, as did a number of Moroi's Hōgaku works. This reliance on indeterminate music unquestionably helped to bring Japanese composers closer to the international mainstream in the late 1960s.[34]

Yet if many of the works written for Japanese instruments by contemporary composers still sounded like Western music, Mayuzumi did the reverse: his well-known *gidayū* (instrumental narrative) *Bunraku* (1960), for cello rather than samisen, amounted to Hōgaku for a Western instrument,[35] blurring both stylistic and technical provenance. Takemitsu, in contrast, used biwa and shakuhachi in his score for the film *Seppuku* (1962), directed by Kobayashi Masaki (1916–1996), developing themes he later adapted in *November Steps* (1967). During this brief period of affinity with Cage's ideas, Takemitsu also composed *Biwa uta (Biwa Song)* for Japanese instruments, using Hōgaku notation, for Kobayashi's movie *Kaidan* (1964), At the same time, certain Hōgaku composers took their cues from Hirose and Moroi: they avidly studied Western music and formed ensembles including such instruments as organ, timpani, and harpsichord to perform new works derived from Japanese musical precedents.[36]

How far these courteous handshakes between genres reached in the direction of genuine crossovers, let alone outright fusions, is questionable. Gendai Hōgaku lost its vigor by the late 1960s, to the delight of essentialist critics such as Koizumi Fumio, who called the movement incapable of "comprehending the true beauty of Japan."[37] The progressive writer Komiya Tamie said it was hard to see by 1970 that Hōgaku had "done much to modernize itself."[38] Meanwhile Mamiya Michio's dream of creating a common language for Japan's art music seemed to have vanished when confronted by the juggernaut of popular music. In contrast to the boom in art Hōgaku during the 1960s, only folk Hōgaku thrives today, thanks to the appeal of folk songs, Taiko drumming, and Tsugaru samisen stirred by NHK and nationwide contests starting in the 1970s.[39]

Still, the success of Moroi's works for the Hōgaku Yonin no Kai and of Takemitsu's *Biwa uta,* with their conventional Hōgaku phrasing, opened fresh fields for contemporary composers trained entirely in Western music. Ichiyanagi

Toshi explained in 2002 how Hōgaku ideas gave performers of his works more latitude:

> Europeans see music as the art of time, painting as the art of space. In the traditional East Asian arts, time and space interpenetrate each other. Yet for a time after World War Two, even shakuhachi players developed a Western sense of timing, because music education in the schools was Western. They also felt an inferiority complex toward the West, which is too bad. I'm trying to promote what we didn't have before [in the 1950s and 1960s]: to bring the idea of space into my music. By this I mean not just physical space — the arrangement of the performers on the stage or the use of strolling musicians — but something more fundamental in context: making each performer freer and more independent. This may have been common in traditional musical concerts in the past.[40]

Starting in 1966 with *Shichuēshon (Situation)* for biwa, koto, violin, bass, and piano, Ichiyanagi implemented this project by writing at least forty-eight works using Japanese instruments through 1998, the year he published his book *Ongaku to iu itonami* (The music business).[41]

Yuasa Jōji likewise discovered in Hōgaku ways of thought and perception not available to him in Western music:

> So then I found compensating techniques to express Japanese ideas of time and space. I didn't need a pentatonic scale or traditional instruments; instead I turned to the structure of Japanese ideas and feelings about time and space. Even using Western instruments and electronic music, I can develop these traditional ideas. *Ma* is best understood as "timing and spacing." Silence is not static or vacant but has intensity. Spacing is like the constant gap between moving kendo swords, called *maai*, or the interval between moving elements in a kinetic sculpture by Alexander Calder.[42]

Yuasa also extended Ichiyanagi's perspective beyond time and space to the timbre, gesture, language, and breathing found in Hōgaku. He maintained that timbre was more important than in a harmonic system because Hōgaku does not differentiate sound from noise. Likewise gestures such as shifts in pitch and tempo support the melodic line. Language expressed in sound, such as the onomatopoeia and tone of voice in the "N to n" section of his *Toi* (1971), creates a paraverbal structure of communication. Rhythms in Hōgaku, he found, are based on "mental breathing" similar to breath and time in both classical Japanese dance and Nō drama.[43] Yuasa may have felt little outright need to use five-tone scales or Hōgaku instruments, but he ended up writing seven works for koto, shakuhachi, and other instruments between 1967 and 1990.

Although the label "ethnic" scarcely fits him, overseas critics often classified Takemitsu as a "Japanese" composer, particularly once Leonard Bernstein and the New York Philharmonic commissioned *November Steps* to commemorate the orchestra's 125th anniversary. After its 1967 premiere, Seiji Ozawa (Ozawa Seiji) recorded this bravura romantic symphony the following year with the Toronto Symphony Orchestra; it briefly rose to third best–selling classical LP album in the United States.[44] *November Steps* alternated Western and Japanese instruments without any attempt to integrate them. "I will keep the ongoing status of my work together," Takemitsu wrote in 1971, "not by resolving the contradictions between the two traditions but by highlighting the contradictions and confronting them."[45] He said, "I must not be trapped by traditional instruments any more than by all other kinds." He sought "to make a living order" of his own, drawing on but not uniting "the fundamentally different musical phenomena of the West and Japan."[46] In developing his quest for a "stream of sounds," Takemitsu used the tone color, timbre, and sound contrasts he found in Hōgaku but without incorporating Japanese scales, melodies, or structural elements, let alone folk or pop music.[47] By liberating sounds and silences from the precision of Western notation, Takemitsu moved toward an unbounded transcultural realm where "it falls to the composer to deal with the real thoughts and emotions of his time."[48]

Even during the 1950s, composers of contemporary music such as Mayuzumi Toshirō (with *Nirvana*, 1958), Hayasaka Fumio, and especially Dan Ikuma occasionally turned to other Asian musics for alternatives to their rigorous Western training. Hayasaka, who wrote mostly film scores between the end of World War Two and his death in 1955 at age forty-one, believed that contemporary composers should use Pan-Asian themes to thwart the dominance of Western music. Takahashi Yūji, born twenty-four years after Hayasaka, similarly turned to Asian musics as alternatives to contemporary Western-style composing. Takahashi began using Hōgaku instruments in his works only well after "it became fashionable to write for traditional instruments in the 1960s."[49] He did so not to recapture an earlier musical consciousness but to repudiate modernism and its globalizing tendencies. He decried the fact that "modern notation" from the West "has been the master plan to be realized."[50] Speaking in 2002, Takahashi maintained:

> We composers began using Asian instruments because they opened up alternatives to modern music, not because of some renewed interest in traditionalism. Instruments from Japan, China, and Southeast Asia offer a different approach to how you use your body in producing sound. This bodily discipline is found also in dance and calligraphy. The importance of Asian musics to us composers

is precisely that there is no unity in the Asian tradition, no single Asian musical value. Modernism began with the Renaissance and terminates in globalism, in which Western instruments and composing methods become uniform, universal norms. Against this tendency, we composers in Asia seek diversity; we seek alternatives to the globalization found in modernism. Various places in Asia such as China and Thailand open up manifold possibilities. This is Asia's contribution to world music.[51]

Here Takahashi brushes aside any hint that, when they tapped into Hōgaku and other Asian musics, Japanese composers were propelled by rearward-looking "ideological notions," indeed romanticized visions, "about the continuity of great traditions."[52] Asian music was not a trapdoor for escaping Western musical hegemony by rushing back to a static and exceptionalist past. Instead the music of Asia, including Hōgaku, staked out a forward path, beyond the concrete universals of modernism, toward the local and contemporary musical environment of their everyday surroundings. If Takahashi and his colleagues seemed to be reversing Fukuzawa Yukichi's 1885 dictum "Shed Asia, Join Europe" (*datsua nyūō*), the Asia they embraced was current, dynamic, and diverse, just as eligible to inform contemporary music as other world regions.

It is easy to come away from a concert of works by Takemitsu, Ichiyanagi, Yuasa, or other similar artists and feel convinced that they use Hōgaku as one of several ways to express thoroughly contemporary musical ideas — often with a firm sense of locale but also a broad transcultural reach. When Japanese composers trained in Western techniques discovered Hōgaku in the late 1950s and 1960s, they retained their contemporary, avant-garde bearings without succumbing to the "return to Japan" phenomenon their intellectual forebears often underwent a half century earlier. The comparative-literature scholar Hirakawa Sukehiro notes that before 1940 "many Japanese writers' returns to Japan from a real or spiritual pilgrimage to the West seem to follow a psychological pattern"[53] of first seeking the fantasized Other, then yearning for Japan and its "traditions" (often partly fabricated). Such was seldom true of Japanese artists, in any genre, after World War Two.

What established their authority as composers was not a rediscovery of a local artistic tradition but their skill at expressing musical ideas of multiple origins through techniques that combined particularity and universality. Thus, just as there is no one Japanese jazz,[54] there is no single contemporary music that can be called Japanese, but instead an astonishing variety of works written by a highly skilled cadre of composers. Here the limits of postcolonial analysis are revealed: few artists slipped into the cultural essentialism to which postcolonialism is susceptible, nor did they succumb to the postcolonial snare of failing "to understand the importance of difference" in place, as Andrew Gordon has written.[55]

Nevertheless Miyake Haruna, who like Takahashi belongs to the slightly younger Shōwa double-digit age group, correctly points out that "Japan has less diversity of viewpoints than abroad. There is a standard model contemporary composers are expected to follow — for a long time Takemitsu defined the model. But in my way of thinking, contemporary music is me. I'm creating it for myself, not to meet some outside standard." She adds, "whereas some people say contemporary music shows a Japanese sensibility, I think it's pretty international. My own work is a bit different from that of my contemporaries trained in Japan, partly because it expresses my own individual nature but also because of the stimulating atmosphere of Juilliard in the 1960s."[56] Yet perhaps Yuasa speaks best for the whole generation of avant-garde composers in the 1950s and 1960s when he shrugs off any real conflict between Hōgaku and Western music: "I define my own identity as based on Japanese culture while, at the same time, maintaining a global point of view as a human being on this planet."[57]

New Dance Routines

Of all the avant-garde arts, contemporary dance and performance art gave their Japanese practitioners the widest scope to define themselves in the context of everyday life, dealing with the realities of living in the tangible matrix of daily interaction with other people. Vanguard choreographers in the 1960s felt the same tugs toward the indigenous classical métier as many contemporary composers felt toward Hōgaku, usually with the same result: juxtaposition, not synthesis, pointing in new directions rather than retracing steps to an imagined past. Both Nihon Buyō (classical Japanese dance) and ballet underwent progressive phases in the 1960s, but the most innovative choreography took shape in three zones of human movement: (1) modern (not necessarily modernist) dance in the style of Martha Graham and Doris Humphrey (1895–1958), known as Modan Dansu; (2) antimodernist or vanguard dance inspired by Trisha Brown (1936–) and Simone Forti (1939–), called Gendai or Zen'ei Buyō; and (3) Gendai or Ankoku Butō, the underground dance of darkness that developed in the 1960s. Artists in each of these zones exhibited a great deal of choice and imagination in the movement they expressed on the stage, approaching the creative freedom posited by mid-century existentialism.

An important stimulus prompting new balletic styles in the 1960s was

generational change, even more than conscious resistance to the modernism found in Western dance theater. Ballet reformers were also affected
by the explosion of contemporary dance, much of it antimodernist, taking
place in Japan at the same time. The result, says the dance historian Yamano
Hakudai, was that "the United States lost the ballet battle with the Soviets
for Japanese audiences in 1957–1958 but won the dance war, thanks to the
impact of the New York City Ballet on choreographers plus visits by American contemporary dancers who streamed into Japan for performances in
the 1960s. It was especially impressive to see black dancers, so that Japanese
could realize ballet wasn't only for white people and thus was something they
could learn."[58]

Except for the traditionalist Tchaikovsky Memorial Tokyo Ballet Company
(founded in 1964), the major ensembles that dominated Japanese ballet for
the rest of the century all sponsored experimental choreography as well as
more orthodox Western productions. The Matsuyama troupe (1948) mod-
eled some of its fresh work on contemporary Chinese theater, whereas the
newer Maki Asami company (1963) relied extensively on the choreography of
its prima ballerina, Tachibana Akiko, who was Maki's mother and a devotee
of Soviet dance. Star Dancers Ballet, founded in 1964 by the prima Tachikawa Ruriko, was the most inventive of the top companies and often reflected
the choreography of Anthony Tudor. Some of the creative choreography, like
certain contemporary-music composing at the time, drew on folk dancing
or other familiar elements in the indigenous arts. From the start the Maki
Asami group staged new works based on Japanese literary themes, as did
the Matsuyama company in numbers such as *Gion matsuri* (*Gion Festival*,
1963).[59]

Classical Japanese choreography also underwent spasms of renewal in the
1960s, somewhat resembling the contemporary Hōgaku composers who were
writing experimental music for Western instruments at the same time. Fresh
works of Nihon Buyō started to be written for ensembles as well as soloists,
vaguely mimicking a corps de ballet. Certain classical-dance choreographers, including Hanayagi Shigeka and Hanayagi Teruna, began working
with counterparts in contemporary dance and sometimes presented "underground" Japanese-style dance at the avant-garde citadel JeanJean in Shibuya.
Hanayagi Chiyo, employing the Graham method, taught her Nihon Buyō
students basic movements before launching them into complete dances,
flouting the centuries-old custom of transmitting a dance tradition intact.[60]
Still, the results of these innovations fell far short of a formal movement comparable to the Hōgaku Yonin no Kai's efforts to refresh Japanese-style music.

By the 1970s both creative ballet and contemporary Nihon Buyō had spent their force, abandoning the stage to more time-honored forms of the "classical" (actually nineteenth-century) versions of each genre.

Somewhat like contemporary musical composition a few years earlier, much of the contemporary-dance choreography in 1960 was still patterned after Western models, but by the end of the decade artists in every zone of dance performance were grappling with current questions of everyday life in their immediate context. In doing so, they put brakes on the tendency to abuse the dancer's body, as in ballet, and insisted instead on what the contemporary choreographer Akiko Kanda called "knowing your own body."[61] After five years' training in New York, including two as a top dancer with the Martha Graham Dance Company, Kanda returned to Tokyo in 1961 to teach and perfect her choreography. Like her mentor, she turned to classical antiquity, both in the Mediterranean and East Asia, as well as to her everyday surroundings for ideas to express in her compositions. After a solo version of *Four Seasons* in October 1969, for example, Kanda drew on Nō and kabuki, accordion music, chansons, and later Chinese instruments as accompaniments.

Even more physical, and amusing, than Kanda was the Osaka choreographer Hanayagi Suzushi (1928–), who returned in 1967 from six years' study in the United States to put on experimental farces spoofing *Swan Lake* and other entertaining celebrations of movement for its own sake, without creating any alternative meaning, reminiscent of the street events of the Neo-Dada group at the beginning of the decade. All that she and her company revealed were seemingly random actions at a certain place with particular people: the dancer crawling, singing, staring, mugging at a bystander, sticking her tongue out at him.[62] Suzushi claimed that there was nothing memorable about what was seen except the routine passage of time; all that endured was the tangible movement of the female body across the flow of unimportant everyday occurrences.[63]

Another innovative choreographer who studied in New York in the 1960s was Ishii Kaoru (1942–), who was the first Japanese dancer to win a Fulbright fellowship. Ishii enrolled at Juilliard during 1964–1966, overlapping there for one year with the composer Miyake Haruna. "The choreographers I worked with at Juilliard and at Connecticut College in the summers, such as Anthony Tudor, Martha Graham, and José Limón, were extraordinarily free and imaginative," Ishii recalled in 2002. She quickly decided to ignore the career pattern expected back home: "I found out that in America it was common for female dancers to have families, whereas in Japan they weren't expected to marry. I realized dance should connect with people's real lives, so I got

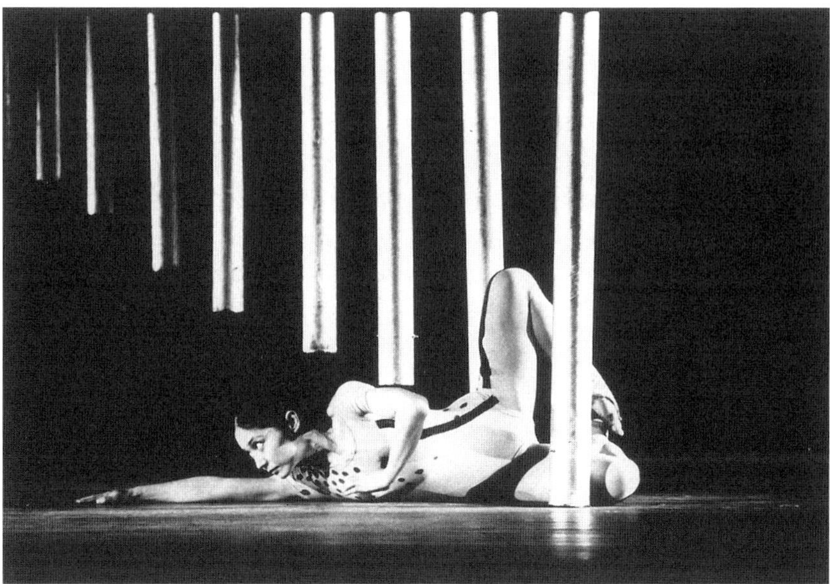

Figure 17. Ishii Kaoru performing her *Composition V*, Toranomon Hall, Tokyo. March 1969. Courtesy Ishii Kaoru.

married and continued my choreography."[64] In 1968 Ishii, who collaborated with many avant-garde composers as well as the poet Tanikawa Shuntarō, portrayed "abnormality and grotesque beauty" in her *Zamuzara*, based on Kafka's *Metamorphosis*, at the underground Jiyū Gekijō in the Roppongi section of Tokyo. Her major work of the decade, *Composition V*, was staged the same year at venerable Toranomon Hall, accompanied by two ensembles led by two conductors, separated by a sound mixer in the center. Ishii says: "This work was inspired by my love of aquariums. The performers unfolded their arms and legs like a crab, stretching out to communicate with one another and with the audience."[65] (See Figure 17.)

Distinct from even the most imaginative modern-dance artists in the 1960s, such as Kanda, Suzushi, and Ishii, were vanguard choreographers who saw themselves as deliberately antimodernist, eclectic, and free to draw on elements of world dance wherever they could be found. The leading exemplar during this decade was Atsugi Bonjin (1936–), one of the most versatile artists of the entire post–World War Two era. In 2002 Atsugi summarized his antimodernism in almost Foucauldian terms: "I've long been concerned with questions such as 'who am I?' and 'what is the body?' I've always refused requests to do choreography unless I can also dance myself. The reason is that my works emanate from my body as I dance, not from Cartesian logic."[66]

In his more mature choreography, Atsugi's antimodernist approach to composing dance self-evidently refused to privilege ideas over their expression in art, in contrast with Suga Kishio's conceptual method of creating sculptures (see Chapter 9) at the same time.

Like Kanda, Suzushi, and Ishii, Atsugi enjoyed a childhood amply exposed to the arts, especially considering the desiccated conditions of wartime and military occupation. He studied dance with the veteran performer Itō Michio, learning ballet as well as modern technique, and in 1964 gave his first recital, mainly of his own choreography but also a work by the Butō artist Hijikata Tatsumi — an early hint of Atsugi's breadth of compass but also of Hijikata's central position among contemporary dancers at the time. By the mid-1960s the experimental mode that began with Neo-Dada and anti-art around 1960 had reached dance, not only via Butō but also in contemporary ballet once Tachikawa Ruriko formed the Star Dancers group in 1964.

When Atsugi returned to Japan in early 1969 after two Fulbright years at Juilliard, he set about creating new works that highlighted the body and its relationship to daily living: "I felt a need to use everyday Japanese customs to do my work. Dance ideas originate in society to an extent and are not found in complete isolation."[67] His trilogy of *Kamu, Haku, Hana wa akai* (*Chew, Vomit, The Flowers Are Red*, 1969–1970) was the landmark work of vanguard dance that nourished antimodernist ideas among Japan's contemporary choreographers and also among young critics, who helped it win recognition and prizes. *Kamu* included two truckloads of cabbages, a toilet fixture, a jalopy, and French bread — redolent of the ordinary artifacts found at Yomiuri Independents early in the decade. *Haku* used a lineup of fluorescent lights and mannequins onstage.

Throughout the trilogy vigorous athleticism alternated with stopping time in its tracks: the performers froze the moment with Polaroid camera shots, then ran endless circles around a gym floor without getting anywhere.[68] Movement was all that counted: their dance of exhaustion seemed to have no purpose except to highlight the physical self. Even though he drew on everyday objects and local customs, Atsugi is firm in denying that he underwent a "return to Japan" experience following his sojourn in New York. "Abroad people often think they see Japanese elements in my work, such as *Kamu*, but actually my dances are completely contemporary and pretty international"[69] — indeed, transcultural, inasmuch as they are portable anywhere, with interchangeable stage props gathered locally. (See Figure 18.)

Atsugi's preoccupation with the body while ignoring settled choreographic routines was matched by the Butō performer Hijikata Tatsumi, who is especially esteemed abroad as a totemic figure in the history of the Japanese

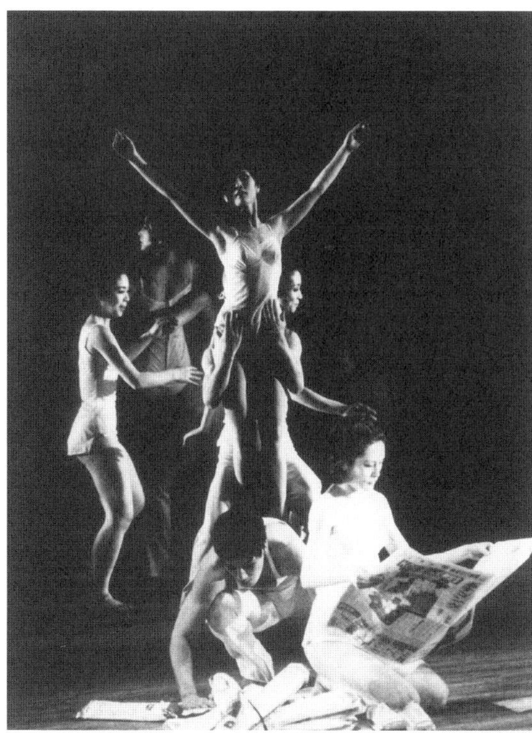

Figure 18. Performance of Atsugi Bonjin's *Kamu (Chew)*, by Atsugi Bonjin Dance Company, Toranomon Hall, Tokyo. April 1969. Courtesy Atsugi Bonjin.

underground arts. Within Japan Hijikata is most often regarded as a prominent innovator in a circle centering on the legendary choreographer Ōno Kazuo.[70] Hijikata was one of the earliest and most antimodernist of the Butō artists, making his debut in May 1959 with *Kinjiki (Forbidden Colors)*, a title borrowed from the Mishima novel of the same name.[71] Other well-known groups populating the Ōno-centered Butō mandala by the mid-1970s were Maro Akaji's Dairakudakan, founded in 1972 by one of Hijikata's pupils; Sankaijuku, formed three years later by Amagatsu Ushio (1949–) after he broke away from Maro's company; and troupes led by Kasai Akira (1943–) and Nishikawa Ukon (1939–).[72]

Hijikata, the single most important choreographer of the Shōwa single-digit cohort, developed Butō in the late 1950s, which "were years of great instability," his widow Motofuji Akiko (1928–) recalled in 2002. "But it was also a very creative period, when we had the opportunity to dance our own ideas, based on a newly discovered energy. We drew some of our inspiration from street theater,"[73] much like the High Red Center artists, who worked closely with Hijikata at the Asbestos Theater (Asubesutokan) in Meguro. Arising at the same moment as anti-art, Butō struck sparks among the artistic underground as a form of guerrilla theater that mocked the stylized movements of both ballet and classical Japanese dance, as well as the flowing movements of modern dancers like Kanda who sometimes still searched for beauty in movement.

Little was stylized, flowing, or beautiful in the Asbestos productions. The architect and Neo-Dada compatriot Isozaki Arata wrote that Hijikata used "the uniquely trained body, a standing corpus, which writhes as if it were placed in the deep darkness of the northern countryside," a style "filled with a resentment deeply interiorized in the Japanese people, who have lived so closely to the damp soil to the point of deformity."[74] (See Figure 19.) Motofuji, herself a leading Butō performer, places Hijikata in the anti–security treaty movement but not in a search for national essences: "Butō addressed themes related to the Japan–United States Mutual Security Treaty and had a political consciousness" similar to other arts groups in 1960,[75] whereas most Western-style dance forms were apolitical — and thus suspect to activists among the avant-garde.[76]

In the same way that certain contemporary composers and choreographers brushed modernism aside and turned to local elements, past and present, to find connections with the routines of daily life, Hijikata drew on near-to-hand dance genres to develop a technique of studied deliberateness: the performers' leisurely movements often seemed closer to kabuki or even Nō than to contemporary dance from abroad. Yet there was little of the truly historical in the social criticism he staged — merely a rebuttal of modernist norms. Butō writ large has unquestionably reestablished ties to premodern times and classical Japanese dance, particularly through Amagatsu's Sankaijuku group in the 1970s, but Hijikata was just as apt to seek meaning in the detritus of ordinary life in the early twentieth century to demonstrate the barrenness and insignificance of Japan's bureaucratically administered society a half century later. Whatever the source of his themes and methods — street performance, Japan's past, the Western stage — the outcome was usually closer to a meticulously planned theater happening than to spontaneous or chaotic movement. In this sense his works from the 1960s more closely resembled the calculated public events of the High Red Center group than the random outbursts of the Neo-Dada followers in the parks and roadways of Tokyo.

"What was remarkable," Motofuji recalls, "was the number of artists from other genres who worked with Hijikata at the Asbestos Theater or the Sōgetsu Art Center in the 1960s: Takemitsu Tōru, Takiguchi Shūzō, Yokoo Tadanori, Tanikawa Shuntarō, Mishima Yukio, Akasegawa Genpei, and many others. Nakanishi Natsuyuki painted spots on Hijikata's back like tattoos."[77] Nakanishi acknowledges that he designed sets for some of Hijikata's produc-

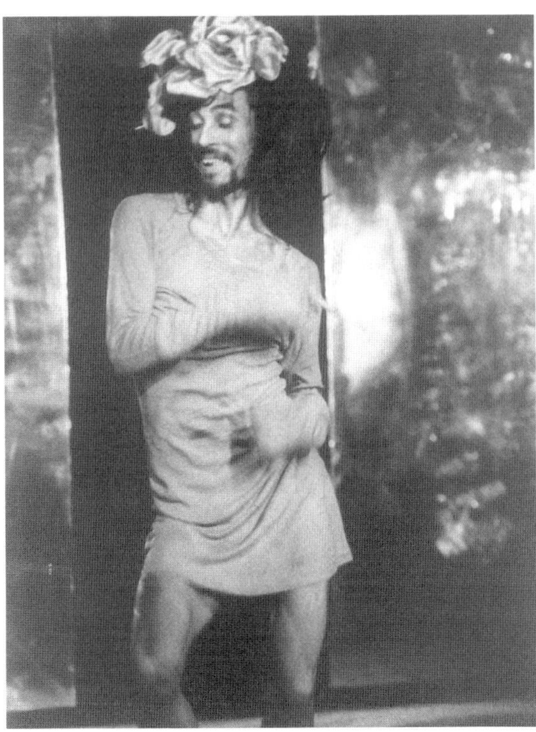

Figure 19. Hijikata Tatsumi performing his *Wan pīsu (One Piece)*, Asubesutokan, Tokyo. 1967. Photo by Nakatani Tadao. Courtesy Keio University Art Center.

tions and, more recently, for Sankaijuku,[78] and he also points out the lack of documentation for so much of what was presented: "As is often said, Butoh only happens once and leaves nothing behind."[79] But Hijikata, as his fellow avant-garde artists recognized, left behind a focus on the ordinary body as it is, dealing with the world as it exists, not as it could be remolded by high-culture choreographers to explore balletic fantasies or smoothed out toward some bland international style of modern dance.

Pure physicality was the hallmark of the shocking performance group Zero Jigen as well. Zero Jigen (Zero Dimension, active 1963–1972) used outrageous happenings, writings, and visual media to break through the boundaries of modern criticism and artistic conventions so as to lead human action to the zero point of nonaction (*wuwei*, the Daoist ideal of nonstriving). Based in Nagoya, its guiding light was the visual artist Katō Yoshihiro (1936–), who studied at Tama Art University at the same time as Sekine Nobuo and other sculptors who later formed the Monoha group.[80] The young painter Iwata Shin'ichi helped Katō set up Zero Jigen and headed its Nagoya activities after 1965. As many as three hundred persons nationwide were associated with this loosely structured organization, of whom twenty or so took part in its first "nonsense" street demonstrations in 1963.

Some of its counterculture events in shopping centers and department stores mixed pornography, near-nude "ceremonies" *(gishiki)*, and obscure references to Buddhist doctrines to create an ill-defined alternative social vision that might appeal to youth in revolt. This bold movement split into two wings in 1965, when Katō moved to Tokyo and took Zero Jigen up from the underground to scandalizing street performances in Hibiya, Shibuya, and Shinjuku and at shrines, parks, and beaches. Zero Jigen's events utilized everyday settings and props to exhibit the body in motion, often with overt sexual metaphor but without the formal choreography found in Butō. By the late 1960s the open-air events grew fewer, as Katō concentrated on joint productions with theater companies, student groups, and film makers. At the end of the decade, Zero Jigen was deeply involved in Hanpaku, an effort by a number of artists to resist the world exposition of science and industry scheduled for Osaka in 1970.[81]

Other performers sympathetic to Zero Jigen's social criticism denounced the group as "too concerned with ritual and not showing enough spontaneity," as the radical artist Ikeda Ichi (1943 —) puts it. After receiving two degrees in polymer chemistry from Kyoto University and designing large sets for the troupe Bara's productions of absurdist plays by Samuel Beckett and Eugene Ionesco (1909–1994), Ikeda became director and playwright for an open theater to promote a new union of art and drama he called the Multi-Play Group. "This group created a feeling of liberation greater than the underground theater of those days," Ikeda says in retrospect.[82] In 1971 he turned his troupe into a mobile community *(idō kyōdōtai)* to ply the Tōkaidō and San'yōdō highways from Tokyo to Himeji in a refitted seventy-five-passenger bus. Rejecting the convention of fixed communities, these itinerant players put on impromptu street performances at bus-side for whatever local audiences they could muster. This unfixed, rambling mode of nonchalant cultural production and unfettered way of life soon led Ikeda to his current preoccupation with water art.[83]

"I'm half Monoha," Ikeda said in 2002. "I like natural materials, but I believe things are dynamic, not static like sculptures — such as the flow of time and events. Performance became my way of challenging the existing institutions of art and theater I encountered during the nap season *(kamin no kisetsu)* that afflicted the worn-out protest movement after its demonstrations against the Japan–United States Mutual Security Treaty in 1960 ended in failure. Likewise, as Japan's economy prospered in the 1960s, consumer society was becoming too goods-oriented and too contented. My energetic antiestablishment radicalism challenged this."[84] Less technically gifted than Hijikata's Butō dancers, yet more improvisational than Zero Jigen's racy performers, the Multi-Play Group and the roaming highway actors shared fully in the common radical critique of Japan's administered society under conservative politicians and prosperous corporations.

The world of Japanese dance, like so many other creative spheres, settled down after 1970 into an artistic and organizational configuration still recognizable today. Dairakudakan and Sankaijuku eventually moved beyond Butō and produced remarkably creative choreography, as did Atsugi Bonjin with his eclectic works utilizing ballet and contemporary dance. Perhaps the most striking new artist to emerge in the 1970s was the vanguard dancer Tanaka Min (1945–), whose "works come from the body" like the choreography of so many of his immediate predecessors.[85] Ballet, however, has presented almost no fresh works since the 1970s, except for a few by the Star Dancers company. "The problem with dance in Japan," says Atsugi, "is that there are no successors to a dance style. The founder of Butō, Hijikata Tatsumi, was very interesting, but after him Butō declined. The same is true of other dance pioneers."[86] In such circumstances, perhaps the veteran dance critic Yamano Hakudai is correct that the most interesting new choreography will arise among small troupes in semirural or rural locations "because dance is always so linked to the soil."[87]

Careers: Composing in the 1960s

Commercial art proved lucrative for some of Japan's best avant-garde painters in the 1960s. The film industry was even more so for the most gifted composers, even though the spread of television led to retrenchment following the golden age of movie making in the 1950s. Takemitsu, for example, wrote at least half of his ninety-three cinema scores during the 1960s (he was an insatiable filmgoer who watched an estimated three to five hundred movies a year).[88] Although he wrote for cinema, stage, and television throughout his career, the early 1970s marked the end of Takemitsu's fervor for contemporary music — and probably the finale of the avant-garde era of composing in Japan. His later works, some of which reflect his fascination with dreams and with Japanese gardens, are often seen as "sensual, aesthetic, and more serene" than before, in keeping with his fondness for Debussy, Johannes Brahms (1833–1897), and George Gershwin (Jacob Gershvin, 1889–1937).[89] In 1973 he began directing a twenty-year-long series at the new 478-seat Seibu (later renamed Parco) theater in Shibuya called Konnichi no Ongaku — Music Today. This annual event, held each June, soon became the most important forum of its era for contemporary music in Japan.[90]

Whether for movies or for the concert hall, Takemitsu said, "when writing music it's impossible to ignore words completely. I try various experiments to grasp my musical ideas and impetus in words. Before putting them into music, I want to put them into words."[91] Like Hayashi Hikaru and others, he worked closely with contemporary writers such as Takiguchi Shūzō, Ōoka Makoto, Ōe Kenzaburō, Tanikawa Shuntarō, and Tamura Ryūichi (1923–1998). "After reading Tanikawa Shuntarō's poems or Ōe Kenzaburō's novels," Takemitsu wrote in 1985, "I aspire to making my own musical expression more multilayered. I want to say not one thing but two different things at the same time."[92] Later he said that "for some years I've felt an inner desire to produce an operatic work,"[93] so he turned to Ōe for the libretto, but because of Takemitsu's illnesses this project never materialized.

In the twelve months following his death in February 1996, Takemitsu was honored at 230 memorial concerts held throughout Japan and another 200 abroad.[94] Yet during his lifetime, his renown even among Japanese seldom spread beyond the arts world to the general public. He told Ozawa Seiji that when he was invited to France in the early 1970s for International Music Week, including three days' performances of his works, the Japanese embassy staff in Paris who showed up at a reception asked, "Who are you?" Likewise, when he sought support from the Cultural Agency of the Japanese Education Ministry for an overseas trip in 1978, government officials "did not recognize my name at all."[95]

Innovative as Takemitsu unquestionably proved to be in his earlier, more experimental works, even more forthright challenges to the modernist canon emerged in the sound installations, improvisations, and electronic-action events promoted by the environmental composers Kosugi Takehisa and Mizuno Shūkō (1934–) during the 1960s. Both helped to found Group On-gaku among disaffected composing students at Geidai in 1960. Beginning with Kosugi's electronic sound event for microphone, *Micro 1* (1961), like-minded musicians put on "anticoncerts" suggestive of the Neo-Dada anti-art performances taking place more or less simultaneously. Kosugi, who gave English-only titles to all his works for theater, instruments, voice, tape, electro-acoustics, and sound sculptures, saw himself as a sound artist. He believed that music developed not in forms but in interactions between individuals and their surroundings as expressed in performative actions such as happenings. "Even when there is no sound," he said, "I believe this is a part of music."[96]

Like most other professions in Japan in the 1950s and 1960s, the avant-garde arts apart from dance were notably dominated by males. Yoko Ono, Enomoto Kazuko, Kusama Yayoi, and Tanaka Atsuko head the short list of females who achieved recognition in visual media. The contemporary composer Tenjinchi (Hirasawa Noriko, 1961–) says, "Not a single female composer of quality works of contemporary music in the 1950s and 1960s comes to mind."[97] Miyake Haruna, herself a well-regarded composer since the mid-1960s, optimistically says that "in some ways being a female composer is probably more interesting than if I were a male. As an outsider — female, foreign-trained — I'm not very well accepted among composers, so I can think more freely and do what I wish." To Miyake, any difficulty she faced in winning professional acceptance was a matter of generation, not gender:

> Although they encountered certain difficulties, the first generation of artists after World War Two found it easy to paint or compose. They were a fresh breeze and could express themselves freely, with few worries about the discredited older establishment. The newcomers soon took over the best spaces, leaving little room for us who started out in the 1960s. I never felt my gender was the reason why I had so little contact with more senior composers in Japan, although objectively I suppose it was a factor. A much clearer reason was that my musical education occurred abroad, so I had no contacts with or patronage from more senior figures. It's funny that Takemitsu and his cohort saw themselves as rebels against the musical establishment long after they themselves had become established, even conservative. Still, I probably managed to get ahead by not fighting the senior composers too much.[98]

The critic Nanjō Fumio agrees that "in all fields of the arts after the 1960s — painting, sculpture, music, theater, film too — the next generation had great difficulty establishing itself because the artists who grew prominent by the 1960s were so powerful."[99] In Miyake's case, the musicologist Chōki Seiji adds, there were two other obstacles: (1) in the 1960s, when it was still hard to make it on one's own, she was not clearly identified with any group of composers or performers; and (2) she wrote mainly chamber music, whereas "to become famous in Japan, you have to compose for orchestras because commissions come mainly for symphonic works."[100]

Miyake contributed most notably to vanguard art music by directing an experimental concert series called Contemporary Music as Myself held at the premier venue for underground productions in the 1960s and 1970s, the JeanJean theater in a grotto beneath the Yamate Church on Park Avenue in Shibuya surrounded by the giant Seibu/Parco/Loft retailing complex. "I organized twenty programs between 1977 and 1985," she recalls. "Those concerts were so different from anything else at the time that people who knew nothing about classical or contemporary music came out of curiosity." Miyake's productions each June coincided almost exactly with Takemitsu's Konnichi no Ongaku — Music Today — series in the nearby Seibu theater, "so contemporary music fans shuttled from one to the other. JeanJean, which finally closed in 2000, had just 120 seats, but my concerts always packed in two hundred people, some seated on the stage and the rest standing in the aisles." Miyake's goal was to provide a mixed-genre event each time:

> I organized the JeanJean series to bring musicians back together after various musical media had become independent, scarcely talking with one another. Today there is a lot of communication among genres, but in the 1970s I saw the need to gather people together, including jazz and even rock artists. I myself began to experiment with improvisation at JeanJean. I also performed my own compositions several times. It's usually difficult to get groups to play your works repeatedly — there's a premiere, and that's it. So JeanJean gave my compositions some audience.[101]

Miyake's programs were part of a larger effort in the mid-1970s "to criticize the narrowly defined contemporary music" world in Japan, as the musicologist Ishida Kazushi notes.[102] But the attempt to bring greater coherence to innovative elements soon yielded to rampant diversification, splintering the avant-garde composing community in the face of a new traditionalism that temporarily washed across most of the arts by the end of that decade. Miyake earned a living from writing scores for TV, radio, and film, from playing piano accompaniment for vocalists at concerts, and from teaching.[103]

Ichiyanagi Toshi, commenting in 1980, said about commissions that "the situation is quite favorable in Japan compared with other countries." Looking back over the two decades since he returned from New York in 1961, he spoke with approval: "Japanese composers are very active and quite original. The creative composers here just now are really creative."[104] He might have added that, despite the brief diversion of traditionalism in the 1970s, the most innovative composers and choreographers could continue their advance toward the transcultural because by the end of the 1960s contemporary dance and art music in Japan were far better grounded locally and far less indebted to modernism than a decade earlier.

chapter nine

The Monoha Moment

Pure physicality and unmediated encounters, so prominent in the noises used by composers and the movements employed by choreographers in the 1960s, enjoyed their most striking visual expression starting in 1968 through the simple avant-garde constructions of a dozen postpolitical, postideological sculptors who eventually became known as the Monoha, or School of Things. Most of these proudly independent artists, who often disagreed with one another and rarely regarded themselves as a formal group, were trained as painters at Tama Art University in the early 1960s — and were thus unfettered by the precepts of existing sculptural approaches. Soon they relinquished the brush and chose assemblages of everyday artifacts as the best vehicle toward their goal: minimizing the artist's role and maximizing the encounter *(deai)* of materials and their surroundings. Like other minimalists, the Monoha adherents played down the act of artistic creation; instead they merely presented physical objects for contemplation. But unlike Marcel Duchamp, who assaulted conventional art by showcasing ordinary items to be pondered in isolation, the Monoha invited reflection on the random relationships between everyday materials and their surrounding environment, both natural and human. In this way the audience became a part of the process of revisualizing and redefining the connections between the materials and their locale.[1]

Although they were based in the Tokyo area, the Monoha artists were less specifically urban in focus than the anti-art Neo-Dada members or the antiestablishment High Red Center. Their minimalism nonetheless owed a good deal to the earlier groups for fixing the place of art in the lived environment. The Monoha triumphed among Japan's avant-garde at the end of the

1960s not because it was popular (it wasn't) but, like minimalism everywhere, because of its "emphasis on contexts," in Peter Schjeldahl's words — "art as a phenomenon in real space and time."[2] In the geographies of postwar Japanese creativity, the Monoha was at once a boundary, marking the furthest extreme of antimodernism, and a beacon, guiding artists who felt no attraction to theory toward the concrete instead. Monoha sculptors valued local materials found in their immediate surroundings and were quite indifferent to contacts with the international avant-garde. Yet the group indulged in the same intergenerational squabbles as other arts organizations of the time and took pains to identify itself as apolitical, however difficult such a stance was to maintain in the conflicted 1960s.

Relationality among tangible objects and their environs, not the materiality of things in themselves, lay at the heart of Monoha approaches to the visual. Daily-use items and derelict jetsam had been deployed in Japanese art works for at least fifteen years before the Monoha began in 1968, particularly in those by the Gutai group. Although the Monoha had a clear connection to the matter *(busshitsu)* championed by Gutai artists, the term Mono ("thing") was now written in kana to distinguish it from ideas of substance or physical object implied by the Chinese character *mono*. At a roundtable convened by the art journal *Bijutsu techō* in early 1970, Monoha artists said the group represented a mood or spirit *(kibun)* of a new artistic age — the direct, unfiltered experience of perceiving the everyday world as it is.[3] "The world being the world as it is," said the Monoha figure Lee Ufan (1936 —), "how am I to create anything? The very most I can do is vividly present the world as it manifests the way it is."[4] Japan's establishment critics took this to mean that Monoha sculptors had abandoned artistry in favor of extolling the physical properties of materials not previously used, such as sheet metal, paper, sand, vinyl, charcoal, and textiles. But the painter Dōmoto Hisao saw much more: "The Monoha was a truly unique movement — not to say 'Japanese,' but definitely imaginative in how it raised questions about existence."[5] Thus it was not the things themselves that mattered but "the disclosure of their existence," the critic Minemura Toshiaki commented.[6]

The Monoha, which gained its name from critics in the early 1970s, issued no manifesto, had no membership list, formed no organizational apparatus, and held no exhibitions as "Monoha." Its affinities with minimalism, although indirect, sometimes bordered on the puritan. In the early 1960s minimalists in the United States such as Donald Judd (1928–1994), Sol LeWitt (1928–), and Richard Serra (1939–) increasingly rejected compositional effects within a work in favor of blank geometric abstractions with a minimum of art content.[7] The Monoha movement was even more antiformalist, de-emphasizing the static, finished work and playing up the relationality of everyday materials in their natural and social contexts.

Perhaps the true analogue was indigenous: the Gutai group in Osaka during its early phase, 1954–1962. The architect Isozaki Arata argues that both the Monoha and the Gutai group lacked structure, emphasized unfinished materials, and focused on artistic process, unlike much modernist art.[8] Chiba Shigeo, the art critic, sees "a clear line of connection" between the two, in that "both sought an alternative approach to art other than European modernism. They shared a new conception of space, more so than material: spacing objects in relation to one another and to an entire room or outdoor area like a garden. Gutai experimented with space in this way; Monoha realized it more fully."[9] Nonetheless, like innovative artists everywhere, the contumacious Monoha sculptors insist on difference from their Kansai forebears. Lee Ufan scoffs, "The Gutai group had the fantasy that they could produce something different from modernist art. The Monoha had no fantasies. It was very practical — we destroyed illusions."[10] Suga Kishio, Lee's antipode among Monoha artists, was eight years old when the Yoshihara Jirō formed the Gutai association in 1954. Yet his alienation from it was more than generational: "I went to see the Pinacotheca in the 1960s, but I found that our content in the Monoha was different from Gutai's. Gutai included a lot of performance, whereas the Monoha was not concerned with human movement. The Monoha was quite original and took very little of its content from abroad or from the Gutai group."[11] What is more, Monoha works were certainly less spontaneous than most of Gutai's, and the Monoha artists were less invested in materiality itself than their Kansai forebears. (See Figure 20.)

The curator Simon Groom is undoubtedly correct that the Monoha's constructions show "resistance to the gradual colonisation of the art work by the idea,"[12] yet their ramrod attention to relationality as a principle meant that the Monoha sculptors often worked in tandem with, not always in opposition to, conceptual artists such as Matsuzawa Yutaka or Kashihara Etsutomu (1941–). Concepts needed things, at least as an afterthought; the Monoha needed thoughts as well as artifacts because it sought ideas about existence through the relations among materials and surroundings. The Monoha regarded the relationship between viewer and material as always contingent, unmediated by language, occurring in the ever-shifting present and immune to permanency or legacy. All that mattered was the instantaneous encounter, at a particular moment, among objects and their social and physical environment. Monoha works were always broken down after being exhibited, prompting the critic Tsuji Nobuo to liken them to "stones in the water, their expressive forms like ripples."[13] Suga Kishio adds, "Japanese museums assem-

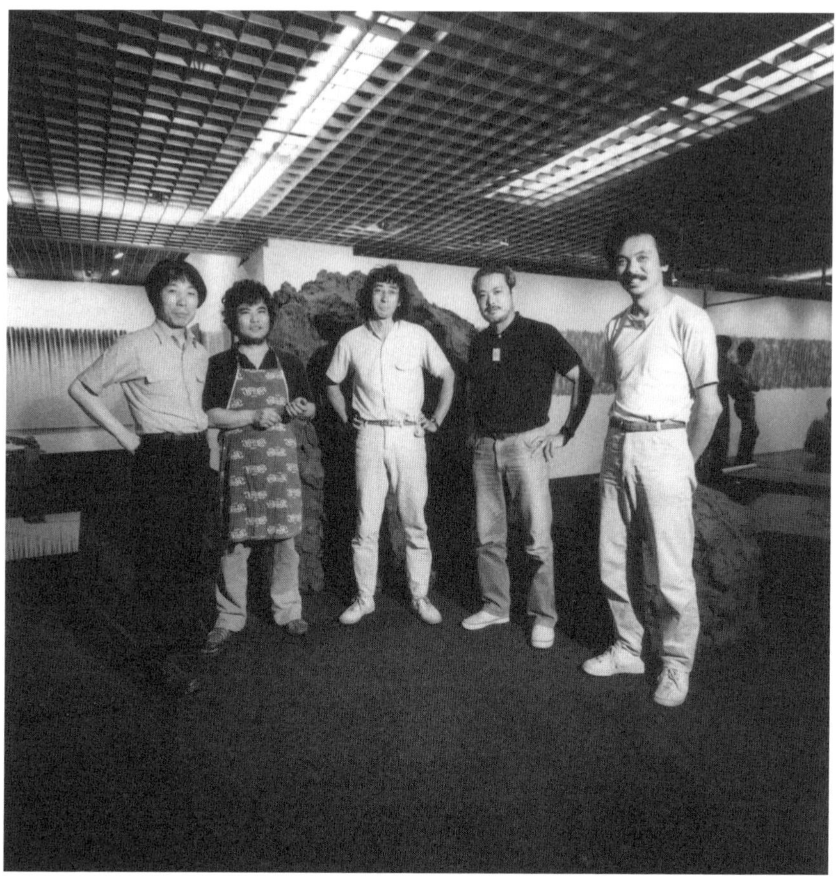

Figure 20. Monoha artists' reunion, Seibu Museum of Art, Tokyo. 1987. From left, Lee Ufan, Sekine Nobuo, Suga Kishio, Koshimizu Susumu, Yoshida Katsurō. Courtesy Anzai Shigeo.

ble temporary exhibits but don't collect very much art, so everybody knows about the Monoha, but there's hardly anywhere you can go to see its works."[14] And when one comes upon them, the encounter occurs in a different present unconnected with the past when they were first produced.

Sekine Nobuo: Making the Unseen Visible

For an art movement with no interest in the past, the Monoha enjoyed a rich intellectual inheritance for its antimodernist, anti-art outlook. A meandering amalgam of ideas from such disparate savants as the philosophers Nishida Kitarō (1870–1945) and Martin Heidegger (1889–1976) and the young media scholar Nicholas Negroponte (1944–) drew the general interest of many

Monoha sculptors, despite their caution about specifically conceptual approaches to art. Most were recent graduates of Tama Art University (Tamabi), where they studied with the High Red Center leader Takamatsu Jirō and especially with the senior abstract artist Saitō Yoshishige (1904–2001).[15] The latter was a towering avant-garde figure who, like Takiguchi Shūzō with the Experimental Workshop fifteen years earlier, never affiliated himself with the Monoha but nonetheless exerted a strong gravitational pull during his decade at Tamabi, 1963–1973, especially because he encouraged his students to experiment. As his pupil Suga attests, "Saitō-sensei introduced us to all sorts of sculpture from around the world. Without Saitō, my development as a sculptor would have been delayed quite a bit."[16]

Saitō Yoshishige belonged to a prewar avant-garde cohort, along with the painter Nanbata Tatsuoki (1905–1997), print maker Hagiwara Hideo (1913–), and sculptor Mukai Ryōkichi, who discovered abstract expressionism in the 1950s "as a means of self-liberation" from earlier modernist strictures.[17] The son of an imperial army officer, Saitō turned to painting in presumed mutiny against his hyperpatriotic schooling. A devotee of both dadaism and constructivism, he became acquainted with the future Gutai leader Yoshihara Jirō during the 1930s. Like the lexicographer Morohashi Tetsuji (1883–1982), whose nearly completed manuscript for the monumental *Dai kanwa jiten* (Great Chinese-Japanese dictionary) was burned in an American air raid near the end of World War Two, Saitō lost all his works to incendiary bombings shortly before the surrender and had to restart from scratch.[18] His *Oni (Demon)* series of oils on plywood, beginning in 1957, showed his new fascination with tangible, almost palpable, raw paints in stunning bold colors. In the 1960s he refocused on expressing reality. *Penchi* (*Pliers*, 1967, lacquer on plywood), which immediately preceded the Monoha period, seems almost kinetic: crimson blades secured by a black bolt are thickly painted in impromptu relief, conveying three-dimensionality and seemingly mechanical action (see Plate 8).[19] This stark everyday item seemed a menacing tool of confinement as well as an indispensable instrument of mechanical culture, a Janus-like emblem of Japan's state-managed consumer society at the time.

Takamatsu Jirō played tricks with vision in his op-art *Shadow* series (see Chapter 7), exploring reality and illusion in ways that often piqued the Monoha sculptors but also made them test the actuality of the relationships between materials and environments. At Tamabi Takamatsu taught students to explore what was absent, dividing representation from what was represented (shadows, not substance),[20] whereas the 1,000-yen note trial had shown that image and reality were interchangeable.[21] Although the Monoha sculptors belonged to the first arts generation raised on television and were preternaturally skeptical of images and the values underlying them, Minemura Toshiaki believes "their greatest contribution was to establish the first thorough perceptual realism, at the very nadir of bad times, in the history of modern Japanese art."[22] Without overtly embracing the indigenous as "Japanese," the Monoha threw off Western-centered approaches in favor of what the philosopher Tsurumi Shunsuke and novelist Oda Makoto (1932–) both call a "bug's-eye view" of the concrete and the local,[23] not the bird's-eye perspective of high modernism.

Like Cromwell's shuttering of the theaters or the shipboard premiere of Handel's *Water Music*, the construction of *Isō — daichi (Phase — Earth)* by Sekine Nobuo in October 1968 was a one-time event that symbolized an artistic era. This sculpture, technically known as *Isō — daichi 2*, consisted of two parts: (1) a hole dug in the surface of Suma Rikyū park in Kobe, 2.7 meters deep and 2.2 meters in diameter, and (2) beside it a vertical column of half oilclay, half concrete of the same dimensions. Looking like something as simple as a child's pegboard — or a Brobdingnagian dirt cylinder plucked from the ground — it quickly became the defining work of the Monoha moment. Sekine was then twenty-six, fresh from graduate school at Tamabi. "Starting in 1968 I began to tap my long-standing interest in topology," he recalled in 2002, "as a way of developing concepts of the structure of space. I began with the *Isō — daichi* series because of my interest in cylindrical forms. It took five of us a week to dig the hole. Everybody's ideas changed when the column of *Isō — daichi 2* stayed up. They realized something new had been born and rushed to use new materials. This was when Monoha began."[24] (See Figure 21.)

Yet at the time, apparently anticipating that later critics might see it as "the first work of conceptual art in Japan,"[25] Sekine tried to brush aside both idea and creation:

> There are times when we see things clearly as if they were enveloped in a magnetic force. A new, fresh encounter with plain ordinary things that are just lying about in reality. . . . We feel then "the desire to create," but this process is definitely not "creating." It is rather sweeping away the conceptual dust that gathers on the surface of things, then turning them into what they really are and presenting clearly the world contained within them. Making visible that which cannot be seen. . . .
>
> The concept of "creating" born out of modern thought: How much has it lost its real meaning? . . . all this because of the tendency of modern thought to emphasize the individuality of consciousness and action. First, we need to stop "creating" and begin "seeing."[26]

As Sekine suggests, vision and observation — how to look and how to see — were standard lessons for artists everywhere in the 1960s, often supplanting

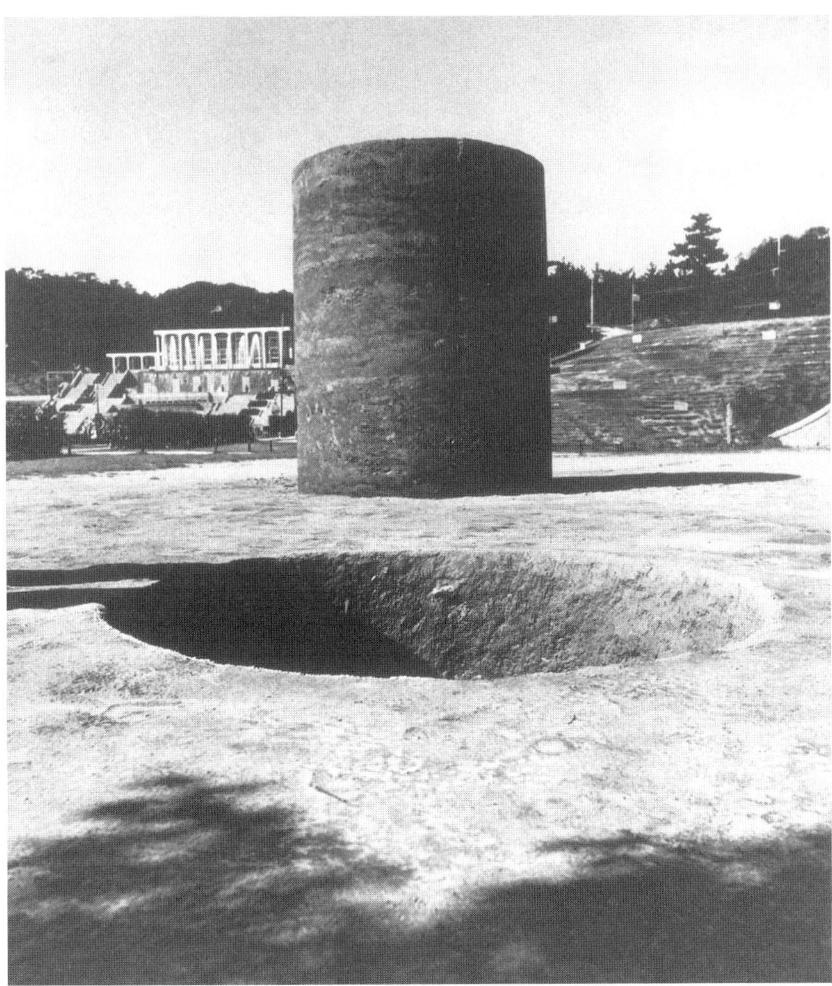

Figure 21. Sekine Nobuo. *Isō daichi (Phase — Earth)*. 1968. Concrete and oilclay. Temporary sculpture, Suma Rikyū Kōen, Ashiya. Courtesy Sekine Nobuo.

the modernist emphasis on creativity and originality. He had labored until 1967 as a studio assistant to Takamatsu Jirō, but now, with *Isō — daichi*, he employed a visual trick to attack art based on modernist ideas, technologies, and images — that is, the works of Takamatsu himself. Monoha was henceforth a "sudden, drastic reversal from a 'world of illusion' to the 'world as it is,'" the critic Tatehata Akira argues: a renunciation of "intellectualised visual manipulations."[27] In effect, *Isō — daichi* was an optical ruse that proved existence, not its absence, thus tearing apart the conflation of illusion and reality by the practitioners of reproduction art and pop art in the early 1960s, particularly High Red Center.

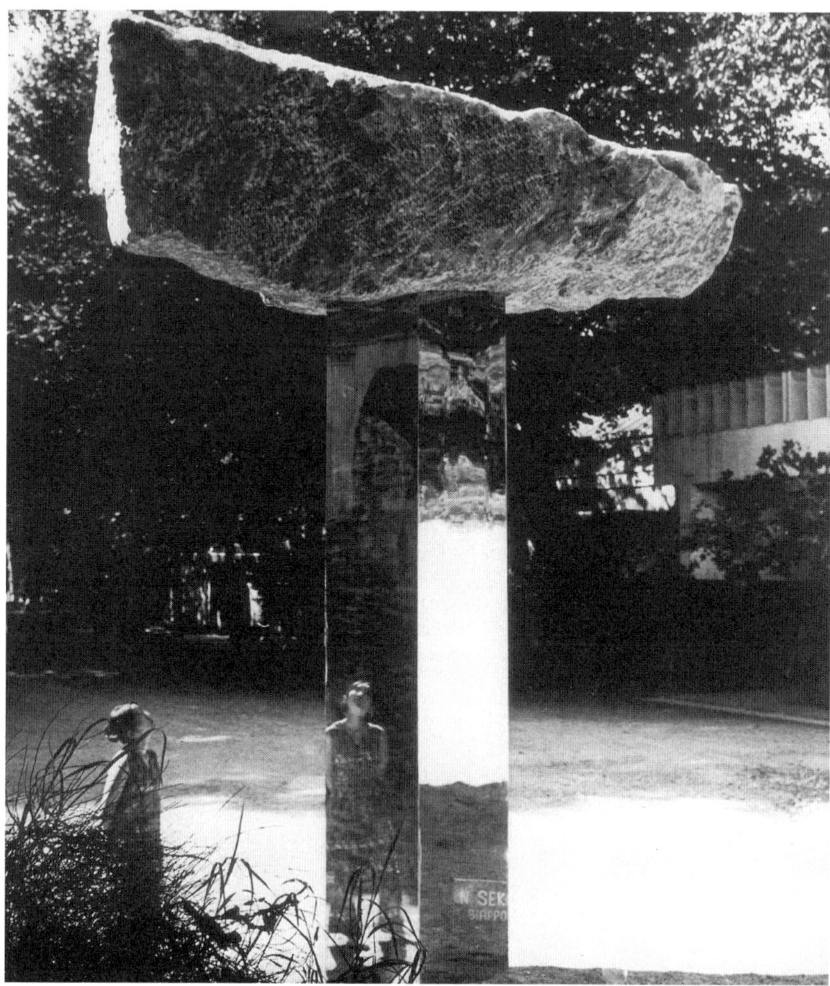

Figure 22. Sekine Nobuo. *Kūsō (Phase — Nothingness)*. 1970. Stone and stainless steel. Louisiana Museum, Copenhagen. Courtesy Sekine Nobuo.

Kūsō (Phase — Nothingness), a series begun at the Hakone Open Air Art Museum when it first opened in 1969 and then carried forward in Venice and Copenhagen, is Sekine's other signature work from the Monoha period (see Figure 22). The surroundings become part of the work because they are reflected in the polished mirror of the square stainless-steel vertical column, showcasing the materiality of the massive rock balanced precariously, almost menacingly, above. "I had worked part-time as a gardener and moved many stones," Sekine recalls. "My mirror column in Venice reflects my belief that rocks have a living spirit, something that is spiritually close to early Shinto ideas. I've also read a great deal of Zen and Daoist thought, both of which affect my approach to the structure of space. Zen and Daoism are more intuitive than topology, but all are important sources for me."[28] Both *Isō — daichi* and *Kūsō*, the sculptor says, reveal "the powerful awesomeness and magnetism of objects" themselves.[29] Both also depend crucially on the properties of physics, especially gravity, as was true of much other Monoha work.

Still one cannot take too seriously Sekine's professed aversion to ideas, because intellectualism lingered ineradicably among the Monoha group. Sekine not only read widely in East Asian philosophic texts but also dwelled on the more elemental "spirit of animism" found in natural objects around himself.[30] Moreover, he concedes, "Lee Ufan became my friend right after *Isō — daichi 2*. We had many debates about art, Heidegger, other German thinkers, and Zen philosophy. His influence on me was very strong. The impact of European and American art was also powerful, but we wanted to express our own ideas."[31] By and by Sekine moved past the Monoha phase to become a public and corporate artist of great repute, whereas most others in the group reverted to inconspicuous sculpting.[32] Two exceptions stand out, Lee Ufan and Suga Kishio. Although thoroughly sophisticated about art theory, each devoted himself in the late 1960s to questions of how to see, and how to present, reality as found in the interdependence among things and their surroundings.

Lee Ufan: Encountering the Everyday

"We were opposed to modernism," Lee recalled in 2002, "because we believed the artist should not make things but merely show them as they are." Born in Korea and trained in philosophy at Nihon University, Lee links his approach as a Monoha artist to alterity, both analytically and personally:

> The Monoha was the first group of artists anywhere to ask, What is the Other *(tasha)* at the moment of encounter *(deai)*? Western concepts of the Other involve human relations and an assumption that people are superior to natural phenomena. Our idea of the Other regarded plants, animals, and rocks as equivalent to humans and as Other in relation to them. As Other, they were not artifacts to be worked, just observed. This idea was easy for me to accept because, as a non-Japanese, I too am Other.[33]

By simply offering materials for observation, Lee reduced his role as artist from modernist originator of ideas to the more humble function of facilitating perception through display.

His sculptures from the Monoha period, 1968 to 1973, graphically reveal how he presented objects and materials just as they were. Between 1968 and

1971 he prepared a series of drawings, called *Relatum,* for sculptural works with the same title in iron plate, stone, and cotton that he continued to put together throughout the next two decades.[34] In these minimalist presentations, as the critic Tani Akira has said, Lee rejects the "symbolic or iconic object,"[35] as well as materiality for its own sake, and instead foregrounds the relationships among the items and their surroundings. *Relatum* (1968) shows a large stone placed atop a sheet of glass that has been spread in articulation with the walls of the exhibit space. The viewer is the random variable in this construction and its successor, *Relatum* (1969), which consists of two dark stones embalmed in a large coffin of unspun cotton, arranged obliquely vis-à-vis the gallery walls. Another in this series, *Work* (1970), perches stones above strategically spaced *zabuton* cushions, some seemingly abjected by being placed near walls rather than at the center of the grouping. The accompanying photograph makes Lee a part of the assemblage, underscoring his belief that rocks are equivalent to, but Other than, humans — erasing the viewer's initial impression that the stones are seated anthropomorphically on furnishings for humans. (See Figure 23.)

Lee Ufan is probably the best-known Japanese visual artist from the 1960s who is still active today, just as celebrated as the composers Yuasa Jōji, Ichiyanagi Toshi, and Hayashi Hikaru or the choreographers Ishii Kaoru and Atsugi Bonjin. In a literal sense Lee was the most truly postcolonial artist of the decade. Born in 1936, when children in colonial Korea were educated in Japanese-language primary schools, he soon discovered an incendiary passion for literature as a field of endeavor. When he failed the entrance examinations for the humanities faculty at Seoul National University, he successfully retook them in art but quit in 1956 after one year's study. He made his way to Japan that same year without knowing much Japanese, acquired a Japanese name, and entered the philosophy department of Nihon University "in order to understand art theory." After graduating in 1961, he went to court to change his name back to Lee, returned briefly to Seoul, then managed to secure a visa so he could go back to Japan. "I had no interest in becoming an artist at that point," Lee recalls today. "I wanted to become a writer, but Japanese was very hard, so eventually I became an artist instead."[36]

Lee's disquiet with informel and action painting from the West doubtless stemmed at least partly from his reaction to the dominance of European thinkers in his studies of philosophy. Writing in the art journal *Dezain hihyō* (Design review) in September 1969, Lee stressed that East Asian aesthetics blurred the distinction between subject and object, a basic difference from Western thought. He criticized conceptual artists for privileging subjectivity while departing from things in the sense of material objects. He dismissed

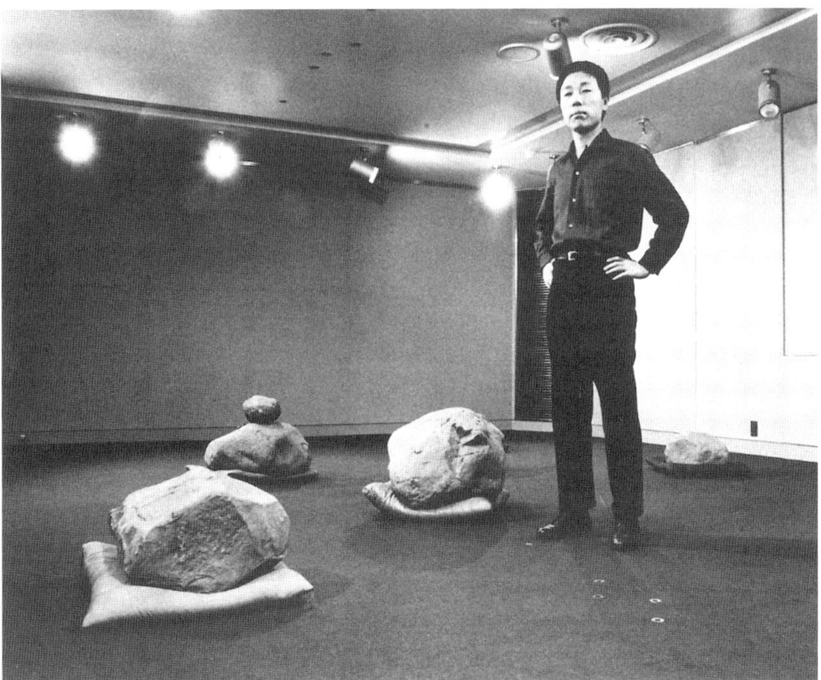

Figure 23. Lee Ufan with his *Work*. 1970. Stones and cushions. Exhibited at Pinar Gallery, Tokyo. Courtesy Lee Ufan.

creation as a principle of art and denied the primacy of modern thought based on consciousness as symbolic action.[37] Many years later Lee acknowledged that conceptual art, like the minimalist Monoha, at least asked, What is art? The conceptual part was good, he said, but the art itself was "strange" because it introduced texts and other extraneous elements.[38]

What mattered to Lee was the "interdependent relationships" between people and their natural environment — the uncontrived "encounters" with the everyday — not the Cartesian distinction between the ideal and the material that gave rise to the false notion of individual creation of plastic forms.[39] With modernism now in full retreat, history mattered even less to Lee and the other Monoha sculptors than it had to anti-art devotees in the Gutaiha, Kyushuha, and Neo-Dada groups a decade earlier. "In the sense that the modernization of Japan's economy and modernism in art originated in the West," Lee commented in 2002, "our antimodernism may have been somewhat anti-Western, but it was not pro-Japan or pro–East Asia. We rejected things that were fabricated and asked ourselves, What are authentic materials? We believed the artist should not build things but instead examine and present the relations among things as they are."[40]

Certainly the Monoha sculptors were more conscious than the Gutai group of their placement in a specific locale[41] — but this stemmed from their focus on everyday materials and surroundings, not from any attachment to a supposed pure Japanese past before Western culture arrived. "It's a mistake to say the Monoha wished to return to something Japanese or East Asian," Lee asserted in 2002. "Our work had nothing to do with nativism or tradition. We asked: What is art? What are the origins of materials? What is the interdependence among materials? Since antiquity Japanese art has been full of non-Japanese elements, so the idea of reverting to something Japanese has no meaning."[42]

Even though there was nothing retrograde or atavistic about the Monoha, the scholar Tatehata Akira is surely correct that the group had no choice but to posit "a Japanese or East Asian art" when it decided "to strike a fiercely antimodernist stance, which can be understood as a kind of critique of cultural colonialism." This "'East Asian-ness' inherently presupposes a sense of opposition"[43] — but not superiority, either historically or currently, only difference. In Lee's terms, modernism itself now became the Other, to be met with a locally developed stance centering on the perception of contemporary reality in a tangible rather than a theoretical context.

More so than any previous arts movement in Japan, the Monoha under Lee Ufan's intellectual guidance tended toward a new, post-Western position that was nevertheless far from fully anti-Western. Minemura Toshiaki cautions against the easy orientalist trap of measuring "Japanese art against a Western yardstick by echoing, without being aware of the harm that's being done, that Euro-American inclination to appraise only non-Western elements in Japanese art."[44] The museum director Hara Toshio concurs, pointing out that when artists such as Lee spoke of nature, encounter, or the cosmos, they signified no nostalgia for an imagined past of Rousseauistic harmony. Instead, they believed that humankind was a mere fraction of the cosmos and that artists should forgo creativity in favor of "an emotional, intuitive process of exploring and exposing the potentialities of the materials themselves."[45] Lee contends that the Monoha was only partially anti-Western, "thoroughly antimodernist, but not postmodern. But after the early 1970s," he concludes wistfully, "the antimodernist movement in Japan fragmented and went in many directions,"[46] of which commercialism was the most evident.

Suga Kishio: Space as Material

The Monoha artist who took relationality to its apex was Suga Kishio, paradoxically the most stoic and the most productive sculptor in the group. Suga was born in the northern city of Morioka in 1944 and studied painting at Tama Art University, graduating in 1968 and later teaching at his alma mater from 1982 to 1989.[47] Paragons of an earlier day such as Takiguchi Shūzō were passé for Suga and his cohort, who also questioned the anti-art mode of the late 1950s. Looking back in 2002, he recalled that "we all used our brains to think about art in the 1960s, not indulging in easy pop art. We asked, How do we look at things? In what forms of existence? How you look at objects in your daily life, and at the relationships among them, depends on your view of the world. When you move your residence to a new area, you see new things in your surroundings, so you do different work depending on where you live."[48] Such complete relativism unhelms modernist constants and proclaims that place and context matter crucially in the expression and experience of art.

The same is true for the artist's wherewithal. "I pick things for my works carefully," Suga says. "Picking good materials is key. Earth, water, wood, even manmade materials like concrete are all okay, but manufactured goods aren't." To these he added another ingredient: space as an almost tangible component. Yet more so than in works by the Russian constructivists, Suga's assemblages incorporated both interior spaces within his sculptures and the exterior milieu in which they were sited.[49] His 1969 work in paraffin, *Heiretsusō (Parallel Phase)*, situated slices of this ordinary household substance, widely used at the time for canning fruits and vegetables, in dynamic interdependence with one another and with the surroundings, constantly changing as the viewer shifted positions. Each time the artist reassembles this temporary work, which was first displayed at the former Tamura Gallery in Nihonbashi, Tokyo, he alters the relationships among elements by recrafting both internal and external space.

Suga understands space as one of his sculptural materials in these terms: "Outdoor sculpture depends on boundaries, not space itself. My system starts with borders, defining them as well as breaking through them. Then I think about the relationships of the objects within borders. Indoor sculpture works with fixed walls as borders, so the variable I work with is vertical space. My thinking starts from the top down. I also think about horizontal vision, how we see through things as we look straight across."[50] Porousness, not liminality, characterizes this view of boundaries in that exterior space is incorporated into the work, not separated from it as somehow different. (The same could be said of how the composers Ichiyanagi and Yuasa used spacing and timing in their 1960s works.) Suga's *Shaisō (Diagonal Phase*, 1969, wood and stone) is one of many structural assemblages from his early career using unpolished materials in dependent relationships to one another. Whether it is placed

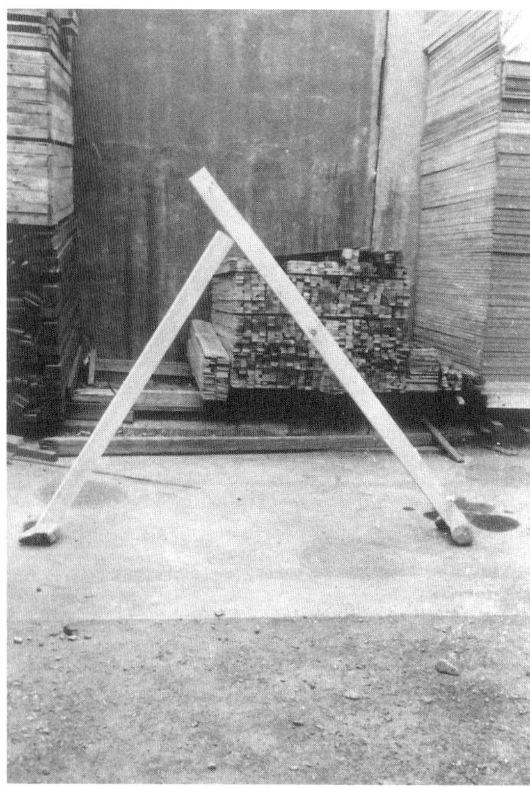

Figure 24. Suga Kishio. *Shaisō (Diagonal Phase).* 1969. Wood and stone. Courtesy Suga Kishio.

almost coyly in front of a lumberyard, as in the accompanying photograph, or in an indoor space, the straightforward geometry of this construction engages its broader surroundings through the openness of the form and the powerful undertow of gravity on which the work relies. (See Figure 24.)

After living for a time in the Ogikubo area of Tokyo, Suga chose semi-isolation in a mountainous area outside Itō, on the Izu peninsula well south of Tokyo, where he continued to churn out gravity studies like *Shaisō* as well as other arrangements of interdependent materials. As the curator Dehara Hitoshi notes, Suga's sculptures used gravity to reveal how materials exist in relation to one another and to their environment, whereas similar assemblages by Lee Ufan "presented the results of gravity,"[51] such as glass shattered by rock. Although he intervened minimally with the unadorned boards, rocks, and other ingredients he selected, Suga did more than simply display items and let them speak for themselves.[52] In 1977 he wrote:

Even if you believe you are creating things as art, it cannot become "art" until it has been exposed to public view. This is because "art" is something that communicates your symbolic language or meaning or opens up a process of recognition to a third person. . . . Although "art" is something that depends on your process of consciousness, if it does not also involve the process of recognition of another person, it is not possible for you to even verify your own self-expression.[53]

In arguing that art conveyed "symbolic language," Suga differed from Lee Ufan and other sculptors who rejected modern thought based on consciousness as symbolic action. But his larger claim, pointing toward subsequent reception theory, was certainly acceptable to the entire Monoha group: art exists in a social content, and the viewer's spatial perception and imagination are crucial parts of the work.

Notwithstanding his flight from the capital, Suga continued to work according to the principles he developed in the Monoha period, generating a substantial output from his hillside studio year after year. Looking back, he says that "in the late 1960s it was quite easy to make art, unlike a decade and a half earlier. But to make a living solely as an artist, without working as a salaryman, was scary. Even when your works sold, it was still terrifying" to lack the security of a predictable niche in Japan's establishment-regulated social system.[54] Like Sekine Nobuo and Lee Ufan, Suga was one of the very few visual artists who attained success by the end of the 1960s. He soon became one of the most discussed artists of his generation (a bibliography of writings about his works includes more than seven hundred items published during 1967–1997),[55] although he did not enjoy the financial rewards from corporate patronage that accrued to Sekine or the public acclaim that was eventually showered on Lee Ufan at the turn of the twenty-first century.

THE SHORT-LIVED Monoha movement soon drew criticism for its seemingly aloof and cerebral stance — in spite of its devotion to everyday materials in their social framework and its disavowal of ideas that subordinated tangible things, as with some conceptual art. Lee himself renounced contemplative encounters by 1972 and resumed painting.[56] Hara Toshio, who has low regard for most Japanese art from the 1950s and 1960s, takes the most gifted Monoha artists seriously. Writing in the catalog of a 1991 exhibition of ten local sculptors held at his art museum, Hara outlined several general characteristics of contemporary Japanese art, of which three seem to trace directly to the Monoha: (1) a convergence of art and craft (the widespread use of natural materials by the Monoha), (2) the aesthetics of space (reworked by all the Monoha sculptors and turned into a veritable construction material by Suga Kishio), and (3) a de-emphasis of the artist as a creative individual (the Monoha preference for presenting materials instead of intervening to re-fine or reshape them).[57] In these ways the brief Monoha movement rejected the modernist inclination to let the artist as subject turn the world into an object, re-creating it in human image.[58] Instead the Monoha asserted the equivalence of people and nature, without hierarchies of domination and submission, awakening a new way of seeing everyday reality among artists and audiences who heretofore were deprived of an entire mode of perception by the staid conventions of established art forms.

chapter ten

Art, Money, and Politics

Artistically speaking, the late 1940s and early 1950s were a time
of rebuilding; the rest of the 1950s and the 1960s were a period
of self-discovery. Nineteen seventy was a big turning point:
it was the end of an era in social movements, labor activism,
student radicalism, the economy, and the arts. The era
shouldn't matter for art, but it does. — Ōoka Makoto,
journalist and poet[1]

Nineteen seventy mattered in Japan for many reasons, perhaps most of all for
the distance traveled in the single decade since the national imbroglio over
the Japan–United States Mutual Security Treaty in May–June 1960. Japan
in 1960 was still beset with ideological contention, labor strife, housing short-
ages, and paltry wages. Then during the next ten years the country enjoyed
undreamed-of prosperity and social sameness, despite lingering inequities
beneath the sunny official pronouncements about the high quality of life in
Japan. To be sure, Japanese continued to debate the nature of constitutional
democracy and their country's place in the world, as they still do today. But
by 1970 their perspective on the years since the Pacific War was subtly yet
unmistakably different from a decade earlier.

Nearly half the national population in 1970 was born since the war, including most of the workers and students who protested in 1968–1970 against
what they believed were the sour fruits of modernity: university elitism, Japanese complicity in a misbegotten American intervention in Southeast Asia,
and semicolonial subordination to the United States through the security
treaty, which was automatically extended in June 1970. But many other Japanese, particularly those who remembered the hardships of wartime and the
early occupation years, found their lives far more satisfactory in 1970 than

ten years earlier. To most of them the discordant issues of the 1950s were now unpleasant, if incompletely resolved, artifacts of a past they preferred to leave safely archived and rarely retrieved, even though the price of forgetting these recent events was to accept an increasingly administered society based on government-brokered compromises with consumer capitalism.

As Ōoka Makoto knew, the era 1968–1970 mattered compellingly for artists no less than for other intellectuals and public figures, in Japan and elsewhere. Japanese artists were buffeted, occasionally even immobilized, by the pushes and pulls of two countervailing magnetic poles. The negative charge emanated from foreign policy. Political protest, nearly dormant after the anti-Anpo movement misfired in 1960, seized center stage again in 1965 when the antiwar group Citizens' Federation for Peace in Vietnam (Betonamu ni Heiwa o! Shimin Rengō, or Beheiren) began shaking many social critics and ordinary citizens from their complacency about external affairs. Although a number of avant-garde artists declined to take part (see overview to Part 2), nearly all seemed skeptical of their government's cooperation with the Americans in Southeast Asia. In the late 1960s radical students on many campuses, exercised about both foreign policy and university governance, began forming independent joint-struggle councils (Zengaku Kyōtō Kaigi, or Zenkyōtō) unaffiliated either with Minsei, a national student organization sponsored by the Japan Communist Party, or with such radical anti-JCP sects as Chūkakuha, Kakumaruha, Shagakudō, and Shaseidō. Graduate students, interns, and young lecturers at art universities established their own affiliates of Zenkyōtō, known as Artists' Joint Struggle Councils (Bijutsuka Kyōtō Kaigi, or Bikyōtō). By 1969 disputes led by one or another student faction had disrupted 152 of Japan's 377 four-year universities.[2]

The positive pole of the public magnet was recognition. However sympathetic they were to the protests about Vietnam, the treaty, or campus affairs, what mattered most to Japan's leading choreographers, composers, painters, and sculptors was the place of the arts at Expo '70, the world exposition of science and industry (Bankoku Hakurankai, or Banpaku) held in Osaka in 1970 at a cost of $335 million. "Nineteen seventy was a turning point for contemporary artists," says the art historian Kondō Yukio. "The Osaka world exposition brought big money to them."[3] The art critic Kanazawa Takeshi agrees: "Artists had long needed a place to show their large-scale works; Banpaku gave them this chance. It was the focus of national attention, so their work could be seen." The exposition also brought to a boil the simmering but long-ignored matter of capitalism and its part in sponsoring art that was frequently antiestablishment and sometimes anticorporate. "Big business and both national and local government had ample budgets for the arts at Banpaku," Kanazawa notes. "Lots of artists were invited to show whatever they wished, without juries."[4] The retailing chieftain and arts patron Tsutsumi Seiji, pointing out that big steel companies were especially generous to the arts at the event, remarks that Banpaku was the first chance for fine artists in Japan to take part in an expo — and the last.[5]

The Osaka fair was a gigantic but controversial tent pitched by the country's political and industrial titans to bring together Japan's best cultural products in every realm of endeavor to dazzle the record 64.2 million paying customers, including visitors from around the world, who trekked to the site in the Senri hills east of the city.[6] A few artists did not fit under the tent, preferring to remain outside in protest of the official approval it conferred. Most who were invited to take part did so, having long since abandoned confrontational protests and reconciled themselves to working within the established order that was now proffering lucrative commissions. More vanguard artists came together for this event than ever before in Japan, but it seems implausible that they recaptured even for a moment the spirit of integrated arts *(geijutsu sōgō)* of the late 1940s or the experimental collaborations of the Jikken Kōbō and Sōgetsu Art Center in the 1950s. Instead, like Hōgaku and Western instruments in Takemitsu Tōru's *November Steps,* various genres at Banpaku were juxtaposed, alternated, but in no sense combined — probably because true intermedia hybridity that synthesizes conventional media, so common today, was not yet possible in an arts milieu still grappling as of 1970 with intercultural creolization as a successor mode to the domination of high modernism.

The Art of Protest

When the novelists Oda Makoto and Ōe Kenzaburō helped to inaugurate Beheiren in 1965 in order to condemn the Vietnam War and their country's considerable role in sustaining American intervention in it, they deliberately renounced the conflictual tactics of the old left in favor of building a voluntary, egalitarian movement of citizens who normally had little to do with politics. (Only later did it become apparent that the group was more male-dominated than egalitarian and more self-absorbed than altruistic.) Some avant-garde artists joined in zealously from the start. Already in 1964 Takemitsu Tōru had composed a five-minute a cappella song for an anti–Vietnam War rally titled *Shinda otoko no nokoshita mono wa* (Things bequeathed by a dead man), based on a poem by Tanikawa Shuntarō of the same title. Hayashi Hikaru arranged this work in its present form in 1971.[7]

Another progressive composer, Mamiya Michio, remembers that "the cultural atmosphere of the 1950s and 1960s was very contentious — the Korean War, security treaty, student movements, Vietnam War. The atmosphere for artists became freer after 1965 as a result of the conflicts between left and right. Many composers participated in Beheiren to support peace in Vietnam."[8] Others from the arts community present at the creation of Beheiren were the painter Okamoto Tarō, film director Shinoda Masahiro (1931–), composer Iida Momo (1926–), and writers Terayama Shūji, Noma Hiroshi, Kaikō Takeshi (1930–1989), Nosaka Akiyuki (1930–), Nakano Shigeharu (1902– 1979), and Komatsu Sakyō (1931–).[9] As in the United States and Western Europe, some artists were suspicious of consumerism and commercialism and regarded Vietnam as an effort to impose capitalist values on a preindustrial society. Yet the poet and art historian Tatehata Akira waves off the contribution of arts professionals to the antiwar movement: "Most artists who took part in the citizens' movement Beheiren after 1965 did so as naïve, vaguely antimodernist protestors whose actual political participation was quite shallow."[10] Deep or shallow, what motives impelled avant-garde artists to participate?

Moroi Makoto, the composer, remembers helping the movement for personal rather than political reasons. Although Moroi thinks "Anpo and Beheiren had very little impact on the music world," he recalls that Iida Momo and his wife ran an antiwar bar where four American naval airmen from the aircraft carrier *Intrepid* took refuge after deserting ship in Japan on October 17, 1967. The four sailors, who said they opposed the war in Vietnam "as true Americans, not affiliated with any political party,"[11] sought help from representatives of Beheiren. "Iida asked me to hide them at my house in Nakano," Moroi says, "so I did so, not as a political act but because of my friendship with Iida." The four deserters eventually made their way to Sweden via Siberia and Moscow. Moroi adds, "I was close to a number of protestors but didn't join any demonstrations." Among those who did, he remembers, a number later went to work for the Shiba Shin'yō Kinko bank in Tokyo; he notes that the senior staff of the Japan Arts talent-management agency are almost entirely veterans of the antiwar movement.[12]

Japanese artists who worked abroad during the 1960s were no more likely to plunge into foreign-policy disputes than their counterparts at home. The sculptor Iida Yoshikuni recalls that, as a result of living in a divided Berlin in 1963, "my desire to evade politics gradually grew stronger, and I finally decided to become an antipolitical person."[13] Atsugi Bonjin, the choreographer, says: "I was in New York at a turbulent time socially and politically [1966–1968], but I was focusing on dance and had almost no interest in politics. The demonstrations in Japan when I came back were more like fashion than true protest."[14] In contrast, the abstract painter Dōmoto Hisao, although no activist, admits to being affected by the antiwar movement in France: "While living in Paris, I began to doubt America's foreign policy, especially in Vietnam. Then I watched the May revolution of 1968 at the Sorbonne. I took no sides; I was neutral. But I began to have big questions about France as well as America, so I moved back to Japan, where things were safer."[15]

Other progressive artists in Japan were alienated to some degree by the conflict in Southeast Asia but chose to express their views through art, not on the streets. The radical painter and performance leader Ikeda Ichi used a refitted school bus for itinerant productions along the Tōkaidō as an alternative vehicle of protest:

> The counterculture movement was very strong in Kyoto, where I was studying in the 1960s. Some people chose direct action and political confrontation. Others like me chose a form of total theater expressing how people should live their lives. I thought it was better to criticize politics through art than through student-led activism. I used unconventional, multiphase staging to rethink space and how people relate to it. I wanted to shake up the structure of ordinary human relations. One way to do this was to invite audience participation via a mobile mike.[16]

Ishii Kaoru, the choreographer, used the Tokyo stage to portray what she called the "abnormality and grotesque beauty" of the times in her Kafka-derived work *Zamuzara* (1968). She recalled in 2002 that

> I've always enjoyed interacting with musicians and poets as well as dancers, especially people with social consciousness. None of my choreography is directly political, but indirectly a work such as *Zamuzara* was affected by the student movement and street demonstrations of those days. My dance students talked a great deal about political activism, so of course I couldn't help being affected in my heart.[17]

Affected in a different way was the art-film director Teshigahara Hiroshi, who was forced to cancel a film festival at the Sōgetsu Art Center in 1969 after protests by radical young people. As a result, Dore Ashton reports, 172 noncommercial films went unscreened.[18] Teshigahara thereafter slighted the arts center and devoted himself during 1971–1972 to collaborating with the Princeton-based director John Nathan in making *Summer Soldiers*, a film about American deserters from the Vietnam War. The cinema historian Donald Richie writes that this production opposes "the quotidian realism of the ordinary and the everyday" to the "raw, wild chaos which exists under the surface of the film."[19] Many other examples of politics in art are to be found in painting, theater, poetry, and fiction.

The Monoha movement in sculpture was the most cutting-blade movement in the visual arts when the nonaligned student organizations known as Zenkyōtō began storming the academy in 1968. Both decried modernity: the Monoha by undermining modernist principles in art, the radical students through self-criticism of the modern in themselves and their society.[20] Yet the Monoha sculptors stayed free of political activism. Suga Kishio explains: "I was a hippie when I was young, but I found that those who are active in protests aren't the most progressive intellectually. The most innovating artists worked out their radical ideas in the studio during this upheaval."[21] But Lee Ufan says a number of student activists began reading his criticism starting in 1969: "Like me, they saw Japan joining the international arena through the U.N., the Olympics, economic growth led by exports, and the world exposition planned for Osaka in 1970. They and I both wondered what sort of country Japan was becoming. Many of them criticized liberals such as Maruyama Masao and socialists such as Ishimoda Shō, while admiring Mishima Yukio"[22] — unmistakable signs of the antimodernist outlook they shared with the Monoha.

In 1968 young art students and lecturers at Tamabi formed an Artists' Joint Struggle Council as an offshoot of Zenkyōtō, with members also from Nihon University, Tokyo University of Fine Arts and Music (Geidai), and universities in Kyoto. This artists' council, or Bikyōtō, shared the Monoha's antipathy to modernism, but the two ended up as rivals despite their common origins at Tamabi. Tatehata Akira believes that "both were opposed to the arts establishment and very opposed to modernism artistically and modernization economically. Both saw the previous avant-garde in Japan as still modernist. Both rejected the manipulation of ideas by the modernist subject and were profoundly antimodernist in overall outlook."[23] For his part, Yoshimura Masunobu, the leader of the Neo-Dada group that young Bikyōtō partisans scorned, ridiculed the latter's anarchism in wishing to destroy the art museums.[24] Lee Ufan points out that "there were conservative as well as progressive elements in Zenkyōtō, and Bikyōtō was rather conservative. It was fairly small, and it criticized the Monoha as 'mystical,' although there was nothing mystical about us."[25] The greatest divergence was doubtless mini-generational: although most had been students just a few years earlier, the Monoha sculptors were starting to establish themselves professionally by 1968 and had little time or taste for campus activism. Bikyōtō, by contrast, produced very little art and mainly issued proclamations about university governance, the war in Southeast Asia, and the extension of Anpo in 1970.

The composer and Beheiren veteran Iida Momo was not fooled by the radical students on Japan's campuses during 1968–1970: "we knew that what was happening was a revolt and not a revolution."[26] But caution is called for when evaluating the recollections of artists such as Iida Yoshikuni, Atsugi Bonjin, or the Monoha sculptors about their noninvolvement in political questions at the end of the 1960s. Proud artists, like most other prominent persons, may not wish to risk public humiliation by being associated with what might seem in retrospect to be failed causes — angry countercurrents that never led to a true sea change. Without question, students, artists, and other intellectuals had little impact on the outcome of public events in 1968–1970: the security treaty was extended automatically and without catharsis, Japan remained a vital staging area for American military operations in Indochina until the 1973 cease-fire, and higher education continued to be largely elitist. Yet the late 1960s were critical for Japanese artists in terms of value and self-assessment. They were forced by events to confront the crisis of modernist assumptions about both art and life. Moreover, as the art historian Chiba Shigeo notes, they were obliged "to rethink what art is, what the place of the artist is in society and politics, to be clear on the artist's role."[27] Although protest via confrontation evaporated after 1970, art remained a valid agent of social criticism and public mobilization for the citizens' movements that replaced street demonstrations as the main vehicle of redress in the 1970s and beyond.

Banpaku as an Arts Festival

The world exposition of science and industry held at Osaka in 1970, like the Tokyo Olympics six years earlier, was the first in any country east of Suez. The event was Osaka's answer to Tokyo in 1964: new subways, highways, and hotels were completed to accommodate international visitors to Japan's latest showcase to the world, even though most who attended were Japanese. Science and technology were the chosen themes, under the slogan "Progress and Harmony of Mankind." A popular centerpiece was an Apollo spacecraft and a rock brought back from the moon after the July 20, 1969, lunar landing by American astronauts. Nearby exhibits displayed Japanese space technology developed at sites in Kagoshima prefecture and on Tanegashima island, as well as model transportation networks and electronic information systems of the future. As with Ichikawa Kon's *Tokyo Olympiad* (1965), documenting the October 1964 games, the subtext at Banpaku was clear: The United States was number one, but Japan was catching up fast.

Banpaku was "a monumental event in which the nation's very prestige was at stake," according to the catalog of a recent retrospective exhibit of its art works. Its supporters, particularly business leaders in the Kansai area, "saw it as an excellent opportunity for further economic development,"[28] backed by heavy donations from the Mitsui, Mitsubishi, and Sumitomo conglomerates as well as a Midas' chest contributed by smaller companies in the Kyoto-Osaka-Kobe region. Okamoto Tarō was named chief producer of the theme pavilion, Progress and Harmony, but admitted he had misgivings because progress "directed eyes only to the future" and harmony might mean pressure to conform. Do progress and harmony "mean human spiritual advancement?" he asked rhetorically. "It's high doubtful." Yet in the end, perhaps relying on his theory of polar oppositions, he said he decided to take a chance on Banpaku despite the huge sums of corporate money involved because "people would gather in one place from all over the world" on a scale much greater than the Olympics for a huge "festival to the oneness of humanity."[29]

Well before the exposition began, a number of other artists expressed misgivings about the potentially controlling influence of corporate capital at Banpaku or the implicit link between participating in its events and supporting the security treaty. A few who were invited to take part declined to do so, despite the exposure and commissions Banpaku offered their works. Hayashi Hikaru remembers that "the Osaka expo was a big turning point for contemporary music. Almost all the composers of my generation except Mamiya Michio and me took part. Haryū Ichirō was strongly opposed to Banpaku; I was less strongly opposed, but just then I was involved in the Kansai folk-song movement and thought I should support its members, so I didn't participate in Banpaku." At the same time, as someone linked to the old-left peace movement of the early 1950s, Hayashi "had no connection with Oda Makoto or Beheiren,"[30] so he likewise declined to attend a counterculture exposition called Hanpaku (Anti-Banpaku) that was held on August 7–11, 1969, on the grounds of Osaka castle.

Hanpaku originated with a February 1969 Beheiren conference seeking to combat "the commercialism and big-power nationalism" of the Osaka exposition taking place the following year. The theme of Hanpaku was "peace and liberation for mankind," in contrast to the official "progress and harmony" slogan of Expo '70.[31] Other signs of opposition to Banpaku began to emerge in the spring of 1969 as well. The performance group Zero Dimension (Zero Jigen) put on a large, seminude "ritual" of resistance in Nagoya. The anti-modernist art group Kumo in Kitakyushu staged erotic happenings in April and May as a part of its Kyushu Rally to Destroy Banpaku (Banpaku Hakai Kyushu Taikai).[32] Hanpaku itself was led by a committee called the Association for the World Exposition to Oppose War (Hansen no Tame no Bankoku-haku Kyōkai). At its August 1969 demonstration in Osaka, some criticized the upcoming Expo '70 as an "avant-garde arts festival" that ignored political questions. Others claimed that "Banpaku is camouflage for the extension of the Japan–United States Mutual Security Treaty in 1970."[33] In contrast to the large antiwar rallies held that year in central Osaka, however, only six thousand people — mainly anti-Vietnam War activists — showed up for Hanpaku. Both Beheiren leaders and participating artists criticized the organizers for selling books at a profit and sounding so shrill an antiestablishmentarian tone as to court a mortal backlash.[34]

Whatever their apprehension about taking part in Banpaku, nearly all artists who received invitations decided to accept them, thus choosing what they believed was realism over radicalism. Sometimes the reason given was artistic pride, sometimes the lucrative commission. The architect and Neo-Dada supporter Isozaki Arata said he sympathized with the Hanpaku movement but decided to participate in Expo '70 as a professional.[35] Perhaps the composer Takahashi Yūji best captures the tortuous thinking of many who elected to present their work at Expo '70:

> Takemitsu Tōru invited Iannis Xenakis and me to prepare music for one of the Banpaku pavilions. He also brought other Japanese and international composers there for a contemporary-music festival in the summer of 1970. Akiyama Kuniharu and Yuasa Jōji were put in charge of music for other pavilions. While I was getting ready for Banpaku in 1969, Oda Makoto asked me to join a rally against the expo, but I told him that I had decided to participate, so we ended up taking different positions. Hanpaku was not a very big thing — one or two rallies and some pamphlets. But we artists discussed a good deal about whether we should take part. Banpaku was a very rare occasion for artists to make big money, so everyone came up with this excuse or that for participating. The music presented there was of high quality.[36]

So too was the amazing variety of visual art, even though it was nonjuried: the paintings, still sculptures, installations, kinetic art, light shows, and photographs were of a surprisingly high standard, many of them submitted by antimodernist or other antiestablishment artists for exhibit in corporate-sponsored pavilions or galleries. The Osaka exposition ended up being the largest display of vanguard visual products since the final Yomiuri Independent in 1963, a fitting climax to the final decade of truly avant-garde art in Japan.

The single art work most closely identified with Banpaku, then and now, was a stunning concrete construction by its main artistic director, Okamoto Tarō. The hallmark edifice of the entire expo, his *Taiyō no tō (Sun Tower)*, was a controversial but unforgettable symbol of the conflicts swirling around Banpaku and the entire country in 1970 (see Plate 9). Okamoto designed this seventy-meter-high humanoid figure with three faces, representing past, present, and future, so that one face could always be seen from anywhere in the expo park. He erected this shocking sculpture as a "challenge" to the modernist theme of progress and harmony. It was meant as an artifact "that would seem to have been there since ancient times, that would reach out to the human soul, and would be 'outrageous.'"[37] His bold tactic worked: after Banpaku closed its doors, the exposition authority and prefectural officials decided to preserve the Sun Tower as it was, even though most of the pavilions and displays were soon dismantled.

Although most of his earlier art was more dissonant than syncretistic, Okamoto saw the Banpaku tower as an opportunity to meld East Asian and Western design principles.[38] He doubtless also realized that, as chief artistic producer for the exposition, he had complete freedom to make an architectural statement. The interior contained a tree of life, with exhibits on the origins of living things, their evolution across time, and the future world of progress. Some critics, such as Hyūga Akiko, applauded *Taiyō no tō*, finding that it "expresses human dreams."[39] The sculptor Iida Yoshikuni, admitting that the Sun Tower "really surprised me," praised it as "a symbol of Japan's rapid economic growth."[40] But the literary critic Etō Jun called it "grotesque," and others ridiculed it as "Tarō Tower" and "Ridiculous (*berabō*) Tower."[41] Okamoto's response was, "I wanted to build something to stir a reaction, not something everybody likes."[42] Improbable as it might seem, the design for the Sun Tower was copied by the Self-Defense Forces in January 1970 as a giant ice sculpture for the twentieth Sapporo Winter Festival, where it was seen by as many as four million people.[43] Similar large works in various materials are still on view at Sukiyabashi, Tokyo, and elsewhere in Japan.

Okamoto, who by now was a media celebrity and Japan's best-known popularizer of the visual arts, was a powerful and self-confident personality who brooked no questions, an ideal figure to make things happen as artistic impresario for the exposition. Ōoka Makoto relates that "Okamoto didn't deal well with people; he was very focused on himself and abrupt with others. But his Sun Tower at Banpaku had a big impact, both positive and negative."[44] Okamoto's widow Toshiko acknowledges that "Tarō's manner put people off a bit. There was relatively little critical interest in him during the last twenty-five years of his life, which ended in 1996."[45] The art critic Haryū Ichirō confirms this lack of esteem, recounting conversations at a televised panel discussion in the 1970s at which Okamoto and several young artists spoke: "The newcomers were very conservative and were taken aback by Okamoto's anti-Picasso, antiestablishment views. They asked incredulously, 'How can you have become so famous?'"[46] But since his death there has been a renaissance of interest in Okamoto's work, which "has a message for today's young people,"[47] his widow believes. The art section of any major bookstore in Japan today boasts a shelf of his writings. Even scholars are beginning to pay his ideas renewed heed: "in the past decade people have begun to see that what Okamoto was saying is correct,"[48] Kanazawa Takeshi says. Today the Sun Tower is a curiosity from the past, not a living statement. What endures is Okamoto's injunction to experiment fearlessly, confront oppositions, and seek lessons from antiquity.

Another figure of considerable prominence at Osaka was the architect Maki Fumihiko (1928–), whose firm designed the district center at Senri New Town near the Banpaku grounds. On the advice of Shimizu Kusuo, owner of the Minami Gallery in Tokyo, Maki selected Iida Yoshikuni to provide a sculpture for the main plaza.[49] The result was *Suteinresu no mori* (*Forest of Stainless Steel*, 1970), a partly kinetic cluster of three columns topped by large square panels, each composed of subpanels, that reflected the sky and the surrounding Senri hills (see Plate 10). This work resembles a communications satellite, in keeping with the exposition's message of technological progress. Iida also organized an international convention of iron sculptors for Expo '70. With financial support from shipbuilding firms, steel companies, and the Industrial Bank of Japan, he brought three Japanese and a dozen international artists to Osaka for four to six weeks each to work on sculptures for the exposition.[50]

It was hardly surprising that members of the Osaka-based Gutai group, led by their distinctly nonpolitical doyen Yoshihara Jirō, participated with gusto in Banpaku, featuring high technology and imaginative lighting in their works. Motonaga Sadamasa remembers "taking part in a Banpaku evening event in 1970 at the festival plaza and the exhibit in the Green Pavilion at Yoshihara Jirō's request. Yoshihara served as producer" for the exhibit.[51] The program in the festival plaza included a performance by Gutai called *Ningen to buttai no dorama* (Drama of humanity and the physique).[52] Separately the art impresario Watanabe Misa arranged a show of paintings by members of the Dōmoto family, centering on the work of the Kyoto Nihonga expert Dōmoto Inshō.[53] Usami Keiji (1940–), a light artist whose laser equipment was provided by Shimizu Kusuo, put on a display as part of the technology exhibit at Banpaku. One spectator, Ōoka Makoto, described it as "more an event than art, but it was also very beautiful."[54]

Advanced technology, especially electronic techniques, also characterized much of the innovative art music presented at Banpaku. The immediate musical precursor to Expo '70 was the Crosstalk series held several times in the late 1960s under Yuasa Jōji's direction and the Tokyo American Center's sponsorship. These performances included a number of new compositions for mixed media, including film, dance, and light images. At Banpaku many of the Crosstalk composers were parceled out to various pavilions for concerts that the critic Chōki Seiji calls "the first rapprochement of contemporary composers with big business."[55] Takemitsu Tōru, for example, consistently feared the power of government and business to rob artistic freedom, yet he readily agreed to take part in Banpaku and, starting in 1973, accepted corporate sponsorship of his Music Today series. Mayuzumi Toshirō, who also appeared at Expo '70, had few such qualms about allying himself with the rich and powerful: he had composed the music for the opening ceremony at the 1964 Olympics, the bell-like jingle for the Shinkansen superexpress trains the same year, and the clock chimes played by the Odakyū department store at the west-exit plaza of Shinjuku station.[56] Ichiyanagi Toshi was another leading composer of art music who played a key part at Banpaku.[57]

ART, MONEY, AND POLITICS converged in 1970 as they had not since the shogun Ashikaga Yoshimitsu (Kitayama-dono, r. 1367–1395) healed the schism between rival imperial lines, lavished his treasury on artists, and represented himself to the Ming court as the virtual king of Japan. Although several decades have elapsed since the Osaka exposition, even today the residue of Banpaku seems problematic. Artists who were not represented at Expo '70 were naturally excluded from the largesse. One of them, the Neo-Dada figure Shinohara Ushio, marvels that "the artists and musicians who took part in Banpaku got rich very suddenly."[58] His colleague Akasegawa Genpei agrees that "Banpaku was good for art sales and for the recognition given to artists. But I didn't think the art displayed there was very interesting, and my own works were not included in the exhibition."[59]

Before Expo '70, Chōki Seiji points out, most "contemporary composers hated the idea of being supported by the government. Banpaku was a major turning point: thereafter commissions came from big businesses like Seibu and governmental units such as the Agency for Cultural Affairs."[60] So profitable was the exposition that in 1971 the Diet established a commemorative fund from the proceeds. By 1980 the endowment was worth $77.5 million, permitting grants of $2.9 million that year for the arts, cultural exchange, academic cooperation, and other international activities.[61] Nonetheless Ōoka Makoto dismisses the Osaka exposition as "a flower that doesn't blossom" (*adabana*).[62] Most artists who participated, regardless of genre, seem to have quickly moved on, "independent of groups, and scattered" in many directions, as Yuasa Jōji has said about composers.[63] As Japan entered the 1970s, vanguard art grew increasingly diverse, while society paradoxically grew more and more integrated. This conundrum remained unresolved for the rest of the twentieth century and continues to vex artists and critics in Japan to this day.

chapter eleven

Radicals and Realists

Looking back in 1979, the outspoken Kyushuha painter Kikuhata Mokuma characterized Japan's quarter century of artistic experience since the end of the American occupation in bittersweet terms:

> In tandem with its popularization, contemporary art continues to develop its social function stunningly, with every genre playing a part in some way or other. It's truly splendid that contemporary art reflects world trends as soon as they occur and that it has close ties with popular culture. Yet I keep wondering if the basis of artistic creativity hasn't begun to lag a bit. Gradually the arts have begun to lose their purity and antiestablishment perspective. . . . The rise of Banpaku and environmental art signals the decline of the logic of the postwar avant-garde arts movement.[1]

Echoing Bourdieu, Kikuhata believed that art was becoming "a kind of social phenomenon," a handmaiden of state and corporation that was no longer "able to offer criticism" of deceptive social practices in the managed structure of the 1970s. He conceded that it was better for the arts to be protected than squashed by the establishment, but he asserted that art should have a paradoxical relationship with authority, not a complaisant one. He correctly noted the irony that artists had to look to a vertical social order and powerful state for guarantees of their artistic freedom and individual rights.[2] Kikuhata pinpointed one of the two major contradictions of Japanese artistic expression in the 1950s and 1960s: the interpenetration of state and society against which many avant-garde figures rebelled also provided them the stability they needed for producing their critical works. This same dilemma faced artists worldwide long before the emergence of the modern state, yet the social integration that was made possible by the technology of government in the twentieth century was unprecedented. This integration reached a heightened state in Japan starting in the mid-1960s and remained in effect for the next three decades, reinforcing the irony that Kikuhata pointed out.

The other big contradiction, stemming from Japan's centuries-long record of fitful interaction with the outside world, was the degree to which culture is national. Whether seeking new trends from the West or renewed inspiration from Asia, most vanguard artists in Japan during the 1950s and 1960s sought cosmopolitan goals yet were confined in practice to working in a national — although rarely nationalist — context. Japanese avant-garde artists in every genre began the 1950s seeking renewed communication across genre boundaries, through the integrated-arts efforts of both Abe Kōbō and the Experimental Workshop inspired by Takiguchi Shūzō. Cheered onward by Okamoto Tarō in the mid-1950s, this movement reached its apex at the Sōgetsu Art Center from 1959 to the mid-1960s, then receded in the face of ever-greater specialization and variegation thereafter. Innovative artists from the Shōwa single-digit generation, born between 1926 and 1934, entered the 1950s parched for up-to-date information about developments abroad after growing up under military censorship and entering adulthood under neocolonial occupation by the United States. Their thirst abated only in the mid-1960s thanks in good part to growing incomes, speedier travel, and improved telecommunications. In the absence of much interaction with the outside world during the early 1950s, some of Japan's most creative figures devised new techniques in parallel with, but distinct from, their overseas counterparts: Takemitsu with a form of musique concrète while apparently unaware of Pierre Schaeffer's work, Moroi Makoto improvising a twelve-tone system in isolation from Darmstadt, or indigenous Gutai art that seemed similar to French informel.

For those able to study abroad or learn about innovations there, the late 1950s and early 1960s were the acme of artistic interaction with the West (dance lagged music and the visual arts by a half decade). Many progressive dancers, musicians, painters, and sculptors at that juncture agreed with Ichiyanagi Toshi that the West supplied excellent tools with which to understand their own arts. Thereafter an antimodernist tide steadily eroded the cultural preeminence of Europe and North America, especially among contemporary Japanese artists born in the Shōwa double-digit years (1935 and after). Much of the resistance to the West, as Nakanishi Natsuyuki indicated, resulted from disenchantment with modernism as an aspect of modernization, with its stepchildren of pollution, inequalities, and materialism. The new antimodernism afforded vanguard individuals space to seek alternative modernities locally, in present time and current context. Most often, artists chose elements close at hand in local folk customs (e.g., Mamiya Michio) or from East Asia (e.g., Dan Ikuma, Takahashi Yūji) to establish difference from the West, only rarely to tout superiority over it. Usually the result was an idiom that was specifically post-Western or, more neutrally, postnational. Yet it was no simple matter to harmonize the global and the local, to become known as a humanist who happened to be Japanese rather than as a Japanese humanist. Only in a limited way were artists able to transcend nationality and participate in the dynamic transcultural interaction known as creolization. As with the struggle between social solidarity and artistic individuality, the question of national culture continued to vex artists for the remainder of the twentieth century and remains incompletely resolved today.

Speaking from secure roots in the premodern Japanese arts, the critic Katō Shūichi argues that typically the artist rebels against the establishment or against traditional styles of art (in Kikuhata's case it was both).[3] Contemporary art as a cultural practice was far from disengaged with social and political issues in the 1950s and 1960s, despite efforts by a few disillusioned elite artists in the Shōwa single-digit generation to dissociate themselves retrospectively from failed causes. If artists' radicalism was tempered by realism in the latter decade, it was often a matter of tactics, not capitulation to authority. To be sure, fewer of them overtly denounced the state after the protests of 1968–1970 fizzled and Banpaku sparkled with corporate gold, but one need look no farther than the amazingly varied visual products and the burgeoning folk music of the 1970s to find evidence of continued resistance and alternative imaginings of reality.[4] Even if Kikuhata is right that Banpaku and technology-driven environmental art brought down the curtain on the avant-garde arts movement of the 1950s and 1960s, the cultural history of Japan after 1970 retained its sharp political blade, whittling more often than hacking as the politics of confrontation gave way to the politics of civic participation.

Anti-art radicals at the turn of the 1960s had only a limited effect on visual production, but they speeded the de-emphasis on artistry that began with the Gutai group in 1954 and produced works showing greater realism, no longer abstraction. They also helped to hone a sharper critical viewpoint in the 1960s, evident in the perspectives of Monoha leaders such as Lee Ufan and Suga Kishio but also in the outlooks of Ichiyanagi Toshi and Hijikata Tatsumi, among many others. The age of grand experiments triggered by Takiguchi, Okamoto, and Yoshihara Jirō in the first half of the 1950s came to a symbolic close when Yomiuri abruptly canceled its independent art exhibition in 1964, in some sense a victim of self-indulgence by anti-art practitioners. By 1970 any consensus on what constituted art was in full rout, and with it disappeared the idea of the avant-garde as a self-conscious cadre in revolt against either established authority or preexisting artistic canons. Thereafter artists in every genre increasingly sought out niches of their own, producing a multiplicity of works and ideas that easily tided over a brief surge of artistic neotraditionalism in the 1970s.

The concrete, the everyday, and the local became entwined in the pell-mell to express the realities of personal experience in rebellion against the certitudes of modernist universalism. Artists as diverse as the composer Yuasa Jōji and the High Red Center painter Akasegawa Genpei redefined timing and spacing as authentic properties of the avant-garde: time was made equivalent to the contemporary (now), space/place to the local (here). Art in the 1960s was widely deemed to be immanent in the everyday, in works by the Gutai, Kyushuha, Neo-Dada, and High Red Center groups, in the compositions of Group Ongaku and the choreography of Hijikata and Atsugi Bonjin, in the prints of Noda Tetsuya, in the bodily focus of performance art, and above all in the presentations of the Monoha sculptors, who sought to establish reality but not value. For better or worse, it was now clear that context matters for art, just as the era matters — even if Ōoka Makoto is right that they shouldn't. In short, the 1950s and 1960s rescued both art and the artist from the borderless and timeless verities of the past and resituated them in the timeful context of current local reality.

Many small movements in the various nonverbal genres sprang up in the 1970s, paralleling a new postmodern mode in Japan that renewed the assault begun by antimodernists a decade earlier without abandoning the humanist concerns that have occupied the core of artistic expression for millennia.[5] Commercial art thrived, painting underwent a revival at the end of the 1970s, and newly affluent Japanese began investing in art and artifacts deemed "authentic." Yet modernism, like figurative art or romantic music or classical ballet, remains far from moribund in Japan today, despite the sudden celebrity of such quintessentially postmodern writers as Murakami Haruki (1949–) in the early 1980s and Yoshimoto Banana (1964–) at the end of the decade.

Ever since, the country has experienced an age of "superstars, in literature, music, architecture, and film — but not painting or sculpture," in the opinion of Tatehata Akira. By coincidence, four of the most celebrated — Okamoto Tarō, Takemitsu Tōru, Akiyama Kuniharu, and the novelist Shiba Ryōtarō — died within months of one another in 1996. Starting in the 1990s came a fresh wave of arts from Asia: first from Indonesia, the Philippines, and Thailand, then from China and Korea. Takahashi Yūji's Water Buffalo project is one example; another is the opening of the Fukuoka Asian Art Museum in 1999. Much of this activity was supported by the Japan Foundation, which promoted a form of multiculturalism termed postmodern "glocalism" — pulling in arts from Japan's former colonies and occupied areas.[6] Continuing the drumbeat of resistance to social management, the painter Murakami Takashi (1962–) debuted in 1991 with superflat art that criticized the infantilization of Japanese culture by consumerism and the mass media.

In the years since 1970 few pacesetters of the early postwar avant-garde have been daunted by the balkanization, commercialization, or diversification of what seems, in retrospect, like a tidy and relatively unified core of innovative artistic activity when they were young. The former Neo-Dada painter Arakawa Shūsaku declared in 2002 that "about ten years ago I quit painting to build neighborhoods for old and not-so-old people in Nagoya, as a kind of 'coordinologist.'"[7] Long after Banpaku drew down its shutters, the choreographer Tachikawa Ruriko said she hoped people would turn to art "as they realize material prosperity isn't fully satisfying."[8] Moroi Makoto, who today serves as director of a major cultural center in suburban Saitama prefecture, affirms that "my religion is the arts. I'm very lucky to be able to embrace all the arts, including poetry. The theater building or concert hall is the church of the twenty-first century; the arts are based in a secular liturgy."[9] For these and many other progressive figures from the 1950s and 1960s, it seems that life is long — and art even longer.

Still, not all is well in Terpsichore's temple. A continuing problem is the lack of true criticism and rigorous scholarship on the contemporary arts. Writing in 2001, Haryū Ichirō complained that Japanese audiences for art were "still immature," lacking "the ability to form appropriate judgments and opinions and respond emotionally to individual works of art."[10] The gallery owner Kawatsuma Sachiko, however, sees Haryū as part of the problem: "Japanese critics from the 1950s and 1960s, such as Tōno Yoshiaki, Segi Shin'ichi, Nakahara Yūsuke, and Haryū Ichirō, became so powerful that no one questioned their views, and their opinions came to carry almost too much weight."[11] A complication, says the expatriate pop artist Shinohara Ushio, is that "the critics dismiss you until foreigners praise your work, whereupon the Japanese critics relax and say 'yes, yes.' To earn recognition in Japan, you have to be praised abroad."[12] "Once an artist gains a powerful reputation in Japan," Miyake Haruna concurs, "it's impossible to criticize him or her. Takemitsu Tōru, for example, was impervious to criticism once he earned a reputation in the West. As a result, there is little free expression or honest assessment of works by senior composers."[13]

Although Takemitsu Tōru is the most famous postwar composer in Japan," the musicologist Chōki Seiji adds, "we must subject him to the same critical standards as other composers, not just praise him because he's well known abroad."[14] The same holds true for dance, Miyake believes: "Ōno Kazuo is in his mid-nineties and above criticism. I've played accompaniment onstage with him since 1990, and he's truly a great dancer, but, like Takemitsu when he was alive, Ōno dominates contemporary dance, leaving very little space for others."[15] If so, little has changed since Hattori Chieko, president of the Japan Ballet Association in 1980, observed that "in Japan no one wants to criticize, so dancers go along without competing very severely."[16] Until recently, most arts criticism was written by reporters, not specialists, and a number of them accepted honoraria in exchange for favorable reviews. Fewer than a dozen senior scholars in Japan's colleges and universities specialize in contemporary art music, and not many more in contemporary visual media. Research on contemporary dance is scarcely recognized in the academy at all. This lack of subject expertise is the main reason for the absence of sophisticated criticism in the nonverbal arts, compared with literature, philosophy, or politics. More generally, avoiding confrontation and criticism is tightly woven into the social fabric of Japan, where honors are bestowed profusely and every child wins a prize for participating in school athletic festivals. The relative lack of head-to-head internal competition within arts groups (as opposed to the heated rivalries between schools or companies) does nothing to refine one's skills, but it reinforces the collective solidarity that undergirds all the arts in Japan.

A second problem involves patronage and the social function of the artist. Japanese choreographers, composers, painters, and sculptors display great dignity and professionalism, expressing a deep love for their vocation and often paying large sums to patronize it themselves when it is not commercially sustainable. Jasper Johns is said to have quipped, "The best criticism of a work of art is another work of art."[17] Lacking better criticism and more serious scholarship by others, a number of Japanese artists seem to have paraphrased Johns by taking the role of critic into their own hands. Suga Kishio says that "artists themselves end up writing their own explanations of their works for the tiny audiences who appreciate the contemporary."[18] Akasegawa Genpei, the celebrated novelist and former radical painter, explains that "I see my main role as a writer of criticism, not just fiction. Almost no one appreciates the Japanese arts, so it's my duty to write about them."[19]

An excellent example of artists patronizing fellow artists is Iwaki Hiroyuki, who has become a major sponsor of contemporary art music through his position as Japan's most famous conductor. "If Beethoven and other avant-garde composers had not been supported in their own time, their work would be lost to history," Iwaki says. "So I've felt an obligation to perform current composers for the benefit of future generations. Altogether I've conducted the Japan premieres of two or three thousand works since the 1950s, mainly by Japanese composers." Iwaki has also commissioned "at least one fifteen-minute work by a contemporary Japanese composer for the past fifteen or sixteen years because I hope to leave a legacy for the future. Japan has more composers than any other country, and many are of high quality."[20]

Fortunately for the muses of the arts, their most perceptive followers in Japan recognize the paradox of the radical artist confronting rampant consumerism, new technologies, and worldwide interconnectedness. Little more than a year before his death in early 1996, Takemitsu shrewdly observed that "the tension between the uniformity of globalization and the diversification of culture gives rise to new human relations that transcend the state. The most important thing for us should be to have the wisdom to understand this tension"[21] — the history, and the promise, of Japan's postwar arts in a nutshell.

Notes

Introduction

1. See Dennis C. Washburn, *The Dilemma of the Modern in Japanese Fiction* (New Haven, Conn.: Yale University Press, 1995), pp. 2–4.

2. Tsutsumi Seiji (penname: Tsujii Takashi) interview, Tokyo, April 8, 2002.

3. Ichiyanagi Toshi interview, Tokyo, April 11, 2002.

4. Tatehata Akira interview, Tokyo, March 4, 2002.

5. Sakai Tadayasu interview, Kamakura, March 5, 2002.

6. See Yoichi Nagashima, ed., *Return to Japan: From "Pilgrimage" to the West* (Aarhus, Denmark: Aarhus University Press, 2001), for a discussion of the West as a concept of fantasy and Japan as one of nostalgia. China was an object of fantasy for Japanese writers in the Edo (1600–1868) period, as was Paris for some Americans after World War One.

7. Enomoto Kazuko letter, February 28, 2002.

8. Sakai Tadayasu interview, Kamakura, March 5, 2002.

9. Terada Tōru regards architecture as the core of contemporary art and points out that, unlike painting, it can't be ignored: people have to walk past it every day. Terada, *Japanese Art in World Perspective*, trans. Thomas Guerin (New York and Tokyo: Weatherhill/Heibonsha, 1976), p. 77.

10. Howard Hibbett interview, Cambridge, Mass., April 21, 2003.

11. Chiba Shigeo interview, Tokyo, March 11, 2002.

12. Deborah Poole, *Vision, Race, and Modernity: A Visual Economy of the Andean Image World* (Princeton, N.J.: Princeton University Press, 1997), p. 7.

13. See Arjun Appadurai, *Modernity at Large: Cultural Dimensions of Globalization* (Minneapolis: University of Minnesota Press, 1996).

14. Carol Gluck, "The Past in the Present," in Andrew Gordon, ed., *Postwar Japan as History* (Berkeley: University of California Press, 1993), p. 78.

15. Ann Sherif, review of Jay Rubin, *Haruki Murakami and the Music of Words* (London: Harvill, 2002), and of Matthew Carl Strecher, *Dances with Sheep: The Quest for Identity in the Fiction of Murakami Haruki* (Ann Arbor: Center for Japanese Studies, University of Michigan, 2002), in *Journal of Japanese Studies* 29:2 (2003), 369.

16. Sōgetsu Bijutsukan, ed., *Hizō shiryō ni miru sengo bijutsu no shōgen* (Tokyo: Sōgetsu Bijutsukan, 2000), p. 1.

17. Pierre Bourdieu, *Distinction: A Social Critique of the Judgement of Taste*, trans. Richard Nice (Cambridge, Mass.: Harvard University Press, 1984), p. 7.

18. See E. Taylor Atkins, *Blue Nippon: Authenticating Jazz in Japan* (Durham, N.C.: Duke University Press, 2001), p. 14.

19. Bourdieu, *Distinction*, p. xi.

20. Randal Johnson, "Editor's Introduction," in Pierre Bourdieu, *The Field of*

Cultural Production: Essays on Art and Literature, ed. Randal Johnson (New York: Columbia University Press, 1993), p. 9.

21. Ibid., p. 13.

22. Marc Bloch, "Toward a Comparative History of European Societies" (1928), in Frederic C. Lane and Jelle C. Riemersma, eds., *Enterprise and Secular Change: Readings in Economic History* (Homewood, Ill.: R. D. Irwin, 1953), pp. 494–512; Henri Pirenne, "What Historians Are Trying to Do," in Stuart A. Rice, ed., *Methods in Social Science: A Case Book* (Chicago: University of Chicago Press, 1931), pp. 444–459; C. Vann Woodward, "The Comparability of American History," in Woodward, ed., *The Comparative Approach to American History* (New York: Basic Books, 1968), pp. 3–17.

23. A path-breaking regionwide study is Stephen N. Hay, *Asian Ideals of East and West: Tagore and His Critics in Japan, China, and India* (Cambridge, Mass.: Harvard University Press, 1970).

24. The classic study is Immanuel M. Wallerstein, *The Modern World-System: Capitalist Agriculture and the Origins of the European World Economy in the Sixteenth Century* (New York: Academic Press, 1974). Two volumes of note are Andre Gunder Frank, *ReOrient: Global Economy in the Asian Age* (Berkeley: University of California Press, 1998), and Kenneth Pomeranz, *The Great Divergence: Europe, China, and the Making of the Modern World Economy* (Princeton, N.J.: Princeton University Press, 2000).

25. Adumbrated in Adam McKeown, *Chinese Migrant Networks and Cultural Change: Peru, Chicago, and Hawaii, 1900–1936* (Chicago: University of Chicago Press, 2001). For an overview of the history of culture in a global context, see Patrick Manning, "Cultural History," in *Navigating World History* (New York: Palgrave Macmillan, 2003).

26. Julie Rivkin and Michael Ryan, eds., *Literary Theory: An Anthology* (Malden, Mass., and Oxford, Eng.: Blackwell Publishers, 1998), p. 3.

27. Victor Brombert, *In Praise of Antiheroes: Figures and Themes in Modern European Literature, 1830–1980* (Chicago: University of Chicago Press, 1999), p. 1.

Chapter One: The Occupation and Modernity

1. Arakawa Shūsaku interview, New York, June 24, 2002.

2. Fukuzawa Yukichi, "Good-Bye Asia (Datsu-a), 1885," in David J. Lu, ed., *Japan: A Documentary History,* vol. 2: *The Late Tokugawa Period to the Present* (Armonk, N.Y.: M. E. Sharpe, 1997), pp. 351–353.

3. Okakura Kakuzō, *The Awakening of Japan* (New York: Century Co., 1904); Okakura, *Ideals of the East, with Special Reference to the Art of Japan* (London: J. Murray, 1905).

4. Naoki Sakai, "Modernity and Its Critique," in Masao Miyoshi and Harry D. Harootunian, eds., *Postmodernism and Japan* (Durham, N.C.: Duke University Press, 1989), pp. 113–114. Emphasis in the original. Sakai's position echoes that of the literary critic Kobayashi Hideo (1902–1983), who in 1933 wrote that "we have become so used to the reception of Western influence that we no longer can identify it as Western influence." Kobayashi, "Literature of the Lost Home," in Paul Anderer,

ed. and trans., *Literature of the Lost Home: Kobayashi Hideo — Literary Criticism,
1924–1939* (Stanford, Calif.: Stanford University Press, 1995), p. 49, quoted in Seiji
M. Lippit, *Topographies of Japanese Modernism* (New York: Columbia University
Press, 2002), p. 4.

5. Kosaku Yoshino, *Cultural Nationalism in Contemporary Japan: A Sociological
Enquiry* (London: Routledge, 1992), p. 11. Such a view presumes that the West is
normative, Japan exceptional.

6. Komiya Tamie, *Kingendai Nihon no ongakushi: juyōshi de wa nai: 1900–1960
nendai* (Tokyo: Sekai no Ongakusha, 2001), p. 157. On occupation censorship, see
John W. Dower, *Embracing Defeat: Japan in the Wake of World War II* (New York:
W. W. Norton, 1999), pp. 405–409, 432–433, 437; Kyoko Hirano, *Mr. Smith Goes to
Tokyo: The Japanese Cinema under the American Occupation, 1945–1952* (Washing-
ton, D.C.: Smithsonian Institute, 1992).

7. Yuasa Jōji interview, Tokyo, February 5, 2002. The composer Mamiya Michio
calls the C I & E library "indispensable. . . . We listened to recordings not just of
the classics but also postwar Soviet composers, like Shostakovich, and Americans
such as Harris, Ives, and Sessions. I especially enjoyed hearing works by Hindemith,
Poulenc, and Stravinsky." Mamiya Michio interview, Tokyo, April 22, 2002.

8. Moroi Makoto interview, Saitamashi, March 30, 2002.

9. Ōoka Makoto interview, Tokyo, March 9, 2002.

10. Tsutsumi Seiji interview, Tokyo, April 8, 2002.

11. Suda Kunitarō, "Waga aburae wa izuko ni yuku ka," *Mizue*, November 1947,
pp. 19–21, quoted in Tatehata Akira, "Mono-ha and Japan's Crisis of the Modern,"
in Simon Groom, ed., *Mono-ha — School of Things*, exh. cat. (Cambridge, Eng.:
Kettle's Yard, University of Cambridge, 2001), p. 27.

12. Etō's research on censorship in occupation archives is summarized in his *Tozasareta gengo kūkan: senryōgun no ken'etsu to sengo Nihon* (Tokyo: Bungei Shunjū,
1989). On censorship, see Donald Keene, "Japanese Writers and the Greater East
Asia War," in Keene, *Landscapes and Portraits: Appreciations of Japanese Culture*
(Tokyo: Kodansha International, 1971), pp. 300–321; Jay Rubin, "From Wholesome-
ness to Decadence: The Censorship of Literature under the Allied Occupation,"
Journal of Japanese Studies 11:1 (1985), 71–103; Dower, *Embracing Defeat*, pp.
405–440; Etō Jun, "The Civil Censorship in Occupied Japan," *Hikaku bunka zasshi
(Annual of Comparative Culture)* 1 (1982): 1–21; Etō Jun, "The Sealed Linguistic
Space: The Occupation Censorship and Post-war Japan," trans. Jay Rubin, part 1,
Hikaku bunka zasshi (Annual of Comparative Culture) 2 (1984): 1–42; part 2, *Hikaku
bunka zasshi (Annual of Comparative Culture)* 3 (1988): 1–23. Some critics have portrayed the American occupation as neocolonialist; others cite U.S. administration of
the Ryukyu Islands until 1972 or the Japan–United States Mutual Security Treaty, in
effect from 1952 to the present, as evidence of American neocolonialism.

13. See Etō Jun, *Amerika to watakushi* (Tokyo: Kōdansha, 1965); Lawrence Olson,
Ambivalent Moderns: Portraits of Japanese Cultural Identity (Savage, Md.: Rowman
and Littlefield, 1992), pp. 20, 34. The art critic Haryū Ichirō points out that Etō abandoned his youthful radicalism in the late 1950s in order to criticize the occupation
"from a very nationalistic viewpoint." He later was a consultant to Prime Minister
Fukuda Takeo in the 1970s. Haryū Ichirō interview, Tokyo, February 12, 2002. Segi

Shin'ichi recalls that Etō was "more antiestablishment than anti-American." Segi Shin'ichi interview, Tokyo, February 11, 2002.

14. Yamashita Fumio, *Atarashii seiji to bunka* (Tokyo: Shin Nihon Shuppansha, 1975), p. 17. See Hidaka Rokurō, "Sengo bunka undōshi no susume," *Iwanami kōza Nihon rekishi geppō* 25 (1977): 5.

15. Dower, *Embracing Defeat*, p. 561. Dower calls postoccupation Japan "a client state in all but name" (p. 552). See also pp. 439, 551–553.

16. Tanaka Takaki interview, Tokyo, February 14, 2002.

17. Washburn, *Dilemma*, p. 8.

18. Kuwabara Takeo, *Gendai Nihon bunka no hansei* (Tokyo: Hakujitsu Shoin, 1947); Hamaguchi Ryūichi, *Hyūmanizumu no kenchiku: Nihon kindai kenchiku no hansei to tenbō* (Tokyo: Ondorisha, 1947). See also Murayama Yasuo, "Japan/I Torn Apart," in *1953: Shedding Light on Art in Japan*, trans. Reiko Tomii, exh. cat. (Tokyo: Tama Art University), p. 15.

19. Katō's views are recapitulated in his *Zasshu bunka: Nihon no chiisa na kibō* (Tokyo: Kōdansha, 1974). See Yoshikuni Igarashi, *Bodies of Memory: Narratives of War in Postwar Japanese Culture, 1945–1970* (Princeton, N.J.: Princeton University Press, 2000), pp. 80–81.

20. See Bert Winther-Tamaki, *Art in the Encounter of Nations: Japanese and American Artists in the Early Postwar Years* (Honolulu: University of Hawai'i Press, 2001), p. 66.

21. Haryū Ichirō interview, Tokyo, February 12, 2002. See Gino K. Piovesana, *Recent Japanese Philosophical Thought 1862–1962: A Survey* (Tokyo: Enderle Bookstore, 1963), pp. 252–253.

22. J. Victor Koschmann, *Revolution and Subjectivity in Postwar Japan* (Chicago: University of Chicago Press, 1996), p. 226.

23. Takeuchi Yoshimi, "Kindaishugi to minzoku no mondai" (1951), in *Takeuchi Yoshimi zenshū* (Tokyo: Chikuma Shobō, 1981) 7:28–37, quoted in Koschmann, *Revolution*, p. 229. Lawrence Olson, while noting that the philosopher Tsurumi Shunsuke (1922–) was a hybrid of Japanese and Western (Harvard 1942) culture, points out that Tsurumi was much taken with the language and customs of farmers as expressed in works by the folklorist Yanagita Kunio (1875–1962). Olson, *Ambivalent Moderns*, pp. xxii, 141.

24. Koschmann, *Revolution*, pp. 203–205, 220–221, 229–230, 236. Maruyama was less sanguine than Takeuchi about the value of race *(minzoku)* in building democracy. Koschmann points out that "Takeuchi clearly believed that ethnic/national identity was capable of providing a far more immediate, visceral experience of historical agency than class ever could." Koschmann, *Revolution*, p. 236. See also Murayama, "Japan/I Torn Apart," p. 16; Curtis Gayle, *Marxist History and Postwar Japanese Nationalism* (London: RoutledgeCurzon, 2002).

25. Washburn, *Dilemma*, p. 1. See also p. 11; Vassiliki Kolocotroni, Jane Goldman, and Olga Taxidou, eds., *Modernism: An Anthology of Sources and Documents* (Chicago: University of Chicago Press, 1998), p. xvii; Jill Lloyd, *German Expressionism: Primitivism and Modernity* (New Haven, Conn.: Yale University Press, 1991), p. vi; Lippit, *Topographies*, p. 5.

26. Washburn, *Dilemma*, p. 35.

27. David Harvey, *The Condition of Postmodernity: An Enquiry into the Origins of Cultural Change* (Oxford, Eng.: Oxford University Press, 1989), p. 22.

28. Rivkin and Ryan, *Literary Theory*, p. 6. See Hazard Adams and Leroy Searle, eds., *Critical Theory since 1965* (Tallahassee: Florida State University Press, 1986), p. 5.

29. Tristan Tzara, "Dada" (1918), in Kolocotroni, Goldman, and Taxidou, *Modernism*, pp. 276–281; Aleksei Gan, "Constructivism" (1922), in Kolocotroni, Goldman, and Taxidou, pp. 298–299.

30. Martin Jay, *The Dialectical Imagination: A History of the Frankfurt School and the Institute of Social Research, 1923–1950* (Berkeley: University of California Press, 1996) (originally published by Little, Brown in 1973), p. 25. See also pp. 176–177.

31. Kolocotroni, Goldman, and Taxidou, *Modernism*, pp. xvii–xviii, 169, 211–213, 276–300; Lippit, *Topographies*, pp. 6–7, 28.

32. Peter Adam, *Art of the Third Reich* (New York: Harry N. Abrams, 1992), p. 38.

33. Rey Chow, *Writing Diaspora: Tactics of Intervention in Contemporary Cultural Studies* (Bloomington: Indiana University Press, 1993), p. 56. See also p. 57.

34. See Kojin Karatani, *Origins of Modern Japanese Literature*, trans. and ed. Brett de Bary (Durham, N.C.: Duke University Press, 1993), p. 192.

35. Harvey, *Postmodernity*, p. 35.

36. For a critique of consensual models of Japanese society, see Befu Harumi, *Ideorogii to shite no Nihon bunkaron* (Tokyo: Shisō no Kagakusha, 1987). See Kolocotroni, Goldman, and Taxidou, *Modernism*, p. xix; Murayama, "Japan/I Torn Apart," p. 15; Nishimoto Masanobu, "Riarizumu to avangyarudo no 50nendai bijutsu," in 1953nen Raito Apputen Jikkō Iinkai, ed., *1953nen raito appu — atarashii sengo bijutsuzō ga miete kita*, exh. cat. (Tokyo: Meguroku Bijutsukan and Tama Bijutsu Daigaku, 1996), p. 42.

37. Minemura Toshiaki, "Introduction," in *1953*, p. 6; Sawaragi Noi, *Nihon gendai bijutsu* (Tokyo: Shinchōsha, 1998), p. 14; Koschmann, *Revolution*, pp. 206–207.

38. Iida Yoshikuni interview, Tokyo, March 26, 2002.

39. Takahashi Yūji interview, Tokyo, June 6, 2002.

40. Iwaki Hiroyuki interview, Tokyo, March 22, 2002.

41. Mamiya Michio interview, Tokyo, April 22, 2002. Mamiya adds that his generation "was greatly affected by the limits on expression during World War Two. The freedom of the postwar period was wonderful. When I entered middle school in 1942, there was no musical education except for a brass band, so I did arrangements for it. There was somewhat greater artistic freedom outside Tokyo during the war, but in any event, all my childhood compositions were destroyed in an American bombing raid on Aomori in 1945."

42. Matsudaira Yoriaki interview, Tokyo, February 13, 2002.

43. Yuasa Jōji interview, Tokyo, February 5, 2002.

44. Tsutsumi Seiji interview, Tokyo, April 8, 2002.

45. Stacy Combs Lynch, *Classical Music for Beginners* (New York: Writers and Readers Publishing, 1994), p. 18.

46. Komiya, *Kingendai*, p. 144.

47. Ongaku no Tomosha, *Nihon no sakkyoku 20seiki* (Tokyo: Ongaku no Tomosha, 1999), pp. 152–153; Judith A. Herd, "The Cultural Politics of Japan's Modern Music:

Nostalgia, Nationalism and Identity in the Interwar Years," unpublished manuscript (2001), pp. 72–76; Chōki Seiji interview, Tokyo, April 17, 2002.

48. Ongaku no Tomosha, *20seiki*, pp. 203–205.

49. Judith A. Herd interview, Tokyo, January 30, 2002.

50. See Herd, "Cultural Politics," pp. 80–82.

51. Judith A. Herd, "The Neonationalist Movement: Origins of Japanese Contemporary Music," *Perspectives of New Music* 27:2 (1989), 150. See Ongaku no Tomosha, *20seiki*, p. 234.

52. Herd, "Neonationalist Movement," p. 150.

53. Komiya, *Kingendai*, pp. 144–164; *Kodansha Encyclopedia of Japan* (Tokyo: Kōdansha, 1983), 5:287; Kuniharu Akiyama, "Japan," in John Vinton, ed., *Dictionary of Contemporary Music* (New York: E. P. Dutton, 1974), pp. 364–365.

54. Yamano Hakudai, "Nihon no baree chizu wa kore kara dō kawaru ka," *Modan dansu*, no. 13 (1974), 14–15; *Asahi nenkan 1964* (Tokyo: Asahi Shinbunsha, 1964), p. 644; Yamano Hakudai interview, Tokyo, March 20, 2002.

55. Gendai Buyō Kyōkai, *Nihon gendai buyō shiryō*, vol. 1: *1971* (Tokyo: Gendai Buyō Kyōkai, 1972), pp. 1, 4, 19, 481; *Nihon gendai buyō shiryō*, vol. 2: *1972* (1973), p. 14. See Machida Takako, *Buyō no ayumi hyakunen* (Tokyo: Ōfūsha, 1968), pp. 51–628, for information on performances.

56. Yamano Hakudai interview, Tokyo, March 20, 2002.

57. See Machida, *Buyō*, pp. 719–792, for early postwar performances; *Nihon gendai buyō nenkan* (Tokyo: Gendai Buyō Kyōkai, 1975–1976), 1:33–35; Gendai Buyō Kyōkai, *Nihon gendai buyō shiryō*, 2, p. 4. On modernist dance in the United States, see Julia L. Foulkes, *Modern Bodies: Dance and American Modernism from Martha Graham to Alvin Ailey* (Chapel Hill: University of North Carolina Press, 2002).

58. Michiaki Kawakita, *Modern Currents in Japanese Art*, trans. Charles S. Terry (New York and Tokyo: Weatherhill/Heibonsha, 1974), pp. 37–39, 118–119, 149–150; *Kodansha Encyclopedia* 6:155–158, 8:146–147, 318; Chiba Shigeo, *Gendai bijutsu itsudatsushi 1945–1985* (Tokyo: Shōbunsha, 1986), p. 17.

59. Ichiro Hariu [Haryū Ichirō], "Progressive Trends in Modern Japanese Art," in David Elliott and Kazu Kaido, eds., *Reconstructions: Avant-Garde Art in Japan 1945–1965*, exh. cat. (Oxford, Eng.: Museum of Modern Art Oxford, 1985), p. 25. See Kazu Kaido, "Reconstruction: The Role of the Avant-Garde in Post-War Japan," in Elliott and Kaido, eds., *Reconstructions*, p. 11; *Kodansha Encyclopedia* 2:347; Miwa Kimitada interview, Tokyo, February 27, 2002.

60. Chiba, *Gendai*, p. 18.

61. Gunma Kenritsu Kindai Bijutsukan and Ehimeken Bijutsukan, eds., *Aru korekutā ga mita sengo Nihon bijutsu* (Takasaki: Gunma Kenritsu Bijutsukan, 2001), p. 64.

62. Sōgetsu Bijutsukan, *Hizō shiryō*, p. 4; Segi Shin'ichi, *Nihon no zen'ei 1945–1999* (Tokyo: Seikatsu no Tomosha, 2000), pp. 150–151, 160–161.

63. Minemura, "Introduction," p. 10; *Mizue*, no. 920 (1981), 39; Kikuhata Mokuma, *Sengo bijutsu to hangeijutsu*, 2nd ed. (Fukuoka: Kaitōsha, 1993 [1979]), pp. 31–34.

64. Matsumoto Tōru, *Senkyūhyakugojū-rokujū nendai no bijutsu* (Tokyo: Tōkyō Kokuritsu Kindai Bijutsukan, 1999), p. 13. See also p. 14; Tōkyō Kokuritsu Kindai

Bijutsukan, ed., *Gushō hyōgen no henbō*, exh. cat. (Tokyo: Tōkyō Kokuritsu Kindai Bijutsukan, 1972), p. 3.

65. Haryū Ichirō interview, Tokyo, February 12, 2002. For Kawara On's *Bathroom (Yokushitsu)* series and closely related works, see 1953nen Raito Apputen Jikkō Iinkai, ed., *1953nen raito appu — atarashii sengo bijutsuzō ga miete kita*, exh. cat. (Tokyo: Meguroku Bijutsukan and Tama Bijutsu Daigaku, 1996), pp. 109, 114, 123.

66. Kikuhata, *Hangeijutsu*, p. 34. See Matsumoto, *Senkyūhyaku*, pp. 28–29.

67. Tōkyō Kokuritsu Kindai Bijutsukan, *Mikan no seiki: 20seiki bijutsuga nokosu mono*, exh. cat. (Tokyo: Yomiuri Shinbunsha, 2002), p. 161. See Ishii Shigeo, "Kanzen hanzai to geijutsu," *Geijutsu nōto*, no. 1 (1961) and no. 2 (1961), reproduced in Āto Gyararī Kan, ed., *Ishii Shigeo sakuhinshū* (Tokyo: Āto Gyararī Kan, 1994), pp. 24–31. See also Āto Gyararī Kan, pp. 4–6; Matsumoto, *Senkyūhyaku*, pp. 29–30. I am grateful to Ishii Yōichi, elder brother of Ishii Shigeo, for insights into the artist's late prints, produced between 1959 and 1962 in a semiconceptual style when he was heavily medicated to treat the asthma that claimed his life. Ishii Yōichi interview, Tokyo, May 6, 2002. During 1959–1962 Ishii Shigeo belonged to the Vanguard Art Association (Zen'ei Bijutsukai). Kawatsuma Sachiko interview, Tokyo, May 6, 2002.

68. Sugiyama Etsuko letter, October 12, 2002. I am grateful to Franziska Seraphim for information about this work.

69. Taki Kōji, "Sekaishi no naka no sengo Nihon to bunka," in Meguroku Bijutsukan, Hyōgo Kenritsu Kindai Bijutsukan, Hiroshimashi Gendai Bijutsukan, Fukuoka Kenritsu Bijutsukan, and Asahi Shinbunsha, eds., *Sengo bunka no kiseki 1945–1995*, exh. cat. (Tokyo: Asahi Shinbunsha, 1995), p. 6.

70. Segi Shin'ichi interview, Tokyo, February 11, 2002.

71. Abe wrote a novel about repatriation from Manchuria, *Kemonotachi wa kokyō o mezasu* (Tokyo: Shinchō Bunko, 1970). This work was originally published in *Gunzō* 12:1–4 (1957). I am grateful to Lori Watt for this reference.

72. Takeuchi Yoshimi, *Takeuchi Yoshimi zenshū*, 7:225–236. See also Takeuchi Yoshimi, *What Is Modernity? Writings of Takeuchi Yoshimi*, trans. Richard Calichman (New York: Columbia University Press, 2005).

73. Hayashi Hikaru interview, Tokyo, June 13, 2002.

74. Herbert Read, "What Is Revolutionary Art?" (1935), in Kolocotroni, Goldman, and Taxidou, *Modernism*, p. 528. See Herschel B. Chipp, comp., *Theories of Modern Art: A Source Book by Artists and Critics* (Berkeley: University of California Press, 1968), pp. 366–374. On dadaism in Taishō, see Gennifer Weisenfeld, *Mavo: Japanese Artists and the Avant-Garde, 1905–1931* (Berkeley: University of California Press, 2002).

75. André Breton, *Le surréalisme et la peinture* (Paris: Gallimard, 1928), translated by Takiguchi Shūzō as *Chōgenjitsushugi to kaiga* (Tokyo: Kōseikaku Shobō, 1930). For Nishiwaki see Hosea Hirata, *The Poetry and Poetics of Nishiwaki Junzaburō* (Princeton, N.J.: Princeton University Press, 1993); for another avant-garde poet, see John P. Solt, *Shredding the Tapestry of Meaning: The Poetry and Poetics of Kitasono Katue (1902–1978)* (Cambridge, Mass.: Harvard University Asia Center, 1999); on surrealism in Japan, see Miryam Sas, *Fault Lines: Cultural Memory and Japanese Surrealism* (Stanford, Calif.: Stanford University Press, 1999), especially pp. 10, 24,

78–79; James A. Fujii, *Complicit Fictions: The Subject in the Modern Japanese Prose Narrative* (Berkeley: University of California Press, 1993). For European surrealism, see Nobert Lynton, *The Story of Modern Art*, 2nd ed. (New York: Phaidon Press, 1989), p. 170.

76. Morris Dickstein interview, *New York Times*, June 22, 2002, p. A15.

77. Piovesana, *Thought*, p. 198. See pp. 197–205.

78. Walter Kaufmann, in Kaufmann, ed., *Existentialism from Dostoevsky to Sartre* (Cleveland and New York: Meridian Books, 1956), p. 42. On early postwar Japanese literary relations with France, see Doug Slaymaker, ed., *Confluences: Postwar Japan and France* (Ann Arbor: Center for Japanese Studies, University of Michigan, 2002).

79. Kanazawa Takeshi interview, Yokohama, April 18, 2002.

80. Sōgetsu Bijutsukan, *Hizō shiryō*, p. 6; Segi Shin'ichi, *Avangyarudo geijutsu — taiken to hihan* (Tokyo: Shichōsha, 1998), pp. 19–20.

81. Takahashi Yūji interview, Tokyo, June 6, 2002. See Sōgetsu Bijutsukan, *Hizō shiryō*, p. 6; Segi, *Avangyarudo*, pp. 15–16.

82. Lectures presented to the Evening Society are collected in Yoru no Kai, *Atarashii geijutsu no tankyū* (Tokyo: Getsuyō Shobō, 1949).

83. Segi, *Nihon no zen'ei*, p. 189. See pp. 176–177, 187–191; Segi, *Avangyarudo*, p. 20.

84. Sōgetsu Bijutsukan, *Hizō shiryō*, p. 6; Kaido, "Reconstruction," p. 17; Segi, *Avangyarudo*, pp. 32–37. As of January 1950, Noma, Sekine, Hanada, and the literary historian Sasaki Kiichi (1914–1993) from the Evening Society belonged to the Japan Communist Party. Segi, *Avangyarudo*, p. 32.

85. Kaido, "Reconstruction," 17; Segi, *Avangyarudo*, p. 35.

86. Iwase Yukio and Yui Kazuto, eds., *Nijūsseiki bukko yōgaka jiten* (Tokyo: Bijutsu Nenkansha, 1997), p. 281.

87. Kaido, "Reconstruction," p. 17; Segi Shin'ichi, *Sengo kūhakuki no bijutsu* (Tokyo: Shichōsha, 1996), p. 100; Segi, *Avangyarudo*, p. 38. See Koschmann, *Revolution*, pp. 48–49. A recent study of art and politics in another capitalist economy hostile to radical movements is Andrew Hemingway, *Artists on the Left: American Artists and the Communist Movement, 1926–1956* (New Haven, Conn.: Yale University Press, 2002).

88. Nishimoto, "Riarizumu," p. 51.

89. Hayashi Hikaru interview, Tokyo, June 13, 2002. The first meeting of the People's Arts group took place on May 13, 1951, at the Socialism Research Institute (Shakaishugi Kenkyūjo) at Tamachi, Tokyo.

90. Abe Kōbō, *Kabe* (Tokyo: Getsuyō Shobō, 1951). See Sōgetsu Bijutsukan, *Hizō shiryō*, p. 6; Segi, *Avangyarudo*, pp. 35–37; Segi, *Sengo*, pp. 101–104; Thomas Schnellbäcker, *Abe Kōbō, Literary Strategist* (Munich: Iudicium, 2004), pp. 487–489.

91. Segi, *Avangyarudo*, pp. 35–36, 42; Segi, *Sengo*, p. 104.

92. Reproduced in Segi, *Sengo*, pp. 104–105.

93. Quoted in ibid., p. 105.

94. Kaido, "Reconstruction," p. 17. See Sawaragi, *Nihon*, p. 314; Sōgetsu Bijutsukan, *Hizō shiryō*, p. 7; Segi, *Avangyarudo*, pp. 41–42; Segi, *Sengo*, pp. 105–108.

95. Kaido, "Reconstruction," p. 17; Segi, *Sengo*, pp. 105–108.

96. Segi, *Avangyarudo,* p. 22.

97. Sawaragi, *Nihon,* p. 314. See Sōgetsu Bijutsukan, *Hizō shiryō,* pp. 7, 15; Tōkyōto Bijutsukan, ed., *Shinkan kaikan 10shūnen kinen: gendai bijutsu no 40nen,* exh. cat. (Tokyo: Tōkyōto Bijutsukan, 1985), p. 15. From 1959 to 1975 the Nippon Exhibition reverted to its original name, Vanguard; in 1976 it joined forces with Scene. Sōgetsu Bijutsukan, *Hizō shiryō,* p. 5.

98. Ichiro Hariu [Haryū], "Progressive Trends in Modern Japanese Art," p. 24. The poet Ōoka Makoto says: "The Japan Communist Party was very strict toward artists — they were not free to express themselves, and there was steady pressure on them, so artists left the party." Ōoka Makoto interview, Tokyo, March 9, 2002.

99. Koschmann, *Revolution,* pp. 223–224; Haryū Ichirō interview, Tokyo, February 12, 2002.

100. Dore Ashton, *The Delicate Thread: Teshigahara's Life in Art* (Tokyo: Kodansha International, 1997), p. 54.

101. Rivkin and Ryan, *Literary Theory,* pp. 238–240; Nakamura Keiji, "Art and Reality," in Kokuritsu Kokusai Bijutsukan, ed., *Geijutsu to nichijō — hangeijutsu/hangeijutsu* (Osaka: Kokuritsu Kokusai Bijutsukan, 1991), p. 21; Minemura Toshiaki, "The Realism of Tactility: Another Japan That Erupted," in *1953,* p. 49.

102. Leo Ou-fan Lee, "The Tradition of Modern Chinese Cinema: Some Preliminary Explorations and Hypotheses," in Chris Berry, ed., *Perspectives on Chinese Cinema* (Ithaca, N.Y.: Cornell University China-Japan Program, 1985), p. 3.

103. See Minemura, "Realism," p. 49; Sawaragi, *Nihon,* pp. 314–315. Haryū Ichirō says that, when *Tale of Akebono Village* was later exhibited at the Pompidou Center in Paris, a curator told him it was the most interesting work on display. Haryū Ichirō interview, Tokyo, February 12, 2002.

104. Ashton, *Thread,* p. 63.

105. Donald Richie, "Teshigahara and the Human Condition," in Teshigahara Productions, *Cinema and Hiroshi Teshigahara* (Tokyo: Teshigahara Productions, 1992), p. 3.

106. Domon Ken (1953), quoted in Iemura Tamayo, "Beyond Genres," in *1953,* p. 35. See pp. 34–40; Taki, "Sekaishi," p. 7.

107. Walter Benjamin, "The Work of Art in the Age of Mechanical Reproduction" (1936), in Benjamin, *Illuminations,* ed. Hannah Arendt, trans. Harry Zohn (New York: Schocken Books, 1969), pp. 217–251. Benjamin's collected works became available in Japanese starting in 1969.

108. Abe Nobuya, in *Tōkyō Shinbun,* February 2, 1960, quoted in Murayama, "Japan/I Torn Apart," p. 27. See Anne Tucker, Dana Friis-Hansen, Kaneko Ryūichi, and Takeba Joe, *History of Japanese Photography* (New Haven: Yale University Press, 2003). For insights into Japanese photography in the 1950s, I am indebted to Yasuda Atsuo, interview, Tokyo, February 20, 2002.

109. Matsumoto, *Senkyūhyaku,* p. 15.

110. Kondō Yukio interview, Yokohama, February 20, 2002. On reportage art, see Nagoyashi Bijutsukan, ed., *Sengo Nihon no riarizumu 1945–1960* (Nagoya: Nagoyashi Bijutsukan, 1998), p. 10.

111. Nakanishi Natsuyuki interview, Tokyo, March 2, 2002.

112. Tsutsumi Seiji interview, Tokyo, April 8, 2002.

113. Bijutsu Shuppansha Henshūbu, ed., *Gendai Nihon āteisuto meikan* (Tokyo: Bijutsu Shuppansha, 1995), p. 79; Legacy Project, http://www.legacy-project.org/artists /display.html?ID=113, November 11, 2002; Nishimoto, "Riarizumu," pp. 46–50.

114. Haryū Ichirō (1955), quoted on this dispute in *Mizue*, no. 921 (1981), 66.

115. Nakahara Yūsuke, in *Mizue*, no. 921 (1981), 67.

116. Haryū Ichirō interview, Tokyo, February 12, 2002.

117. The term is used somewhat differently by Andrew Barshay in *The Social Sciences in Modern Japan: The Marxian and Modernist Traditions* (Berkeley: University of California Press, 2004), p. 32. See also Nakamura, "Art and Reality," p. 21.

118. Nishimoto, "Riarizumu," p. 52.

119. Segi, *Sengo*, pp. 105–108. On the importance of artists' groups, see Blake Stimson and Gregory Sholette, eds., *Collectivism after Modernism* (Minneapolis: University of Minnesota Press, 2005).

Part One: Overview

1. *Asahi shinbun*, morning edition, April 28, 1952, p. 1.

2. See Robert J. C. Young, *Postcolonialism: A Very Short Introduction* (Oxford, Eng.: Oxford University Press, 2003), pp. 4–8.

3. See Ueno Chizuko, *Nationalism and Gender*, trans. Beverley Yamamoto (Melbourne: Trans Pacific Press, 2004), pp. xiii, 62, 172, 225. Cultural studies as practiced in Japan, while acknowledging the colonizer/subaltern dyad, focuses instead on cultural interactions through zones of contact.

4. See, for example, Dower, *Embracing Defeat*, pp. 551–561.

5. Ichiyanagi Toshi interview, Tokyo, April 11, 2002. See Leo Ou-fan Lee, *The Romantic Generation of Modern Chinese Writers* (Cambridge, Mass.: Harvard University Press, 1973); Hirakawa Sukehiro, ed., *Lafcadio Hearn in International Perspectives* (Tokyo: Comparative Literature and Culture Program, University of Tokyo, 2001), p. 1; Nagashima, *Return*, passim.

6. The painter Sugai Kumi (1919–1996) was warmly welcomed in France. See Gunma, *Aru Korekutā*, p. 42, on the orientalism of early postwar Europe.

7. Judith A. Herd, "Change and Continuity in Contemporary Japanese Music" (Ph.D. dissertation, Brown University, 1987), p. 190; Chōki Seiji interview, Tokyo, April 17, 2002; Akiyama Kuniharu, *Nihon no sakkyokukatachi* (Tokyo: Ongaku no Tomosha, 1978–1979), 2:35–40; Ongaku no Tomosha, *20seiki*, pp. 166–167.

8. Moroi Makoto interview, Saitamashi, March 30, 2002.

9. Ongaku no Tomosha, *20seiki*, p. 241; Peter Burt, *The Music of Tōru Takemitsu* (Cambridge, Eng.: Cambridge University Press, 2001), p. 18; Robin J. Heifetz, "Post–World War II Japanese Composition" (D.M.A. dissertation, University of Illinois, 1978), pp. 14–15, 26; Paul Griffiths, *Modern Music and After* (Oxford, Eng.: Oxford University Press, 1995), pp. 17–18; Paul Griffiths, *Modern Music: The Avant Garde since 1945* (London: J. M. Dent and Sons, 1981), p. 11.

10. Chōki Seiji interview, Tokyo, April 17, 2002; Ongaku no Tomosha, *20seiki*, p. 241; Burt, *Takemitsu*, p. 18; Heifetz, "Composition," p. 26.

11. Nanjō Fumio interview, Tokyo, March 15, 2002.

12. Ichikawa Masanori, "Nijūsseiki bunmei to bunka no hazama ni," in *Tōkyō Kokuritsu Kindai Bijutsukan, Mikan*, p. xx.

13. Kanagawa Kenritsu Kindai Bijutsukan, *Kindai Nihon bijutsu retsuden* (Tokyo: Bijutsu Shuppansha, 1999), p. 68.

14. *Asahi shinbun*, evening ed., April 1, 2002, p. 3. See Haryū Ichirō, "The Kagami Collection in the Context of Postwar Japanese Art History," trans. Stanley N. Anderson, in Gunma, *Aru Korekutā*, p. 14; Miki Tamon, "The 1960's — a Decade of Change in Contemporary Japanese Art," in Tōkyō Kokuritsu Kindai Bijutsukan, ed., *1960nendai — gendai bijutsu no tenkanki*, exh. cat. (Tokyo: Tōkyō Kokuritsu Kindai Bijutsukan, 1981), p. 24.

15. Haga Tōru interview, Tokyo, June 2, 2002.

16. Hirakawa Sukehiro interview, Tokyo, June 2, 2002. The haute-couture designer Koshino Junko agrees that Imai's energy was cyclonic: "I first met Imai in France in 1968. For someone who painted so prolifically, he certainly loved the night life of Paris." Koshino Junko interview, Tokyo, June 2, 2002.

17. *Asahi shinbun*, evening ed., April 1, 2002, p. 3.

18. Dōmoto Hisao interview, Tokyo, March 15, 2002.

19. Seibu Bijutsukan, ed., *Dōmoto Hisao 30nen*, exh. cat. (Tokyo: Seibu Bijutsukan, 1987), pp. 25–27.

20. Nakahara Yūsuke, "The Sculpture of Yoshikuni Iida," trans. Susan Pulvers, in Iida Yoshikuni, *Iida Yoshikuni: Mirā mobiru* (Tokyo: Bijutsu Shuppansha, 1987), p. 155.

21. Iida Yoshikuni interview, Tokyo, March 26, 2002.

22. Iida Yoshikuni, "The Art of Iida Yoshikuni," in Miekenritsu Bijutsukan, Meguroku Bijutsukan, and Kyōto Kokuritsu Kindai Bijutsukan, eds., *Iida Yoshikuniten*, exh. cat. (Tsū: Miekenritsu Bijutsukan, 1988), p. 2.

23. Iwase and Yui, *Nijūsseiki bukko*, pp. 67, 238; Segi, *Nihon no zen'ei*, pp. 217–219. See Winther-Tamaki, *Encounter*, pp. 26, 39–43.

24. "Yoko Ono: A Biography," http://www.kaapeli.fi/aiu/onolife2.html, December 18, 2002.

25. "There are no words to express my shock when I saw Martha's dancing at the old Sankei Hall in Ōtemachi in October 1955," Kanda has written. Well known for her motto "to dance is to live," Kanda has devoted her career to Graham technique. Kanda Akiko, *Onna o odoru* (Kyoto: Shinshindō, 1980), p. 15. See also pp. 16–17, 49.

26. Ichiyanagi Toshi interview, Tokyo, April 11, 2002.

27. Miyake Haruna interview, Tokyo, February 24, 2002.

28. Ichiyanagi Toshi interview, Tokyo, April 11, 2002.

29. Donald Richie, "One Hundred Years of Japanese Film," lecture, International House of Japan, Tokyo, February 22, 2002.

30. Hara Toshio interview, Tokyo, February 20, 2002.

31. Yano Tomoo, *Han'ei o motomete: hyakumannin no keizai hakusho* (Tokyo: Shiseidō, 1956), p. 1.

32. Minemura Toshiaki interview, Tokyo, March 25, 2002. Minemura adds, "There was no one on the Geidai faculty comparable to Professor Saitō Yoshishige at Tama Art University, the other main source of the avant-garde."

33. Mamiya Michio interview, Tokyo, April 22, 2002.

34. Hayashi Hikaru interview, Tokyo, June 13, 2002.

35. Koyano Masako, telephone interview, Tokyo, February 14, 2002. See Sōgetsu Bijutsukan, *Hizō shiryō*, p. 1.

36. Segi, *Sengo*, pp. 44–45.

37. Taki Teizō, *Nihon no yōga nanajūnen: gaka to gashō no monogatari* (Tokyo: Nikkei Jigyō Shuppansha, 2000), p. 225; Segi, *Sengo*, pp. 60–68. For details of early postwar shows of Western art in Japan, see Sōgetsu Bijutsukan, *Hizō shiryō*, p. 3.

38. Taki, *Nihon no yōga*, p. 273. See Segi Shin'ichi, *Nihon Andepandanten zenkiroku 1949–1963* (Tokyo: Sōbisha, 1993), p. 276; Segi, *Sengo*, pp. 250–251.

39. Taki, *Nihon no yōga*, p. 225; Segi, *Nihon no zen'ei*, pp. 239–240.

40. Sōgetsu Bijutsukan, *Hizō shiryō*, p. 21; Tōkyōto Bijutsukan, ed., *Gendai bijutsu no dōkō*, vol. 1: *1950nendai: sono ankoku to kōbō* (Tokyo: Tōkyōto Bijutsukan, 1981), p. 77; Ebizuka Kōichi, "Shuzo Takiguchi and the Takemiya Gallery," in *1953*, pp. 59–61.

41. Satani Kazuhiko interview, Tokyo, February 4, 2002.

42. Ōoka Makoto interview, Tokyo, March 9, 2002. See *Shimizu Kusuo to Minami Garō* (Tokyo: Shimizu Kusuo to Minami Garō Kankōkai, 1985); Maki Fumihiko, "Yoshikuni Iida, the Artist of Perpetual Youth," trans. Watanabe Hiroshi, in Iida Yoshikuni, *Iida Yoshikuni: Mirā mobiru* (Tokyo: Bijutsu Shuppansha, 1987), p. 150; K. Mitsuyama-Wdowiak, "The Critical Reception of Exhibitions of Japanese Contemporary Art in the West during the 1980s" (unpublished manuscript, 2000), p. 1.

43. Mitsuyama-Wdowiak, "Reception," p. 1; Tōkyōto, *1950nendai*, p. 77; Segi, *Nihon no zen'ei*, pp. 241–242.

44. Mamiya Michio interview, Tokyo, April 22, 2002.

45. Tanikawa Shuntarō letter, March 5, 2002.

46. Kawatsuma Sachiko interview, Tokyo, May 6, 2002.

Chapter Two: The Experimental Workshop

1. Satani Garō, ed., *Dai 11kai omāju Takiguchi Shūzōten: Jikken Kōbō to Takiguchi Shūzō*, exh. cat. (Tokyo: Satani Garō, 1991), p. 33. See Matsumoto, *Senkyūhyaku*, p. 24.

2. See Weisenfeld, *Mavo*.

3. Yuasa Jōji interview, Tokyo, February 5, 2002.

4. Tatehata Akira interview, Tokyo, March 4, 2002.

5. Yuasa Jōji interview, Tokyo, February 5, 2002.

6. Tatehata Akira interview, Tokyo, March 4, 2002. Yuasa Jōji states flatly, "Jikken Kōbō members felt no resentment toward American culture. We felt no imperialism from America. Possibly some people resented the United States in the 1960s." Yuasa Jōji interview, Tokyo, February 5, 2002.

7. Okamoto Tarō, in *Atelier*, May 1951, pp. 24–25, quoted in Kaido, "Reconstruction," p. 21. See Satani Kazuhiko, "Takiguchi Shūzō to Jikken Kōbō no shigoto," *Kokubungaku* 44:10 (1999), 109.

8. Minemura, "Realism," p. 50.

9. Minemura, "Introduction," p. 7. See Kaido, p. 20.

10. Walter Gropius, "Manifesto of the Bauhaus" (1919), in Kolocotroni, Goldman, and Taxidou, *Modernism*, pp. 301–302.

11. Yamaguchi Katsuhiro, "Experimental Workshop," in *1953*, p. 76.

12. Segi, *Avangyarudo*, p. 30; Yamaguchi, "Workshop," pp. 76–77.

13. Takahashi Yūji interview, Tokyo, June 6, 2002. See Ongaku no Tomosha, *20seiki*, p. 51; Satani, "Takiguchi," p. 107.

14. Kōno Yasuo, *Oto to Nihonjin* (Tokyo: Geijutsu Gendaisha, 2001), p. 72.

15. Satani, "Takiguchi," p. 106.

16. Yuasa Jōji interview, Tokyo, February 5, 2002.

17. Herbert Edward Read, *Icon and Idea: The Function of Art in the Development of Human Consciousness* (Cambridge, Mass.: Harvard University Press, 1955). See Kōno, *Oto*, p. 73; Yuasa Jōji, "'Jikken Kōbō' no koto, sono wakai sakkyokuka e no teigen," part 1, *Ongaku gendai* 27:15 (1997), 113.

18. Kanagawa, *Kindai*, p. 284; Satani Kazuhiko interview, Tokyo, February 4, 2002; *Daily Yomiuri*, January 10, 2002, p. 12.

19. Chiba Shigeo interview, Tokyo, March 11, 2002. See Kanagawa, *Kindai*, p. 285; Setagaya Bungakukan, ed., *Takiguchi Shūzō to Takemitsu Tōruten*, exh. cat. (Tokyo: Setagaya Bungakukan, 1999), p. 96.

20. Takiguchi Shūzō, "Jikken no seishin ni tsuite," program for Jikken Kōbō Dainikai Happyōkai, January 1952, in Takiguchi Shūzō, *Korekushon Takiguchi Shūzō* (Tokyo: Misuzu Shobō, 1992), 7:3–4.

21. Takiguchi Shūzō, in *Bijutsu hihyō*, May 1952, in Takiguchi, *Korekushon*, 7:6.

22. Ibid., 7:7–9.

23. Kōno, *Oto*, p. 276.

24. Sawaragi, *Nihon*, p. 316.

25. Sugino Hideki and Mitsuda Yuri, eds., *Takiguchi Shūzō no zōkeiteki jikken*, exh. cat. (Toyama: Toyama Kenritsu Kindai Bijutsukan and Tokyo: Shibuya Kuritsu Shōtō Bijutsukan, 2001), pp. 4, 229; Kanagawa, *Kindai*, p. 285; Ebizuka, "Takiguchi," pp. 62–63. Sugino and Mitsuda calculate that Takiguchi focused on poetry during 1927–1931 and, to a lesser extent, 1968–1975; during the latter period he also produced paintings and objets. Otherwise he concentrated on the visual arts. Sugino and Mitsuda, *Takiguchi*, pp. 227–230.

26. Akiyama, *Nihon no sakkyokukatachi*, 1:47; Akiyama Kuniharu, "Jikken Kōbō ni yoru henkaku to ongaku no kakuchō," *Ongaku geijutsu* 45:1 (1987), 24–25; Sōgetsu Bijutsukan, *Hizō shiryō*, p. 7; Yamaguchi, "Workshop," p. 77. Satani, "Takiguchi," pp. 110–111, provides a full catalog of Jikken Kōbō events.

27. Haryū Ichirō interview, Tokyo, February 12, 2002; Yamaguchi, "Workshop," p. 78.

28. Iwaki Hiroyuki interview, Tokyo, March 22, 2002.

29. Yamaguchi Katsuhiro, quoted in Satani Garō, *Dai 11kai*, p. 27. See Ongaku no Tomosha, *20seiki*, p. 57; Yamaguchi, "Workshop," pp. 77–78.

30. Satani Kazuhiko interview, Tokyo, February 4, 2002.

31. Yamaguchi Katsuhiro, cited in Yamashita Yūji, "Sengo geijutsu undō no naka no Takemitsu Tōru," in Chōki Seiji and Higuchi Ryūichi, eds., *Takemitsu Tōru: oto no kawa no yukue* (Tokyo: Heibonsha, 2000), p. 212.

32. Yamaguchi Katsuhiro, quoted in Satani Garō, *Dai 11kai*, p. 28.

33. Iwaki Hiroyuki interview, Tokyo, March 22, 2002.

34. Akiyama, "Japan," p. 365.

35. Ongaku no Tomosha, *20seiki*, pp. 50–52, 220; *Kodansha Encyclopedia* 2:366; Burt, *Takemitsu*, p. 19.

36. Yuasa, "'Jikken Kōbō' no koto," part 1, p. 112.

37. Toru Takemitsu, *Confronting Silence: Selected Writings*, trans. Yoshiko Kakudo and Glenn Glasow (Berkeley, Calif.: Fallen Leaf Press, 1995), p. xii.

38. Akiyama, "Jikken," p. 28. See Akiyama, *Nihon no sakkyokukatachi*, 1:48; Yamaguchi, "Workshop," p. 79; Segi, *Sengo*, p. 194; Ongaku no Tomosha, *20seiki*, p. 57.

39. Biographical details are taken from Ongaku no Tomosha, *20seiki*, p. 180; Burt, *Takemitsu*, pp. 21–23; Takemitsu Tōru, *Oto chinmoku to hakariaeru hodo ni* (Tokyo: Shinchōsha, 1971), quoted in Takemitsu, *Confronting*, p. 11. Other helpful sources include James Siddons, *Toru Takemitsu: A Bio-Bibliography* (Westport, Conn.: Greenwood, 2001); Hugh de Ferranti and Yōko Narazaki, eds., *A Way a Lone: Writings on Tōru Takemitsu* (Tokyo: Academica Music, 2002); and Alison McQueen Tokita and David W. Hughes, eds., *Japanese Music: History, Performance, Research* (New York: Cambridge University Press, 2003). For movie music, see Takemitsu Tōru, *Music for Movies: Toru Takemitsu*, vols. 1–2, ed. Tetsuo Ohara, 21 CDs (Tokyo: Shogakkan, 2003).

40. Tsutsumi Seiji interview, Tokyo, April 8, 2002.

41. Takemitsu Tōru, in Ozawa Seiji and Takemitsu Tōru, *Ongaku* (Tokyo: Shinchōsha, 1984), p. 139.

42. Takemitsu Tōru, *Takemitsu Tōru chosakushū* (Tokyo: Shinchōsha, 2000), 1:288–290.

43. Ibid., 1:282–284.

44. Takemitsu, *Oto chinmoku*, p. 25.

45. Sano Kōji, "Joron — Nihongo de kataru ongaku e no kiseki," in Chōki and Higuchi, *Takemitsu*, p. 11.

46. "Probably I was the first to introduce Messiaen to Japan," Takemitsu told Ozawa Seiji in 1984. Ozawa and Takemitsu, *Ongaku*, p. 149. See Takemitsu, *Confronting*, p. xii; Burt, *Takemitsu*, pp. 41–42.

47. Burt, *Takemitsu*, p. 30.

48. Takemitsu Tōru, program notes for the score of *Saegirarenai kyūsoku* (Tokyo: Ongaku no Tomosha, 1962), quoted in Kawaguchi Yoshiharu, "Takemitsu Tōru to shururearizumu," in Chōki and Higuchi, *Takemitsu*, p. 190. The poem "Saegirarenai kyūsoku" is contained in Takiguchi Shūzō, *Yōsei no kyori* (Tokyo: Shunchōkai, 1937), reprinted in *Korekushon Takiguchi Shūzō*, v. 12.

49. Kawaguchi, "Takemitsu," pp. 188–190.

50. Setagaya Bungakukan, *Takiguchi*, pp. 108, 150.

51. Takemitsu, *Oto chinmoku*, quoted in Takemitsu, *Confronting*, p. 28.

52. Sano, "Joron," p. 12; Heifetz, "Composition," pp. 26–27; Burt, *Takemitsu*, pp. 44–45. Takemitsu is said to have preferred using sounds recognizable to audiences; in this he differed from both Schaeffer and Karlheinz Stockhausen, the latter of whom often used electronically generated sounds. Burt, p. 44; Heifetz, p. 27.

53. Quoted in Sano, "Joron," p. 13.

54. Burt, *Takemitsu*, p. 51. See pp. 50, 57; Sano, "Joron," pp. 13–14; Ongaku no Tomosha, *20seiki*, p. 180; Kanagawa, *Kindai*, p. 66.

55. Ongaku no Tomosha, *20seiki*, pp. 182–185.

56. Takemitsu Tōru, quoted in Kōno, *Oto*, p. 99.

57. Takemitsu, *Confronting*, p. xii. See Chōki Seiji, "Seiyō zen'ei ongaku no naka no Takemitsu Tōru," in Chōki and Higuchi, *Takemitsu*, pp. 286–288.

58. See Burt, *Takemitsu*, p. 43.

59. Yuasa Jōji interview, in Kōno, *Oto*, p. 71. For biographical details, see Ongaku no Tomosha, *20seiki*, pp. 267–268.

60. Yuasa Jōji interview, in Kōno, *Oto*, p. 71. See also pp. 67–70. Yuasa's first contact with the Experimental Workshop was through the music critic Akiyama Kuniharu: "I knew Akiyama when he was a student at Waseda and came to Keiō for composers' meetings." Yuasa Jōji interview, Tokyo, February 5, 2002.

61. Yuasa Jōji interview, Tokyo, February 5, 2002.

62. Yuasa Jōji, quoted in Ongaku no Tomosha, *20seiki*, p. 268. See Kanagawa, *Kindai*, p. 117.

63. Ongaku no Tomosha, *20seiki*, pp. 268–269.

64. Yuasa Jōji, "Music as a Reflection of a Composer's Cosmology," *Perspectives of New Music* 27:2 (1989), 176. See Stanley Sadie, ed., *The New Grove Dictionary of Music and Musicians* (London: Macmillan, 1980), 20:584; Ongaku no Tomosha, *20seiki*, pp. 267–268.

65. Yuasa Jōji interview, Tokyo, February 5, 2002. For a study of *enka*, a popular ballad form that emerged early in the twentieth century with Western instruments and Japanese scales, melodies, and poetry, see Christine R. Yano, *Tears of Longing: Nostalgia and the Nation in Japanese Popular Song* (Cambridge, Mass.: Harvard University Asia Center, 2002), esp. pp. 103–109.

66. Yuasa Jōji interview, Tokyo, February 5, 2002.

67. *Japan Times Online*, February 19, 2003.

68. Performed on March 20, 2002, by the Tokyo Philharmonic Chorus, conducted by Iwaki Hiroyuki, at Daiichi Seimei Hall in Kachidoki, Tokyo.

69. Yuasa Jōji, *Ongaku no kosumorojī e* (Tokyo: Seidosha, 1981). See Ongaku no Tomosha, *20seiki*, p. 269.

70. See Ongaku no Tomosha, *20seiki*, p. 52, for a discussion of premodern Japanese aesthetics and contemporary music.

71. Dan Ikuma, *Watakushi no Nihon ongakushi* (Tokyo: Nihon Hōsō Shuppan Kyōkai, 1999), pp. 358, 363.

72. Akutagawa Yasushi, quoted in Nihon Ongaku Buyō Kaigi, *Sakkyokuka to no taiwa* (Tokyo: Shin Nihon Shuppansha, 1982), p. 73.

73. Ongaku no Tomosha, *20seiki*, p. 53; Akiyama, *Nihon no sakkyokukatachi*, 2:16; Herd, "Change," p. 131.

74. Mayuzumi Toshirō, *Puripeado piano to gengaku no tame no shōhin* (1957), published as *Pieces for Prepared Piano and Strings* (New York: C. F. Peters Corp., 1958).

75. See Ongaku no Tomosha, *20seiki*, pp. 57, 242; Akiyama, *Nihon no sakkyokukatachi*, 2:81; Herd, "Change," pp. 138, 141; Herd, "Neonationalist," p. 137.

76. Ongaku no Tomosha, *20seiki*, p. 242.

77. Ibid., pp. 122–123. See Akiyama, *Nihon no sakkyokukatachi*, 2:16–21.

78. Akutagawa Yasushi, in *Ongaku geijutsu*, November 1966, quoted in Akiyama, *Nihon no sakkyokukatachi*, 2:18.

79. Dan, *Watakushi*, p. 362. See Ongaku no Tomosha, *20seiki*, pp. 186–187; *Bijutsu techō nenkan 2002* (Tokyo: Bijutsu Shuppansha, 2002), p. 57.

80. Dan Ikuma interview, Tokyo, December 23, 1980. See Ongaku no Tomosha, *20seiki*, p. 53.

81. Dan Ikuma, "The Influence of Japanese Traditional Music on the Development of Western Music in Japan," trans. Dorothy G. Britton, *Transactions of the Asiatic Society of Japan*, 3rd ser. (1961), 8:207. Dan expressed similar views in Dan Ikuma and Koizumi Fumio, *Nihon ongaku no saihakken* (Tokyo: Kōdansha, 1976), p. 101, and to Kōno Yasuo, in Kōno, *Oto*, pp. 243–244. See Nihon Geijutsuin, ed., *Nihon Geijutsuinshi*, rev. ed. (Tokyo: Nihon Geijutsuin, 1979–1980 [1963]), 2:224.

82. Dan, "Influence," 8:204.

83. Ibid., 8:201, 216–217.

84. Ibid., 8:201.

85. Herd, "Neonationalist," p. 140.

86. Tone Yasunao, "Toward Anti-Music," trans. Reiko Tomii, program notes from a 1961 concert held at Sōgetsu Kaikan, Tokyo, in Munroe, *Scream*, p. 376.

87. Chōki Seiji interview, Tokyo, April 17, 2002; Kōno, *Oto*, p. 71.

88. Takahashi Yūji interview, Tokyo, June 6, 2002. See Komiya, *Kingendai*, p. 175.

89. Moroi Makoto interview, Saitamashi, March 30, 2002. See Ongaku no Tomosha, *20seiki*, pp. 55–56, 60–63; Sano, "Joron," p. 9; Komiya, *Kingendai*, pp. 189–190.

90. Sawaragi, *Nihon*, p. 315; Satani Garō, *Dai 11kai*, passim; Komiya, *Kingendai*, pp. 168–169.

Chapter Three: Avant-Garde Visual Culture

1. Reprinted in Okamoto Tarō, *Okamoto Tarō no me* (Tokyo: Asahi Shinbunsha, 1966), extracted in Kawagiri Nobuhiko, *Okamoto Tarō — geijutsu wa bakuhatsu ka* (Tokyo: Chūsekisha, 2000 [1978]), p. 214.

2. Okamoto Tarō, *Konnichi no geijutsu: seikatsu o sōzō suru enerugī no gensen*, 2nd ed. (Tokyo: Kōbunsha, 1963 [1954]), p. 235.

3. Ibid., p. 245.

4. Okamoto Tarō, *Okamoto Tarō no me*, in Kawagiri, *Okamoto*, pp. 70–71.

5. Segi Shin'ichi interview, Tokyo, February 11, 2002.

6. Yoshimasu Gōzō interview, Tokyo, May 22, 2002.

7. Kanagawa, *Kindai*, p. 314; Omuka Toshiharu, *Nihon no avangyarudo geijutsu* (Tokyo: Seidosha, 2001), p. 264; Ashton, *Thread*, p. 46. Okamoto was born in Kawasaki in 1911, the son of the poet and novelist Okamoto Kanoko and the manga artist Okamoto Ippei. He quit the Tokyo School of Fine Arts after a half year and traveled to France with his parents in 1929 at age eighteen. He stayed behind by himself to study and paint until 1940. Kanagawa, *Kindai*, p. 314.

8. Omuka, *Avangyarudo*, pp. 264–265; Murayama, "Japan/I Torn Apart," p. 18; Kaido, "Reconstruction," p. 14; Matsumoto, *Senkyūhyaku*, p. 27.

9. Okamoto Tarō, catalog of a solo exhibition held in 1952 at the Osaka Takashimaya department store, quoted in Murayama, "Japan/I Torn Apart," p. 17. Okamoto rejected Noma Hiroshi's impression that the zipper in this work stood for fascist violence. Ibid., p. 18.

10. See Matsumoto, *Senkyūhyaku*, p. 27.

11. Okamoto Tarō, in Kanagawa, *Kindai*, p. 315. See Kaido, "Reconstruction," p. 25.

12. Winther-Tamaki, *Encounter*, p. 25.

13. Okamoto Tarō, quoted in Omuka, *Avangyarudo*, p. 267.

14. See Kawagiri, *Okamoto*, p. 68.

15. Isozaki Arata, "As Witness to Postwar Japanese Art," in Munroe, *Scream*, p. 28.

16. Matsumoto Tōru, "The Contemporariness of Postwar Art," trans. Ogawa Kikuko, in Tōkyō Kokuritsu, *Mikan*, supplement, p. 14. On realism and the avantgarde, see Nakamura Yoshikazu, *Nihon kindai bijutsu ronsōshi* (Tokyo: Kyūryūdō, 1981), pp. 265–266. Sce also Minemura, "Introduction," p. 9. The Neo-Dada painter and subsequent urban planner Arakawa Shūsaku says: "Okamoto Tarō introduced me to Mishima Yukio when I was seventeen years old. Okamoto was one of the most intellectual artists of that era. He brought Takiguchi Shūzō to my apartment to meet me when I was showing my work at the Yomiuri Independent in the late 1950s. Takiguchi was very romantic in his approach to art; Hanada Kiyoteru was more political. I argued a great deal with Takiguchi." Arakawa Shūsaku interview, New York, June 24, 2002.

17. Okamoto Toshiko interview, Tokyo, March 25, 2002.

18. Okamoto Tarō, "Jōmon dokiron," *Mizue*, February 1952, quoted in Murayama, *Japan/I Torn Apart*, p. 17. At this time the architect Tange Kenzō was likewise drawn to the spirit of prehistoric Japan.

19. Okamoto, *Okamoto Tarō no me*, in Kawagiri, *Okamoto*, p. 68.

20. Okamoto Tarō, *Nihon no dentō* (Tokyo: Kōbunsha, 1956).

21. Okamoto Tarō, "Dentō to wa nani ka," in *Watakushi no gendai geijutsu* (Tokyo: Shinchōsha, 1963), in Kawagiri, *Okamoto*, pp. 210, 212. On p. 210 of the same work Okamoto added: "The idea of tradition as formulated in the Meiji era was hurriedly given substance by the national bureaucracy. It was created in response to Westernization and the modern structure of the times."

22. Murayama, *Japan/I Torn Apart*, p. 24.

23. Kondō Yukio interview, Yokohama, February 20, 2002.

24. Chiba Shigeo interview, Tokyo, March 11, 2002. See Murayama, *Japan/I Torn Apart*, pp. 21–23.

25. Ōoka Makoto interview, Tokyo, March 9, 2002.

26. Okamoto Tarō, *Wasurerareta Nihon — Okinawa bunkaron* (Tokyo: Chūō Kōronsha, 1961). A revised edition appeared as *Okinawa bunkaron — wasurerareta Nihon* from the same publisher in 1972. See Kamakura, *Kindai*, p. 315.

27. Kondō Yukio interview, Yokohama, February 20, 2002.

28. Ibid. Also affected by Okamoto's focus on the past were Mori Bushirō (1923–), who produced unpolished cast-iron sculptures in the 1950s, and Murata Saburō (1928–), who worked in rough cast iron in the 1960s.

29. Okamoto Toshiko interview, Tokyo, March 25, 2002.

30. Okamoto Tarō, "What Is Tradition?" trans. Reiko Tomii, in Munroe, *Scream*, p. 381. See Sawaragi, *Nihon*, p. 311.

31. Haryū Ichirō interview, Tokyo, February 12, 2002. The Congress for Cultural Freedom was founded by intellectuals meeting in West Berlin in June 1950. Headquartered in Paris, this group argued that communism was the enemy of art and artists. The Central Intelligence Agency ended its covert sponsorship of the congress in 1966. The French scholar Pierre Emmanuel (1916–1984) was a prominent leader of the congress in the 1960s. See "Origins of the Congress for Cultural Freedom,

1949–1950," http://www.sfsu.edu/fischer/IR%20360/Readings/Congress%20Cultur al%20Freedom.htm, February 19, 2003.

32. Segi, *Avangyarudo*, p. 39; Segi, *Nihon no zen'ei*, p. 187.

33. Okamoto Tarō, quoted in Segi, *Avangyarudo*, p. 40.

34. Segi, *Avangyarudo*, pp. 39–41; Segi Shin'ichi interview, Tokyo, February 11, 2002.

35. Minemura, "Introduction," p. 9.

36. *Gendai hihyō*, quoted in Segi, *Sengo*, p. 233. See Kawasakishi Okamoto Tarō Bijutsukan, ed., *Okamoto Tarō Expo'70 Taiyō no tō kara no messējiten*, exh. cat. (Kawasaki: Kawasakishi Okamoto Tarō Bijutsukan, 2000), p. 62.

37. Segi, *Sengo*, p. 236.

38. Segi, *Avangyarudo*, pp. 42–43; Segi, *Sengo*, pp. 228–234.

39. Kokusai Āto Kurabu, *Sengen*, July 25, 1953, in Segi, *Nihon no zen'ei*, p. 221.

40. Taki, *Nihon*, p. 236; Sōgetsu Bijutsukan, *Hizō shiryō*, p. 4; Segi, *Nihon no zen'ei*, pp. 220–235; Segi, *Sengo*, pp. 184–186.

41. Gendai Geijutsu no Kai, *Nyūsu*, January 10, 1956, in Segi, *Sengo*, p. 189.

42. Gendai Geijutsu Kenkyūjo, ed., *Gendai geijutsu kōza*, 4 vols. (Tokyo: Kawade Shobō, 1955–1956).

43. Segi, *Sengo*, pp. 189, 192–193.

44. Theodor W. Adorno, "Aesthetic Theory" (1970), in Adams and Searle, *Critical Theory*, p. 232. See Kanagawa, *Kindai*, p. 315.

45. Tatehata, "Mono-ha," pp. 27–28.

46. Ashton, *Thread*, p. 10.

47. Katō Shūichi, *Form, Style, Tradition: Reflections on Japanese Art and Society*, trans. John Bester (Berkeley: University of California Press, 1971), pp. 3–4.

48. *Genshoku Nihon no bijutsu 33 gendai* (Tokyo: Shōgakukan, 1994), pp. 225–226. See Iwasaki Yoshikazu, *Kindai Nihonga no kōbō* (Kyoto: Kyōto Shinbunsha, 1995), pp. 66–69; Tsuruta Heihachirō, "Sengo no Nihonga," in *Shōwa no bunka isan* (Tokyo: Gyōsei, 1991), p. 110. Nakamura Tanio provides a more essentialist reading of Nihonga in *Contemporary Japanese-Style Painting*, trans. Itō Mikio (Tokyo: Tokyo International Publishers and New York: Tudor Publishing, 1969), pp. 12–17.

49. Hara Toshio interview, Tokyo, February 20, 2002.

50. Iwasaki, *Nihonga*, p. 51.

51. Haryū Ichirō interview, Tokyo, February 12, 2002. See Iwasaki, *Nihonga*, pp. 51–55; Tsuruta, "Sengo," pp. 114–115; Haryū, "Nihonga kakumei no undō," *Bijutsu techō* 30:7, expanded no. (1978), 157.

52. Haryū, "Nihonga," p. 158. See Sōgetsu Bijutsukan, *Hizō shiryō*, p. 12; Matsumoto, *Senkyūhyaku*, p. 24; Tsuruta, "Sengo," p. 114.

53. Matsumoto, *Senkyūhyaku*, p. 25. See Tsuruta, "Sengo," p. 115.

54. Matsumoto, *Senkyūhyaku*, p. 21. See also p. 20; Iwasaki, *Nihonga*, pp. 199–200; Yui Kazuto, ed., *Nijūsseiki bukko Nihon gaka jiten* (Tokyo: Bijutsu Nenkansha, 1998), pp. 135–136, 422; J. Thomas Rimer, "Postwar Developments: Absorption and Amalgamation, 1945–1968," in Ellen P. Conant, ed., *Nihonga: Transcending the Past: Japanese-Style Painting, 1868–1968* (St. Louis: St. Louis Art Museum, 1995), pp. 62–71.

55. Winther-Tamaki, *Encounter*, p. 68.

56. Ibid., pp. 77–78; Sugawara Norio, *Nihon no gendai bijutsu* (Tokyo: Maruzen,

1995), pp. 23–29; Segi, *Sengo*, p. 147. See also Louise Allison Cort and Bert Winther-Tamaki, *Isamu Noguchi and Modern Japanese Ceramics: A Close Embrace of the Earth* (Washington, D.C.: Smithsonian Institution and Berkeley: University of California Press, 2003).

57. Matsumoto, *Senkyūhyaku*, p. 24; Moroyama Masanori, "Trends in the Living Arts and Modern Crafts in the 1950s," in Tōkyō Kokuritsu Kindai Bijutsukan Kōgeikan, ed., *Crafts in Everyday Life in the 1950s and 1960s*, exh. cat. (Tokyo: Tōkyō Kokuritsu Kindai Bijutsukan, 1995), pp. 21–22. See Winther-Tamaki, *Encounter*, pp. 89–94.

58. Moroyama, "Trends," p. 19.

59. Ibid., pp. 16–18.

Chapter Four: Concrete Abstractions, Abstract Expressions

1. Haryū Ichirō, "'Chihō' konpurekkusu o kowase," *Bijutsu techō* 20:4 (1968), 83.

2. Chiba Shigeo, "Japanese Art in the 1950's and 1960's," in *Gutai 1955/56: Nihon gendai bijutsu no risutāto chiten* (Tokyo: Penrose Institute of Contemporary Art, 1993), p. 20.

3. Hikosaka Naoyoshi, "Tojirareta enkan no anata wa — 'Gutai' no kiseki kara nani o . . . ," *Bijutsu techō* 25:8 (1973), 90–92. See Segi, *Nihon no zen'ei*, p. 335.

4. Haryū Ichirō, "Kyūshūha tenmatsuki," in Fukuokashi Bijutsukan, ed., *Kyūshūhaten: hangeijutsu purojekuto*, exh. cat. (Fukuoka: Fukuokashi Bijutsukan, 1988), p. 6. See Haryū, "'Chihō,'" pp. 85–86, for a map displaying out-of-town art groups in the 1950s and 1960s. See also Segi, *Sengo*, pp. 110–115.

5. Motonaga Sadamasa letter, May 3, 2002.

6. Akasegawa Genpei interview, Tokyo, May 22, 2002.

7. See George Orwell, *The Lion and the Unicorn: Socialism and the English Genius* (London: Secker and Warburg, 1941). H. D. Harootunian discusses everydayness in interwar Japan in *History's Disquiet: Modernity, Cultural Practice, and the Question of Everyday Life* (New York: Columbia University Press, 2000). See J. Victor Koschmann's review of Harootunian's book in *Journal of Asian Studies* 60:4 (2001), 1188–1189, which notes the key role of Walter Benjamin in identifying everydayness. See also Henri Lefebvre, *Everyday Life in the Modern World*, trans. Sacha Rabinovitch (New York: Harper and Row, 1971), for a discussion of leisure and consumption in post–World War Two industrial societies.

8. Munroe, *Scream*, p. 84. See Chiba, *Gendai*, p. 82; Segi, *Sengo, Hizō shiryō*, p. 130; Sōgetsu Bijutsukan, p. 11; Taki, *Nihon no yōga*, pp. 236–237.

9. Kanagawa, *Kindai*, p. 294.

10. Yoshihara Jirō, quoted in David Kung, *The Contemporary Artist in Japan* (Honolulu: East-West Center Press, 1966), p. 137.

11. Yamamoto Atsuo, "Gutai 1954–1972," in Ashiya Shiritsu Bijutsu Hakubutsukan, ed., *Gutai I, II, III*, exh. cat. (Ashiya: Ashiya Shiritsu Bijutsu Hakubutsukan, 1994), p. 27.

12. Haryū Ichirō, *Sengo bijutsu seisuishi* (Tokyo: Tōkyō Shoseki, 1979), p. 96; Tatehata Akira interview, Tokyo, March 4, 2002; Tatehata Akira, "The Eve of Gutai," in *1953*, pp. 67–68.

13. Segi, *Sengo*, p. 131; Chiba, *Gendai*, p. 58; Hikosaka, "Tojirareta enkan," p. 73.

14. Matsumoto, *Senkyūhyaku*, p. 31; Matsumoto, "Contemporariness," p. 16. See Chiba, *Gendai*, p. 58.

15. Motonaga Sadamasa letter, May 3, 2002. See Kuroda Raiji, "Gutai ura no konseputo," *Bijutsu techō* 42:5 (1990), 110; Chiba, *Gendai*, p. 45.

16. Daniel Bell, "Tetsuya Noda: An Appreciation," in Fuji Terebi Gyayarī, *Noda Tetsuya zensakuhin III 1992–2000*, exh. cat. (Tokyo: Fuji Terebi Gyararī, 2001), p. 15.

17. "The Gutai Manifesto" ("Sengen"), from *Geijutsu shinchō* 7:12 (1956), in Ashiya Shiritsu Bijutsu Hakubutsukan, ed., *Gutai shiryōshū — dokyumento 1954–1972* (Ashiya: Ashiya Bunka Shinkō Zaidan, 1993), p. 8. See Chiba, *Gendai*, pp. 55–56.

18. "Gutai Manifesto," p. 8.

19. Ibid., p. 9. See Chiba, *Gendai*, p. 55. Establishing a purpose for art, as opposed to art for its own sake, was a goal of proletarian art and literature in Japan between the world wars.

20. *Gutai 1955/56*, p. 15.

21. Ashiya, *Gutai shiryōshū*, pp. 406–424.

22. Osaki Shin'ichiro, "Art in Gutai; Action into Painting," in Ashiya, *Gutai shiryōshū*, pp. 20–21; Sōgetsu Bijutsukan, *Hizō shiryō*, p. 12; Kuroda, "Gutai," p. 119. See Munroe, *Scream*, pp. 83, 89–90; Chiba, *Gendai*, pp. 55–56.

23. Gutai Bijutsu no 18nen Kankō Iinkai, ed., *Gutai bijutsu no 18nen* (Osaka: Gutai Bijutsu no 18nen Kankō Iinkai, 1976), p. 50; *Gutai 1955/56*, pp. 50–51.

24. Shimamoto Shōzō, "My Avant Garde," http://www.sukothai.com/X.SA.16/X.16.Shimamoto.html, March 7, 2003.

25. Takahashi Yūji interview, Tokyo, June 6, 2002. See Yamamoto, "Gutai," p. 33; *Gutai bijutsu no 18nen*, pp. 31–51; Osaki, "Art in Gutai," p. 22; Shimamoto, "My Avant Garde."

26. *Gutai bijutsu no 18nen*, pp. 31–51. See Yamamoto, "Gutai," p. 35; Osaki, "Art in Gutai," p. 23.

27. Osaki, "Art in Gutai," p. 23; Segi, *Sengo*, p. 133.

28. Yamamoto, "Gutai," p. 35.

29. Motonaga Sadamasa, quoted in Kung, *Contemporary Artist*, p. 79. See Tōkyō Kokuritsu Kindai Bijutsukan, ed., *Sengo bijutsu no tenkai: chūshō hyōgen no tayōka*, exh. cat. (Tokyo: Tōkyō Kokuritsu Kindai Bijutsukan, 1973), p. 53; Kanazawa Takeshi interview, Yokohama, April 18, 2002.

30. Tōno Yoshiaki, "Artists in the Early Sixties," in Takashina Shūji, Tōno Yoshiaki, Nakahara Yūsuke, and Tomiyama Hideo, eds., *Art in Japan Today* (Tokyo: Japan Foundation and Kinokuniya Bookstore, 1974), p. 18. See Tōkyō Kokuritsu Kindai Bijutsukan, *Sengo*, p. 52.

31. Tōkyō, *Sengo*, p. 51; Kung, *Contemporary Artist*, p. 109; Kanazawa Takeshi interview, Yokohama, April 18, 2002.

32. Gian Carlo Calza, *Tanaka Ikko: Graphic Master* (London: Phaidon Press, 1997), pp. 18–19.

33. Motonaga Sadamasa letter, May 3, 2002. See Chiba, *Gendai*, pp. 56–57.

34. Hikosaka, "Tojirareta enkan," p. 72.

35. Okamoto Tarō, quoted in Kuroda, "Gutai," p. 110. See Sugawara, *Nihon*, pp. 35–36; Osaki, *Art*, pp. 19, 22–23; Kokuritsu Kokusai Bijutsukan, ed., *Kaiga no arashi*

1950nendai: anfuorumeru/Gutai bijutsu/kobura kaiga no arashi, exh. cat. (Osaka: Kokuritsu Kokusai Bijutsukan, 1985).

36. See Hikosaka, "Tojirareta enkan," pp. 72–92; Chiba, *Gendai*, pp. 24–25.

37. See Harold Rosenberg, *The Tradition of the New* (New York: Horizon Press, 1959).

38. Taki, *Nihon no yōga*, pp. 238–239. See Chiba, *Gendai*, pp. 58–62. Taki credits Michel Tapié with recognizing the significance of informel painting earlier than other authorities. *Nihon no yōga*, pp. 239–240.

39. See Terada, *Japanese Art*, p. 39.

40. Lynton, *Story*, p. 234.

41. Erika Doss, *Benton, Pollock, and the Politics of Modernism: From Regionalism to Abstract Expressionism* (Chicago: University of Chicago Press, 1991), p. 6. See Lynton, *Story*, p. 227.

42. Clement Greenberg, "Abstract, Representational, and So Forth" (1961), in Chipp, *Theories*, p. 577; Michael Archer, *Art since 1960* (London: Thames and Hudson, 1997), pp. 41–42. The art historian Kajiya Kenji has established that Greenberg's writings were first translated into Japanese in the 1960s; Greenberg visited Japan in 1966. Kajiya Kenji, "Gosado suru buki: Kuremento Gurinbāgu, bunka reisen, guro-barizeshon," *Amerika kenkyū*, no. 37 (2003), pp. 83–105.

43. Winther-Tamaki, *Encounter*, pp. 19–22. See Taki, *Nihon no yōga*, p. 238.

44. Miki, "1960's," p. 24. See Miyakawa Atsushi, "Anfuorumeru igo," *Bijutsu techō* 15:5 (1963), 90. The writer is also known as Miyakawa Jun.

45. Akasegawa Genpei interview, Tokyo, May 22, 2002.

46. Haryū, *Sengo*, p. 100; Segi, *Nihon no zen'ei*, pp. 225–226; Segi, *Sengo*, p. 187; Segi Shin'ichi, *Gendai bijutsu no sanjūnen* (Tokyo: Bijutsu Kōronsha, 1978), pp. 207–208; Taki, *Nihon no yōga*, pp. 237, 240–241; Dōmoto Hisao interview, Tokyo, March 15, 2002; Satani Kazuhiko interview, Tokyo, February 4, 2002. According to Satani, the art critic Tōno Yoshiaki, who was married for a time to Idemitsu's eldest daughter, first introduced his father-in-law to Francis' paintings.

47. Shinohara Ushio interview, Tokyo, April 16, 2002.

48. Chiba, *Gendai*, p. 27. See Sawaragi, *Nihon*, pp. 258–262; Segi, *Sengo*, p. 187.

49. Ashton, *Thread*, p. 65. See Segi, *Sengo*, pp. 184–185; Setagaya Bijutsukan, ed., *Teshigahara Sōfū — sengo Nihon o kakenuketa ishoku no zen'ei*, exh. cat. (Tokyo: Setagaya Bijutsukan and Sōgetsukai, 2001), 1:94–96; "Teshigahara Sōfū: avangyarudo no kōseki," *Asahi gurafu*, October 13, 2000, p. 9.

50. Akasegawa Genpei interview, Tokyo, May 22, 2002.

51. Dōmoto Hisao interview, Tokyo, March 15, 2002.

52. Taki, *Nihon no yōga*, p. 241; Gunma, *Aru korekutā*, p. 23.

53. Tōkyōto, *Shinkan*, p. 17; Terada, *Japanese Art*, pp. 50, 57, 88.

54. Chiba, *Gendai*, p. 62; Sawaragi, *Nihon*, p. 260.

55. Taki, *Nihon no yōga*, p. 242.

56. On architecture, see Stan Allen, "Focus on the School of Architecture," *Princeton Alumni Weekly* 103:11 (2003), 2.

57. Sawaragi, *Nihon*, p. 260. On the rise of critics, see *Mizue*, no. 920, November 1981, p. 64; Chiba, *Gendai*, pp. 22–23; Yoshida Yoshie, *Kaitaigeki no maku orite: 60nendai zen'ei bijutsushi* (Tokyo: Zōkeisha, 1982), p. 75.

58. Hariū [Haryū] Ichirō, "Reflections on the Season of Neo Dada," in Mito Geijutsukan, *Nihon no natsu — 1960–1964* (Mito: Mito Geijutsukan, 1997), p. 78.

59. Segi, *Gendai*, p. 47; Segi Shin'ichi interview, Tokyo, February 11, 2002.

60. Segi, *Gendai*, p. 41. See pp. 30–32, 44.

61. See Hariū [Haryū] Ichirō, "The Phases of Neo-Dada in Postwar Art," trans. Yamazaki Yumiko, in Ōitashi Bijutsukan, ed., *Neo-Dada Japan 1958–1998: Isozaki Arata to Howaito Hausu no menmen*, exh. cat. (Ōita: Ōitashi Bijutsukan, 1998), p. 276.

62. See Chiba, *Gendai*, pp. 32–36.

63. Haryū Ichirō, in *Bijutsu techō* 15:10, expanded ed. (1963), 65.

64. Minemura Toshiaki interview, Tokyo, March 25, 2002.

65. Mitsuyama-Wdowiak, "Reception," p. 2; Chiba, *Gendai*, pp. 29–31; Segi, *Sengo*, pp. 119, 216.

66. Miyakawa, "Anfuorumeru," pp. 86–96.

67. Yamazaki Akiko interview, Tokyo, June 2, 2002.

68. Kikuhata, *Hangeijutsu*, p. 72.

69. Kuroda Raiji, "Isetsu bijutsu undō to shite no Kyūshūha," in Fukuokashi, *Kyūshūhaten*, p. 15.

70. Chiba, *Gendai*, p. 67. See Mito, *Nihon no natsu*, p. 68.

71. Sawaragi, *Nihon*, p. 279; Kuroda, "Isetsu," pp. 14–15.

72. Kikuhata Mokuma, *Sengo bijutsu no genshitsu* (Fukuoka: Ashi Shobō, 1982), pp. 26–27.

73. Kikuhata Mokuma, "Tsūzokusei ni taishite," in Kikuhata, *Hangeijutsu*, p. 31.

74. Ibid., pp. 39–40.

75. Kuroda, "Isetsu," pp. 20–21. See Mito, *Nihon no natsu*, p. 68. Cf. Munroe, *Scream*, pp. 156, 395.

76. Tatehata Akira interview, Tokyo, March 4, 2002; Chiba, *Gendai*, p. 67; Mito, *Nihon no natsu*, p. 68; Kuroda, "Isetsu," p. 18.

77. Sōgetsu Bijutsukan, *Hizō shiryō*, p. 14.

78. Kikuhata, *Hangeijutsu*, p. 96.

79. Mito, *Nihon no natsu*, p. 69.

80. Kikuhata, *Hangeijutsu*, pp. 76–80.

81. Kuroda, "Gutai," p. 110.

Chapter Five: The Sōgetsu Art Center

1. Teshigahara Hiroshi, quoted in Setagaya Bijutsukan, *Teshigahara*, 1:182.

2. Tsutsumi Seiji interview, Tokyo, April 8, 2002.

3. Hara Toshio interview, Tokyo, February 20, 2002.

4. See Setagaya Bijutsukan, *Teshigahara*, vol. 1, passim.

5. Sugiyama Etsuko, "Sōfū to wa, ittai nanimono datta no ka," in Setagaya Bijutsukan, *Teshigahara*, 2:37.

6. Sakai Tadayasu interview, Kamakura, March 5, 2002.

7. Ichiyanagi Toshi interview, Tokyo, April 11, 2002.

8. Teshigahara Sōfū, *Kadensho* (Tokyo: Sōgetsu Shuppan, 1979), p. 55. He used the characters for *zōkei* (forms) to write *ikeru* (to cause to live). See Setagaya Bi-

jutsukan, *Teshigahara*, 1:84, 139; Sugiyama, "Sōfū," pp. 39–40; Iemura, "Beyond Genres," pp. 36–37; "Teshigahara Sōfū: avangyarudo no kōseki," pp. 6–9.

9. Ōshima Seiji, "In a Chaos of Creation," in Setagaya Bijutsukan, *Teshigahara*, 1:15. Donald Richie notes that, after Teshigahara Hiroshi's death in 2001, "the Sōgetsu school has made an industry of canonizing its long-deceased headmaster Teshigahara Sōfū as founder, no longer innovator. It sponsors exhibits and produces publications establishing him as a preexisting authoritative voice." Richie, "One Hundred."

10. Setagaya Bijutsukan, *Teshigahara*, 1:44.

11. Ibid., 1:59; Sugiyama, "Sōfū," p. 42.

12. Iemura, "Beyond Genres," p. 38.

13. Setagaya Bijutsukan, *Teshigahara*, 1:66.

14. Teshigahara Sōfū, *Sōfū no chōkoku Kojiki*, exh. cat. (1966), reprinted in Setagaya Bijutsukan, *Teshigahara*, 2:70–71.

15. Setagaya Bijutsukan, *Teshigahara*, 1:116. See Sugiyama, "Sōfū," pp. 42–43.

16. Haryū Ichirō, "Zōkeika seikatsu geijutsuka," *Sōgetsu*, no. 22 (1955), pp. 213–214. See Setagaya Bijutsukan, *Teshigahara*, 1:178.

17. Takiguchi Shūzō, "Obuje no hakken," *Sōgetsu*, special number, February 1953, reprinted in Setagaya Bijutsukan, *Teshigahara*, 1:204–205. Sōfū's granddaughter Teshigahara Akane, the fourth head of the Sōgetsu school, points out that he had a greater artistic reputation abroad than in Japan, where he was known mainly as an ikebana headmaster. Some of his wooden sculptures are so huge that they must be kept in warehouses and are seldom seen. Teshigahara Akane, "Time to Find Sōfū," in Setagaya Bijutsukan, *Teshigahara*, 1:18–19.

18. "Teshigahara Sōfū: avangyarudo no kōseki," p. 16; Ashton, *Thread*, p. 45.

19. Segi Shin'ichi interview, Tokyo, February 11, 2002.

20. Ōoka Makoto interview, Tokyo, March 9, 2002. See "Teshigahara Sōfū: avangyarudo no kōseki," p. 16.

21. Ashton, *Thread*, pp. 68–73.

22. Sōgetsukai, ed., *Kokoro wa itsumo runesansu hyōgen jiyūjin Teshigahara Hiroshi* (Tokyo: Sōgetsu Shuppan, 1989), p. 45; "Teshigahara Sōfū: avangyarudo no kōseki," pp. 12–13; Ashton, *Thread*, p. 102; Setagaya Bijutsukan, *Teshigahara*, 1:174–175. A revisionist reading of Teshigahara's *Suna no onna* is Chigusa Kimura-Steven, "The Otherness of Women in the Avant-Garde Film *Woman in the Dunes*," in Joshua S. Mostow, Norman Bryson, and Maribeth Graybill, eds., *Gender and Power in the Japanese Visual Field* (Honolulu: University of Hawai'i Press, 2003), pp. 155–178, 250–254.

23. Setagaya Bijutsukan, *Teshigahara*, 1:107, 176–177. See Sōgetsu Bijutsukan, *Hizō shiryō*, p. 10.

24. Teshigahara Hiroshi, quoted in Sugiyama, "Sōfū," p. 44.

25. Sōgetsukai, ed., *Sōgetsu 60th Anniversary: Saigen Sōgetsu Āto Sentā* (Tokyo: Sōgetsukai, 1987), pp. 30–34. See p. 1; Ongaku no Tomosha, *20seiki*, p. 65; Setagaya Bijutsukan, *Teshigahara*, 1:182; Sōgetsu Bijutsukan, *Hizō shiryō*, p. 10; Ashton, *Thread*, p. 75.

26. Tōno Yoshiaki, quoted in Sōgetsukai, *60th*, p. 7.

27. Ongaku no Tomosha, *20seiki*, pp. 65, 136, 183; Sōgetsukai, *60th*, pp. 30–34.

Iwaki points out that "the Sōgetsu Art Center group of experimental composers were wonderful. There were nineteen composers plus I, the only conductor. Ichiyanagi was not a part of this group, but it was splendid when he brought John Cage to Japan." Iwaki Hiroyuki interview, Tokyo, March 22, 2002.

28. Bijutsu Shuppansha, *Gendai*, p. 42.

29. Ibid.; Ongaku no Tomosha, *20seiki*, p. 155; Sōgetsu Bijutsukan, *Teshigahara*, p. 10.

30. Sōgetsukai, *60th*, p. 6. See Ongaku no Tomosha, *20seiki*, p. 136; Bijutsu Shuppansha, *Gendai*, p. 12.

31. Sōgetsukai, *60th*, p. 7; Ashton, *Thread*, pp. 116–117. See Ashiya Shiritsu Bijutsu Hakubutsukan and Chibashi Bijutsukan, eds., *Sōgetsu to sono jidai 1945–1970*, exh. cat. (Ashiya: Ashiya Shiritsu Bijutsu Hakubutsukan, 1998), for exhibition materials on this period.

32. Ongaku no Tomosha, *20seiki*, pp. 66–67; Tone Yasunao, *Gendai geijutsu no isō: geijutsu wa shisō tariuru ka* (Tokyo: Tabata Shoten, 1970), pp. 20, 23; David Pogue and Scott Speck, *Classical Music for Dummies* (New York: Hungry Minds, 1997), p. 90; Griffiths, *Modern Music and After*, p. 25.

33. Ichiyanagi Toshi (1961), quoted in Ongaku no Tomosha, *20seiki*, p. 66.

34. Chōki Seiji interview, Tokyo, April 17, 2002.

35. Yuasa Jōji interview, Tokyo, February 5, 2002.

36. Ichiyanagi Toshi interview, Tokyo, April 11, 2002.

37. Ibid.

38. Iwaki Hiroyuki interview, Tokyo, March 22, 2002.

39. Ongaku no Tomosha, *20seiki*, p. 69.

40. Sōgetsukai, *60th*, pp. 12–24, 30–34; Setagaya Bijutsukan, *Teshigahara*, 1:182, 185–187; Sōgetsu Bijutsukan, *Hizō shiryō*, p. 10.

41. Mamiya Michio interview, Tokyo, April 22, 2002.

42. Griffiths, *Modern Music and After*, p. 126.

43. Heifetz, "Composition," p. 50. See Ongaku no Tomosha, *20seiki*, p. 136; Bijutsu Shuppansha, *Gendai*, p. 12.

44. Ichiyanagi Toshi, quoted in Takemitsu, *Oto chinmoku*, p. 44.

45. Akiyama Kuniharu, *Gendai ongaku o dō kiku ka* (Tokyo: Shōbunsha, 1973), p. 155. See Bijutsu Shuppansha, *Gendai*, p. 12; Ongaku no Tomosha, *20seiki*, pp. 136–137.

46. Ongaku no Tomosha, *20seiki*, pp. 137–139.

47. Takemitsu, *Oto chinmoku*, p. 98.

48. Sano, "Joron," pp. 14–15; Ongaku no Tomosha, *20seiki*, pp. 180–181, 183.

49. Chōki Seji, "Seiyō zen'ei ongaku no naka Takemitsu Tōru," in Chōki and Higuchi, eds., *Takemitsu*, p. 288.

50. Takemitsu Tōru, "Contemporary Music in Japan," *Perspectives of New Music* 27:2 (1989), 198.

51. Burt, *Takemitsu*, pp. 96–97.

52. Griffiths, *Modern Music and After*, p. 91; Bijutsu Shuppansha, *Gendai*, p. 62.

53. Takahashi Yūji interview, Tokyo, June 6, 2002. Hayashi Hikaru points out that the festival was the inaugural event held at the new Tokyo Bunka Kaikan (Tokyo Metropolitan Festival Hall), opened in 1961 in Ueno Park: "I declined to participate." Hayashi Hikaru interview, Tokyo, June 13, 2002.

54. Takahashi Yūji interview, Tokyo, June 6, 2002.

55. Takahashi Yūji, "Movements, Colors and Nearness" (1998), www.ne.jp/asahi/kerbau/kerbau21/texts(e)/mcn.html, June 24, 2003.

56. Takahashi Yūji interview, Tokyo, June 6, 2002. See Ongaku no Tomosha, *20seiki*, pp. 176–179.

57. Munroe, *Scream*, p. 218.

58. Griffiths, *Modern Music and After*, p. 94; Peter Frank, "The Fluxus Movement," www.artcommotion.com/Issue2/VisualArts/, April 5, 2003. See Ken Friedman, *The Fluxus Reader* (New York: Academy Editions, 1998); Hannah Higgins, *Fluxus Experience* (Berkeley: University of California Press, 2002), the latter of which emphasizes performance.

59. Teshigahara Hiroshi, quoted in Sōgetsukai, *60th*, p. 1. See Sugiyama, "Sōfū," p. 44; Setagaya Bijutsukan, *Teshigahara*, 1:182.

Part Two: Overview

1. Rivkin and Ryan, *Theory*, pp. 1025–1026.

2. Hariū [Haryū], "Progressive," p. 27.

3. Andrew Gordon, *A Modern History of Japan from Tokugawa Times to the Present* (New York: Oxford University Press, 2003), p. 252.

4. In 1995, 15,298,000 Japanese traveled overseas. Kawai Nobukazu, ed., *Asahi shinbun Japan arumanakku 1999* (Tokyo: Asahi Shinbunsha, 1998), p. 273.

5. See Simon Partner, *Assembled in Japan: Electrical Goods and the Making of the Japanese Consumer* (Berkeley: University of California Press, 1999), pp. 186–188.

6. Yano Tomoo, *Han'ei*, p. 1.

7. *Kodansha Encyclopedia of Japan* 2:323.

8. Walt W. Rostow, *The Stages of Economic Growth, a Non-Communist Manifesto* (London: Cambridge University Press, 1960). On social management, see Deborah J. Milly, *Poverty, Equality, and Growth: The Politics of Economic Need in Postwar Japan* (Cambridge, Mass.: Harvard University Asia Center, 1999), esp. pp. 15–24; see also Sheldon Garon, *Molding Japanese Minds: The State in Everyday Life* (Princeton, N.J.: Princeton University Press, 1997).

9. Kano Masanao, *Nihon no gendai* (Tokyo: Iwanami Shoten, 2000), p. 78. See pp. 75–77; Hariū [Haryū], "Progressive," p. 27.

10. See Yoshimi Shun'ya, "Reisen taisei to 'Amerika' no shōhi," in Komori Yōichi et al., eds., *Reisen taisei to shihon no bunka: 1955nen igo 1 Iwanami kōza kindai Nihon no bunkashi 9* (Tokyo: Iwanami Shoten, 2002), pp. 1–60. I am grateful to J. Victor Koschmann for insights into this question (Modern Japanese History Workshop, Harvard University, April 10, 2004). In Yoshimi's analysis the integration of state and society began to break apart in Japan after 1990. Yoshimi is a leading Japanese specialist in cultural studies, the impact of which has been especially felt in the study of Japanese colonialism, emphasizing zones of contact and cultural interaction rather than unidirectional domination by the metropole.

11. Colin Gordon, "Governmental Rationality: An Introduction," in Graham Burchall, Colin Gordon, and Peter Miller, eds., *The Foucault Effect: Studies in Governmentality with Two Lectures by and an Interview with Michel Foucault* (London: Harvester Wheatsheaf, 1991), p. 3.

12. James Scott, *Seeing Like a State: How Certain Schemes to Improve the Human Condition Have Failed* (New Haven: Yale University Press, 1998), pp. 3, 54, 92.

13. Mark Overmyer-Velázquez, "Visions of the Emerald City: Politics, Culture, and Alternative Modernities in Oaxaca City, Mexico, 1877–1920" (Ph.D. dissertation, Yale University, 2002), p. 13. See also p. 32. Brian J. McVeigh extends the analysis to Japanese nationalism, finding its sources in the everyday interactions of state and society rather than in properties unique to Japan. *Nationalisms of Japan: Managing and Mystifying Identity* (Lanham, Md.: Rowman and Littlefield, 2004).

14. See Frank J. Schwarz and Susan J. Pharr, eds., *The State of Civil Society in Japan* (New York: Cambridge University Press, 2003).

15. Young, *Postcolonialism*, pp. 113–114.

16. Harvey, *Condition*, p. 38.

17. Tsutsumi Seiji interview, Tokyo, April 8, 2002. See Munroe, *Scream*, pp. 23–24.

18. Yukio Kondo, "Thoughts on Kazuo Kadonaga from a Japanese Perspective: Beyond Exoticism," in Japanese American Cultural and Community Center, Los Angeles, and Salt Lake Art Center, Salt Lake City, eds., *Kazuo Kadonaga*, exh. cat. (2001), p. 43.

19. Washburn, *Dilemma*, p. 211.

20. Katō, *Form*, p. 35.

21. Jay, *Imagination*, p. xxvii.

22. Using a postcolonial perspective, Ueno Chizuko notes that by "cleverly deploying femininity as a resource," Mahatma Gandhi perpetuated sexual discrimination even as he led a highly effective anticolonial movement for Indian independence. See *Nationalism and Gender*, p. 140. Gender equality was similarly retarded in the avant-garde arts, antiwar organizations, and citizens' movements in Japan during the 1960s.

23. David G. Goodman, *Japanese Drama and Culture in the 1960s: The Return of the Gods* (Armonk, N.Y.: M. E. Sharpe, 1988), p. 3. See pp. 4–9; Minemura Toshiaki, "Tōji, kūkansu," in Ōitashi Bijutsukan, ed., *Yoshimura Masunobu no jikkenten — ōtō to hen'yō*, exh. cat. (Ōita: Ōitashi Bijutsukan, 2000), pp. 16–17.

24. Minemura Toshiaki, "Kaitai to soshikika no kurikaeshi," *Mizue*, no. 921 (1981), pp. 74–75. See also Chiba, *Gendai*, p. 100.

25. Catherine Millet, quoted in Tōno Yoshiaki, "Mono-ha and Post-Mono-ha Developments: An On-the-Scene Commentary," trans. Alfred Birnbaum, in Tama Bijutsu Daigaku and Seibu Bijutsukan, eds., *Monoha to posutomonoha no tenkai*, exh. cat. (Tokyo: Tama Bijustu Daigaku and Seibu Bijutsukan, 1987), p. 188.

26. Nakanishi Natsuyuki interview, Tokyo, March 2, 2002.

27. Brombert, *Antiheroes*, pp. 1–2.

28. Nanjō Fumio interview, Tokyo, March 15, 2002.

29. Moroi Makoto interview, Saitamashi, March 30, 2002.

30. Yuasa Jōji interview, Tokyo, February 5, 2002.

31. Hara Toshio interview, Tokyo, February 20, 2002.

32. Tachikawa Ruriko letter, March 10, 2002.

33. Matsudaira Yoriaki interview, Tokyo, February 13, 2002.

34. See Sugiyama, "Sōfū," pp. 38–39.

35. Minemura, "Introduction," p. 5.

36. Ishiguro Kenji interview, Tokyo, June 6, 2002.

37. Ōoka Makoto interview, Tokyo, March 9, 2002.

38. Ishiguro Kenji interview, Tokyo, June 6, 2002.

39. Suga Akira, "Jikken no bunseki — ōtō to sekinin," in Ōitashi, *Yoshimura*, p. 116.

40. Komiya, *Kingendai*, p. 209.

41. Ongaku no Tomosha, *20seiki*, p. 123; Komiya, *Kingendai*, p. 183.

42. *Nihon kingendaishi jiten* (Tokyo: Tōyō Keizai Shinpōsha, 1978), p. 175; Komiya, *Kingendai*, pp. 207–208.

43. Konuma Jun'ichi, *Takemitsu Tōru* (Tokyo: Seidosha, 1999), pp. 56–57.

44. Ongaku no Tomosha, *20seiki*, pp. 63–64.

45. Hayashi Hikaru interview, Tokyo, June 13, 2002; Komiya, *Kingendai*, pp. 207–209. On writers and Anpo, see Isoda Kōichi, *Sengoshi no kūkan* (Tokyo: Shinchōsha, 1993), pp. 145–165.

46. George R. Packard III, *Protest in Tokyo* (Princeton, N.J.: Princeton University Press, 1966), p. 261; Ishida Takeshi, "Emerging or Eclipsing Citizenship?" *The Developing Economies* 6:4 (1968), 416.

47. Yamano Hakudai interview, Tokyo, March 20, 2002. See Yamano Hakudai, "Nihon yōbu ryakushi," part 3, *Kisetsu dansāto*, no. 11 (August 1998), pp. 1–2.

48. Komiya, *Kingendai*, pp. 211–214.

49. Akasegawa Genpei interview, Tokyo, May 22, 2002.

50. Arakawa Shūsaku interview, New York, June 24, 2002. See Hariū [Haryū], "Phases," p. 277.

51. Isozaki Arata, "Imprint of 1960," trans. Yamazaki Yumiko and David B. Stewart, in Ōitashi, *Neo-Dada*, p. 274.

52. Nakanishi Natsuyuki interview, Tokyo, March 2, 2002.

53. Ibid.

54. Chiba Shigeo interview, Tokyo, March 11, 2002.

55. Isozaki Arata, "Runaway System," in Mito, *Nihon no natsu*, p. 81.

56. Sekine Nobuo interview, Tokyo, February 21, 2002.

57. Yoshimasu Gōzō interview, Tokyo, May 22, 2002.

58. *Bijutsu techō* 30:7 (1978), expanded no., p. 198.

59. Tone Yasunao, "Geijutsu no chikaku hendō," *Bijutsu techō* 19:11 (1967), 101.

60. Ishiguro Kenji interview, Tokyo, June 6, 2002.

61. Joe B. Moore, "Japan, Jazz, and Creolization," in Takeshi Matsuda, ed., *The Age of Creolization in the Pacific* (Hiroshima: Keisuisha, 2001), p. 157. See also Michael S. Molasky, *Sengo Nihon no jazu bunka — eiga, bungaku, sabukaruchā* (Tokyo: Seidosha, 2005).

62. Kara Jūrō interview, Tokyo, November 10, 1980. Situationalism derives from France in the 1930s.

63. Sekine Nobuo interview, Tokyo, February 21, 2002.

Chapter Six: Beyond Form and Formality

1. Kokuritsu Kokusai Bijutsukan, ed., *Geijutsu to nichijō — hangeijutsu/hangeijutsu*, exh. cat. (Osaka: Kokuritsu Kokusai Bijutsukan, 1991), p. 6.

2. Chow, *Writing*, p. 41.

3. Nakamura Keiji, "Art," p. 22. See Sawaragi, *Nihon*, pp. 233–234.

4. Tōno's review appeared in *Yomiuri* on March 2, 1960, evening ed., and Takiguchi's on March 4, 1960, evening ed., quoted in Taki, *Nihon no yōga*, p. 273.

5. See Chiba, *Gendai*, pp. 80–81; Iwase and Yui, *Nijūsseiki*, p. 102; Gunma, *Aru korekutā*, p. 82.

6. Shinohara Ushio, *Zen'ei no michi* (Tokyo: Bijutsu Shuppansha, 1968), p. 61.

7. Kikuhata, *Hangeijutsu*, p. 110. See Nakamura Keiji, "Art," pp. 24–25; Sugawara, *Nihon*, pp. 39–41.

8. Miyakawa, "Anfuorumeru," pp. 86–96.

9. Miyakawa Atsushi, "Hangeijutsu: sono nichijōsei e no kakō," *Bijutsu techō* 16:4 (1964), 48. Portions of this article appear in translation in Munroe, *Scream*, p. 385. See Miki, "1960s," p. 27; Chiba, *Gendai*, p. 64.

10. Miyakawa, "Hangeijutsu," p. 48.

11. Ibid., p. 50.

12. Ibid., p. 57. See pp. 53–56.

13. See Chiba, *Gendai*, pp. 64–66; Sawaragi, *Nihon*, pp. 202–203.

14. Tōno Yoshiaki, "Isetsu 'hangeijutsu' — 'Miyakawa Atsushi' igo," *Bijutsu techō* 16:5 (1964), 46–49, summarizing Haryū's criticism as well as his own.

15. Chiba, *Gendai*, p. 43.

16. *Mizue*, no. 921 (December 1981), p. 67.

17. Tone, *Gendai*, p. 19.

18. Kikuhata, *Hangeijutsu*, p. 107. See Sugawara, *Nihon*, pp. 38–39.

19. Matsumoto, "Contemporariness," pp. 18–19.

20. Chipp, *Theories*, pp. 367–368; Archer, *Art*, p. 10.

21. Chipp, *Theories*, p. 376.

22. Benjamin, "Work," pp. 237–238. See Lynton, *Story*, pp. 124–128; Chipp, *Theories*, pp. 368–369.

23. Sekine Nobuo interview, Tokyo, February 21, 2002.

24. Dōmoto Hisao interview, Tokyo, March 15, 2002.

25. Tōkyō, *Sengo*, p. 3.

26. Kondō Yukio interview, Yokohama, February 20, 2002.

27. Chiba, *Gendai*, pp. 73–74; Hariū [Haryū], "Phases," pp. 276–277.

28. Iwata Shin'ichi, quoted in Kuroda Raiji, "Akarui satsurikisha, sono shunkan gei no jutsu," in Fukuokashi Bijutsukan, ed., *Ryūdō suru bijutsu III: Neo-Dada no shashin*, exh. cat. (Fukuoka: Fukuokashi Bijutsukan, 1993), p. 9.

29. See Akasegawa, *Hangeijutsu*, passim.

30. Hariū [Haryū], "Phases," p. 277. See Sōgetsu Bijutsukan, *Hizō shiryō*, p. 9; Suga Akira, "Why the Current Interest in Neo-Dada?" in Ōitashi, *Neo-Dada*, p. 289; Kuroda, "Akarui," p. 12.

31. William A. Marotti, "Politics and Culture in Postwar Japan: Akasegawa Genpei and the Artistic Avant-garde, 1958–1970" (Ph.D. dissertation, University of Chicago, 2001), p. 136. See Mito, *Nihon*, pp. 86–87; Munroe, *Scream*, pp. 157, 396; Sawaragi, *Nihon*, p. 45; Hariū [Haryū], "Reflections," p. 78.

32. Hyūga Akiko interview, Kawasaki, March 21, 2002.

33. Shinohara Ushio interview, Tokyo, April 16, 2002.

34. Isozaki, "Witness," p. 28. See Shinohara, *Zen'ei*, pp. 56–62, 73–74; Kanagawa, *Kindai*, p. 51; Hiroshimashi Gendai Bijutsukan, ed., *Shinohara Ushioten zuroku*, exh. cat. (Tokyo: Asahi Shinbunsha, 1992), pp. 5–9, 96, 101.

35. Yoshimura Masunobu, "Neo-Dada Oruganaizāsu," *Bijutsu techō* 23:10 (1971), 56–57.

36. Quoted in Kuroda, "Akarui," p. 10.

37. See Akasegawa Genpei and Otsuji Katsuhiko, *Tōkyō rojō tankenki*, 2nd ed. (Tokyo: Shinchōsha, 1989 [1986]), pp. 194–196. Otsuji Katsuhiko is Akasegawa's pen name.

38. Mito, *Nihon*, p. 63.

39. Kuroda, "Akarui," p. 10.

40. Shinohara, *Zen'ei*, p. 60.

41. Ōitashi, *Neo-Dada*, p. 67. For *Mudai*, see Matsumoto, *Senkyūhyaku*, pp. 41–42.

42. Tōno, "Artists," p. 20.

43. See Kanagawa, *Kindai*, p. 7; Mito, *Nihon*, p. 63.

44. Suga, "Jikken," pp. 117, 126; Kuroda, "Akarui," p. 9; Hariū [Haryū], "Phases," p. 278; Tatehata Akira, "Neo-Dada Since Then," in Ōitashi, *Neo-Dada*, pp. 287–288.

45. Akasegawa Genpei interview, Tokyo, May 22, 2002.

46. Haryū Ichirō, "Zen'ei geijutsu ni tsukaremashita," *Geijutsu shinchō* 12:8 (1962), 151.

47. Akasegawa Genpei, "Toshi kūkan no naka no shintai," *Yuriika*, September 1984, quoted in Kuroda, "Gutai," p. 110. See Kuroda, "Akarui," pp. 10, 13.

48. Hara Toshio interview, Tokyo, February 20, 2002.

49. Tatehata, "Neo-Dada," p. 286; Sugawara, *Nihon*, pp. 10–11.

50. Arakawa Shūsaku interview, New York, June 24, 2002.

51. Shinohara Ushio interview, Tokyo, April 16, 2002.

52. Suga, "Why?" p. 290.

53. Shinohara Ushio interview, Tokyo, April 16, 2002.

54. Akasegawa Genpei, *Hangeijutsu anpan* (Tokyo: Chikuma Shobō, 1994), p. 10. Originally published by Chikuma in 1985 as *Ima ya akushon aru nomi! — "Yomiuri Andepandan" to iu genshō*.

55. Sawaragi, *Nihon*, p. 232. See Segi, *Sengo*, pp. 278–279.

56. Miki Tamon, "Japanese Contemporary Art — the 1950s and 1960s," in Kokuritsu, *Geijutsu*, p. 13.

57. Akasegawa Genpei, "The 1960s: The Art Which Destroyed Itself: An Intimate Account," trans. John Clark, in Elliott and Kaido, *Reconstructions*, p. 86. See Marotti, "Politics," pp. 89–91, 99–106, 112, 124–134.

58. Taki, *Nihon no yōga*, p. 274; Segi, *Sengo*, pp. 279–282.

59. Hariū [Haryū], "Phases," p. 279.

60. Tōno Yoshiaki, "Sayōnara Yomiuri andepandanten," *Bijutsu techō* 16:4 (1964), 13.

61. Sawaragi, *Nihon*, pp. 235–236; Taki, *Nihon no yōga*, pp. 274–275.

62. Yomiuri Shinbun statement, January 12, 1964, in Segi, *Sengo*, p. 282.

63. Akasegawa, "1960s," p. 88.

64. Sawaragi, *Nihon*, p. 244.

65. See Ibid., pp. 236, 247–248.

66. See Miller and Lieberman, *Painting and Sculpture*; Sugawara, *Nihon*, pp. 5–8.

67. See Segi, *Sengo*, pp. 285–286; Taki, *Nihon no yōga*, pp. 289–290.

Chapter Seven: Events, Objects, and Concepts

1. Quoted in Taki, *Nihon no yōga*, p. 280.

2. Miki Tamon, "Major Trends in Modern Japanese Sculpture Since the 1950s," in Kumon Yasuo, ed., *Nihon gendai bijutsu: chōkoku* (Tokyo: Keishōsha, 1985), p. 7.

3. Matsumoto, *Senkyūhyaku*, p. 23. See also p. 22; Segi, *Sengo*, pp. 265–266.

4. Yoshimasu Gōzō interview, Tokyo, May 22, 2002.

5. Chiba, *Gendai*, pp. 94–97.

6. Minemura Toshiaki interview, Tokyo, March 25, 2002.

7. Tatehata Akira interview, Tokyo, March 4, 2002.

8. Akasegawa Genpei, *Tōkyō mikisā keikaku* (Tokyo: Chikuma Shobō, 1994), p. 8. This title was originally published in Tokyo by Parco in 1984. See Sawaragi, *Nihon*, p. 206.

9. Akasegawa Genpei, "1960s," p. 88. The German physicist Werner Heisenberg (1901–1976) proposed his uncertainty principle in 1939.

10. Mito, *Nihon*, p. 87.

11. Kaido, "Reconstruction," p. 20; Chiba, *Gendai*, p. 87; Sawaragi, *Nihon*, p. 201.

12. Nakanishi Natsuyuki interview, Tokyo, March 2, 2002. See Akasegawa, *Tōkyō*, pp. 17, 21–26; Tsuji Nobuo, ed., *Manga Nihon bijutsu 3 Meiji-gendai no bijutsu* (Tokyo: Bijutsu Shuppansha, 1996), pp. 214–215; Marotti, "Politics," p. 139.

13. Akasegawa, *Hangeijutsu*, p. 9.

14. Akasegawa, *Tōkyō*, p. 111. See pp. 17, 99–130; Sōgetsu Bijutsukan, *Hizō shiryō*, p. 9; *Bijutsu techō* 15:10 (1963), expanded no., p. 38.

15. See Akasegawa, *Tōkyō*, pp. 134–135.

16. Akasegawa, "1960s," p. 89.

17. Ibid. Cf. Elliott and Kaido, *Reconstructions*, p. 10.

18. See Marotti, "Politics," pp. 228–229; Sawaragi, *Nihon*, pp. 204–205. Also see Marotti, pp. 231–242 for a detailed account of this exhibit.

19. Akasegawa, "1960s," pp. 89–90; Yuasa Jōji interview, Tokyo, February 5, 2002.

20. Akasegawa, *Tōkyō*, pp. 177–200.

21. Ibid., p. 216.

22. Ibid., pp. 215–227; Yaguchi Kunio, "The 1964 Tokyo Olympics and a Turning Point in Japanese Art," in Tōkyōto Gendai Bijutsukan, ed., *Nihon no bijutsu: yomigaeru 1964*, exh. cat. (Tokyo: Tōkyōto Gendai Bijutsukan, 1996), p. 185. Yaguchi reports that Dr. Miyata Kunio, the former clinic owner, was an acquaintance of Nakanishi.

23. Akasegawa, *Tōkyō*, p. 246. See pp. 229–245.

24. Ibid., p. 251. See Hirata Minoru, *Chōgeijutsu* (Tokyo: Sangokan, 2005), for photos of vanguard artists.

25. Nakanishi Natsuyuki interview, Tokyo, March 2, 2002. See Tsuji, *Manga*, pp. 214–215.

26. Akasegawa, *Tōkyō*, p. 268. See pp. 249–267.

27. Nakanishi Natsuyuki interview, Tokyo, March 2, 2002. See Kanagawa, *Kindai*, p. 78. The art critic Kanazawa Takeshi points out that "at the Nishimura Gallery in the 1980s, Nakanishi painted huge works with a long brush, standing far back from the canvas, to avoid control by his hand and thus to mask his ability." Kanazawa Takeshi interview, Yokohama, April 18, 2002.

28. Marotti, "Politics," p. 3.

29. Nakanishi Natsuyuki interview, Tokyo, March 2, 2002.

30. Okamoto Tarō, "Sukyandaru to Dali" (1955), quoted in Kaido, "Reconstruction," p. 20.

31. Akasegawa, "1960s," p. 90.

32. Sawaragi, *Nihon*, p. 200.

33. Akasegawa, *Tōkyō*, p. 269.

34. *Concerned Theatre Japan* 1:3 (1970), 35. See Sawaragi, *Nihon*, pp. 206–207.

35. Sōgetsu Bijutsukan, *Hizō shiryō*, p. 9. For a detailed study of the investigation and trial, see Marotti, "Politics," pp. 22–35, 43–47, 59, 74, 77–86, 194–226, 273. For an incisive discussion of the artistic issues at stake, see Reiko Tomii, "State v. (Anti-)Art: Model 1,000-Yen Note Incident by Akasegawa Genpei and Company," *positions* 10:1 (2002), 141–172. See also Akasegawa, *Tōkyō*, pp. 271–293.

36. Tōkyōto, *Shinkan*, p. 18.

37. Akasegawa Genpei, "Capitalist Realism," *Concerned Theatre Japan* 1:3 (1970), 35 (translation of "'Shihonshugi rearizumu'ron," *Dokusho shinbun*, February 1964). See Marotti, "Politics," p. 199.

38. Rand Castile, "Thinking of Shinohara," in Hiroshimashi, *Shinohara*, p. 107. The American painter Andy Warhol (1928–1987) turned to reproduction art in 1962.

39. Benjamin, "Work," pp. 217–251. See Chow, *Writing*, p. 43; Rivkin and Ryan, *Theory*, pp. 282–285.

40. Noguchi Reiichi, "Japanese Art of 1964: The Reaction to *Art Informel* and Further Developments," in Tōkyōto, *Nihon*, p. 190.

41. Akasegawa, *Tōkyō*, p. 271.

42. Akasegawa, "1960s," p. 87.

43. Akasegawa, "Capitalist," pp. 32, 35.

44. *Concerned Theatre Japan* 1:3 (1970), 49.

45. Takiguchi's writings on the thousand-yen note case amplify his testimony. Takiguchi, *Korekushon*, 7:445–489. *Bijutsu techō* 23:10–11 (1971) published a retrospective on the trial and appeals.

46. Akasegawa, *Tōkyō*, p. 283. See Sawaragi, *Nihon*, pp. 212–225; Chiba, *Gendai*, p. 87.

47. Akasegawa, *Tōkyō*, pp. 286–293; Sawaragi, *Nihon*, p. 201.

48. Akasegawa, *Tōkyō*, p. 293.

49. Sekine Nobuo interview, Tokyo, February 21, 2002.

50. See Matsumoto, *Senkyūhyaku*, p. 44. Plato's cave reduces phenomena to shadows. See Yomi Braester, *Witness against History: Literature, Film, and Public Discourse in Twentieth-Century China* (Stanford, Calif.: Stanford University Press, 2003), p. 5.

51. Nakanishi Natsuyuki interview, Tokyo, March 2, 2002.

52. Akasegawa, "1960s," p. 90.

53. Minemura Toshiaki interview, Tokyo, March 25, 2002.

54. Sakai Tadayasu interview, Kamakura, March 5, 2002.

55. Tanaka Takaki interview, Tokyo, February 14, 2002; Miki, "Major," p. 5.

56. Sakai Tadayasu interview, Kamakura, March 5, 2002. See Sakai Tadayasu, "Sengo no gendai chōkoku," in *Genshoku Nihon no bijutsu 33 gendai* (Tokyo: Shōgakukan, 1994), pp. 238–246.

57. See Lynton, *Story*, p. 340.

58. Takashina Shūji, "Modern Sculpture," in Takashina, Tōno, Nakahara, and Tomiyama, *Art in Japan Today*, pp. 12–14.

59. Mito, *Nihon*, p. 86; Sakai, "Sengo," pp. 240–242; Geijutsu no Mori Bijutsukan, ed., *20seiki Nihon chōkoku monogatari* (Sapporo: Geijutsu no Mori Bijutsukan, 2000), p. 120.

60. Miki, "Major," p. 9. See Yaguchi, "Olympics," pp. 188–189. *Rittai* also means "solid" or "cubic."

61. Terada, *Japanese Art*, pp. 132–133.

62. Iino Kiichi interview, Tokyo, December 16, 1980.

63. Kanagawa, *Kindai*, p. 22.

64. Iida Yoshikuni, "Dialogue with the Infinite," trans. Susan Pulvers, in Iida, *Mirā mobiru*, p. 159.

65. Matsumoto, *Senkyūhyaku*, p. 40; Tanaka Takaki interview, Tokyo, February 14, 2002; Kanagawa, *Kindai*, pp. 316–317.

66. Iino Kiichi interview, Tokyo, December 16, 1980.

67. Tanaka Takaki interview, Tokyo, February 14, 2002; Kanagawa, *Kindai*, p. 18.

68. Iida, "Art," unnumbered pp. 4, 8.

69. Ibid., unnumbered p. 5; Arayashiki Tōru, "The Rediscovered Mirror Sculpture by Yoshikuni Iida," in Mie, *Iida*, unnumbered p. 2.

70. Archer, *Art*, p. 6.

71. Tōkyōto, *Shinkan*, p. 18; Taki, *Nihon no yōga*, p. 275; Archer, *Art*, pp. 13, 17; Miki, "1960s," pp. 27–28; Chiba, *Gendai*, p. 99.

72. Haryū, "Kagami," p. 15; *Bijutso techō* 25:8 (1973), 65; Matsumoto, *Senkyūhyaku*, p. 43.

73. Noda Tetsuya interview, Tokyo, April 24, 2002. See Miki, "1960s," p. 30.

74. Bell, "Noda," pp. 13–15.

75. Matsumoto, *Senkyūhyaku*, pp. 38–39. See Archer, *Art*, pp. 44–60.

76. Yoshimasu Gōzō interview, Tokyo, May 22, 2002. See Munroe, *Scream*, p. 215.

77. Minemura Toshiaki interview, Tokyo, March 25, 2002.

78. See Chiba, *Gendai*, p. 107; Tsuji, *Manga*, pp. 217–218; Archer, *Art*, pp. 69, 76, 84–85.

79. Chiba, *Gendai*, p. 108; Reiko Tomii, "Infinity Nets: Aspects of Contemporary Japanese Painting," in Munroe, *Scream*, p. 312.

80. Suga Kishio interview, Itō, March 22, 2002.

81. Tsuji, *Manga*, p. 218; Chiba, *Gendai*, p. 108.

82. See *Pusai no saidan* (*Altar of Psi*, 1960–1961, mixed media), in Tōkyō, *Mikan*, p. 202.

83. Okabayashi Hiroshi, *Nihon no gendai āto* (Tokyo: Maruzen, 1998), pp. 129, 136; Chiba, *Gendai*, pp. 108–110.

84. Okabayashi, *Nihon*, pp. 136–139.

85. Tomii, "Infinity Nets," p. 312.

86. Hyūga Akiko interview, Kawasaki, March 21, 2002. See Segi, *Nihon no zen'ei*, pp. 373–375, for a chart of avant-garde art groups in the 1960s.

87. Akasegawa, *Hangeijutsu*, p. 174.

88. Chiba, *Gendai*, pp. 106, 114–117.

89. Segi, *Nihon no zen'ei*, pp. 338–340; Chiba, *Gendai*, pp. 103–105.

90. Segi, *Nihon no zen'ei*, p. 340.

91. Tōkyōto, *Shinkan*, p. 18; Geijutsu, *20seiki*, p. 120; Miki, "1960s," pp. 29–30.

92. See Archer, *Art*, p. 7.

Chapter Eight: Contemporary Art Music and Dance in the 1960s

1. Ichiyanagi Toshi interview, Tokyo, April 11, 2002.

2. Ongaku no Tomosha, *20seiki*, p. 53.

3. Hayashi Hikaru, *Gakushi no seki kara: watakushi no sengo ongakushi* (Tokyo: Shōbunsha, 1978), p. 275. See also p. 276.

4. Ibid., pp. 283–284.

5. Hayashi Hikaru interview, Tokyo, June 13, 2002.

6. Mamiya Michio interview, Tokyo, April 22, 2002; Ongaku no Tomosha, *20seiki*, pp. 190–193.

7. Akiyama, *Nihon no sakkyokukatachi*, 1:282; Ongaku no Tomosha, *20seiki*, pp. 205–211.

8. Judith Herd interview, Tokyo, January 30, 2002; Ongaku no Tomosha, *20seiki*, p. 209.

9. Hayashi Hikaru, "Introduction" to *Genbaku shōkei*, trans. David G. Goodman, program for Hayashi Hikaru–Tokyo Konsei Gasshōdan August Festival, August 5, 2001, at Aichi Global Peace Festival and August 9, 2001, in Tokyo. I am grateful to David Goodman for sharing this introduction. "Genbaku shōkei" is the title of nine poems by Hara Tamiki published in 1950, in *Hara Tamiki zenshū* (Tokyo: Haga Shoten, 1965), 1:474–479. On Hara and Tōge, see Karen L. Thornber, "Atomic Bomb Writers," in Jay Rubin, ed., *Modern Japanese Writers* (New York: Charles Scribner's Sons, 2001), pp. 49–70.

10. Hayashi Hikaru interview, Tokyo, June 13, 2002.

11. Hayashi, *Gakushi*, pp. 256–257.

12. Hayashi, "Introduction."

13. "Mizu o kudasai" (1958) is four minutes, twenty-four seconds, in length. See Hayashi Hikaru, *Genbaku shōkei—Hayashi Hikaru gasshō sakuhinshū*, compact disc (Tokyo: Fontec FOCD 3294, 1996), containing three parts from 1958 to 1971 but not the final version of "Towa no midori" (2001).

14. Iwaki Hiroyuki interview, Tokyo, March 22, 2002. On Hara's suicide, see Thornber, "Writers," p. 53.

15. Mamiya Michio interview, Tokyo, April 22, 2002.

16. Mamiya Michio, *Nihon min'yōshū*, compact disc (Tokyo: Fontec FOCD 3481, 2001), liner notes, p. 13; Mamiya Michio interview, Tokyo, April 22, 2002. Mamiya researched scores in Nihon Hōsō Kyōkai, ed., *Nihon min'yō taikan*, 12 vols. (Tokyo: Nihon Hōsō Kyōkai, 1952–1993), and Nihon Hōsō Kyōkai, ed., *Tōhoku min'yōshū*, 6

vols. (Tokyo: Nihon Hōsō Shuppan Kyōkai, 1955–1967). See Mamiya Michio, *Nihon min'yōshū*, 2nd ed. (Tokyo: Zen'on Gakufu Shuppansha, 2002 [1975]), p. 140. Bartók is said to have studied seven thousand Hungarian folk songs.

17. Mamiya, *Nihon min'yōshū*, pp. 139–140.

18. Ongaku no Tomosha, *20seiki*, p. 238. See Akiyama, *Nihon no sakkyokukatachi*, 1:135.

19. Mamiya, *Nihon min'yōshū*, p. 140.

20. Mamiya Michio interview, Tokyo, April 22, 2002.

21. Mamiya Michio, in Kamei Katsuichirō, ed., *Tōyō shisō kōza 5* (Tokyo: Shibundō, 1958), quoted in Komiya, *Kingendai*, pp. 202–203.

22. Takahashi, "Movements."

23. William P. Malm, *Traditional Japanese Music and Musical Instruments*, 2nd ed. (Tokyo: Kodansha International, 2000), p. 45 (originally published as *Japanese Music and Musical Instruments* in 1959 by C. E. Tuttle Co., Tokyo).

24. William P. Malm, "Layers of Music in Japan since 1945," in *The Fourth Kyushu International Cultural Conference: Proceedings* (Fukuoka: Fukuoka UNESCO Association, 1978), p. 96.

25. Malm, *Traditional*, pp. 44–45; *Kodansha Encyclopedia of Japan* 5:285.

26. Takahashi, "Movements."

27. Atkins, *Blue*, p. 39; Christopher Yohmei Blasdel, "We're Talking the Real Thing," *Japan Times*, June 16, 2002, p. 13.

28. Ongaku no Tomosha, *20seiki*, p. 266; Sano, "Joron," p. 18.

29. Sano, "Joron," p. 16. See Ongaku no Tomosha, *20seiki*, p. 58; Kojima Tomiko, *Nihon no ongaku o kangaeru*, 2nd ed. (Tokyo: Ongaku no Tomosha, 1999 [1976]), pp. 133–135.

30. Moroi Makoto interview, Saitamashi, March 30, 2002.

31. Chōki Seiji interview, Tokyo, April 17, 2002.

32. Ibid.

33. Kojima, *Ongaku*, pp. 134–135.

34. Ongaku no Tomosha, *20seiki*, p. 70.

35. Ibid., pp. 70, 242. See Heifetz, "Composition," pp. 40–42, 47. Mayuzumi spent more time on conservative politics than music after 1970, opposing communism, supporting constitutional revision, and chairing a right-wing group called Nippon o Mamoru Kokuminkai (National Association to Defend Japan) from 1981 to 1991. See Ongaku no Tomosha, *20seiki*, p. 242; Burt, *Takemitsu*, p. 19.

36. Sano, "Joron," p. 17; Koizumi Fumio, *Nihon no oto: sekai no naka no Nihon ongaku* (Tokyo: Seidosha, 1977), p. 219 (a second edition was issued in 1994 by Heibonsha in Tokyo). Chōki Seiji (interview, Tokyo, April 17, 2002) emphasizes that film was the most lucrative source of income for contemporary composers in the 1950s and 1960s, giving them opportunities to experiment in their scores, then incorporate ideas into their more formal works.

37. Koizumi, *Nihon no oto*, p. 222.

38. Komiya, *Kingendai*, p. 204.

39. Blasdel, "Real Thing," p. 13.

40. Ichiyanagi Toshi interview, Tokyo, April 11, 2002.

41. Ichiyanagi Toshi, *Ongaku to iu itonami* (Tokyo: NTT Shuppan, 1998). See Ongaku no Tomosha, *20seiki*, p. 138.

42. Yuasa Jōji interview, Tokyo, February 5, 2002.

43. Yuasa, "Music," pp. 178, 187, 192, 196. See Ongaku no Tomosha, *20seiki*, p. 269.

44. Akiyama Kuniharu, "Nihon no gendai ongaku o kikō," *Bijutsu techō* 20:11 (1968), 128–129. See Narazaki Yōko, "Takemitsu Tōru sōsakushi gaisetsu," in Chōki and Higuchi, *Takemitsu*, p. 100; Sano, "Joron," pp. 16–18. Paul Griffiths says Takemitsu's acceptance in the West "may have to do not only with his music's quality but also with western expectations of Asian art as serene, passive, decorative and subsidiary." Griffiths, *Modern Music and After*, p. 157.

45. Takemitsu, *Oto chinmoku*, p. 197.

46. Takemitsu, quoted in Akiyama, "Japan," p. 365.

47. Judith Ann Herd, "Interpreting Tradition: The Use of Traditional Japanese Music in the Compositions of Takemitsu," manuscript, p. 3. This manuscript is an English translation of Herd, "Takemitsu Tōru to Nihon no dentō ongaku," in Chōki and Higuchi, *Takemitsu*, pp. 84–93. See also Burt, *Takemitsu*, pp. 235–236.

48. Takemitsu, *Oto chinmoku*, quoted in Takemitsu, *Confronting*, p. 4.

49. Takahashi Yūji interview, Tokyo, June 6, 2002.

50. Takahashi, "Movements."

51. Takahashi Yūji interview, Tokyo, June 6, 2002.

52. Chow, *Writing*, p. 138.

53. Hirakawa Sukehiro, "Return to Japan or Return to the West? — Lafcadio Hearn's 'A Conservative,'" in Hirakawa, ed., *Lafcadio Hearn*, pp. 16–17, 29. Theodore Bestor, in *Neighborhood Tokyo* (Stanford, Calif.: Stanford University Press, 1989), p. 10, writes that inventing a tradition is "a common Japanese cultural device for managing or responding to social change."

54. Atkins, *Blue*, p. 41.

55. Andrew Gordon, "Rethinking Area Studies, Once More," *Journal of Japanese Studies* 30:2 (2004), 423.

56. Miyake Haruna interview, Tokyo, February 24, 2002.

57. Yuasa, "Music," p. 197.

58. Yamano Hakudai interview, Tokyo, March 20, 2002.

59. *Buyō nenkan, IV*, 1980, pp. 7–10; *Asahi nenkan 1964*, p. 644.

60. *Asahi nenkan 1965*, p. 622; Gendai Buyō Kyōkai, *Nihon gendai buyō shiryō, II*, 1972, p. 4; *Ongaku nenkan 1977*, pp. 59–61; *Buyō nenkan, IV*, 1980, p. 2.

61. Kanda Akiko, "Akiko no modan dansu I," *Modan dansu*, no. 11 (1972), 36. See also "Akiko no modan dansu II," *Modan dansu*, no. 12 (1973), 30–32; "Akiko no modan dansu III," *Modan dansu*, no. 13 (1974), 45–48; Akiko Kanda interview, Tokyo, November 28, 1980.

62. Gōda Nario, "Yōbu," in *Ongaku nenkan 1977*, pp. 76–77.

63. Horikiri Yoshiko, "Kihyō," *Modan dansu*, no. 15 (1975), 52–53; *Dansu wāku*, no. 16 (1976), 12–13.

64. Ishii Kaoru interview, Tokyo, May 16, 2002.

65. Ibid.

66. Atsugi Bonjin interview, Tokyo, March 8, 2002.

67. Ibid. See Fukuzawa, "Good-Bye," p. 85.

68. Satō Shigeru, "Atsugi Bonjinron," *Modan dansu*, no. 9 (1971), 34–37; Fukuzawa, "Good-Bye," pp. 12, 19.

69. Atsugi Bonjin interview, Tokyo, March 8, 2002.

70. Yoshimasu Gōzō interview, Tokyo, May 22, 2002. Ōno's connections with Hijikata are discussed in Kazuo Ohno and Yoshito Ohno, *Kazuo Ohno's World: From Within and Without,* trans. John Barrett (Middletown, Conn.: Wesleyan University Press, 2004). Key documents for Hijikata's career are found in Hijikata Tatsumi, *Hijikata Tatsumi zenshū,* ed. Tanemura Suehiro, Tsuruoka Yoshihisa, and Motofuji Akiko, 2 vols. (Tokyo: Kawade Shobō Shinsha, 1998); Hijikata Tatsumi, *Hijikata Tatsumi shō: "nikki" to "inyō" ni yoru,* ed. Yoshioka Minoru (Tokyo: Chikuma Shobō, 1987); Motofuji Akiko, *Hijikata Tatsumi to tomo ni* (Tokyo: Chikuma Shobō, 1990).

71. Mishima Yukio, *Kinjiki* (Tokyo: Shinchōsha, 1951–1953; trans. Alfred H. Marks as *Forbidden Colors* [New York: Knopf, 1968]).

72. In 2003 there were five major schools of Butō in Japan, even though as an artistic movement Butō peaked in the late 1970s. The big five were so well established that the Nagoya regional taxation bureau accused Nishikawa Ukon of failing to report more than $1.2 million in revenue earned by his dance school between 1997 and 2001. *Japan Times Online,* June 15, 2003.

73. Motofuji Akiko interview, Tokyo, March 2, 2002.

74. Isozaki, "Witness," p. 28.

75. Motofuji Akiko interview, Tokyo, March 2, 2002.

76. See Susan Blakeley Klein, *Ankoku Butō: The Premodern and Postmodern Influences on the Dance of Utter Darkness* (Ithaca, N.Y.: Cornell University East Asia Program, 1988), p. 10.

77. Motofuji Akiko interview, Tokyo, March 2, 2002.

78. Nakanishi Natsuyuki interview, Tokyo, March 2, 2002.

79. Nakanishi Natsuyuki, quoted in Sas, *Fault Lines,* p. 165.

80. See Mizuma Art Gallery, http://mizuma-art.co.jp/_artist/kato_e.html, June 21, 2003. See also *Gendai bijutsu kīwādo, Zero Jigen,* http://www.dnp.co.jp/museum/nmp/artscape/artwords/u_z/zero_jigen.html, June 21, 2003.

81. Kuroda Raiji, "1960nendai Nihon no pafuōmansu kenkyū I: bunka to shite no 'Zero Jigen' joron e no hashirigaki," *Kajima bijutsu kenkyū, nenpō,* no. 18 (2001), *bessatsu,* 362–368.

82. Ikeda Ichi interview, Tokyo, March 27, 2002.

83. See Ikeda Ichi, *Mizu kagami* (Sagamiharashi: G-Day Plan, 1988).

84. Ikeda Ichi interview, Tokyo, March 27, 2002.

85. Yamano Hakudai interview, Tokyo, March 20, 2002.

86. Atsugi Bonjin interview, Tokyo, March 8, 2002.

87. Yamano, "Ryakushi," part 4 (November 1998), p. 3.

88. Peter Grilli, "Takemitsu's Film Music," Harvard University Composers' Seminar, Cambridge, Mass., November 13, 2000. See Ongaku no Tomosha, *20seiki,* pp. 183–184.

89. Sano, "Joron," p. 22.

90. Ibid., p. 21.

91. Takemitsu Tōru, in Takemitsu and Kawada Junzō, *Oto, kotoba, ningen* (Tokyo: Iwanami Shoten, 1980), reprinted in Takemitsu, *Takemitsu Tōru chosakushū,* 4:186.

92. Takemitsu Tōru, *Ongaku o yobisamasu mono* (Tokyo: Shinchōsha, 1985), quoted in Konuma, *Takemitsu,* p. 121.

93. Takemitsu Tōru, in Takemitsu and Ōe Kenzaburō, *Opera o tsukuru* (Tokyo: Iwanami Shoten, 1990), reprinted in *Takemitsu Tōru chosakushū* 4:207. See Konuma, *Takemitsu*, pp. 114–116, 120–121, 126, 137.

94. Sano, "Joron," p. 32.

95. Takemitsu, in Ozawa and Takemitsu, *Ongaku*, pp. 169–170.

96. Kosugi Takehisa, quoted in Akiyama, *Nihon no sakkyokukatachi*, 1:63. See 1:60; Ongaku no Tomosha, *20seiki*, pp. 155–156.

97. Tenjinchi letter, February 26, 2002. Miyake Haruna cites three: Kanai Kikuko (1906–1986), who wrote an opera based on Okinawan folk stories; Ōsawa Kazuko (1926–), who composed for NHK radio dramas and wrote art music for saxophone; and Yoshida Takako (1910–1956), who produced works honoring the martyred proletarian writer Kobayashi Takiji (1903–1933) after police tortured him to death in February 1933. Yoshida herself was detained by the authorities during the war, fell ill, and then recovered after the surrender to write operatic and chamber music. To this trio Judith Herd adds the koto composer Chikushi Katsuko (1904–1984), unusual for her generation of Hōgaku artists in being able to write for Western orchestras as well as Japanese ensembles and even more unusual, for a female composer, in being permitted to found her own school of koto performance after the war. Herd notes that the 1970s were the real breakthrough decade for emerging female composers. Miyake Haruna interview, Tokyo, February 24, 2002; Ongaku no Tomosha, *20seiki*, pp. 296, 306; Judith Herd interview, Tokyo, January 30, 2002. A web site, "Japanese Women Composers," lists several dozen, a few of whom were active in the 1950s and 1960s: http://music.acu.edu/www/iawm/pages/earth/comp/japancomp.html, June 11, 2003.

98. Miyake Haruna interview, Tokyo, February 24, 2002.

99. Nanjō Fumio interview, Tokyo, March 15, 2002.

100. Chōki Seiji interview, Tokyo, April 17, 2002.

101. Miyake Haruna interview, Tokyo, February 24, 2002.

102. Ishida Kazushi, *Performing Arts in Japan Now: Present Condition of Japanese Contemporary Music* (Tokyo: Japan Foundation, 1994), p. 6.

103. Miyake Haruna interview, Tokyo, February 24, 2002.

104. Ichiyanagi Toshi interview, Tokyo, November 30, 1980.

Chapter Nine: The Monoha Moment

1. On Duchamp, see Chipp, *Theories*, pp. 367–368. See Toshiaki Minemura, "Measuring Up to the Mono-ha — and Beyond," trans. Alfred Birnbaum, in Tama Bijutsu Daigaku and Seibu Bijutsukan, *Monoha to posutomonoha no tenkai*, exh. cat. (Tokyo: Tama Bijutsu Daigaku and Seibu Bijutsukan, 1987), p. 191.

2. Peter Schjeldahl, "Bare Minimal," *The New Yorker*, May 3, 2004, p. 108.

3. Sawaragi, *Nihon*, pp. 143–145. See Minemura Toshiaki, "Objects and Events: Twins in the Same Egg," in Mito, *Nihon no natsu*, p. 83.

4. Lee Ufan, quoted in Minemura, "Measuring," p. 191. A major archive of Monoha materials is in the Contemporary Art Resource Center of Tama Art University.

5. Dōmoto Hisao interview, Tokyo, March 15, 2002. See Sawaragi, *Nihon*, p. 144. The art critic Kanazawa Takeshi (interview, Yokohama, April 18, 2002) believes that

"the Monoha appealed to native attitudes toward natural materials, uncut and un-adorned." But the critic Nanjō Fumio (interview, Tokyo, March 15, 2002), points out that that "the Monoha artists got a lot of ideas from abroad." See also *Mizue*, no. 921 (December 1981), p. 67, on the Monoha and foreign art.

6. Minemura Toshiaki, "What Was Monoha?" trans. Jean Campignon, in Tama Bijutsu Daigaku IRAC Kenkyūjo, ed., *"Monoha" katarogu*, exh. cat. (Tokyo: Kamakura Garō, 1986), p. 7.

7. Tsuji, *Manga*, p. 220; Archer, *Art*, pp. 44–47. See Tatehata, "Mono-ha," pp. 28–29; Miki, "1960s," p. 30.

8. Isozaki, "Witness," p. 29.

9. Chiba Shigeo interview, Tokyo, March 11, 2002.

10. Lee Ufan interview, Kamakura, March 5, 2002.

11. Suga Kishio interview, Itō, March 22, 2002.

12. Simon Groom, "Encountering Mono-ha," in Groom, *Mono-ha*, p. 5.

13. Tsuji, *Manga*, p. 221. See Moriguchi Akira, "Mono-ha: Insights on Re-production," trans. Alfred Birnbaum, in Tama Bijutsu Daigaku and Seibu Bijutsukan, *Monoha*, pp. 195–196; Chiba, "Japanese," p. 21; Chiba, *Gendai*, p. 160. Segi Shin'ichi agrees that "the Monoha pointed in the direction of conceptual art." Segi interview, Tokyo, February 11, 2002. See also Munroe, *Scream*, pp. 261–265.

14. Suga Kishio interview, Itō, March 22, 2002.

15. Segi, *Sengo*, pp. 269, 272; Tatehata, "Mono-ha," pp. 33–35; Kondō Yukio interview, Yokohama, February 20, 2002. Minemura Toshiaki (interview, Tokyo, March 25, 2002), who is the group's leading critical champion, believes that "Saitō Yoshishige's influence was quite indirect."

16. Suga Kishio interview, Itō, March 22, 2002.

17. Miki, "1960s," p. 25.

18. Kanagawa, *Kindai*, pp. 286–287; Tōkyō, *Sengo*, pp. 1–3; Gunma, *Aru korekutā*, pp. 64–71; Taki, *Nihon no yōga*, p. 271.

19. See Matsumoto, *Senkyūhyaku*, p. 34.

20. Tatehata, "Mono-ha," p. 35. See Janet Koplos, *Contemporary Japanese Sculpture* (New York: Abbeville Press, 1991), pp. 39–40.

21. Minemura, "What?" p. 7.

22. Minemura, "Kaitai," p. 74.

23. See Oda Makoto, *Nanshi no shisō* (Tokyo: Bungei Shunjū, 1969), p. 545, citing Tsurumi. See also Oda Makoto, *Nani o watakushitachi wa hajimete iru no ka* (Tokyo: San'ichi Shobō, 1970), p. 88. I am grateful to Simon Avenell for these references.

24. Sekine Nobuo interview, Tokyo, February 21, 2002. See Tatehata, "Mono-ha," p. 29.

25. Sakai Tadayasu interview, Kamakura, March 5, 2002.

26. Sekine Nobuo, 1969, in *Sekine Nobuo 1968–1978* (Tokyo: Yuria Pemuperu Kōbō, 1978), pp. 82, 85.

27. Tatehata, "Mono-ha," p. 32.

28. Sekine Nobuo interview, Tokyo, February 21, 2002.

29. Sekine Nobuo, "The Message of Environmental Art," in Hayashi Yoshifumi, ed., *Sekine: A Message from Environmental Art Studio* (Tokyo: Purosesu Ākitekuchua, 1992), p. 10. Sekine's environmental art *(kankyō geijutsu)* meant public sculp-

ture in corporate plazas, not the high-technology works usually associated with environmental art in Japan or the land art sometimes found in Sekine's settings.

30. Ibid. See Minemura, "What?" p. 8.

31. Sekine Nobuo interview, Tokyo, February 21, 2002.

32. Chiba Shigeo interview, Tokyo, March 11, 2002.

33. Lee Ufan interview, Kamakura, March 5, 2002.

34. See Hara Bijutsukan, ed., *Lee Ufan*, exh. cat. (Tokyo: Arukanshiēru Zaidan, 1991), especially Tani Akira, "A Presence That Eclipses Subject," pp. 4–7.

35. Tani, "Presence," p. 7. See Groom, "Encountering," pp. 9–10.

36. Lee Ufan interview, Kamakura, March 5, 2002. See Kamakura, *Kindai*, p. 121; Tani, "Presence," p. 4.

37. Lee Ufan, "Sekai no kōzō," *Dezain hihyō*, September 1969, quoted in Chiba, *Gendai*, pp. 142–144. See Kamakura, *Kindai*, p. 121.

38. Lee Ufan interview, Kamakura, March 5, 2002.

39. Lee U-fan [Lee Ufan], "Foreshadowings and Premonitions: Mono-ha," in Groom, *Mono-ha*, p. 21; Sawaragi, *Nihon*, pp. 147–148.

40. Lee Ufan interview, Kamakura, March 5, 2002.

41. Sugawara, *Nihon*, p. 57.

42. Lee Ufan interview, Kamakura, March 5, 2002.

43. Tatehata, "Mono-ha," p. 28.

44. Minemura, "What?" p. 9.

45. Hara Toshio, "Preface," in Howard N. Fox, *A Primal Spirit: Ten Contemporary Japanese Sculptors*, exh. cat. (Los Angeles: Los Angeles County Museum of Art, 1991), p. 14.

46. Lee Ufan interview, Kamakura, March 5, 2002.

47. Suga Kishio, *Suga Kishio*, 2nd ed. (Tokyo: Yomiuri Shinbunsha and Bijutsukan Renraku Kyōgikai, 1998 [1977]), p. 2.

48. Suga Kishio interview, Itō, March 22, 2002.

49. See Minemura Toshiaki, "Why Do We Call It Art?" trans. Reiko Tomii, in Suga, *Suga*, p. 307.

50. Suga Kishio interview, Itō, March 22, 2002.

51. Dehara Hitoshi, "Interrelationships within the Aspect of Time," trans. Yamazaki Yumiko, in Suga, *Suga*, p. 309.

52. See Minemura, "Why?" p. 305.

53. Suga Kishio, "Bundling Together Surroundings to Open the Edges of a New World," trans. Robert Reed, in Suga, *Suga*, p. 313.

54. Suga Kishio interview, Itō, March 22, 2002.

55. Suga, *Suga*, pp. 286–301.

56. Minemura "Meaning," pp. 192–193.

57. Hara, "Preface," pp. 9–10.

58. Ibid., p. 13.

Chapter Ten: Art, Money, and Politics

1. Ōoka Makoto interview, Tokyo, March 9, 2002.

2. Tsurumi Kazuko, "Student Movements in 1960 and 1969," in Takayanagi

Shun'ichi and Miwa Kimitada, eds., *Postwar Trends in Japan* (Tokyo: University of Tokyo Press, 1975), p. 205.

3. Kondō Yukio interview, Yokohama, February 20, 2002.

4. Kanazawa Takeshi interview, Yokohama, April 18, 2002.

5. Tsutsumi Seiji interview, Tokyo, April 8, 2002.

6. For details on the exposition, see *Kodansha Encyclopedia* 2:237–238; *Japan Times Online*, April 17, 2005. The 64,210,000 paid attendance surpassed the New York (1964) and Montreal (1967) expositions by nearly 15 million visitors. The Shanghai exposition scheduled for 2010 is expected to break the Osaka mark, which still stood as of 2006.

7. Hayashi, *Genbaku*, liner notes, p. 5.

8. Mamiya Michio interview, Tokyo, April 22, 2002.

9. Shisō Undō Kenkyūjo, *Bōhatsu suru shinsayoku* (Tokyo: Zenbōsha, 1969), pp. 131–135.

10. Tatehata Akira interview, Tokyo, March 4, 2002.

11. Betonamu ni Heiwa o! Shimin Rengō, *Shiryō "Beheiren" undō* (Tokyo: Kawade Shobō Shinsha, 1974), 1:274.

12. Moroi Makoto interview, Saitamashi, March 30, 2002.

13. Iida Yoshikuni interview, Tokyo, March 26, 2002.

14. Atsugi Bonjin interview, Tokyo, March 8, 2002.

15. Dōmoto Hisao interview, Tokyo, March 15, 2002.

16. Ikeda Ichi interview, Tokyo, March 27, 2002.

17. Ishii Kaoru interview, Tokyo, May 16, 2002.

18. Ashton, *Thread*, p. 117.

19. Donald Richie, "Hiroshi Teshigahara and the Film . . . ," in Sōgetsukai, ed., *Kokoro wa itsumo runesansu hyōgen jiyūjin Teshigahara Hiroshi* (Tokyo: Sōgetsu Shuppan, 1989), p. 39.

20. Tatehata, "Mono-ha," p. 42.

21. Suga Kishio interview, Itō, March 22, 2002.

22. Lee Ufan interview, Kamakura, March 5, 2002.

23. Tatehata Akira interview, Tokyo, March 4, 2002.

24. Yoshimura, "Neo-Dada," pp. 56–57.

25. Lee Ufan interview, Kamakura, March 5, 2002.

26. Iida Momo, quoted in Tessa Morris-Suzuki, *Showa* (London: Athlone Press, 1984), p. 307.

27. Chiba Shigeo interview, Tokyo, March 11, 2002.

28. Kawasakishi, *Expo*, p. 3.

29. Okamoto Tarō, *Nihon Bankokuhaku* (Tokyo: Shōbunsha, 1971), extracted in Okamoto Tarō, "Bankokuhaku ni kaketa mono," in Kawasakishi, *Expo*, p. 7.

30. Hayashi Hikaru interview, Tokyo, June 13, 2002. See Murata Keinosuke, "Hajime ni Expo '70 to Tarō no tō to . . . ," in Kawasakishi, *Expo*, p. 11.

31. Haryū Ichirō, "Hanpaku," *Gendai no me*, vol. 10, no. 10 (1969), 126. See *Asahi jānaru*, February 16, 1969, p. 114.

32. Mito, *Nihon no natsu*, p. 69; "'Shūdan Kumo' no kisekiten," *Fukuokashi Bijutsukan jōsetsu tenji*, no. 188 (1997), p. 1.

33. Kawasakishi, *Expo*, p. 80.

34. Haryū, "Hanpaku," pp. 127, 133; Shisō, *Bōhatsu*, p. 113.

35. Isozaki, "Imprint," p. 272. See Taki, "Sekaishi," p. 6.

36. Takahashi Yūji interview, Tokyo, June 6, 2002.

37. Kawasakishi, *Expo*, p. 3.

38. Okamoto, *Nihon Bankokuhaku*, p. 9.

39. Hyūga Akiko interview, Kawasaki, March 21, 2002.

40. Iida Yoshikuni interview, Tokyo, March 26, 2002.

41. Murata, "Hajime," p. 11. See Kawasakishi, *Expo*, pp. 43–61, for a detailed description of the interior of the Sun Tower.

42. Okamoto Tarō, quoted in Murata, "Hajime," p. 11.

43. Kawasakishi, *Expo*, p. 79.

44. Ōoka Makoto interview, Tokyo, March 9, 2002.

45. Okamoto Toshiko interview, Tokyo, March 25, 2002.

46. Haryū Ichirō interview, Tokyo, February 12, 2002.

47. Okamoto Toshiko interview, Tokyo, March 25, 2002.

48. Kanazawa Takeshi interview, Yokohama, April 18, 2002.

49. Maki, "Iida," p. 150.

50. Iida Yoshikuni interview, Tokyo, March 26, 2002.

51. Motonaga Sadamasa letter, May 3, 2002.

52. Segi, *Sengo*, p. 133.

53. Watanabe Misa interview, Tokyo, June 2, 2002.

54. Ōoka Makoto interview, Tokyo, March 9, 2002.

55. Chōki Seiji interview, Tokyo, April 17, 2002.

56. Chōki, "Seiyō," pp. 282–283; Akiyama, *Gendai*, p. 153.

57. Kawasakishi, *Expo*, p. 80, includes a list of prominent artists from many genres who took part in Banpaku.

58. Shinohara Ushio interview, Tokyo, April 16, 2002.

59. Akasegawa Genpei interview, Tokyo, May 22, 2002.

60. Chōki Seiji interview, Tokyo, April 17, 2002.

61. Nihon Bankoku Hakurankai Kinen Kikin, *Shōwa 55nendo Nihon Bankoku Hakurankai Kinen Kikin jigyō* (Tokyo: Nihon Bankoku Hakurankai Kinen Kikin, 1980).

62. Ōoka Makoto interview, Tokyo, March 9, 2002.

63. Yuasa Jōji interview, Tokyo, February 5, 2002.

Chapter Eleven: Radicals and Realists

1. Kikuhata, *Hangeijutsu*, pp. 26–27.

2. Ibid., p. 27.

3. Katō, *Form*, p. 2.

4. See Rivkin and Ryan, *Theory*, pp. 1026–1027.

5. See Lynton, *Story*, p. 339.

6. Tatehata Akira interview, Tokyo, March 4, 2002.

7. Arakawa Shūsaku interview, New York, June 24, 2002.

8. Tachikawa Ruriko interview, Tokyo, December 8, 1980.

9. Moroi Makoto interview, Saitamashi, March 30, 2002.

10. Haryū, "Kagami," p. 13.

11. Kawatsuma Sachiko interview, Tokyo, May 6, 2002.

12. Shinohara Ushio interview, Tokyo, April 16, 2002.

13. Miyake Haruna interview, Tokyo, February 24, 2002.

14. Chōki Seiji interview, Tokyo, April 17, 2002.

15. Miyake Haruna interview, Tokyo, February 24, 2002.

16. Hattori Chieko interview, Tokyo, December 6, 1980.

17. Jasper Johns, quoted in Tōno, "Mono-ha," p. 189.

18. Suga Kishio interview, Itō, March 22, 2002.

19. Akasegawa Genpei interview, Tokyo, May 22, 2002.

20. Iwaki Hiroyuki interview, Tokyo, March 22, 2002.

21. Takemitsu Tōru, from *Mainichi shinbun*, evening ed., January 23, 1995, re-printed in Takemitsu Tōru, *Toki no entei* (Tokyo: Shinchōsha, 1996), p. 77.

Sources Cited

Interviews

Akasegawa Genpei. Painter, novelist, arts critic. Pen name as novelist: Otsuji Katsuhiko. Tokyo, May 22, 2002.
Arakawa Shūsaku. Painter, sculptor, urban planner. New York, June 24, 2002.
Atsugi Bonjin. Choreographer, dancer. Tokyo, March 8, 2002.
Chiba Shigeo. Art historian. Tokyo, March 11, 2002.
Chōki Seiji. Musicologist. Tokyo, April 17, 2002.
Dan Ikuma. Composer. Tokyo, December 23, 1980.
Dōmoto Hisao. Painter. Tokyo, March 15, 2002.
Haga Tōru. Literary critic. Tokyo, June 2, 2002.
Hara Toshio. Director, Hara Museum of Contemporary Art. Tokyo, February 20, 2002.
Haryū Ichirō. Art critic. Tokyo, February 12, 2002.
Hattori Chieko. President, Japan Ballet Association. Tokyo, December 6, 1980.
Hayashi Hikaru. Composer. Tokyo, June 13, 2002.
Herd, Judith. Musicologist. Tokyo, January 30, 2002.
Hibbett, Howard. Literary critic. Cambridge, Mass., April 21, 2003.
Hirakawa Sukehiro. Literary critic. Tokyo, June 2, 2002.
Hyūga Akiko. Art critic. Kawasaki, March 21, 2002.
Ichiyanagi Toshi. Composer. Tokyo, November 30, 1980; April 11, 2002.
Iida Yoshikuni. Sculptor, painter. Tokyo, March 26, 2002.
Ikeda Ichi. Theater director, water artist. Tokyo, March 27, 2002.
Ishiguro Kenji. Photographer. Tokyo, June 6, 2002.
Ishii Kaoru. Choreographer, dancer. Tokyo, May 16, 2002.
Ishii Yōichi. Historian. Tokyo, May 6, 2002.
Iwaki Hiroyuki. Life conductor, NHK Symphony Orchestra. Tokyo, December 27, 1980; March 22, 2002.
Kanazawa Takeshi. Art curator, critic. Yokohama, April 18, 2002.
Kanda Akiko. Choreographer. Tokyo, November 28, 1980.
Kara Jūrō. Playwright. Tokyo, November 10, 1980.
Kawatsuma Sachiko. President, Art Gallery Kan. Tokyo, May 6, 2002.
Kondō Yukio. Art historian. Yokohama, February 20, 2002.
Koshino Junko. Fashion designer. Tokyo, June 2, 2002.
Koyano Masako. Art conservationist. Tokyo, February 14, 2002 by telephone.
Lee Ufan. Sculptor. Kamakura, March 5, 2002.
Mamiya Michio. Composer. Tokyo, April 22, 2002.
Matsudaira Yoriaki. Composer. Tokyo, February 13, 2002.
Minemura Toshiaki. Art critic. Tokyo, March 25, 2002.
Miwa Kimitada. Historian, painter. Tokyo, February 27, 2002.

Miyake Haruna. Composer. Tokyo, February 24, 2002.

Moroi Makoto. Composer; Director, Saitama Arts Theater. Saitamashi, March 30, 2002.

Motofuji Akiko. Dancer; Director, Asbestos Theater. Tokyo, March 2, 2002.

Nakanishi Natsuyuki. Sculptor, painter. Tokyo, March 2, 2002.

Nanjō Fumio. Art critic. Tokyo, March 15, 2002.

Noda Tetsuya. Print maker. Tokyo, April 24, 2002.

Okamoto Toshiko. Director, Okamoto Tarō Museum, Aoyama. Tokyo, March 25, 2002.

Ōoka Makoto. Journalist, poet. Tokyo, March 9, 2002.

Sakai Tadayasu. Director, Museum of Modern Art, Kamakura. Kamakura, March 5, 2002.

Satani Kazuhiko. President, Satani Gallery. Tokyo, February 4, 2002.

Segi Shin'ichi. Art critic. Tokyo, February 11, 2002.

Sekine Nobuo. Sculptor. Tokyo, February 21, 2002.

Shinohara Ushio. Sculptor, painter. Tokyo, April 16, 2002.

Suga Kishio. Sculptor. Itō, March 22, 2002.

Takahashi Yūji. Composer. Tokyo, June 6, 2002.

Tanaka Takaki. Managing Director, Contemporary Sculpture Center. Tokyo, February 14, 2002.

Tatehata Akira. Art historian, poet. Tokyo, March 4, 2002.

Tsutsumi Seiji. Chair, Saison Foundation; novelist, poet. Pen name as writer: Tsujii Takashi. Tokyo, April 8, 2002.

Watanabe Misa. Chair, Watanabe Productions. Tokyo, June 2, 2002.

Yamano Hakudai. Dance critic. Tokyo, March 20, 2002.

Yamazaki Akiko. Associate Curator, Nakagawa Village Informel Museum. Tokyo, June 2, 2002.

Yasuda Atsuo. Curator, Hara Museum of Contemporary Art. Tokyo, February 20, 2002.

Yoshimasu Gōzō. Poet, photographer. Tokyo, May 22, 2002.

Yuasa Jōji. Composer. Tokyo, February 5, 2002.

Correspondence

Enomoto Kazuko. Painter. Letter, February 28, 2002.

Motonaga Sadamasa. Painter. Letter, May 3, 2002.

Sugiyama Etsuko. Curator, Setagaya Art Museum. Letter, October 12, 2002.

Tachikawa Ruriko. President, Star Dancers Ballet Foundation. Letter, March 10, 2002.

Tanikawa Shuntarō. Poet. Letter, March 5, 2002.

Tenjinchi (Hirasawa Noriko). Composer. Letter, February 26, 2002.

Published Sources

Abe Kōbō. *Kabe*. Tokyo: Getsuyō Shobō, 1951.

———. *Kemonotachi wa kokyō o mezasu*. Tokyo: Shinchō Bunko, 1970.

Adam, Peter. *Art of the Third Reich.* New York: Harry N. Abrams, 1992.

Adams, Hazard, and Leroy Searle, eds. *Critical Theory since 1965.* Tallahasse, Florida State University Press, 1986.

Adorno, Theodor W. "Aesthetic Theory" (1970). In Hazard Adams and Leroy Searle, eds., *Critical Theory since 1965,* pp. 232–237. Tallahassee: Florida State University Press, 1986.

Akasegawa Genpei. "Capitalist Realism." *Concerned Theatre Japan,* vol. 1, no. 3 (1970), pp. 32–35.

———. *Hangeijutsu anpan.* Tokyo: Chikuma Shobō, 1994. Originally published as *Ima ya akushon aru nomi! — "Yomiuri andepandan" to iu genshō.* Tokyo: Chikuma Shobō, 1985.

———. "The 1960s: The Art Which Destroyed Itself: An Intimate Account." Trans. John Clark. In David Elliott and Kazu Kaido, eds., *Reconstructions: Avant-Garde Art in Japan 1945–1965,* exh. cat., pp. 85–90. Oxford, Eng.: Museum of Modern Art Oxford, 1985.

———. *Tōkyō mikisā keikaku.* Tokyo: Chikuma Shobō, 1994. Originally published in Tokyo by Parco in 1984.

Akasegawa Genpei and Otsuji Katsuhiko. *Tōkyō rojō tankenki.* 2nd ed. Tokyo: Shinchōsha, 1989 (1986).

Akiyama Kuniharu. *Gendai ongaku o dō kiku ka.* Tokyo: Shōbunsha, 1973.

———. "Japan." In John Vinton, ed., *Dictionary of Contemporary Music,* pp. 364–367. New York: E. P. Dutton, 1974.

———. "Jikken Kōbō ni yoru henkaku to ongaku no kakuchō." *Ongaku geijutsu,* vol. 45, no. 1 (1987), pp. 24–28.

———. "Nihon no gendai ongaku o kikō." *Bijutsu techō,* vol. 20, no. 11 (1968), pp. 128–131.

———. *Nihon no sakkyokukatachi.* 2 vols. Tokyo: Ongaku no Tomosha, 1978–1979.

Allen, Stan. "Focus on the School of Architecture." *Princeton Alumni Weekly,* vol. 103, no. 11 (2003), p. 2.

Appadurai, Arjun. *Modernity at Large: Cultural Dimensions of Globalization.* Minneapolis: University of Minnesota Press, 1996.

Arayashiki Tōru. "The Rediscovered Mirror Sculpture by Yoshikuni Iida." In Mie Kenritsu Bijutsukan, Meguroku Bijutsukan, and Kyōto Kokuritsu Kindai Bijutsukan, ed., *Iida Yoshikuniten,* exh. cat., unnumbered pp. 1–4. Tsū: Mie Kenritsu Bijutsukan, 1988.

Archer, Michael. *Art since 1960.* London: Thames and Hudson, 1997.

Ashiya Shiritsu Bijutsu Hakubutsukan, ed. *Gutai I, II, III.* Exh. cat. Ashiya: Ashiya Shiritsu Bijutsu Hakubutsukan, 1994.

———, ed. *Gutai shiryōshū — dokyumento 1954–1972.* Ashiya: Ashiyashi Bunka Shinkō Zaidan, 1993.

Ashiya Shiritsu Bijutsu Hakubutsukan and Chibashi Bijutsukan, eds. *Sōgetsu to sono jidai 1945–1970.* Exh. cat. Ashiya: Asihiya Shiritsu Bijutsu Hakubutsukan, 1998.

Ashton, Dore. *The Delicate Thread: Teshigahara's Life in Art.* Tokyo: Kodansha International, 1997.

Atkins, E. Taylor. *Blue Nippon: Authenticating Jazz in Japan.* Durham, N.C.: Duke University Press, 2001.

Āto Gyararī Kan, ed. *Ishii Shigeo sakuhinshū*. Tokyo: Āto Gyararī Kan, 1994.

Barshay, Andrew. *The Social Sciences in Modern Japan: The Marxian and Modernist Traditions*. Berkeley: University of California Press, 2004.

Befu Harumi. *Hegemony of Homogeneity: An Anthropological Analysis of "Nihonjinron."* Melbourne: Trans Pacific Press, 2001.

———. *Ideorogii to shite no Nihon bunkaron*. Tokyo: Shisō no Kagakusha, 1987.

Bell, Daniel. "Tetsuya Noda: An Appreciation." In Fuji Terebi Gyararī, *Noda Tetsuya zensakuhin III 1992–2000*, pp. 13–18. Tokyo: Fuji Terebi Gyararī, 2001.

Benjamin, Walter. "The Work of Art in the Age of Mechanical Reproduction" (1936). In Benjamin, *Illuminations*, ed. Hannah Arendt, trans. Harry Zohn, pp. 217–251. New York: Schocken Books, 1969. This title was originally published in New York by Harcourt, Brace and World in 1968.

Bestor, Theodore. *Neighborhood Tokyo*. Stanford: Stanford University Press, 1989.

Betonamu ni Heiwa o! Shimin Rengō. *Shiryō "Beheiren" undō*. Vol. 1. Tokyo: Kawade Shobō Shinsha, 1974.

Bijutsu Shuppansha Henshūbu, ed. *Gendai Nihon āteisuto meikan*. Tokyo: Bijutsu Shuppansha, 1995.

Bijutsu techō nenkan 2002. Tokyo: Bijutsu Shuppansha, 2002.

Blasdel, Christopher Yohmei. "We're Talking the Real Thing." *Japan Times*, June 16, 2002, p. 13.

Bloch, Marc. "Toward a Comparative History of European Societies" (1928). In Frederic C. Lane and Jelle C. Riemersma, eds., *Enterprise and Secular Change: Readings in Economic History*, pp. 494–512. Homewood, Ill.: R. D. Irwin, 1953.

Bourdieu, Pierre. *Distinction: A Social Critique of the Judgement of Taste*. Trans. Richard Nice. Cambridge, Mass.: Harvard University Press, 1984.

———. *The Field of Cultural Production: Essays on Art and Literature*. Ed. Randal Johnson. New York: Columbia University Press, 1993.

Braester, Yomi. *Witness against History: Literature, Film, and Public Discourse in Twentieth-Century China*. Stanford, Calif.: Stanford University Press, 2003.

Breton, André. *Chōgenjitsushugi to kaiga*. Trans. Takiguchi Shūzō. Tokyo: Kōseikaku Shobō, 1930.

———. *Le surréalisme et la peinture*. Paris: Gallimard, 1928.

Brombert, Victor. *In Praise of Antiheroes: Figures and Themes in Modern European Literature, 1830–1980*. Chicago: University of Chicago Press, 1999.

Burt, Peter. *The Music of Tōru Takemitsu*. Cambridge, Eng.: Cambridge University Press, 2001.

Calza, Gian Carlo. *Tanaka Ikko: Graphic Master*. London: Phaidon Press, 1997.

Castile, Rand. "Thinking of Shinohara." In Hiroshimashi Gendai Bijutsukan, ed., *Shinohara Ushioten zuroku*, exh. cat., p. 107. Tokyo: Asahi Shinbunsha, 1992.

Chiba Shigeo. *Gendai bijutsu itsudatsushi 1945–1985*. Tokyo: Shōbunsha, 1986.

———. "Japanese Art in the 1950's and 1960's." In *Gutai 1955/56: Nihon gendai bijutsu no risutāto chiten*, pp. 20–21. Tokyo: Penrose Institute of Contemporary Art, 1993.

Chipp, Herschel B., comp. *Theories of Modern Art: A Source Book by Artists and Critics*. Berkeley: University of California Press, 1968.

Chōki Seiji. "Seiyō zen'ei ongaku no naka no Takemitsu Tōru." In Chōki and Higuchi Ryūichi, eds., *Takemitsu Tōru: oto no kawa no yukue*, pp. 276–293. Tokyo: Heibonsha, 2000.

Chōki Seiji and Higuchi Ryūichi, eds. *Takemitsu Tōru: oto no kawa no yukue.* Tokyo: Heibonsha, 2000.

Chow, Rey. *Writing Diaspora: Tactics of Intervention in Contemporary Cultural Studies.* Bloomington: Indiana University Press, 1993.

Conant, Ellen P., ed. *Nihonga: Transcending the Past: Japanese-Style Painting, 1868–1968.* St. Louis: St. Louis Art Museum, 1968.

Cort, Louise Allison, and Bert Winther-Tamaki. *Isamu Noguchi and Modern Japanese Ceramics: A Close Embrace of the Earth.* Washington, D.C.: Smithsonian Institution and Berkeley: University of California Press, 2003.

Dan Ikuma. "The Influence of Japanese Traditional Music on the Development of Western Music in Japan." Trans. Dorothy G. Britton. *Transactions of the Asiatic Society of Japan*, 3rd ser., vol. 8 (1961), pp. 201–217.

———. *Watakushi no Nihon ongakushi.* Tokyo: Nihon Hōsō Shuppan Kyōkai, 1999.

Dan Ikuma and Koizumi Fumio. *Nihon ongaku no saihakken.* Tokyo: Kōdansha, 1976.

de Ferranti, Hugh, and Yōko Narazaki, eds. *A Way a Lone: Writings on Tōru Takemitsu.* Tokyo: Academica Music, 2002.

Dehara Hitoshi. "Interrelationships within the Aspect of Time." Trans. Yamazaki Yumiko. In Suga Kishio, *Suga Kishio*, 2nd ed., pp. 308–312. Tokyo: Yomiuri Shinbunsha and Bijutsukan Renraku Kyōgikai, 1998 [1977].

Doss, Erika. *Benton, Pollock, and the Politics of Modernism: From Regionalism to Abstract Expressionism.* Chicago: University of Chicago Press, 1991.

Dower, John W. *Embracing Defeat: Japan in the Wake of World War II.* New York: W. W. Norton, 1999.

Ebizuka Kōichi. "Shuzo Takiguchi and the Takemiya Gallery." In *1953: Shedding Light on Art in Japan*, trans. Reiko Tomii, exh. cat., pp. 59–66. Tokyo: Tama Art University, 1997.

Elliott, David, and Kazu Kaido, eds. *Reconstructions: Avant-Garde Art in Japan 1945–1965.* Exh. cat. Oxford, Eng.: Museum of Modern Art Oxford, 1985.

Etō Jun. *Amerika to watakushi.* Tokyo: Kōdansha, 1965.

———. "The Civil Censorship in Occupied Japan." *Hikaku bunka zasshi (Annual of Comparative Culture)*, vol. 1 (1982), pp. 1–21.

———. "The Sealed Linguistic Space: The Occupation Censorship and Post-war Japan." Trans. Jay Rubin. *Hikaku bunka zasshi (Annual of Comparative Culture)*, part 1: vol. 2 (1984), pp. 1–42; part 2: vol. 3 (1988), pp. 1–23.

———. *Tozasareta gengo kūkan: senryōgun no ken'etsu to sengo Nihon.* Tokyo: Bungei Shunjū, 1989.

Foulkes, Julia L. *Modern Bodies: Dance and American Modernism from Martha Graham to Alvin Ailey.* Chapel Hill: University of North Carolina Press, 2002.

Frank, Andre Gunder. *ReOrient: Global Economy in the Asian Age.* Berkeley: University of California Press, 1998.

Friedman, Ken. *The Fluxus Reader.* New York: Academy Editions, 1998.

Fuji Terebi Gyararī. *Noda Tetsuya zensakuhin III 1992–2000.* Exh. cat. Tokyo: Fuji Terebi Gyararī, 2001.

Fujii, James A. *Complicit Fictions: The Subject in the Modern Japanese Prose Narrative*. Berkeley: University of California Press, 1993.

Fukuokashi Bijutsukan, ed. *Kyūshūhaten: hangeijutsu purojekuto*. Exh. cat. Fukuoka: Fukuokashi Bijutsukan, 1988.

———, ed. *Ryūdō suru bijutsu III: Neo-Dada no shashin*. Exh. cat. Fukuoka: Fukuokashi Bijutsukan, 1993.

Fukuzawa Yukichi. "Good-bye Asia (Datsu-a), 1885." In David J. Lu, ed., *Japan: A Documentary History*, vol. 2: *The Late Tokugawa Period to the Present*, pp. 351–353. Armonk, N.Y.: M. E. Sharpe, 1997.

Gan, Aleksei. "Constructivism" (1922). In Vassiliki Kolocotroni, Jane Goldman, and Olga Taxidou, eds., *Modernism: An Anthology of Sources and Documents*, pp. 298–299. Chicago: University of Chicago Press, 1998.

Garon, Sheldon. *Molding Japanese Minds: The State in Everyday Life*. Princeton, N.J.: Princeton University Press, 1997.

Gayle, Curtis. *Marxist History and Postwar Japanese Nationalism*. London: RoutledgeCurzon, 2002.

Geijutsu no Mori Bijutsukan, ed. *20seiki Nihon chōkoku monogatari*. Sapporo: Geijutsu no Mori Bijutsukan, 2000.

Gendai Buyō Kyōkai. *Nihon gendai buyō shiryō*, vol. 1: 1971. Tokyo: Gendai Buyō Kyōkai, 1972.

———. *Nihon gendai buyō shiryō*, vol. 2: 1972. Tokyo: Gendai Buyō Kyōkai, 1973.

Gendai Geijutsu Kenkyūjo, ed. *Gendai geijutsu kōza*. 4 vols. Tokyo: Kawade Shobō, 1955–1956.

Genshoku Nihon no bijutsu 33 gendai. Tokyo: Shōgakukan, 1994.

Gluck, Carol. "The Past in the Present." In Andrew Gordon, ed., *Postwar Japan as History*, pp. 64–95. Berkeley: University of California Press, 1993.

Gōda Nario. "Yōbu." *Ongaku nenkan 1977*, pp. 72–82.

Goodman, David G. *Japanese Drama and Culture in the 1960s: The Return of the Gods*. Armonk, N.Y.: M. E. Sharpe, 1988.

Gordon, Andrew. *A Modern History of Japan from Tokugawa Times to the Present*. New York: Oxford University Press, 2003.

———. "Rethinking Area Studies, Once More." *Journal of Japanese Studies*, vol. 30, no. 2 (2004), pp. 417–429.

Gordon, Colin. "Governmental Rationality: An Introduction." In Graham Burchell, Colin Gordon, and Peter Miller, eds., *The Foucault Effect: Studies in Governmentality with Two Lectures by and an Interview with Michel Foucault*, pp. 1–51. London: Harvester Wheatsheaf, 1991.

Greenberg, Clement. "Abstract, Representational, and So Forth" (1961). In Herschel B. Chipp, comp., *Theories of Modern Art: A Source Book by Artists and Critics*, pp. 577–581. Berkeley: University of California Press, 1968.

Griffiths, Paul. *Modern Music and After*. Oxford, Eng.: Oxford University Press, 1995.

———. *Modern Music: The Avant Garde since 1945*. London: J. M. Dent and Sons, 1981.

Grilli, Peter. "Takemitsu's Film Music." Harvard University Composers' Seminar, Cambridge, Mass., November 13, 2000.

Groom, Simon. "Encountering Mono-ha." In Groom, ed., *Mono-ha — School of Things*, exh. cat., pp. 5–19. Cambridge, Eng.: Kettle's Yard, University of Cambridge, 2001.

———, ed. *Mono-ha — School of Things*. Exh. cat. Cambridge, Eng.: Kettle's Yard, University of Cambridge, 2001.

Gropius, Walter. "Manifesto of the Bauhaus" (1919). In Vassiliki Kolocotroni, Jane Goldman, and Olga Taxidou, eds., *Modernism: An Anthology of Sources and Documents*, pp. 301–303. Chicago: University of Chicago Press, 1998.

Gunma Kenritsu Kindai Bijutsukan and Ehimeken Bijutsukan, eds. *Aru korekutā ga mita sengo Nihon bijutsu*. Takasaki: Gunma Kenritsu Kindai Bijutsukan, 2001.

Gutai Bijutsu no 18nen Kankō Iinkai, ed. *Gutai bijutsu no 18nen*. Osaka: Gutai Bijutsu no 18nen Kankō Iinkai, 1976.

Gutai 1955/56: Nihon gendai bijutsu no risutāto chiten. Tokyo: Penrose Institute of Contemporary Art, 1993.

Hamaguchi Ryūichi. *Hyūmanizumu no kenchiku: Nihon kindai kenchiku no hansei to tenbō*. Tokyo: Ondorisha, 1947.

Hara Bijutsukan, ed. *Lee Ufan*. Exh. cat. Tokyo: Arukanshiēru Bijutsu Zaidan, 1991.

Hara Tamiki. *Hara Tamiki zenshū*. Vol. 1. Tokyo: Haga Shoten, 1965.

Hara Toshio. "Preface." In Howard N. Fox, *A Primal Spirit: Ten Contemporary Japanese Sculptors*, exh. cat., pp. 9–14. Los Angeles: Los Angeles County Museum of Art, 1991.

Hariū Ichirō [Haryū Ichirō]. "The Phases of Neo-Dada in Postwar Art." Trans. Yamazaki Yumiko, in Ōitashi Bijutsukan, ed., *Neo-Dada Japan 1958–1998: Isozaki Arata to Howaito Hausu no menmen*, exh. cat., pp. 276–281. Ōita: Ōitashi Bijutsukan, 1998.

———. "Progressive Trends in Modern Japanese Art." In David Elliott and Kazu Kaido, eds., *Reconstructions: Avant-Garde Art in Japan 1945–1965*, exh. cat., pp. 23–27. Oxford, Eng.: Museum of Modern Art Oxford, 1985.

———. "Reflections on the Season of Neo Dada." In Mito Geijutsukan, *Nihon no natsu — 1960–1964*, exh. cat., pp. 78–79. Mito: Mito Geijutsukan, 1997.

Harootunian, H. D. *History's Disquiet: Modernity, Cultural Practice, and the Question of Everyday Life*. New York: Columbia University Press, 2000.

Harvey, David. *The Condition of Postmodernity: An Enquiry into the Origins of Cultural Change*. Oxford, Eng.: Oxford University Press, 1989.

Haryū Ichirō. "Avangyarudo no rinen to geijutsu," *Bijutsu techō*, vol. 30, no. 7 (1978), expanded no., pp. 148–156.

———. "'Chihō' konpurekkusu o kowase." *Bijutsu techō*, vol. 20, no. 4 (1968), pp. 82–94.

———. "Hanpaku." *Gendai no me*, vol. 10, no. 10, (1969), pp. 126–135.

———. "The Kagami Collection in the Context of Postwar Japanese Art History." Trans. Stanley N. Anderson. In Gunma Kenritsu Kindai Bijutsukan and Ehimeken Bijutsukan, eds., *Aru korekutā ga mita sengo Nihon bijutsu*, pp. 12–15. Takasaki: Gunma Kenritsu Kindai Bijutsukan, 2001.

———. "Kyūshūha tenmatsuki." In Fukuokashi Bijutsukan, ed., *Kyūshūhaten:*

hangeijutsu purojekuto, exh. cat., pp. 6–9. Fukuoka: Fukuokashi Bijutsukan, 1988.

———. "Nihonga kakumei no undō." *Bijutsu techō*, vol. 30, no. 7 (1978), expanded no., pp. 157–159.

———. *Sengo bijutsu seisuishi*. Tokyo: Tōkyō Shoseki, 1979.

———. "Zen'ei geijutsu ni tsukaremashita." *Geijutsu shinchō*, vol. 12, no. 8 (1962), pp. 148–153.

———. "Zōkeika seikatsu geijutsuka." *Sōgetsu*, no. 22 (1955), pp. 213–214.

Hay, Stephen N. *Asian Ideals of East and West: Tagore and His Critics in Japan, China, and India*. Cambridge, Mass.: Harvard University Press, 1970.

Hayashi Hikaru. *Gakushi no seki kara: watakushi no sengo ongakushi*. Tokyo: Shōbunsha, 1978.

———. *Genbaku shōkei — Hayashi Hikaru gasshō sakuhinshū*. Compact disk. Tokyo: Fontec FOCD 3294, 1996.

———. "Introduction." Trans. David G. Goodman. In *Genbaku shōkei*, program for Hayashi Hikaru–Tokyo Konsei Gasshōdan August Festival, August 5, 2001, at Aichi Global Peace Festival and August 9, 2001, in Tokyo.

Heifetz, Robin J. "Post–World War II Japanese Composition." D.M.A. dissertation, University of Illinois, Urbana, 1978.

Hemingway, Andrew. *Artists on the Left: American Artists and the Communist Movement, 1926–1956*. New Haven, Conn.: Yale University Press, 2002.

Herd, Judith Ann. "Change and Continuity in Contemporary Japanese Music." Ph.D. dissertation, Brown University, 1987.

———. "The Cultural Politics of Japan's Modern Music: Nostalgia, Nationalism and Identity in the Interwar Years." Unpublished manuscript, 2001.

———. "Interpreting Tradition: The Use of Traditional Japanese Music in the Compositions of Takemitsu." English translation of Herd, "Takemitsu Tōru to Nihon no dentō ongaku," in Chōki Seiji and Higuchi Ryūichi, eds., *Takemitsu Tōru: oto no kawa no yukue*, pp. 84–93. Tokyo: Heibonsha, 2000.

———. "The Neonationalist Movement: Origins of Japanese Contemporary Music." *Perspectives of New Music*, vol. 27, no. 2 (1989), pp. 118–163.

Hidaka Rokurō. "Sengo bunka undōshi no susume." *Iwanami kōza Nihon rekishi geppō*, no. 25 (1977), pp. 3–7.

Higgins, Hannah. *Fluxus Experience*. Berkeley: University of California Press, 2002.

Hijikata Tatsumi. *Hijikata Tatsumi shō: "nikki" to "inyō" ni yoru*. Ed. Yoshioka Minoru. Tokyo: Chikuma Shobō, 1987.

———. *Hijikata Tatsumi zenshū*. Ed. Tanemura Akihiro, Tsuruoka Yoshihisa, and Motofuji Akiko. 2 vols. Tokyo: Kawade Shobō Shinsha, 1998.

Hikosaka Naoyoshi. "Tojirareta enkan no anata wa — 'Gutai' no kiseki kara nani o . . . ." *Bijutsu techō*, vol. 25, no. 8 (1973), pp. 72–92.

Hirakawa Sukehiro, ed. *Lafcadio Hearn in International Perspectives*. Tokyo: Comparative Literature and Culture Program, University of Tokyo, 2001.

———. "Return to Japan or Return to the West? — Lafcadio Hearn's 'A Conservative.'" In Hirakawa, ed., *Lafcadio Hearn in International Perspectives*, pp. 11–17, 29. Tokyo: Comparative Literature and Culture Program, University of Tokyo, 2001.

Hirano, Kyoko. *Mr. Smith Goes to Tokyo: The Japanese Cinema under the American Occupation, 1945–1952*. Washington, D.C.: Smithsonian Institute, 1992.

Hirata, Hosea. *The Poetry and Poetics of Nishiwaki Junzaburō*. Princeton, N.J.: Princeton University Press, 1993.

Hirata Minoru. *Chōgeijutsu*. Tokyo: Sangokan, 2005.

Hiroshimashi Gendai Bijutsukan, ed. *Shinohara Ushioten zuroku*. Exh. cat. Tokyo: Asahi Shinbunsha, 1992.

Horikiri Yoshiko. "Kihyō." *Modan dansu*, no. 15 (1975), pp. 52–53.

Ichikawa Masanori. "Nijūsseiki bunmei to bunka no hazama ni." In Tōkyō Kokuritsu Kindai Bijutsukan, ed., *Mikan no seiki: 20seiki bijutsu ga nokosu mono*, exh. cat., pp. xiii–xxii. Tokyo: Yomiuri Shinbunsha, 2002.

Ichiyanagi Toshi. *Ongaku to iu itonami*. Tokyo: NTT Shuppan, 1998.

Iemura Tamayo. "Beyond Genres." In *1953: Shedding Light on Art in Japan*, trans. Reiko Tomii, exh. cat., pp. 33–42. Tokyo: Tama Art University, 1997.

Igarashi, Yoshikuni. *Bodies of Memory: Narratives of War in Postwar Japanese Culture, 1945–1970*. Princeton, N.J.: Princeton University Press, 2000.

Iida Yoshikuni. "The Art of Iida Yoshikuni." In Mie Kenritsu Bijutsukan, Meguroku Bijutsukan, and Kyōto Kokuritsu Kindai Bijutsukan, eds., *Iida Yoshikuniten*, exh. cat., pp. 1–9. Tsū: Mie Kenritsu Bijutsukan, 1988.

———. "Dialogue with the Infinite." Trans. Susan Pulvers. In Iida, *Iida Yoshikuni: Mirā mobiru*, pp. 159–161. Tokyo: Bijutsu Shuppansha, 1987.

———. *Iida Yoshikuni: Mirā mobiru*. Tokyo: Bijutsu Shuppansha, 1987.

Ikeda Ichi. *Mizu kagami*. Sagamiharashi: G-Day Plan, 1988.

Ishida Kazushi. *Performing Arts in Japan Now: Present Condition of Japanese Contemporary Music*. Tokyo: Japan Foundation, 1994.

Ishida Takeshi. "Emerging or Eclipsing Citizenship?" *The Developing Economies*, vol. 6, no. 4 (1968), pp. 410–424.

Ishii Shigeo. "Kanzen hanzai to geijutsu." *Geijutsu nōto*, no. 1 (1961) and no. 2 (1961). Reproduced in Āto Gyararī Kan, ed., *Ishii Shigeo sakuhinshū*, pp. 24–31. Tokyo: Āto Gyararī Kan, 1994.

Isoda Kōichi. *Sengoshi no kūkan*. Tokyo: Shinchōsha, 1993.

Isozaki Arata. "As Witness to Postwar Japanese Art." In Alexandra Munroe, *Japanese Art after 1945: Scream against the Sky*, exh. cat., pp. 27–31. New York: Harry N. Abrams, 1994.

———. "Imprint of 1960." Trans. Yamazaki Yumiko and David B. Stewart. In Ōitashi Bijutsukan, ed., *Neo-Dada Japan 1958–1998: Isozaki Arata to Howaito Hausu no menmen*, exh. cat., pp. 272–275. Ōita: Ōitashi Bijutsukan, 1998.

———. "Runaway System." In Mito Geijutsukan, *Nihon no natsu — 1960–1964*, exh. cat., pp. 80–81. Mito: Mito Geijutsukan, 1997.

Iwasaki Yoshikazu. *Kindai Nihonga no kōbō*. Kyoto: Kyōto Shinbunsha, 1995.

Iwase Yukio and Yui Kazuto, eds. *Nijūsseiki bukko yōgaka jiten*. Tokyo: Bijutsu Nenkansha, 1997.

Jay, Martin. *The Dialectical Imagination: A History of the Frankfurt School and the Institute of Social Research, 1923–1950*. Berkeley: University of California Press, 1996. Originally published in Boston by Little, Brown in 1973.

Johnson, Randal. "Editor's Introduction." In Pierre Bourdieu, *The Field of Cultural*

Production: Essays on Art and Literature, ed. Randal Johnson, pp. 1–42. New York: Columbia University Press, 1993.

Kaido, Kazu. "Reconstruction: The Role of the Avant-Garde in Post-war Japan." In David Elliott and Kaido, eds., *Reconstructions: Avant-Garde Art in Japan 1945–1965*, exh. cat., pp. 11–22. Oxford, Eng.: Museum of Modern Art Oxford, 1985.

Kajiya Kenji. "Gosado suru buki: Kuremento Gurinbāgu, bunka reisen, guroba-rizeshon." *Amerika kenkyū*, no. 37 (2003), pp. 83–105.

Kanagawa Kenritsu Kindai Bijutsukan. *Kindai Nihon bijutsuka retsuden.* Tokyo: Bijutsu Shuppansha, 1999.

———. *The Museum of Modern Art, Kamakura.* Kamakura: Kanagawa Kenritsu Kindai Bijutsukan, 1994.

Kanda Akiko. "Akiko no modan dansu." Part 1: *Modan dansu*, no. 11 (1972), pp. 36–40; part 2: *Modan dansu*, no. 12 (1973), pp. 30–32; part 3: *Modan dansu*, no. 13 (1974), pp. 45–49.

———. *Onna o odoru.* Kyoto: Shinshindō, 1980.

Kano Masanao. *Nihon no gendai.* Tokyo: Iwanami Shoten, 2000.

Karatani, Kojin. *Origins of Modern Japanese Literature.* Trans. and ed. Brett de Bary. Durham, N.C.: Duke University Press, 1993.

Katō Shūichi. *Form, Style, Tradition: Reflections on Japanese Art and Society.* Trans. John Bester. Berkeley: University of California Press, 1971.

———. *Zasshu bunka: Nihon no chiisa na kibō.* Tokyo: Kōdansha, 1974.

Kaufmann, Walter, ed. *Existentialism from Dostoevsky to Sartre.* Cleveland and New York: Meridian Books, 1956.

Kawagiri Nobuhiko. *Okamoto Tarō — geijutsu wa bakuhatsu ka.* Tokyo: Chūsekisha, 2000 [1978].

Kawaguchi Yoshiharu. "Takemitsu Tōru to shururearizumu." In Chōki Seiji and Higuchi Ryūichi, eds., *Takemitsu Tōru: oto no kawa no yukue*, pp. 188–201. Tokyo: Heibonsha, 2000.

Kawai Nobukazu, ed. *Asahi shinbun Japan arumanakku 1999.* Tokyo: Asahi Shin-bunsha, 1998.

Kawakita Michiaki. *Modern Currents in Japanese Art.* Trans. Charles S. Terry. New York and Tokyo: Weatherhill/Heibonsha, 1974.

Kawasakishi Okamoto Tarō Bijutsukan, ed. *Okamoto Tarō Expo '70 Taiyō no tō kara no messējiten.* Exh. cat. Kawasaki: Kawasakishi Okamoto Tarō Bijutsukan, 2000.

Keene, Donald. "Japanese Writers and the Greater East Asia War." In Keene, *Landscapes and Portraits: Appreciations of Japanese Culture*, pp. 300–321. Tokyo: Kodansha International, 1971.

Kikuhata Mokuma. *Sengo bijutsu no genshitsu.* Fukuoka: Ashi Shobō, 1982.

———. *Sengo bijutsu to hangeijutsu.* 2nd ed. Fukuoka: Kaitōsha, 1993 [1979].

Kimura-Steven, Chigusa. "The Otherness of Women in the Avant-Garde Film *Woman in the Dunes.*" In Joshua S. Mostow, Norman Bryson, and Maribeth Graybill, eds., *Gender and Power in the Japanese Visual Field*, pp. 155–178, 250–254. Honolulu: University of Hawai'i Press, 2003.

Klein, Susan Blakeley. *Ankoku Butō: The Premodern and Postmodern Influences on the Dance of Utter Darkness*. Ithaca, N.Y.: East Asia Program, Cornell University, 1988.

Kodansha Encyclopedia of Japan. 9 vols. Tokyo: Kōdansha, 1983.

Koizumi Fumio. *Nihon no oto: sekai no naka no Nihon ongaku*. Tokyo: Seidosha, 1977.

Kojima Tomiko. *Nihon no ongaku o kangaeru*. 2nd ed. Tokyo: Ongaku no Tomosha, 1999 [1976].

Kokuritsu Kokusai Bijutsukan, ed. *Geijutsu to nichijō — hangeijutsu/hangeijutsu*. Exh. cat. Osaka: Kokuritsu Kokusai Bijutsukan, 1991.

———, ed. *Kaiga no arashi 1950nendai: Anfuorumeru/Gutai bijutsu/kobura kaiga no arashi*. Exh. cat. Osaka: Kokuritsu Kokusai Bijutsukan, 1985.

Kolocotroni, Vassiliki, Jane Goldman, and Olga Taxidou, eds. *Modernism: An Anthology of Sources and Documents*. Chicago: University of Chicago Press, 1998.

Komiya Tamie. *Kingendai Nihon no ongakushi: juyōshi de wa nai: 1900–1960nendai*. Tokyo: Sekai no Ongakusha, 2001.

Komori Yōichi et al., eds. *Reisen taisei to shihon no bunka: 1955nen igo*. Vol. 1. *Iwanami kōza kindai Nihon no bunkashi 9*. Tokyo: Iwanami Shoten, 2002.

Kondo, Yukio. "Thoughts on Kazuo Kadonaga from a Japanese Perspective: Beyond Exoticism." In Japanese American Cultural and Community Center, Los Angeles, and Salt Lake Art Center, Salt Lake City, eds., *Kazuo Kadonaga*, exh. cat., pp. 42–45. Los Angeles: Japanese American Cultural and Community Center, Los Angeles, and Salt Lake City: Salt Lake Art Center, Salt Lake City, 2001.

Kōno Yasuo. *Oto to Nihonjin*. Tokyo: Geijutsu Gendaisha, 2001.

Konuma Jun'ichi. *Takemitsu Tōru*. Tokyo: Seidosha, 1999.

Koplos, Janet. *Contemporary Japanese Sculpture*. New York: Abbeville Press, 1991.

Koschmann, J. Victor. Review of H. D. Harootunian, *History's Disquiet* (New York: Columbia University Press, 2000). *Journal of Asian Studies*, vol. 60, no. 4 (2001), pp. 1188–1189.

———. *Revolution and Subjectivity in Postwar Japan*. Chicago: University of Chicago Press, 1996.

Kung, David. *The Contemporary Artist in Japan*. Honolulu: East-West Center Press, 1966.

Kuroda Raiji. "Akarui satsurikisha, sono shunkan gei no jutsu." In Fukuokashi Bijutsukan, ed., *Ryūdō suru bijutsu III: Neo-Dada no shashin*, exh. cat., pp. 8–13. Fukuoka: Fukuokashi Bijutsukan, 1993.

———. "Gutai ura no konseputo." *Bijutsu techō*, vol. 42, no. 5 (1990), pp. 109–122.

———. "Isetsu bijutsu undō to shite no Kyūshūha." In Fukuokashi Bijutsukan, ed., *Kyūshūhaten: hangeijutsu purojekuto*, exh. cat., pp. 14–23. Fukuoka: Fukuokashi Bijutsukan, 1988.

———. "1960nendai Nihon no pafuōmansu kenkyū I: bunka to shite no 'Zero Jigen' joron e no hashirigaki." *Kajima bijutsu kenkyū, nenpō*, no. 18 (2001), *bessatsu*, pp. 362–376.

Kuwabara Takeo. *Gendai Nihon bunka no hansei*. Tokyo: Hakujitsu Shoin, 1947.

Lee, Leo Ou-fan. *The Romantic Generation of Modern Chinese Writers*. Cambridge, Mass.: Harvard University Press, 1973.

———. "The Tradition of Modern Chinese Cinema: Some Preliminary Explorations and Hypotheses." In Chris Berry, ed., *Perspectives on Chinese Cinema*, pp. 1–20. Ithaca, N.Y.: Cornell University China-Japan Program, 1985.

Lee Ufan. "Foreshadowings and Premonitions: Mono-ha." In Simon Groom, ed., *Mono-ha — School of Things*, exh. cat., pp. 21–25. Cambridge, Eng.: Kettle's Yard, University of Cambridge, 2001.

Lefebvre, Henri. *Everyday Life in the Modern World.* Trans. Sacha Rabinovitch. New York: Harper and Row, 1971.

Lippit, Seiji M. *Topographies of Japanese Modernism.* New York: Columbia University Press, 2002.

Lloyd, Jill. *German Expressionism: Primitivism and Modernity.* New Haven, Conn.: Yale University Press, 1991.

Lynch, Stacy Combs. *Classical Music for Beginners.* New York: Writers and Readers Publishing, 1994.

Lynton, Norbert. *The Story of Modern Art.* 2nd ed. New York: Phaidon Press, 1989 [1980].

Machida Takako. *Buyō no ayumi hyakunen.* Tokyo: Ōfūsha, 1968.

Maki Fumihiko. "Yoshikuni Iida, the Artist of Perpetual Youth." Trans. Watanabe Hiroshi. In Iida Yoshikuni, *Iida Yoshikuni: Mirā mobiru*, pp. 150–151. Tokyo: Bijutsu Shuppansha, 1987.

Malm, William P. "Layers of Music in Japan since 1945." In *The Fourth Kyushu International Cultural Conference: Proceedings*, pp. 91–96. Fukuoka: Fukuoka UNESCO Association, 1978.

———. *Traditional Japanese Music and Musical Instruments.* 2nd ed. Tokyo: Kodansha International, 2000. Originally published in Tokyo by C. E. Tuttle in 1959 as *Japanese Music and Musical Instruments.*

Mamiya Michio. *Nihon min'yōshū.* 2nd ed. Tokyo: Zen'on Gakufu Shuppansha, 2002 [1975].

———. *Nihon min'yōshū.* Compact disk. Tokyo: Fontec FOCD 3481, 2001.

Manning, Patrick. *Navigating World History.* New York: Palgrave Macmillan, 2003.

Marotti, William A. "Politics and Culture in Postwar Japan: Akasegawa Genpei and the Artistic Avant-garde, 1958–1970." Ph.D. Dissertation, University of Chicago. Chicago, 2001.

Matsumoto Tōru. "The Contemporariness of Postwar Art." Trans. Ogawa Kikuko. In Tōkyō Kokuritsu Kindai Bijutsukan, ed., *Mikan no seiki: 20seiki bijutsu ga nokosu mono*, exh. cat., supplement, pp. 14–20. Tokyo: Yomiuri Shinbunsha, 2002.

———. *Senkyūhyakugojū-rokujū nendai no bijutsu.* Tokyo: Tōkyō Kokuritsu Kindai Bijutsukan, 1999.

Mayuzumi Toshirō. *Puripeado piano to gengaku no tame no shōhin* (1957). Published as *Pieces for Prepared Piano and Strings.* New York: C. F. Peters Corp., 1958.

McKeown, Adam. *Chinese Migrant Networks and Cultural Change: Peru, Chicago, and Hawaii, 1900–1936.* Chicago: University of Chicago Press, 2001.

McVeigh, Brian J. *Nationalisms of Japan: Managing and Mystifying Identity.* Lanham, Md.: Rowman and Littlefield, 2004.

Meguroku Bijutsukan, Hyōgo Kenritsu Kindai Bijutsukan, Hiroshimashi Gendai Bijutsukan, Fukuoka Kenritsu Bijutsukan, and Asahi Shinbunsha, eds. *Sengo bunka no kiseki 1945–1995*. Exh. cat. Tokyo: Asahi Shinbunsha, 1995.

Mie Kenritsu Bijutsukan, Meguroku Bijutsukan, and Kyōto Kokuritsu Kindai Bijutsukan, ed., *Iida Yoshikuniten*. Exh. cat. Tsū: Mie Kenritsu Bijutsukan, 1988.

Miki Tamon. "Japanese Contemporary Art — the 1950s and 1960s." In Kokuritsu Kokusai Bijutsukan, ed., *Geijutsu to nichijō — hangeijutsu/hangeijutsu*, exh. cat., pp. 12–15. Osaka: Kokuritsu Kokusai Bijutsukan, 1991.

———. "Major Trends in Modern Japanese Sculpture since the 1950s." In Kumon Yasuo, ed., *Nihon gendai bijutsu: chōkoku*, pp. 4–11. Tokyo: Keishōsha, 1985.

———. "The 1960's — a Decade of Change in Contemporary Japanese Art." In Tōkyō Kokuritsu Kindai Bijutsukan, ed., *1960nendai — gendai bijutsu no tenkanki*, exh. cat., pp. 23–31. Tokyo: Tōkyō Kokuritsu Kindai Bijutsukan, 1981.

Miller, Dorothy C., and William S. Lieberman, eds. *The New Japanese Painting and Sculpture*. Exh. cat. New York: Museum of Modern Art, 1966.

Milly, Deborah J. *Poverty, Equality, and Growth: The Politics of Economic Need in Postwar Japan*. Cambridge, Mass.: Harvard University Asia Center, 1999.

Minemura, Toshiaki. "Introduction." In *1953: Shedding Light on Art in Japan*, trans. Reiko Tomii, exh. cat., pp. 5–12. Tokyo: Tama Art University, 1997.

———. "Kaitai to soshikika no kurikaeshi." *Mizue*, no. 921 (1981), pp. 74–79.

———. "Measuring Up to the Mono-ha — and Beyond." Trans. Alfred Birnbaum. In Tama Bijutsu Daigaku and Seibu Bijutsukan, eds., *Monoha to posutomonoha no tenkai*, exh. cat., pp. 190–194. Tokyo: Tama Bijutsu Daigaku and Seibu Bijutsukan, 1987.

———. "Objects and Events." In Mito Geijutsukan, *Nihon no natsu — 1960–1964*, exh. cat., pp. 82–83. Mito: Mito Geijutsukan, 1997.

———. "The Realism of Tactility: Another Japan That Erupted." In *1953: Shedding Light on Art in Japan*, trans. Reiko Tomii, exh. cat., pp. 45–56. Tokyo: Tama Art University, 1997.

———. "Tōji, kūkansu." In Ōitashi Bijutsukan, ed., *Yoshimura Masunobu no jikkenten — ōtō to hen'yō*, exh. cat., pp. 16–21. Ōita: Ōitashi Bijutsukan, 2000.

———. "What Was Monoha?" Trans. Jean Campignon. In Tama Bijutsu Daigaku IRAC Kenkyūjo, ed., *"Monoha" katarogu*, pp. 6–9. Tokyo: Kamakura Garō, 1986.

———. "Why Do We Call It Art?" Trans. Reiko Tomii. In Suga Kishio, *Suga Kishio*, 2nd ed., pp. 302–307. Tokyo: Yomiuri Shinbunsha and Bijutsu Renraku Kyōgikai, 1998 [1977].

Mishima Yukio. *Forbidden Colors*. Trans. Alfred H. Marks. New York: Knopf, 1968.

———. *Kinjiki*. Tokyo: Shinchōsha, 1951–1953.

Mito Geijutsukan. *Nihon no natsu — 1960–1964*. Exh. cat. Mito: Mito Geijutsukan, 1997.

Mitsuyama-Wdowiak, K. "The Critical Reception of Exhibitions of Japanese Contemporary Art in the West during the 1980s." Unpublished manuscript, 2000.

Miyakawa Atsushi. "Anfuorumeru igo." *Bijutsu techō*, vol. 15, no. 5 (1963), pp. 86–96.

———. "Hangeijutsu: sono nichijōsei e no kakō." *Bijutsu techō*, vol. 16, no. 4 (1964), pp. 48–57.

———. "Henbō no suii — montajū fū ni." *Bijutsu techō*, vol. 15, no. 10 (1963), expanded no., pp. 49–64.

Molasky, Michael S. *Sengo Nihon no jazu bunka — eiga, bungaku, sabukaruchā*. Tokyo: Seidosha, 2005.

Moore, Joe B. "Japan, Jazz, and Creolization." In Takeshi Matsuda, ed., *The Age of Creolization in the Pacific*, pp. 135–165. Hiroshima: Keisuisha, 2001.

Moriguchi Akira. "Mono-ha: Insights on Re-production." Trans. Alfred Birnbaum. In Tama Bijutsu Daigaku and Seibu Bijutsukan, eds., *Monoha to posutomonoha no tenkai*, exh. cat., pp. 195–196. Tokyo: Tama Bijutsu Daigaku and Seibu Bijutsukan, 1987.

Moroyama Masanori. "Trends in the Living Arts and Modern Crafts in the 1950s." In Tōkyō Kokuritsu Kindai Bijutsukan Kōgeikan, ed., *Crafts in Everyday Life in the 1950s and 1960s*, exh. cat., pp. 16–23. Tokyo: Tōkyō Kokuritsu Kindai Bijutsukan, 1995.

Morris-Suzuki, Tessa. *Showa*. London: Athlone Press, 1984.

Mostow, Joshua S., Norman Bryson, and Maribeth Graybill, eds., *Gender and Power in the Japanese Visual Field*. Honolulu: University of Hawai'i Press, 2003.

Motofuji Akiko. *Hijikata Tatsumi to tomo ni*. Tokyo: Chikuma Shobō, 1990.

Munroe, Alexandra. *Japanese Art after 1945: Scream against the Sky*. Exh. cat. New York: Harry N. Abrams, 1994.

Murata Keinosuke. "Hajime ni Expo '70 to Tarō no tō to . . . ." In Kawasakishi Okamoto Tarō Bijutsukan, ed., *Okamoto Tarō Expo '70 Taiyō no tō kara no messējiten*, exh. cat., p. 11. Kawasaki: Kawasakishi Okamoto Tarō Bijutsukan, 2000.

Murayama Yasuo. "Japan/I Torn Apart." In *1953: Shedding Light on Art in Japan*, trans. Reiko Tomii, exh. cat., pp. 15–29. Tokyo: Tama Art University, 1997.

Nagashima, Yoichi, ed. *Return to Japan: From "Pilgrimage" to the West*. Aarhus, Denmark: Aarhus University Press, 2001.

Nagoyashi Bijutsukan, ed. *Sengo Nihon no riarizumu 1945–1960*. Nagoya: Nagoyashi Bijutsukan, 1998.

Nakahara Yūsuke. "The Sculpture of Yoshikuni Iida." Trans. Susan Pulvers. In Iida Yoshikuni, *Iida Yoshikuni: Mirā mobiru*, pp. 155–158. Tokyo: Bijutsu Shuppansha, 1987.

Nakamura Keiji. "Art and Reality." In Kokuritsu Kokusai Bijutsukan, ed., *Geijutsu to nichijō — hangeijutsu/hangeijutsu*, exh. cat., pp. 21–26. Osaka: Kokuritsu Kokusai Bijutsukan, 1991.

Nakamura Tanio. *Contemporary Japanese-Style Painting*. Trans. Itō Mikio. Tokyo: Tokyo International Publishers and New York: Tudor Publishing, 1969.

Nakamura Yoshikazu. *Nihon kindai bijutsu ronsōshi*. Tokyo: Kyūryūdō, 1981.

Narazaki Yōko. "Takemitsu Tōru sōsakushi gaisetsu." In Chōki Seiji and Higuchi Ryūichi, eds., *Takemitsu Tōru: oto no kawa no yukue*, pp. 94–114. Tokyo: Heibonsha, 2000.

Nihon Bankoku Hakurankai Kinen Kikin. *Shōwa 55nendo Nihon Bankoku Hakurankai Kinen Kikin jigyō*. Tokyo: Nihon Bankoku Hakurankai Kinen Kikin, 1980.

Nihon Geijutsuin, ed. *Nihon Geijutsuinshi*. Rev. ed., 3 vols. Tokyo: Nihon Geijutsuin, 1979–1980 [1963].

Nihon gendai buyō nenkan. 2 vols. Tokyo: Gendai Buyō Kyōkai, 1975–1976.

Nihon Hōsō Kyōkai, ed. *Nihon min'yō taikan.* 12 vols. Tokyo: Nihon Hōsō Kyōkai, 1952–1993.

———, ed. *Tōhoku min'yōshū.* 6 vols. Tokyo: Nihon Hōsō Shuppan Kyōkai, 1955–1967.

Nihon kingendaishi jiten. Tokyo: Tōyō Keizai Shinpōsha, 1978.

Nihon Ongaku Buyō Kaigi. *Sakkyokuka to no taiwa.* Tokyo: Shin Nihon Shuppansha, 1982.

1953: Shedding Light on Art in Japan. Trans. Reiko Tomii. Exh. cat. Tokyo: Tama Art University, 1997.

Nishimoto Masanobu. "Riarizumu to avangyarudo no 50nendai bijutsu." In 1953nen Raito Apputen Jikkō Iinkai, ed., *1953nen raito appu — atarashii sengo bijutsuzō ga miete kita,* exh. cat., pp. 42–55. Tokyo: Meguroku Bijutsukan and Tama Bijutsu Daigaku, 1996.

Noguchi Reiichi. "Japanese Art of 1964: The Reaction to *Art Informel* and Further Developments." In Tōkyōto Gendai Bijutsukan, ed., *Nihon no bijutsu: yomi-gaeru 1964,* exh. cat., pp. 190–196. Tokyo: Tōkyōto Gendai Bijutsukan, 1996.

Oda Makoto. *Nani o watakushitachi wa hajimete iru no ka.* Tokyo: San'ichi Shobō, 1970.

———. *Nanshi no shisō.* Tokyo: Bungei Shunjū, 1969.

Ohno, Kazuo, and Yoshito Ohno. *Kazuo Ohno's World: From Within and Without.* Trans. John Barrett. Middletown, Conn.: Wesleyan University Press, 2004.

Ōitashi Bijutsukan, ed. *Neo-Dada Japan 1958–1998: Isozaki Arata to Howaito Hausu no menmen.* Exh. cat. Ōita: Ōitashi Bijutsukan, 1998.

———, ed. *Yoshimura Masunobu no jikkenten — ōtō to hen'yō.* Exh. cat. Ōita: Ōitashi Bijutsukan, 2000.

Okabayashi Hiroshi. *Nihon no gendai āto.* Tokyo: Maruzen, 1998.

Okakura Kakuzō [Tenshin]. *The Awakening of Japan.* New York: Century Co., 1904.

———. *Ideals of the East, with Special Reference to the Art of Japan.* London: J. Murray, 1905.

Okamoto Tarō. "Bankokuhaku ni kaketa mono." In Kawasakishi Okamoto Tarō Bijutsukan, ed., *Okamoto Tarō Expo '70 Taiyō no tō kara no messējiten,* exh. cat., pp. 6–9. Kawasaki: Kawasakishi Okamoto Tarō Bijutsukan, 2000.

———. *Konnichi no geijutsu: seikatsu o sōzō suru enerugī no gensen.* 2nd ed. Tokyo: Kōbunsha, 1963 [1954].

———. *Nihon Bankokuhaku.* Tokyo: Shōbunsha, 1971.

———. *Nihon no dentō.* Tokyo: Kōbunsha, 1956.

———. *Okamoto Tarō no me.* Tokyo: Asahi Shinbunsha, 1966.

———. *Okinawa bunkaron — wasurerareta Nihon.* Tokyo: Chūō Kōronsha, 1972.

———. *Wasurerareta Nihon — Okinawa bunkaron.* Tokyo: Chūō Kōronsha, 1961.

———. "What Is Tradition?" Trans. Reiko Tomii. In Alexandra Munroe, *Japanese Art after 1945: Scream against the Sky,* exh. cat., pp. 381–382. New York: Harry N. Abrams, 1994.

Olson, Lawrence. *Ambivalent Moderns: Portraits of Japanese Cultural Identity.* Savage, Md.: Rowman and Littlefield, 1992.

Omuka Toshiharu. *Nihon no avangyarudo geijutsu.* Tokyo: Seidosha, 2001.

Ongaku no Tomosha. *Nihon no sakkyoku 20seiki.* Tokyo: Ongaku no Tomosha, 1999.

Orwell, George. *The Lion and the Unicorn: Socialism and the English Genius.* London: Secker and Warburg, 1941.

Osaki Shin'ichirō. "Art in Gutai; Action into Painting." In Ashiya Shiritsu Bijutsu Hakubutsukan, ed., *Gutai shiryōshū — dokyumento 1954–1972*, pp. 19–28. Ashiya: Ashiyashi Bunka Shinkō Zaidan, 1993.

Ōshima Seiji. "In a Chaos of Creation." In Setagaya Bijutsukan, ed., *Teshigahara Sōfū — sengo Nihon o kakenuketa ishoku nozen'ei*, exh. cat., vol. 1, pp. 14–15. Tokyo: Setagaya Bijutsukan and Sōgetsukai, 2001.

Overmyer-Velázquez, Mark. "Visions of the Emerald City: Politics, Culture, and Alternative Modernities in Oaxaca City, Mexico, 1877–1920." Ph.D. dissertation, Yale University, 2002.

Ozawa Seiji and Takemitsu Tōru. *Ongaku.* Tokyo: Shinchōsha, 1984.

Packard, George R. III. *Protest in Tokyo.* Princeton, N.J.: Princeton University Press, 1966.

Paik, Nam June. "To Catch Up or Not to Catch Up with the West: Hijikata and Hi Red Center." In Alexandra Munroe, *Japanese Art after 1945: Scream against the Sky*, exh. cat., pp. 77–81. New York: Harry N. Abrams, 1994.

Partner, Simon. *Assembled in Japan: Electrical Goods and the Making of the Japanese Consumer.* Berkeley: University of California Press, 1999.

Piovesana, Gino K. *Recent Japanese Philosophical Thought 1862–1962: A Survey.* Tokyo: Enderle Bookstore, 1963.

Pirenne, Henri. "What Historians Are Trying to Do." In Stuart A. Rice, ed., *Methods in Social Science: A Case Book*, pp. 444–459. Chicago: University of Chicago Press, 1931.

Pogue, David, and Scott Speck. *Classical Music for Dummies.* New York: Hungry Minds, 1997.

Pomeranz, Kenneth. *The Great Divergence: Europe, China, and the Making of the Modern World Economy.* Princeton, N.J.: Princeton University Press, 2000.

Poole, Deborah. *Vision, Race, and Modernity: A Visual Economy of the Andean Image World.* Princeton, N.J.: Princeton University Press, 1997.

Read, Herbert Edward. *Icon and Idea: The Function of Art in the Development of Human Consciousness.* Cambridge, Mass.: Harvard University Press, 1955.

———. "What Is Revolutionary Art?" (1935). In Vassiliki Kolocotroni, Jane Goldman, and Olga Taxidou, eds., *Modernism: An Anthology of Sources and Documents*, pp. 526–529. Chicago: University of Chicago Press, 1998.

Richie, Donald. "Hiroshi Teshigahara and the Film . . . ." In Sōgetsukai, ed., *Kokoro wa itsumo runesansu hyōgen jiyūjin Teshigahara Hiroshi*, p. 39. Tokyo: Sōgetsu Shuppan, 1989.

———. "One Hundred Years of Japanese Film." Lecture, International House of Japan, Tokyo, February 22, 2002.

———. "Teshigahara and the Human Condition." In Teshigahara Productions, *Cinema and Hiroshi Teshigahara*, p. 3. Tokyo: Teshigahara Productions, 1992.

Rimer, J. Thomas. "Postwar Developments: Absorption and Amalgamation,

1945–1968." In Ellen P. Conant, ed., *Nihonga: Transcending the Past: Japanese-Style Painting, 1868–1968*, pp. 62–71. St. Louis: St. Louis Art Museum, 1968.

Rivkin, Julie, and Michael Ryan, eds. *Literary Theory: An Anthology*. Malden, Mass., and Oxford, Eng.: Blackwell, 1998.

Rosenberg, Harold. *The Tradition of the New*. New York: Horizon Press, 1959.

Rostow, Walt W. *The Stages of Economic Growth, a Non-Communist Manifesto*. London: Cambridge University Press, 1960.

Rubin, Jay. "From Wholesomeness to Decadence: The Censorship of Literature under the Allied Occupation." *Journal of Japanese Studies*, vol. 11, no. 1 (1985), pp. 71–103.

Sadie, Stanley, ed. *The New Grove Dictionary of Music and Musicians*. London: Macmillan, 1980.

Sakai, Naoki. "Modernity and Its Critique." In Masao Miyoshi and Harry D. Harootunian, eds., *Postmodernism and Japan*, pp. 93–122. Durham, N.C.: Duke University Press, 1989.

Sakai Tadayasu. "Sengo no gendai chōkoku." In *Gendai no bijutsu*, pp. 238–246. *Genshoku Nihon no bijutsu* 33. Tokyo: Shōgakukan, 1994.

Sano Kōji. "Joron — Nihongo de kataru ongaku e no kiseki." In Chōki Seiji and Higuchi Ryūichi, eds., *Takemitsu Tōru: oto no kawa no yukue*, pp. 8–33. Tokyo: Heibonsha, 2000.

Sas, Miryam. *Fault Lines: Cultural Memory and Japanese Surrealism*. Stanford, Calif.: Stanford University Press, 1999.

Satani Garō, ed. *Dai 11kai omāju Takiguchi Shūzōten: Jikken Kōbō to Takiguchi Shūzō*. Exh. cat. Tokyo: Satani Garō, 1991.

Satani Kazuhiko. "Takiguchi Shūzō to Jikken Kōbō no shigoto." *Kokubungaku*, vol. 44, no. 10 (1999), pp. 104–111.

Satō Shigeru. "Atsugi Bonjinron." *Modan dansu*, no. 9 (1971), pp. 33–37.

Sawaragi Noi. "The Heat of Passion and Thermal Dynamics." In Mito Geijutsukan, *Nihon no natsu — 1960–1964*, exh. cat., pp. 72–77. Mito: Mito Geijutsukan, 1997.

———. *Nihon gendai bijutsu*. Tokyo: Shinchōsha, 1998.

Schjeldahl, Peter. "Bare Minimal." *The New Yorker*, May 3, 2004, pp. 108–109.

Schnellbächer, Thomas. *Abe Kōbō, Literary Strategist*. Munich: Iudicium, 2004.

Schwarz, Frank J., and Susan J. Pharr, eds. *The State of Civil Society in Japan*. New York: Cambridge University Press, 2003.

Scott, James. *Seeing Like a State: How Certain Schemes to Improve the Human Condition Have Failed*. New Haven, Conn.: Yale University Press, 1998.

Segi Shin'ichi. *Avangyarudo geijutsu — taiken to hihan*. Tokyo: Shichōsha, 1998.

———. *Gendai bijutsu sanjūnen*. Tokyo: Bijutsu Kōronsha, 1978.

———. *Nihon Andepandanten no zenkiroku 1949–1963*. Tokyo: Sōbisha, 1993.

———. *Nihon no zen'ei 1945–1999*. Tokyo: Seikatsu no Tomosha, 2000.

———. *Sengo kūhakuki no bijutsu*. Tokyo: Shichōsha, 1996.

Seibu Bijutsukan, ed. *Dōmoto Hisao 30nen*. Exh. cat. Tokyo: Seibu Bijutsukan, 1987.

Sekine Nobuo. "The Message of Environmental Art." In Hayashi Yoshifumi, ed., *Sekine: A Message from Environmental Art Studio*, pp. 9–12. Tokyo: Purosesu Ākitekuchua, 1992.

———. *Sekine Nobuo 1968–1978*. Tokyo: Yuria Pemuperu Kōbō, 1978.

1953nen Raito Apputen Jikkō Iinkai, ed. *1953nen raito appu — atarashii sengo bijutsuzō ga miete kita*. Exh. cat. Tokyo: Meguroku Bijutsukan and Tama Bijutsu Daigaku, 1996.

Setagaya Bijutsukan, ed. *Teshigahara Sōfū — sengo Nihon o kakenuketa ishoku no zen'ei*. Exh. cat., 2 vols. Tokyo: Setagaya Bijutsukan and Sōgetsukai, 2001.

Setagaya Bungakukan, ed. *Takiguchi Shūzō to Takemitsu Tōruten*. Exh. cat. Tokyo: Setagaya Bungakukan, 1999.

Sherif, Ann. Review of Jay Rubin, *Haruki Murakami and the Music of Words* (London: Harvill, 2002), and Matthew Carl Strecher, *Dances with Sheep: The Quest for Identity in the Fiction of Murakami Haruki* (Ann Arbor: Center for Japanese Studies, University of Michigan, 2002). *Journal of Japanese Studies*, vol. 29, no. 2 (2003), pp. 368–372.

Shimizu Kusuo to Minami Garō. Tokyo: Shimizu Kusuo to Minami Garō Kankōkai, 1985.

Shinohara Ushio, *Zen'ei no michi*. Tokyo: Bijutsu Shuppansha, 1968.

Shisō Undō Kenkyūjo. *Bōhatsu suru shinsayoku*. Tokyo: Zenbōsha, 1969.

Shōwa no bunka isan. Tokyo: Gyōsei, 1991.

"'Shūdan Kumo' no kisekiten." *Fukuokashi Bijutsukan jōsetsu tenji*, no. 188 (1997), pp. 1–6.

Siddons, James, *Tōru Takemitsu: A Bio-Bibliography*. Westport, Conn.: Greenwood, 2001.

Slaymaker, Doug, ed. *Confluences: Postwar Japan and France*. Ann Arbor: Center for Japanese Studies, University of Michigan, 2002.

Sōgetsu Bijutsukan, ed. *Hizō shiryō ni miru sengo bijutsu no shōgen*. Tokyo: Sōgetsu Bijutsukan, 2000.

Sōgetsukai, ed. *Kokoro wa itsumo runesansu hyōgen jiyūjin Teshigahara Hiroshi*. Tokyo: Sōgetsu Shuppan, 1989.

———. *Sōgetsu 60th Anniversary: Saigen Sōgetsu Āto Sentā*. Tokyo: Sōgetsukai, 1987.

Solt, John P. *Shredding the Tapestry of Meaning: The Poetry and Poetics of Kitasono Katue (1902–1978)*. Cambridge, Mass.: Harvard University Asia Center, 1999.

Stimson, Blake, and Gregory Sholette, eds. *Collectivism after Modernism*. Minneapolis: University of Minnesota Press, 2005.

Suga Akira. "Jikken no bunseki — ōtō to sekinin." In Ōitashi Bijutsukan, ed., *Yoshimura Masunobu no jikkenten — ōtō to hen'yō*, exh. cat., pp. 113–130. Ōita: Ōitashi Bijutsukan, 2000.

———. "Why the Current Interest in Neo-Dada?" In Ōitashi Bijutsukan, ed., *Neo-Dada Japan 1958–1998: Isozaki Arata to Howaito Hausu no menmen*, exh. cat., pp. 289–294. Ōita: Ōitashi Bijutsukan, 1998.

Suga Kishio. "Bundling Together Surroundings to Open the Edges of a New World." Trans. Robert Reed. In Suga, *Suga Kishio*, 2nd ed., pp. 313–316. Tokyo: Yomiuri Shinbunsha and Bijutsukan Renraku Kyōgikai, 1998 [1977].

———. *Suga Kishio*. 2nd ed. Tokyo: Yomiuri Shinbunsha and Bijutsukan Renraku Kyōgikai, 1998 [1977].

Sugawara Norio. *Nihon no gendai bijutsu*. Tokyo: Maruzen, 1995.

Sugino Hideki and Mitsuda Yuri, eds. *Takiguchi Shūzō no zōkeiteki jikken.* Exh. cat. Toyama: Toyama Kenritsu Kindai Bijutsukan and Tokyo: Shibuya Kuritsu Shōtō Bijutsukan, 2001.

Sugiyama Etsuko. "Sōfū to wa, ittai nanimono datta no ka." In Setagaya Bijutsukan, ed. *Teshigahara Sōfū — sengo Nihon o kakenuketa ishoku no zen'ei,* exh. cat., vol. 2, pp. 30–49. Tokyo: Setagaya Bijutsukan and Sōgetsukai, 2001.

Takashina Shūji. "Modern Sculpture." In Takashina, Tōno Yoshiaki, Nakahara Yūsuke, and Tomiyama Hideo, eds., *Art in Japan Today,* pp. 11–15. Tokyo: Japan Foundation and Kinokuniya Bookstore, 1974.

Takashina Shūji, Tōno Yoshiaki, Nakahara Yūsuke, and Tomiyama Hideo, eds. *Art in Japan Today.* Tokyo: Japan Foundation and Kinokuniya Bookstore, 1974.

Takemitsu Tōru. *Confronting Silence: Selected Writings.* Trans. Yoshiko Kakudo and Glenn Glasow. Berkeley, Calif.: Fallen Leaf Press, 1995.

———. "Contemporary Music in Japan." *Perspectives of New Music,* vol. 27, no. 2 (1989), pp. 198–204.

———. *Music for Movies: Toru Takemitsu.* Vols. 1–2. Ed. Tetsuo Ohara. 21 CDs. Tokyo: Shogakkan, 2003.

———. *Oto chinmoku to hakariaeru hodo ni.* Tokyo: Shinchōsha, 1971.

———. *Takemitsu Tōru chosakushū.* 5 vols. Tokyo: Shinchōsha, 2000.

———. *Toki no entei.* Tokyo: Shinchōsha, 1996.

Takemitsu Tōru and Kawada Junzō. *Oto, kotoba, ningen.* Tokyo: Iwanami Shoten, 1980.

Takemitsu Tōru and Ōe Kenzaburō. *Opera o tsukuru.* Tokyo: Iwanami Shoten, 1990.

Takeuchi Yoshimi. *Takeuchi Yoshimi zenshū.* Vol. 7. Tokyo: Chikuma Shobō, 1981.

———. *What Is Modernity? Writings of Takeuchi Yoshimi.* Trans. Richard Calichman. New York: Columbia University Press, 2005.

Taki Kōji. "Sekaishi no naka no sengo Nihon to bunka." In Meguroku Bijutsukan, Hyōgo Kenritsu Kindai Bijutsukan, Hiroshimashi Gendai Bijutsukan, Fukuoka Kenritsu Bijutsukan, and Asahi Shinbunsha, eds., *Sengo bunka no kiseki 1945–1995,* exh. cat., pp. 4–8. Tokyo: Asahi Shinbunsha, 1995.

Taki Teizō. *Nihon no yōga nanajūnen: gaka to gashō no monogatari.* Tokyo: Nikkei Jigyō Shuppansha, 2000.

Takiguchi Shūzō. "Jikken no seishin ni tsuite." Program for *Jikken Kōbō Dainikai Happyōkai,* January 1952, in Takiguchi, *Korekushon Takiguchi Shūzō,* vol. 7, pp. 3–4. Tokyo: Misuzu Shobō, 1992.

———. *Korekushon Takiguchi Shūzō.* 14 vols. Tokyo: Misuzu Shobō, 1991–1998.

———. "Obuje no hakken." *Sōgetsu,* special number, February 1953. In Setagaya Bijutsukan, ed., *Teshigahara Sōfū — sengo Nihon o kakenuketa ishoku no zen'ei,* exh. cat., vol. 1, pp. 204–205. Tokyo: Setagaya Bijutsukan and Sōgetsukai, 2001.

———. *Yōsei no kyori.* Tokyo: Shunchōkai, 1937.

Tama Bijutsu Daigaku and Seibu Bijutsukan, eds. *Monoha to posutomonoha no tenkai.* Exh. cat. Tokyo: Tama Bijutsu Daigaku and Seibu Bijutsukan, 1987.

Tama Bijutsu Daigaku IRAC Kenkyūjo, ed. "*Monoha*" katarogu. Tokyo: Kamakura Garō, 1986.

Tani Akira. "A Presence That Eclipses Subject." In Hara Bijutsukan, ed., *Lee Ufan,* exh. cat., pp. 4–8. Tokyo: Arukanshiēru Bijutsu Zaidan, 1991.

Tatehata Akira. "The Eve of Gutai." In 1953: *Shedding Light on Art in Japan*, trans. Reiko Tomii, exh. cat., pp. 67–74. Tokyo: Tama Art University, 1997.

——. "Mono-ha and Japan's Crisis of the Modern." In Simon Groom, ed., *Mono-ha — School of Things*, exh. cat., pp. 27–45. Cambridge, Eng.: Kettle's Yard, University of Cambridge, 2001.

——. "Neo-Dada Since Then." In Ōitashi Bijutsukan, ed., *Neo-Dada Japan 1958–1998: Isozaki Arata to Howaito Hausu no menmen*, exh. cat., pp. 286–288. Ōita: Ōitashi Bijutsukan, 1998.

Terada Tōru. *Japanese Art in World Perspective*. Trans. Thomas Guerin. New York and Tokyo: Weatherhill/Heibonsha, 1976.

Teshigahara Akane. "Time to Find Sōfū." In Setagaya Bijutsukan, ed., *Teshigahara Sōfū — sengo Nihon o kakenuketa ishoku no zen'ei*, exh. cat., vol. 1, pp. 18–19. Tokyo: Setagaya Bijutsukan and Sōgetsukai, 2001.

Teshigahara Sōfū. *Kadensho*. Tokyo: Sōgetsu Shuppan, 1979.

——. *Sōfū no chōkoku Kojiki*. Exh. cat. (1966). In Setagaya Bijutsukan, ed., *Teshigahara Sōfū — sengo Nihon o kakenuketa ishoku no zen'ei*, exh. cat., vol. 2, pp. 70–71. Tokyo: Setagaya Bijutsukan and Sōgetsukai, 2001.

"Teshigahara Sōfū: avangyarudo no kōseki." *Asahi gurafu*, October 13, 2000, pp. 1–25, 99–111.

Thornber, Karen L. "Atomic Bomb Writers." In Jay Rubin, ed., *Modern Japanese Writers*, pp. 49–70. New York: Charles Scribner's Sons, 2001.

Tokita, Alison McQueen, and David W. Hughes, eds. *Japanese Music: History, Performance, Research*. New York: Cambridge University Press, 2003.

Tōkyō Kokuritsu Kindai Bijutsukan, ed. *Gushō hyōgen no henbō*. Exh. cat. Tokyo: Tōkyō Kokuritsu Kindai Bijutsukan, 1972.

——, ed. *Mikan no seiki: 20seiki bijutsu ga nokosu mono*. Exh. cat. and supplement. Tokyo: Yomiuri Shinbunsha, 2002.

——, ed. *Sengo bijutsu no tenkai: chūshō hyōgen no tayōka*. Exh. cat. Tokyo: Tōkyō Kokuritsu Kindai Bijutsukan, 1973.

——, ed. *1960nendai — gendai bijutsu no tenkanki*. Exh. cat. Tokyo: Tōkyō Kokuritsu Kindai Bijutsukan, 1981.

Tōkyō Kokuritsu Kindai Bijutsukan Kōgeikan, ed. *Crafts in Everyday Life in the 1950s and 1960s*. Exh. cat. Tokyo: Tōkyō Kokuritsu Kindai Bijutsukan, 1995.

Tōkyōto Bijutsukan, ed. *Gendai bijutsu no dōkō*, vol. 1: *1950nendai: sono ankoku to kōbō*. Exh. cat. Tokyo: Tōkyōto Bijutsukan, 1981.

——, ed. *Gendai bijutsu no dōkō*, vol. 2: *1960nendai: tayōka e no shuppatsu*. Exh. cat. Tokyo: Tōkyōto Bijutsukan, 1983.

——, ed. *Shinkan kaikan 10shūnen kinen: gendai bijutsu no 40nen*. Exh. cat. Tokyo: Tōkyōto Bijutsukan, 1985.

Tōkyōto Gendai Bijutsukan, ed. *Nihon no bijutsu: yomigaeru 1964*. Exh. cat. Tokyo: Tōkyōto Gendai Bijutsukan, 1996.

Tomii, Reiko. "Infinity Nets: Aspects of Contemporary Japanese Painting." In Alexandra Munroe, *Japanese Art after 1945: Scream against the Sky*, exh. cat., pp. 307–319. New York: Harry N. Abrams, 1994.

——. "State v. (Anti-)Art: Model 1,000-Yen Note Incident by Akasegawa Genpei and Company." *Positions*, vol. 10, no. 1 (2002), pp. 141–172.

Tone Yasunao. "Geijutsu no chikaku hendō." *Bijutsu techō*, vol. 19, no. 11 (1967), pp. 97–109.

———. *Gendai geijutsu no isō: geijutsu wa shisō tariuru ka.* Tokyo: Tabata Shoten, 1970.

———. "Toward Anti-Music." Trans. Reiko Tomii. In Alexandra Munroe, *Japanese Art after 1945: Scream against the Sky*, exh. cat., p. 376. New York: Harry N. Abrams, 1994.

Tōno Yoshiaki. "Artists in the Early Sixties." In Takashina Shūji, Tōno Yoshiaki, Nakahara Yūsuke, and Tomiyama Hideo, eds., *Art in Japan Today*, pp. 16–21. Tokyo: Japan Foundation and Kinokuniya Bookstore, 1974.

———. "Isetsu 'hangeijutsu' — 'Miyakawa Atsushi' igo." *Bijutsu techō*, vol. 16, no. 5 (1964), pp. 46–49.

———. "Mono-ha and Post-Mono-ha Developments: An On-the-Scene Commentary." Trans. Alfred Birnbaum. In Tama Bijutsu Daigaku and Seibu Bijutsukan, eds., *Monoha to posutomonoha no tenkai*, exh. cat., pp. 188–189. Tokyo: Tama Bijutsu Daigaku and Seibu Bijutsukan, 1987.

———. "Sayōnara Yomiuri Andepandanten." *Bijutsu techō*, vol. 16, no. 4 (1964), pp. 11–27.

Tsuji Nobuo, ed. *Manga Nihon bijutsushi*, vol. 3: *Meiji-gendai no bijutsu*. Tokyo: Bijutsu Shuppansha, 1996.

Tsurumi Kazuko. "Student Movements in 1960 and 1969." In Takayanagi Shun'ichi and Miwa Kimitada, eds., *Postwar Trends in Japan*, pp. 195–227. Tokyo: University of Tokyo Press, 1975.

Tsuruta Heihachirō. "Sengo no Nihonga." In *Shōwa no bunka isan*, pp. 110–125. Tokyo: Gyōsei, 1991.

Tucker, Anne, Dana Friis-Hansen, Kaneko Ryūichi, and Takeba Joe. *History of Japanese Photography*. New Haven, Conn.: Yale University Press, 2003.

Tzara, Tristan. "Dada" (1918). In Vassiliki Kolocotroni, Jane Goldman, and Olga Taxidou, eds., *Modernism: An Anthology of Sources and Documents*, pp. 276–281. Chicago: University of Chicago Press, 1998.

Ueno Chizuko. *Nationalism and Gender*. Trans. Beverley Yamamoto. Melbourne: Trans Pacific Press, 2004.

Wallerstein, Immanuel M. *The Modern World-System: Capitalist Agriculture and the Origins of the European World Economy in the Sixteenth Century*. New York: Academic Press, 1974.

Washburn, Dennis C. *The Dilemma of the Modern in Japanese Fiction*. New Haven, Conn.: Yale University Press, 1995.

Weisenfeld, Gennifer S. *Mavo: Japanese Artists and the Avant-Garde, 1905–1931*. Berkeley: University of California Press, 2002.

Winther-Tamaki, Bert. *Art in the Encounter of Nations: Japanese and American Artists in the Early Postwar Years*. Honolulu: University of Hawai'i Press, 2001.

Woodward, C. Vann. "The Comparability of American History." In Woodward, ed., *The Comparative Approach to American History*, pp. 3–17. New York: Basic Books, 1968.

Yaguchi Kunio. "The 1964 Tokyo Olympics and a Turning Point in Japanese Art." In Tōkyōto Gendai Bijutsukan, ed., *Nihon no bijutsu: yomigaeru 1964*, exh. cat., pp. 183–189. Tokyo: Tōkyōto Gendai Bijutsukan, 1996.

Yamaguchi Katsuhiro. "Experimental Workshop." In *1953: Shedding Light on Art in Japan*, trans. Reiko Tomii, exh. cat., pp. 75–80. Tokyo: Tama Art University, 1997.

Yamamoto Atsuo. "Gutai 1954–1972." In Ashiya Shiritsu Bijutsu Hakubutsu-kan, ed., *Gutai I, II, III*, exh. cat., pp. 27–47. Ashiya: Ashiya Shiritsu Bijutsu Hakubutsukan, 1994.

Yamano Hakudai. "Baree no gaikyō." *Buyō nenkan*, vol. 1: 1977, pp. 36–40.

———. "Nihon no baree chizu wa kore kara dō kawaru ka." *Modan dansu*, no. 13 (1974), pp. 11–16.

———. "Nihon yōbu ryakushi." *Kisetsu dansāto.* Part 1: no. 9 (1998), pp. 1–3; part 2: no. 10 (1998), pp. 1–4; part 3: no. 11 (1998), pp. 1–3; part 4: no. 12 (1998), pp. 1–3.

Yamashita Fumio. *Atarashii seiji to bunka.* Tokyo: Shin Nihon Shuppansha, 1975.

Yamashita Yūji. "Sengo geijutsu undō no naka no Takemitsu Tōru." In Chōki Seiji and Higuchi Ryūichi, eds., *Takemitsu Tōru: oto no kawa no yukue*, pp. 202–221. Tokyo: Heibonsha, 2000.

Yano, Christine R. *Tears of Longing: Nostalgia and the Nation in Japanese Popular Song.* Cambridge, Mass.: Harvard University Asia Center, 2002.

Yano Tomoo. *Han'ei o motomete: hyakumannin no keizai hakusho.* Tokyo: Shiseidō, 1956.

Yoru no Kai. *Atarashii geijutsu no tankyū.* Tokyo: Getsuyō Shobō, 1949.

Yoshida Yoshie. *Kaitaigeki no maku orite: 6onendai zen'ei bijutsushi.* Tokyo: Zōkeisha, 1982.

Yoshimi Shun'ya. "Reisen taisei to 'Amerika' no shōhi." In Komori Yōichi et al., eds., *Reisen taisei to shihon no bunka: 1955nen igo*, vol. 1, pp. 1–60. *Iwanami kōza kindai Nihon no bunkashi* 9. Tokyo: Iwanami Shoten, 2002.

Yoshimura Masunobu. "Neo-Dada Oruganaizāsu." *Bijutsu techō*, vol. 23, no. 10 (1971), pp. 56–57.

Yoshino, Kosaku. *Cultural Nationalism in Contemporary Japan: A Sociological Enquiry.* London: Routledge, 1992.

Young, Robert J. C. *Postcolonialism: A Very Short Introduction.* Oxford, Eng.: Oxford University Press, 2003.

Yuasa Jōji. "'Jikken Kōbō' no koto, sono wakai sakkyokuka e no teigen." Part 1. *Ongaku gendai*, vol. 27, no. 15 (1997), pp. 111–113.

———. "Music as a Reflection of a Composer's Cosmology." *Perspectives of New Music*, vol. 27, no. 2 (1989), pp. 176–197.

———. *Ongaku no kosumorojī e.* Tokyo: Seidosha, 1981.

Yui Kazuto, ed. *Nijūsseiki bukko Nihon gaka jiten.* Tokyo: Bijutsu Nenkansha, 1998.

Zusetsu Nihon bunkashi taikei, vol. 13: *Gendai.* Tokyo: Shōgakukan, 1968.

Digital Sources

Frank, Peter. "The Fluxus Movement." http://www.artcommotion.com/Issue2/VisualArts/. April 5, 2003.

Gendai bijutsu kīwādo, Zero Jigen. http://www.dnp.co.jp/museum/nmp/artscape/artwords/u_z/zero_jigen.html. June 21, 2003.

Japan Times Online. http://www.japantimes.co.jp/.

"Japanese Women Composers." http://music.acu.edu/www/iawm/pages/earth/comp/japancomp.html. June 11, 2003.

Legacy Project. http://www.legacy-project.org/artists/display.html?ID=113. November 11, 2002.

Mizuma Art Gallery. http://mizuma-art.co.jp/_artist/kato_e.html. June 21, 2003.

"Origins of the Congress for Cultural Freedom, 1949–1950." http://www.sfsu.edu/fischer/IR%20360/Readings/Congress%20Cultural%20Freedom.htm. February 19, 2003.

Shimamoto Shōzō. "My Avant Garde." http://www.sukothai.com/X.SA.16/X.16.Shimamoto.html. March 7, 2003.

Takahashi Yūji. "Movements, Colors and Nearness" (1998). http://www.ne.jp/asahi/kerbau/kerbau21/texts(e)/mcn.html. June 24, 2003.

"Yoko Ono: A Biography." http://www.kaapeli.fi/aiu/onolife2.html. December 18, 2002.

Index

About the Author

Thomas R. H. Havens is a professor of history at Northeastern University. In 1960 he made his first visit to Tokyo's Shinjuku district, the seedbed of Japan's avant-garde arts discussed in *Radicals and Realists.* Arriving in Japan a week after a nationwide strike of six million workers protesting the Japan–United States Mutual Security Treaty, he first encountered the postwar arts as an English tutor of three apprentice geisha at the Hasegawa Teahouse in central Tokyo. He is the author of a previous book on arts patronage in postwar Japan *(Artist and Patron in Postwar Japan: Dance, Music, Theater, and the Visual Arts, 1955–1980)* (1982) and another on the Seibu-Saison retailing empire *(Architects of Affluence: The Tsutsumi Famly and the Seibu-Saison Enterprises in Twentieth-Century Japan)* (1994), whose chieftain, Tsutsumi Seiji, was Japan's leading sponsor of avant-garde art for more than two decades. His other book-length writings include *Nishi Amane and Modern Japanese Thought* (1970), *Farm and Nation in Modern Japan: Agrarian Nationalism, 1870–1940* (1974), *Valley of Darkness: The Japanese People and World War Two* (1978, 1986), *The Historical Encyclopedia of World War II* (coauthor) (1980), *Fire Across the Sea: The Vietnam War and Japan, 1965–1975* (1987), and *The Ambivalence of Nationalism: Modern Japan between East and West* (coeditor) (1990).

Production Notes for HAVENS | RADICALS AND REALISTS IN
THE JAPANESE NONVERBAL ARTS
Cover and interior design by April Leidig-Higgins in Electra Type,
    with display type in Champion
Composition by Copperline Book Services, Inc.
Printing and binding by Thomson-Shore, Inc.
Printed on 60# Finch White Opaque Bright White Smooth, 500 ppi